Judith-Elisa Kaufmann

Dancing & Teaching Dance based on **Dance Medicine & Science**

The Symbiosis of the Future

VOLUME 1

BASIC ASPECTS
OF THE DISCIPLINES

Judith-Elisa Kaufmann

Dancing & Teaching Dance

based on

Dance Medicine & Science

The Symbiosis of the Future

VOLUME 1

BASIC ASPECTS
OF THE DISCIPLINES

Rediroma-Verlag

ISBN 978-3-98527-100-9

Translation of German excerpts for the English series:
Sarah Magdalena Huber & Theodoros Sakalidis

Cover Photo Judith-Elisa Kaufmann: Studio Furgler

Rediroma Publisher
Kremenholler Str. 53
42857 Remscheid, Germany

For

Charlie, Michael, Imela, Anja
My beloved Parents & Family
Annkathrin, Summy & Anita
with love and gratitude for always believing in me

for my dancers & my students,
with special thanks for your trust and affection

dedicated to
Anja Laskus, MD

With special thanks to:

Larissa Arens, MD
Stefan Arens, MD
Elisabeth Exner-Grave, MD
Holger Förster, MD
Monika Löffelholz, MD

Annkathrin Dehn, Sabine „Summy" Riegler, Nathalie-Sylvie Hödl,
Viktoria Luckinger, Verena Kalcher, Emma Tschuschnigg

Academy for Ballet Pedagogy
Dance Pedagogy
bdp + Dance Medicine
www.tanzpaedagogik.eu

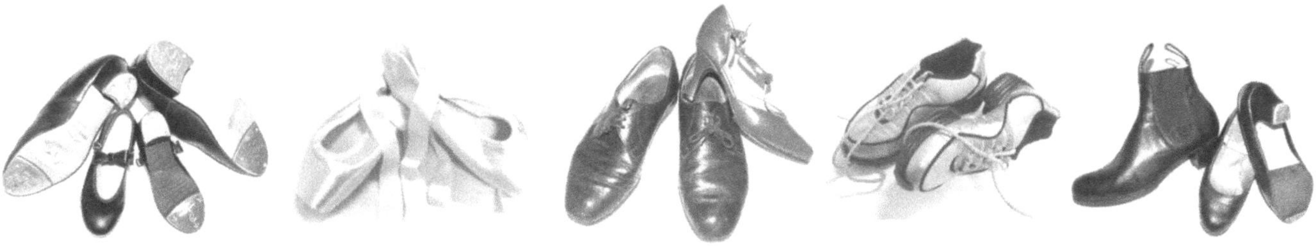

The dancer is the most extraordinary fusion of cognitive and physical ability and creativity, of artistic virtuosity and athletic performance.
As such, dancers don't fit into any generalization, they are dependent on specialization.
Dance medicine and science acknowledge this specificity and place it center stage.
The goal is a maximum of health in dancers for a maximum of performance!

Judith-Elisa Kaufmann, 2008

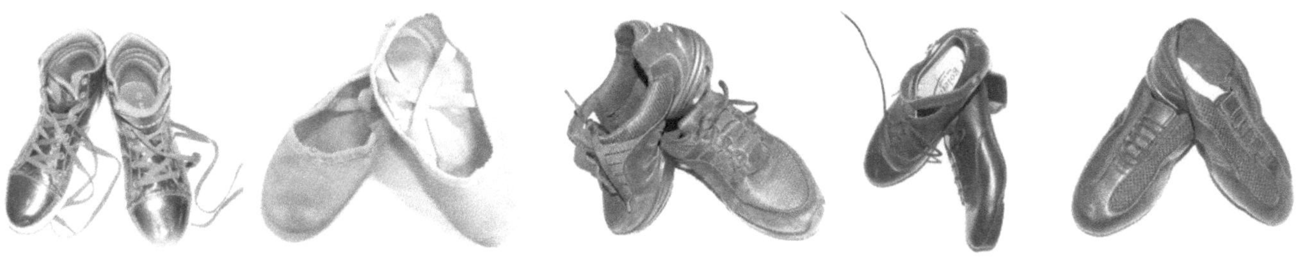

PREFACE

As an orthopaedic physician and enthusiastic dance follower, I'm very pleased to introduce this book series to you. I have known Judith-Elisa since she was a young dancer and student in my dance anatomy and dance medicine courses. Over the years she has become an experienced presenter, working with dance students, professional dancers, teachers and health care practitioners and impresses with an exceptional knowledge in both areas, dance pedagogy and dance medicine.

This book series includes several volumes, more than 800 pages of information, thousands of scholarly references, an extensive bibliography, and specials such as the introduction on how to search, find and use scientific literature for those who want to start into dance medicine and science. As such, it serves dancers, teachers, trainers, medical professionals, parents, and many more, providing an extensive compilation of topics, which benefit from the symbiosis between dance, teaching dance, and dance science. Judith-Elisa Kaufmann skillfully bridges dance, dance medicine and dance teaching.

Volume 1 provides an overview of the definition of terms in dance medicine and science and the objectives of dance education. The book focuses on injury prevention and performance enhancement through the recognition and classification of the respective cognitive, psychological and physical development of dancers with the influence on their individual dance potential, taking intrinsic and extrinsic factors into account.

In Volume 2, the author dedicates herself to the neuropsychological aspects and in Volume 3 to the performance physiological and biomechanical aspects of dancing and teaching, from a dual perspective of a dance medicine specialist and pedagogue. Both volumes present extensive practical information and exercises. Theory and practice are linked in such a way that what has been learned can be applied immediately, clearly illustrated by photos.

Volume 4 discusses the health and wellbeing of teachers and trainers in dance, offering a comprehensive collection of support for these hard-working professions.

Equally comprehensive indexes enable you to quickly find the details you are looking for with the information you have been taught, and offers the opportunity to deepen your knowledge.

In summary, this series gives the reader the chance to receive an excellent information and reference work for dance, dance pedagogy, and dance medicine.

A perfect symbiosis for those dancers, educators, trainers, and medical professionals who turn dancing into the greatest possible, individual benefit for the practitioner.

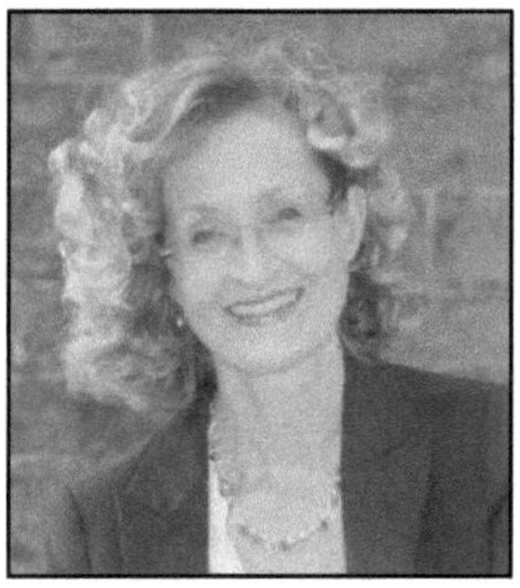

Elisabeth Exner-Grave, MD
February 2021

INTRODUCTION TO THIS SERIES

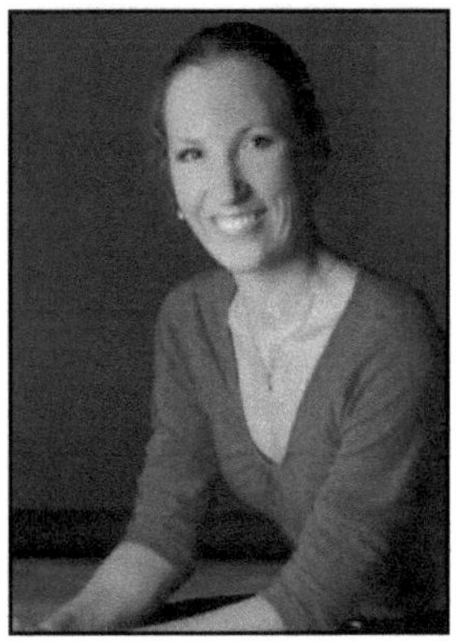

The following book series is a result of 25 years of teaching and researching dance, dance pedagogy, dance medicine and dance science around the globe. I have been blessed being allowed to guide thousands of dancers and those working with dancers towards (and through) the beneficial symbiosis between dance medicine, science, teaching or dancing. It has always led to wellbeing, performance enhancement, injury prevention, or rehabilitation. So many, including myself, were able to open new doors or safely push their own limits beyond borders, which have before appeared to be final.

Many people I meet have at least heard of the concept of dance medicine. However, most of them also immediately state: "I don't need it, I'm not injured!"

Dance medicine and dance science reach far beyond the diagnosis, treatment, and rehabilitation of injuries. This aspect is one of the numerous possibilities they can offer. The even bigger part, however, is what dance medicine can provide to enhance performance and prevent injuries in dancers of all levels and styles, teachers, instructors, choreographers – and everyone, who wants to benefit from insights into

- **Dance technique** (e.g., basing technique on individuality to achieve highest levels of performance)
- **Movement analysis** (e.g., screening dancers' technique for individual errors which endanger or already impair performance and/or health)
- **Biomechanics** (e.g., economy of alignment and dynamic control of motion)
- **Neuro-/Psychology** (e.g., working with imagery, learning, coping skills for stress situations)
- **Nutrition** (e.g., how to fuel your body and mind for daily work and exercise)
- **Science of training** (e.g., compiling your own training plan, learning how to stretch or warm-up)
- **Dance management and administration** (e.g., reduce costs for injuries and related administrative issues by evidence-based scheduling or compiling of curricula)
- **Injury prevention** (e.g., which risk factors are to be identified and eliminated in the course of targeted practical implementation of preventive measures)
- **Injury management** (e.g., how to best cooperate among medical and teaching professionals; how to deal with first aid, or transition training)
- and so many more

Very often dancers/performers or dance teachers/trainers/masters/choreographers as well as clinicians tell me that they have reached a plateau. Either in their own development, or in guiding others in their development. The moment they come in touch with the fusion of dance, dance pedagogy and dance medicine through my rehearsals, lectures, or seminars, new perspectives for performance analysis and enhancement, or injury prevention and management open up.

Dance medicine and science serve all dance styles, all levels of expertise, dancers and non-dancers, other disciplines such as medicine, sports medicine and science, physiotherapy, movement analysis and many more, and offer a huge spectrum of different topics, professions, and possibilities. For that matter, the fusion of science and practice of dance is a symbiosis for the benefit of all parties involved.

A great number of impressive publications exist describing aspects of dance medicine or dance science. But so many people are still not sure, how dance science can be practically implemented into daily dance routines, or the world of teaching and training dance in general. "We had dance medicine. We had to learn all those stupid muscles by heart." – One of the many quotes of dancers, who had to deal with a lack of content knowledge on dance medicine and science in their teachers or trainers. Dance medicine is so much more than that.

This series addresses all dancers, teachers, physicians, therapists, parents, administrators, and everyone working in the dance field. It wants to help to enhance performance, prevent physical, psychological, and mental ill-health in all those dancing and teaching, and give clear information how to include these goals into daily practice. This book and series neither aim to be a dogma for all teaching dance, nor can it replace active learning from a specialist in the field of dance medicine, science, and dance medical dance pedagogy. But it should provide fundamental theoretical and practical information of what dance medicine and science can do to support dancers and teachers alike.

If somebody really wants to train a dancer to their individual best while preventing their injuries with a maximum effort, they have to have very profound knowledge of the above listed topics and many more aspects related. And those who diagnose and treat dancers (and dance teachers) need to know the world of dance, its language, its thoughts and techniques, its needs, its assets and liabilities. It doesn't matter whether the dancers are professional or recreational (amateurs), children, adolescents, adults, or older adults. In order to enhance performance and prevent and manage injuries, very profound content knowledge of dance medicine and science is indispensable.

Moreover, this book series wants to put the dance teacher, trainer, master, and choreographer into the spotlight, their own health and wellbeing as well as their duties. Teaching dance or training dancers means to carry a load of responsibilities and cover way more tasks than what is known and visible to the outside world. And it also implies to stay in the shadow, while the dancer flies out into the limelight. However, teachers as well as masters and trainers are the significant others with the closest contact to and the highest influence on dancers, their education, training, and attitudes. They should therefore be the first and foremost to include dance medicine into daily practice through in-depth knowledge and the self-reflective willingness to engage in dance science. For their own performance enhancement and injury prevention as well as the safety and wellbeing of their dancers.

Dance medical dance pedagogy, i.e., teaching dance based on the evidence of dance medicine and science, is a science in itself. This book series aims to support all those, who have realized that teaching dance is not an inevitable thing to follow the own dancing career but a different, high-level profession, which needs specific knowledge and in-depth study. Hence, another goal of this publication is to lay the basis for dance medical dance pedagogy as a field of dance science, evolving from a mere passing-on of (often unreflected) training traditions, former dancers have experienced from their teachers.

For that matter, this book and series are especially dedicated to all those dance teachers and pedagogues, who have already pushed that fusion forward: your motivation to include dance medicine into teaching has proofed your sense of responsibility and love for your dancers!

HOW TO USE THIS BOOK

This book series focusses on the bridges between dance, dance medicine, science, and the art of dance medical dance pedagogy. For that purpose, most of the aspects of performance enhancement and injury prevention are discussed from two different angles with the aim of fusing them for practice: the scientific and basic background and the practical implementation of these basics.

Volume 1 consists of five main parts and lays the groundwork for the understanding and the use of the other volumes of this series.

Part 1 presents the ***"The Characteristics & Objectives of the Disciplines – The Fundament"***, which gives background information on the underlying sciences that are meant to be cooperating. The characteristic focus of this series lies on their influence on teaching and training environments, surrounding the dancer.

Part 2, ***"Performance Enhancement & Injury Prevention – The Background"***, discusses injuries, etiology and risk factors, relevant for the practical injury preventive and performance enhancing measures.

Part 3 introduces ***"Performance Enhancement & Injury Prevention – The Implementation"***, looking into aspects of practical transfer and its status quo of dance medicine and science into training and education.

Part 4 offers a ***"Getting Started: How to Find and Use Science – The Inspiration Part I"*** for all (novices) who want to know how to find, read and use academic literature.

Part 5 will provide a list of ***"Bibliography & Recommended Reading – The Inspiration Part II"*** for all interested in literature on dance and related sciences.

Since this book aims to serve dancers, teachers, and all other professions involved in the dance world, some things will be repeatedly discussed in various contexts, because they have a relevant influence on multiple aspects. Short introductions at the beginning of the main chapters should help to get an overview and summarize important aspects of what can be expected to be found in the upcoming pages. Bold key words as well as relevant hints or cross-references to other volumes of this series in boxes should help to navigate. Furthermore, this series cites thousands of scientific references, which should kindle motivation for further reading and inspire to study various aspects of dance medicine and science in more details. Due to so many requests, and since this book can and should be used as a textbook, the cited references can be found as footnotes on the same page rather than at the end of the book. As such, the reader can enjoy making notes or highlighting references for further reading on the very page of interest while reading, without having to search for the references at the end of the book. Many gave the feedback that searching for endnotes disturbs their flow of reading, which is why they do not look up references. Thus, this decision should support one of the many goals of the series, namely to introduce dancers, teachers, trainers and all other readers to the world of science and give support, how to actively access this world. Searching for further reading is one of those actions.

May this book and series serve as an inspiration to dive head first into the world of dance sciences, such as dance medical dance pedagogy, and detect all the assets, dance medicine and science holds at the ready for dancers, teachers, and everyone involved and interested in dance and healthy motion.

Thanks that you are here!

Judith-Elisa Kaufmann March 2021

TABLE OF CONTENT

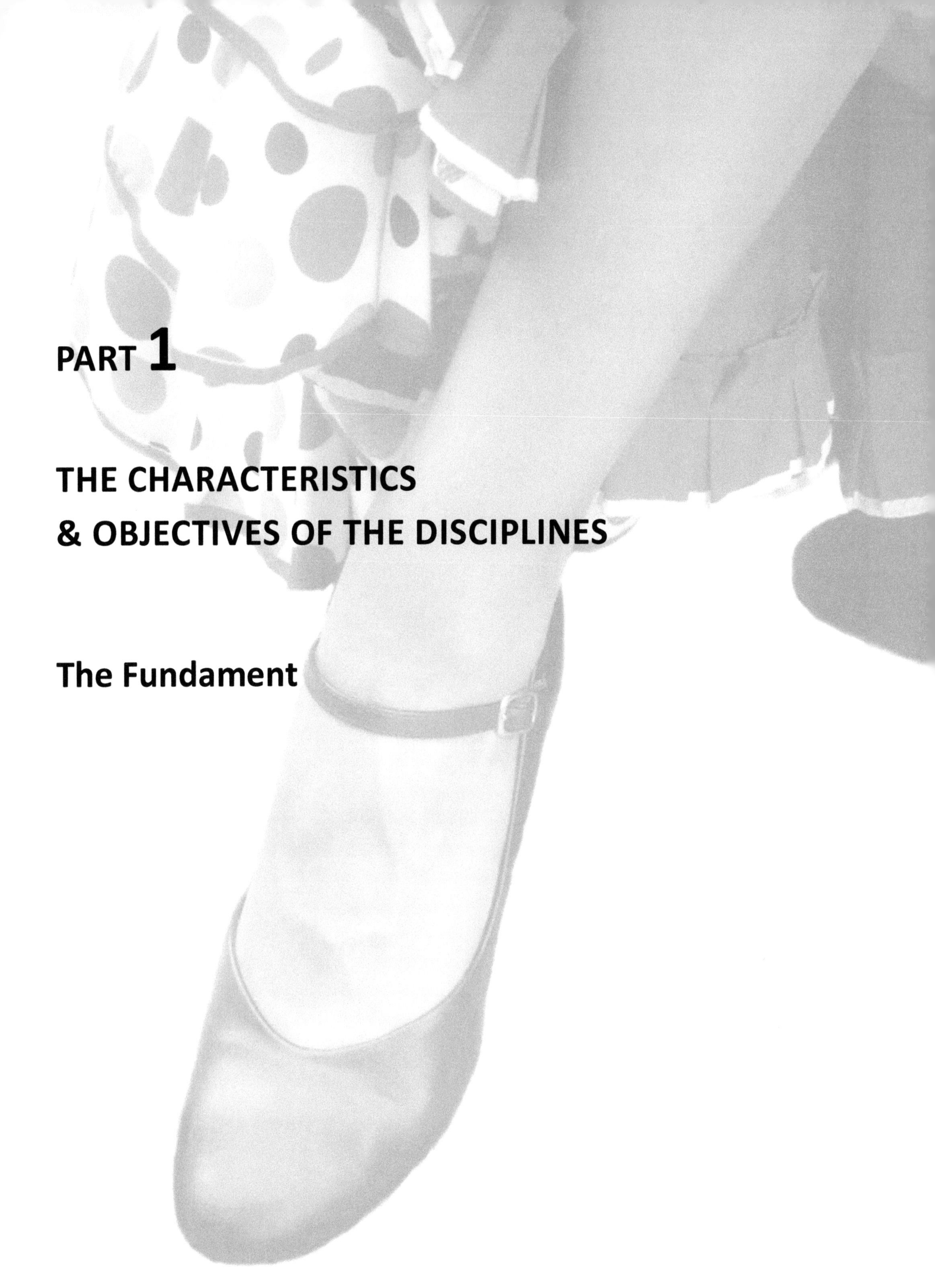

PART 1

THE CHARACTERISTICS & OBJECTIVES OF THE DISCIPLINES

The Fundament

PART 1 THE CHARACTERISTICS & OBJECTIVES OF THE DISCIPLINES – THE FUNDAMENT

The following chapters give an overview on the history, goals and purposes of dance medicine and science, dance education and dance pedagogy. The essence of dance, its holistic effect on health and wellbeing of dancers of all ages, genders, styles, cultures, backgrounds and levels of expertise is discussed. And the dancer, as the visible protagonist is defined, while the role of the teacher, trainer, pedagogue, ballet master, artistic director, chorographer, etc., as the commonly invisible protagonist is investigated.

Taking it from there, the connections between the disciplines are pointed out, through the eyes of dance medical dance pedagogy. The goal is to show, why a symbiosis of the disciplines is so important for the dancer's as well as teacher's/trainer's health and wellbeing. Moreover, the chapters show why health and wellbeing are always directly related to performance enhancement in all parties involved, which is why injury prevention and performance enhancement actually go hand in hand. While a symbiosis supports health and wellbeing in dancers, who can thus achieve individual, optimal levels of performance, implementation of dance medicine and science into the realms of dance and teaching dance reduces physiological, psychological, financial and social burden of injuries. Through several scholarly examples provided by dance medicine and science this overall goal is presented to the reader. However, a fusion of the disciplines is also essential to support the scholarly development of the disciplines themselves, supporting the important notion of teamwork and cooperation.

'Preventing injuries is not easy. But prospective studies in dance science done by scientists dedicated to help dancers show how efficiently it can be done. However, for those who do not engage in dance science, it seems that there is nothing to be seen, because with good prevention 'just nothing happens' to the dancer, meaning that in the best case, there is no injury at all. Society, media, and politics always want to see results. They must learn to see the results of prevention, the "nothing happened", as the most valuable of all results! The hero on this successful path is the responsible and knowledgeable dance teacher or trainer.'

(Judith-Elisa Kaufmann 2008)

The terms "dance medicine" and "dance science" repeatedly appear in this book and series – of course. For that matter, a look behind the curtains of the underlying concepts and disciplines is the first step towards the goal to be achieved: their fusion with dance practice.

The goal of dance medicine and science is to maximize dance performance by maximizing the health of dancers and all involved in training and teaching dance. Moreover, health through dance and dance for health has received a big focus of attention within the last 10 years.

The term "dance medicine" has become widely known in the last decades, yet many people still ask themselves – and me – what it really means. First, dance medicine does not equal dance therapy. Dance medicine [1, 2, 3] is a specialized branch of medicine that deals with all the health and performance concerns of dancers and dance professionals and should not be confused with "dance therapy", which is a form of psychotherapy. Dance medicine is **part of performing arts medicine, dedicated to evaluating, preventing, treating, rehabilitating, and documenting dance injuries and injury risks, as well as involved aspects of dancers' lives, work, and training. Dance medicine serves all dance styles, genders, and age groups, and aims for implementation of dance as source for health and wellbeing among all ages, genders, and cultures**.

As such, dance medicine can be compared to sports medicine. Some refer to it as a part of sports medicine, which specializes in dancers.[4] There are specialists for specific dance styles and related issues among physicians, therapists, teachers, trainers, dance medical consultants and practitioners. Just as there are many different types of sports, which depend on specialists in the sports medicine sector, there must be specialists in dance medicine for the many disciplines in dance. A ballet dancer has other injuries and requires different medical professionals and teachers' expertise than does, for instance, a flamenco or tap dancer. For that matter, specific content knowledge of dance medicine and dance science for all those working with dancers, from teachers to physicians, is vital.

Part II of this book, with its chapters on injury prevention and dance style specifics, will address such aspects in detail.

Dance science is a broader concept or umbrella term, which spans and represents a variety of aspects of dance medicine, such as science of training, biomechanics or nutrition in dance, but also researches culture and identity of dance and dancers, philosophy or pedagogy, again comparable to sports science. Ideally, former dancers choose to study aspects of dance medicine and/or science, after their active careers and then dedicate their professional knowledge to support dancers and those working in dance. Examples would be dance pedagogy based on dance science, medicine, therapy, law, career transition consultant, or other.

In the fields of sports medicine and science, athletes have already benefited from sports medical and scientific research and knowledge before. Considering such advantages for dancers, a focus on specific research in dance medicine and dance science evolved in the middle to late 20th century.

However, the first publications on the intersection between dance and health date back to as early as 1824[5], 1898[6], and 1935[7]. And in 1661, when Louis XIV founded the first ballet academy in Paris, the first dance masters began to write scripts that already dealt with something close to teaching dance or **dance pedagogy, the science of dance education**. They as well as famous later representatives, such as Jean-Georges Noverre[8] already addressed early thoughts related to dance medicine in the broadest sense, such as safety in cases of

[1] Miller C. *Dance Medicine. Current Concepts.* Physical Medicine and Rehabilitation Clinics of North America. 17. 803-811.2006.

[2] Ryan AJ. *Early History of Dance Medicine.* J Dance Med Sci. 1(1). 30-34. 1997.

[3] Kravitz SR. *Dance medicine.* Clin Podiatry. 1(2). 417-430. 1984.

[4] Hahnengress ML. *Musik- und Tanzmedizin - Künstlerisches Pendant der Sportmedizin.* Dte Zeitschr Sportmedizin. 62(6). 141-142. 2011.

[5] Magriel PD. *A Selected Bibliography of the Dance in Health, Hygiene, and Physiology.* Research Quarterly. American Association for Health, Physical Education and Recreation. 10(2). 1939.

[6] Blanchard G. La danseuse. Considérations sur quelques accidents professionnels de ses tendons et ligaments du pied. Thèse de doctorat en médecine. Paris. Henri Jouve. 1898.

[7] Pressman LP. *Neurovascular factor and limitations of muscle exertion in ballet dancers.* Klin Med. 13. 43-50. 1935.

[8] Noverre, Jean-Georges. Lettres sur la danse, et sur les ballets. Lyon. Aimé Delaroche. 1760.

emergencies like fire outbreaks in theatres, or aspects of training in dance classes.

Several authors can be regarded as the pioneers in publications on dance medicine and science. Among them are the Frenchman Remy who wrote the first dissertation on dance medicine and published his work at the medical faculty in Paris in 1824.[9] Mabel Elsworth Todd [10], a pioneer in movement sciences, published her book "The Thinking Body" in 1937, which has become a classic for dancers and all involved in dance and movement sciences.

In 1948, the first German publication followed, entitled "Arbeitsmedizinische Untersuchungen an Balletttänzern" (Examinations of ballet dancers in the field of occupational medicine), which already dealt with topics that are still highly relevant today, such as malnutrition and eating disorders in dancers.[11] In 1987, Robert L. Stephens and Allen J. Ryan [12] published their comprehensive guide on dance medicine, offering the term "dance medicine" in the title.

Josef Huwyler is considered a pioneer of dance medicine in German speaking countries, which still was more of a "ballet medicine"[13] in 1995. However, the new edition of his 1995 publication was published in 2005 already presenting the term "dance medicine" in the title: "Tanzmedizin: Anatomische Grundlagen und gesunde Bewegung" (Dance medicine: anatomical principles and healthy movement).

To date, dance medicine and science has been able to provide a huge body of research[14] dealing with an equally high number of issues and aspects related to performance enhancement and injury prevention in dancers of all backgrounds. The following list can only serve as an example, given the thousands of research articles published.

Among relevant topics are documentations of injury prevalence, causes, and risks[15,16,17,18,19,20], aspects of pain[21,22], injury rehabilitation, and dancing through pain, an issue, which seems to be enculturated into dance[23,24] and add to the high risk of overuse and repetitive injury[25,26]; the psychological, physical, and financial burden that comes with injuries for all parties involved.[27,28,29] Dance medicine stresses the importance of evidence based science of training for dancers[30,31], which addresses aspects such as fitness[32,33], screening[34],

[9] Magriel PD. *A Selected Bibliography of the Dance in Health, Hygiene, and Physiology.* Research Quarterly. American Association for Health, Physical Education and Recreation. 10(2). 1939.

[10] Todd, Mabel Elsworth. The Thinking Body. Princeton Book Company. 1937.

[11] Wanke E, and Groneberg DA. *Tanzmedizin. Maximale Anforderungen.* Deutsches Ärzteblatt. 109(37). 1835. 2012.

[12] Stephens, Robert E., and Allan J. Ryan. Dance medicine: a comprehensive guide. Chicago. Pluribus Press. 1987.

[13] Huwyler J. Der Tänzer und sein Körper. Aspekte des Tanzens aus ärztlicher Sicht. Balingen. Perimed-spitta Verlag. 1995.

[14] Solomon, Ruth, and John Solomon. Dance Medicine & Science Bibliography, 7th Edition. International Association for Dance Medicine & Science. 2017.

[15] Hincapie CA, Morton EJ, and Cassidy JD. *Musculoskeletal injuries and pain in dancers: a systematic review.* Arch Phys Med Rehabil. 89(9). 1819-1829. 2008.

[16] Allen N, Nevill A, Brooks J, Koutedakis Y, and Wyon M. *Ballet injuries: injury incidence and severity over 1 year.* J Orthop Sports Phys Ther. 42(9). 781-790. 2012.

[17] Jacobs CL, Cassidy JD, Côté P, Boyle E, Ramel E, Ammendolia C, Hartvigsen J, and Schwartz I. *Musculoskeletal Injury in Professional Dancers: Prevalence and Associated Factors: An International Cross-Sectional Study.* Clin J Sport Med. 27(2). 153-160. 2017.

[18] Leanderson C, Leanderson J, Wykman A, Strender LE, Johansson SE, and Sundquist K. *Musculoskeletal injuries in young ballet dancers.* Knee Surg Sports Traumatol Arthrosc. 19(9). 1531-1535. 2011.

[19] Nilsson C, Leanderson J, Wykman A, and Strender LE. *The injury panorama in a Swedish professional ballet company.* Knee Surg Sports Traumatol Arthrosc. 9(4). 242-246. 2001.

[20] Bowling A. *Injuries to dancers: prevalence, treatment, and perceptions of causes.* BMJ. 298(6675). 731-734. 1989.

[21] Lampe J, Ohlendorf D, Groneberg DA, Borgetto BM, and Wanke EM. *[Musculoskeletal Pain in Dance: Prevalence, Localisation and Development Over Time in Amateur Dancers and Professional Dance Teachers].* Sportverletz Sportschaden. 2018.

[22] Tajetfoxell B., and Rose FD. *Pain and Pain Tolerance in Professional Ballet Dancers.* British Journal of Sports Medicine. 29(1). 31-34. 1995.

[23] Thomas H., and Tarr J. *Dancers' perceptions of pain and injury: positive and negative effects.* J Dance Med Sci. 13(2). 51-59. 2009.

[24] Rivera DC, Alexander JL, Nehrenz GM, and Fields BJ. *Dancers' perceptions of injuries.* Journal of Music and Dance. 2(1). 9-12. 2012.

[25] Negus V, Hopper D, and Briffa NK. *Associations between turnout and lower extremity injuries in classical ballet dancers.* Journal of Orthopaedic & Sports Physical Therapy. 35(5). 307-318. 2005.

[26] Garrick JG. *Early identification of musculoskeletal complaints and injuries among female ballet students.* Journal Dance Medicine & Science. 3(2). 80-83. 1999.

[27] Ekegren CL, Quested R, and Brodrick A. *Injuries in pre-professional ballet dancers: Incidence, characteristics and consequences.* J Sci Med Sport. 17(3). 271-275. 2014.

[28] Solomon R, Solomon J, Micheli LJ, and McGray Jr E. *The 'cost' of injuries in a professional ballet company: A five-year study (Dancers, medical problems).* Medical Problems of Performing Artists. 14(4). 164-169. 1999.

[29] Garrick JG, and Requa RK. *Ballet injuries – an analysis of epidemiology and financial outcome.* Am J Sports Med. 21(4). 586-590. 1993.

[30] Wyon MA, and Redding E. *Physiological monitoring of cardiorespiratory adaptations during rehearsal and performance of contemporary dance.* J Strength Cond Res. 19(3). 611-614. 2005.

[31] Allen N, Nevill AM, Brooks JH, Koutedakis Y, and Wyon MA. *The effect of a comprehensive injury audit program on injury incidence in ballet: a 3-year prospective study.* Clin J Sport Med. 23(5). 373-378. 2013.

[32] Twitchett EA, Koutedakis Y, and Wyon MA. *Physiological fitness and professional classical ballet performance: a brief review.* J Strength Cond Res. 23(9). 2732-2740. 2009.

[33] Twitchett E, Brodrick A, Nevill AM, Koutedakis Y, Angioi M, and Wyon M. *Does physical fitness affect injury occurrence and time loss due to injury in elite vocational ballet students?* J Dance Med & Sci. 14(1). 26-31. 2010.

[34] Armstrong R, and Relph N. *Screening Tools as a Predictor of Injury in Dance: Systematic Literature Review and Meta-analysis.* Sports Med Open. 4(1). 33. 2018.

biomechanics[35, 36, 37] or the importance of healthy nutrition as well as the danger of eating disorders, and related hormonal changes.[38,39] The roles of fatigue, rest and overuse injuries[40,41], anxiety, post-injury-distress[42], and many other issues related to injury prevention and etiology of injuries or ill-health are further topics of investigation in the ongoing pursuit of dance medicine and science to provide comprehensive care for dancers and related professions.[43,44,45]

Starting in the late 20th century, societies, associations, and organizations evolved, dedicated to the wellbeing of all involved in dance through research and networking. In 1990, "**IADMS**", the International Association for Dance Medicine & Science, was founded, dedicated to uniting representatives of dance medicine and science from all around the globe. Shortly after that, in 1997, "**ta.med**", the organization for dance medicine in German-speaking countries (from the German word **tan**z**med**izin, i.e., dance medicine), and many more followed. Among them are the Australian Society for Performing Arts Healthcare (ASPAH); Athletes and the Arts; AusDANCE; British Association for Performing Arts Medicine (BAPAM); Centro italiano interdisciplinare di Medicina dell'Arte (CEIMArs); Dance Science Net; Dance USA; Harkness Center for Dance Injuries; Healthy Dancer Canada (HDC); International Dance Association (I.D.A.); Médecine des Arts; National Centre Performing Arts (NCPA); Nederlandse Vereniging voor Dans- en Muziek Geneeskunde (NVDMG), or One Dance UK.

In addition to research on and the vital treatment of dancers' injuries, dance medicine deals with the essential field of prevention, i.e., **precautionary measures to prevent injuries and illbeing**.[46] That comprises the training of dancers as well as dance teachers, trainers, or choreographers, medical professionals, insurances, caregivers, and **parents**, who are especially important in the fields of dancers' injury prevention. Many dance styles, such as those described by the umbrella term "Urban Dance Styles" or dance philosophies such as Flamenco, Irish dance, or Tango argentino, very often work without **teachers** and are based on evolving technical repertoire by their dancers and choreographers, who often simultaneously engage as teachers. Such styles are challenging for dance medicine as far as injury prevention is concerned, because they depend on the dancers themselves, often lacking trained teachers or educated trainers.

However, dancers have become increasingly involved in dance medicine and science realizing the benefit, and practice has shown that many dancers already have more in-depth knowledge than some of their teachers.

While many styles depend on dancers as choreographers or trainers, teacher-focused styles such as classical ballet, are equally challenging for dance medicine and the implementation of injury preventive measures. Due to a lack of content knowledge, many teachers, trainers or masters insist on regarding dance as art form only rather than the high-performance artistic discipline it has become, denying the importance of dance medicine, science, and education for teachers and trainers.

Demands on dancers are constantly rising, while in traditional environments training and education of dancers often remain unadjusted, resulting in the high numbers of dancers' injuries, dance medicine and science are still recording. To date, dance as an art form has become a highly artistic and virtuous but nonetheless highly athletic discipline, in which many outdated training traditions must be overcome to protect dancers' health and wellbeing. This aspect of dance medicine is the main link to dance education and training, making it all the more critical for dance education and dance medicine to forge a collective path.

---

[35] Koutedakis Y. *Biomechanics in dance. Journal of Dance Medicine and Science.* J Dance Med Sci. 12. 73-74. 2008.

[36] Grossman G, Krasnow D, and Welsh TM. *Effective Use of Turnout: Biomechanical, Neuromuscular, and Behavioral Considerations.* Journal of Dance Education. 5(1). 15-27. 2005.

[37] Krasnow D, Wilmerding MV, Stecyk S, Wyon M, and Koutedakis Y. *Biomechanical research in dance: a literature review.* Med Probl Perform Art. 26(1). 3-23. 2011.

[38] Kadel NJ, Teitz CC, and Kronmal RA. *Stress fractures in ballet dancers.* Am J Sports Med. 20(4). 445-449. 1992.

[39] Thomas JJ, Keel PK, and Heatherton TF. *Disordered eating and injuries among adolescent ballet dancers.* Eating and Weight Disorders-Studies on Anorexia Bulimia and Obesity. 16(3). E216-E222. 2011.

[40] Liederbach M, Schanfein L, and Kremenic IJ. *What is known about the effect of fatigue on injury occurrence among dancers?* Journal Dance Medicine & Science. 17(3). 101-108. 2013.

[41] Murgia C. *Overuse, fatigue, and injury: neurological, psychological, physiological, and clinical aspects.* J Dance Med Sci. 17(2). 51-2. 2013.

[42] Air ME. *Psychological distress among dancers seeking outpatient treatment for musculoskeletal injury.* J Dance Med Sci. 17(3). 115-125. 2013.

[43] Hancox JE, Quested E, Ntoumanis N, and Duda JL. *Teacher-created social environment, basic psychological needs, and dancers' affective states during class: A diary study.* Personality and Individual Differences. 115. 137-143. 2017.

[44] Liederbach M, Gleim GW, and Nichols JA. *Physiologic and psychological measurements of performance stress and onset of injuries in professional ballet dancers.* Med Probl Perform Art. 9(1). 10-14. 1994.

[45] Lai RY, Krasnow D, and Thomas M. *Communication between medical practitioners and dancers.* J Dance Med Sci. 12(2). 47-53. 2008.

[46] Scott WA. *Maximizing performance and the prevention of injuries in competitive athletes.* Current Sports Med Rep. 1(3). 184-190. 2002.

For amateurs and for professionals, dance is one of the most demanding (high-performance) activities. It requires great dedication and discipline from the dancers involved, based on high quality motivation at best. Even though dance as an amateur and recreational activity is considered even less of a sport than professional dance, dance training places high demands on dancers, including amateurs. Unfortunately, injuries happen frequently, as in all sportive activities. However, to say they are part of or in the nature of dance has to be rejected. As in any (competitive) sport, it is possible to prevent dance injuries, acute or traumatic injuries (accidents) and especially chronic injuries resulting from overtraining and overuse.[47,48,49,50,51,52,53] Many factors must be considered since injuries are usually multifactorial, i.e., they do not depend on one cause only. Such contributing factors can be exogenous, external, or extrinsic, i.e., resulting from the dancers' environment, or endogenous, internal, or intrinsic, i.e., resulting from dancers themselves.

Injuries are neither a measure for ambition, dedication, motivation, or discipline in dancers or teachers/trainers, nor do they characterize a dancer as specifically artistic. Injuries are simply a part of sportive activity and performance, which can happen, but the first and foremost goal is to prevent them: **preventing injuries means learning to understand the mechanisms underlying their etiology** (i.e., why and how they happened or developed).

The time available to dancers for their activity is minimal. Either because time for active careers is naturally limited, or because amateurs only have restricted time to invest into their hobby. Simultaneously, the demands placed on dancers, from competitive sports and health points of view, are enormously high [54] and they keep rising. Comparable to rugby/American football, dance is one of the most demanding high-performance activities. [55] Approximately 80-90% of all professional dancers sustain at least one serious injury in their careers and a majority of injuries result from overuse as well as fatigue, since exhaustion and sleep deprivation are significant issues for vocational and professional dancers.[56] The dance usually is the dancers' passion and often happens to become their identity. Their body is their instrument, and their mind is their conductor. If one part is injured, it always affects all other parts without exception. As such, the psychological correlations of physical injury must not be underestimated.[57,58]

Dancers fear injuries, which often leads them to try and ignore the pain for long periods.[59,60] That, sure, is exactly the wrong way to deal with injuries and pain.[61] On the one hand, dancers are afraid to admit their injuries to themselves, knowing that a break or restrictions of their training and a possible correction of underlying wrong dance technique would be necessary, which costs time and energy. On the other hand, both employed dancers and young dancers in training fear that their "weak points" might become known and cost them a job, role, or training opportunity. Even the ambition of many recreational dancers can lead them to hide injuries or dance through pain.[62] Shockingly enough, many dancers feel deeply ashamed for their injuries[63], which shows to

[47] Russel JA. *Preventing Dance Injuries: current perspectives.* J Sports Med. 4. 199-210. 2013.

[48] Sohl P, and Bowling A. *Injuries to dancers: prevalence, treatment and prevention.* Sports Med. 9. 317-322. 1990.

[49] Rietveld ABM, Macfarlane JD, and de Haas GJF. *Some thoughts on the prevention of complaints in musicians and dancers.* Clin Rheumatol. 32. 449-452. 2013.

[50] Robinson D, Zander J, and Research BC. *Preventing musculoskeletal injury (MSI) for muscians and dancers: A resource guide Vancouver.* Safety and Health in Arts Production and Entertainment (SHAPE). 36–50. 2002.

[51] Scialom M, Goncalves A, and Padovan CR. *Work and injuries in dancers.* Med Probl Perform Art. 21(1). 29-33. 2006.

[52] Garrick JG. *Early identification of musculoskeletal complaints and injuries among female ballet students.* J Dance Med Sci. 3(2). 80-83. 1999.

[53] Kaufmann JE, and Kiselka A. *Dance Medical Demands.* Dancer's Magazine. 2. 98-99. 2015.

[54] Wyon MA, Deighan MA, Nevill AM, Doherty M, Morrison SL, Allen N, Jobson SJ, and George S. *The cardiorespiratory, anthropometric, and performance characteristics of an international/national touring ballet company.* J Strength Cond Res. 21(2). 389 – 393. 2007.

[55] Blankenstein T, Grainger A, Dube B, Evans R, and Robinson P. *MRI hip findings in asymptomatic professional rugby players, ballet dancers, and age-matched controls.* Clin Radiol. 75(2). 116-122. 2020.

[56] Harkness Center for dance injuries. Newsletter 1(1). 2. 2005.

[57] Mainwaring L, Kerr G, and Krasnow D. *Psychological correlates of dance injuries.* Med probl perform Art. 8. 3-6. 1993.

[58] Mainwaring L, Krasnow D, and Kerr G. *And the dance goes on: Psychological impact of injury.* J Dance Med & Sci. 5(4). 105-115. 2001.

[59] Kelman BB. *Occupational hazards in female ballet dancers. Advocate for a forgotten population.* AAOHN J. 48(9). 430-434. 2000.

[60] Vassallo AJ, Pappas E, Stamatakis E, Hiller CE. *Injury Fear, Stigma, and Reporting in Professional Dancers.* Saf Health Work. 10(3). 260-264. 2019.

[61] Wainwright SP, Williams C, and Turner BS. *Fractured identities: injury and the balletic body.* Health (London). 9(1). 49-66. 2005.

[62] Lampe J, Groneberg DA, Ohlendorf D, and Wanke EM. *Pain in female dancers and dance teachers: Perception, assessment, and related behavior.* Scand J Med Sci Sports. 29(4). 623-632. 2019.

[63] Thomson P, and Jaque SV. *Exposing shame in dancers and athletes: shame, trauma, and dissociation in a nonclinical population.* J Trauma Dissociation. 2013;14(4):439-54.

which extent injuries in dance are regarded as personal weakness, making matters worse. **However, all the reasons for covering up and working through injury pain as the body's warning signals of overuse are ultimately harming the dancers, resulting in the specifically high numbers of overuse injuries in dance, especially to the lower extremities and spine.**[64,65,66,67] Moreover, such wrong coping strategies increase injury frequency, severity, and duration until full recovery[68], very often severely underestimated by dancers.[69,70]

What is needed here is for trainers, teachers and artistic directors, choreographers, and theater personnel to be experienced enough in dance medicine and fair enough to help (young) dancers make the right choices – among other, by **installing a climate, which fosters health and wellbeing through the support of the dancers' autonomy, their social, psychological, cognitive, and physical needs**. Sanctions, pressure, or threats resulting from injuries (or anything else) must not happen in a good institution![71] If pain, overuse reactions, or even injuries are already present, dancers must be given all the support they need to recover, and immediately at that.

Then again, schools, theatres or companies must never educate or force their dancers to work through pain or injury, erroneously claiming such behavior as sign for a good dancer, or using any other misleading and irresponsible interpretation imaginable. Many beginning complaints are shrugged off by teachers/trainers as bagatelles or trifles (and consequently then by dancers, because that is what they learn to do!). However, they lay the foundation of severe injuries to follow, when underlying factors are not detected and eliminated immediately (e.g., faults in dance technique).

Very often injuries begin as "minor" signs of overwork. Too often, acute and recurrent sore and hardened muscles or even pulled muscles are shrugged off easily.[72] But they already are muscle injuries, which can have far-reaching consequences and can severely influence dancers' health and wellbeing, or terminate their careers / joyful leisure activity. Instant search for the underlying causes by professionals, earliest possible identification, elimination, and the rehabilitation (i.e., healing) are decisive first actions to be taken immediately.[73] As immediate first aid is the most crucial factor for the chances of healing in acute injuries, it also is the foundation of the prevention of overuse injuries, which very often start as "minor" (acute or repetitive) injuries and end as severe chronic manifestations, when they are left unattended.

Are dancers artists or athletes?[74,75,76] This question is asked recurrently and hard to answer. However, dance medicine wants to ask that question to set the record straight for the overall benefit of dancers. To call dancers athletes is right with reference to the high levels of athletic performance they have to manage and which must not go unmentioned. To reduce dancers to artists only diminishes their reputation as much as it shortens the long list of opportunities how dance medicine and science can help them. However, the world of dance mostly uses "artists", stressing the artistic background, mostly with desperate vehemence, as if the athletic connotation ruined their artistic reputation. Dance medicine and science call dancers artistic athletes, athletic artists, or **performing athletes**, because leaving the athletic component away would diminish their stunning, diversified skills, while it bereaves them of so

---

[64] Hincapié CA, Morton EJ, and Cassidy JD. *Musculoskeletal injuries and pain in dancers: a systematic review.* Arch Phys Med Rehabil. 89(9). 1819-1829. 2008.

[65] Allen N, Nevill A, Brooks J, Koutedakis Y, and Wyon M. *Ballet injuries: injury incidence and severity over 1 year.* J Orthop Sports Phys Ther. 42(9). 781-790. 2012.

[66] Ekegren CL, Quested R, and Brodrick A. *Injuries in pre-professional ballet dancers: Incidence, characteristics and consequences.* J Sci Med Sport. 17(3). 271-275. 2014.

[67] Nilsson C, Leanderson J, Wykman A, and Strender LE. *The injury panorama in a Swedish professional ballet company.* Knee Surg Sports Traumatol Arthrosc. 9(4). 242-246. 2001.

[68] Jacobs CL, Hincapié CA, Cassidy JD. *Musculoskeletal injuries and pain in dancers: a systematic review update.* J Dance Med Sci. 16(2). 74-84. 2012.

[69] Askling C, Tengvar M, Saartok T, and Thorstensson A. *Sports related hamstring strains--two cases with different etiologies and injury sites.* Scand J Med Sci Sports. 10(5). 304-307. 2000.

[70] Askling CM, Tengvar M, Saartok T, and Thorstensson A. *Acute first-time hamstring strains during slow-speed stretching: clinical, magnetic resonance imaging, and recovery characteristics.* Am J Sports Med. 35(10). 1716-1724. 2007.

[71] Jenkins JB, Wyon M, and Nevill A. *Can turnout measurements be used to predict physiotherapist-reported injury rates in dancers?* Med Probl Perform Art. 28(4). 230-235. 2013.

[72] Askling C, Lund H, Saartok T, and Thorstensson A. *Self-reported hamstring injuries in student-dancers.* Scand J Med Sci Sports. 12(4).230-235. 2002.

[73] Garrick JG. *Early identification of musculoskeletal complaints and injuries among female ballet students.* J Dance Med Sci. 3(2). 80-83. 1999.

[74] Wyon MA, and Allen N. *Dance Medicine – Athlete or Artist?* SportEx Medicine 35(1).6-9. 2008.

[75] Turner BS, and Wainwright SP. *Corps de ballet: the case of the injured ballet dancer.* Sociol Health Illn. 25(4). 269-88. 2003.

[76] Russel JA. *Preventing Dance Injuries: current perspectives.* J Sports Med. 4. 199-210. 2013.

much, dance medicine and science can support them with.[77]

There is a point in the dancer's wish to stress the art component. (Professional) dancers are so exceptional that no new word creation could do them justice. They achieve the indescribable and, through their dedication and discipline, make dreams come true – for the outside world, while all such artistic virtuosity is but based on highest levels of athleticism, no other profession has to deliver to such an extent. Combining these two sides of art and sports makes dance probably the most demanding high impact sport ever. Professional, employed dancers usually face an enormous training load and work more hours a week than most other athletes, too often even without longer timeout such as summer vacation.[78,79] But not only that: they train and perform more hours than other athletes, while they manage to "hide" exactly that incredible athletic effort under the lightness and beautiful ease of artistic virtuosity – which is what is left and visible to the outside world, still making some people believe that dance is not much more than an easy physical activity.

The dancer is a fascinating target to study and research. Dancers are unique in all dimensions, offering insights into what is possible with regard to human cognitive and physical capacities but cannot be found in many people.[80] Dancers unify high-performance sport with artistic components, requiring exceptional neurocognitive skills: They fuse elite motion with music, rhythm, dramatic interpretation, the inclusion of costumes, props, partners and so much more, that makes them outstanding among all other athletes of the world. Which is why **dancers do never need to fear to be called athletes. They are exceptional anyway and the artistic component can never be taken away from them because it is the naturally underlying basis of their athleticism**! However, the physical and cognitive demands on dancers are continuously increasing, demanding athletic skills, such as high-level acrobatics, from today's ballet dancers, which were unthinkable 60 years ago. That is why they need support to be able to present their art with pain-and-strain-free enjoyment. Dancers perform all that is asked of them with pretended ease due to the constant strive for an overall focus on esthetics and excellence. That requires more from dancers than most other athletes have to give to do their job. And the audiences as well as the media insists, criticizes, and asks for more. But then, how is it possible that dancers, in particular, are entirely underserved, medically or financially, and that too often than not dancers and dance teachers are denied the social and financial recognition they deserve?

This is the reason why dance medicine refuses to reduce the dancer to an artist only (and teachers and trainers to people, "who love to jump around with children and adolescents in their spare time"). **Dance medicine and science want to show, how incredible dancers really are, and what a load of responsibility is imposed on and how much scholarly and practical knowledge is needed in a teacher/trainer**. On the one hand to do them justice. On the other, to be able to support them and call for others to do the same, by offering them solutions how to help. The rejection of the athletic part of dancers means to somehow deny or ignore much of the work dance scientists are doing every day for dancers. And this is also, why dance medicine is still so often misinterpreted as "dance therapy for the expression of feelings" or "only for those who are injured". – With regard to the latter, that would mean that actually dance medicine is the right thing for at least 90% of all dancers.

Despite all knowledge about dance medicine, dancers are not treated as the **high-performance artistic athletes** they are. And this includes amateurs as well. Not in the elite and high-performance levels, but dance as a hobby is nevertheless based on an impressive fusion of demanding physical activity paired with impressive neuro-cognitive demands. However, neither elite dancers not dance clubs or studios receive as much media attention and financial support through sponsors as team or individual sports do. As a result, financial resources are in short supply, as is the case everywhere in the arts. However, **many of these cost-cutting measures affect dancers' and dance teachers' health alike**, inflicting immediate and long-term worries or damage. It is or should be clear to everyone, who deals with the matter, that only maximum health can guarantee top performance. Therefore, the reverse conclusion should be that administrations, institutions, politics, and society, (as well as teachers and trainers), who have the maximum

[77] Koutedakis Y, and Jamuertas A. *The dancer as a performing athlete: Psychological considerations.* Sports Med. 34. 651-661. 2004.

[78] Ekegren C, Quested R, and Brodrick A. *Injuries in pre-professional ballet dancers: Incidence, characteristics, and consequences.* J Sci Med in Sports / Sports Med Australia. 17(3). 271-275. 2014.

[79] Twitchett E, Angioi M, Koutedakis Y, and Wyon MA.*The demands of a working day among female professional ballet dancers.* J Dance Med Sci. 14(4). 127-132. 2010.

[80] Bläsing B, Calvo-Merino B, Cross ES, Jola C, Honisch J, and Stevens CJ. *Neurocognitive control in dance perception and performance.* Acta Psychol (Amst). 139(2). 300-308. 2012.

performance of their dancers in mind, hopefully also try to strive for their maximum of health.

Exactly that is what dance medicine and science are talking about and doing every day: They research and implement means of prevention as well as performance enhancement. That is equally important for amateur and professional education as well as training. Both, amateur and professional dancers, are the representatives of their respective schools, studios, or institutions, thus indirectly shedding light on their administrations', teachers' and trainers' working methods and management. An accumulation of injuries or "drop-outs" in an institution or class should make management (as well as media, society, insurances etc.) reflect on the situation.

In amateur dance, it is common practice to stop dancing when something hurts. Nevertheless, even in amateur dance, many very ambitious young dancers very well work through pain and demotivation in a dogged effort to fulfill their dream of the stage. In professional schools, in companies or performance classes, dancers are admitted through auditions, performances, competitions, and aptitude tests, and the selection procedures are very tough and much feared because of, among other things, the large number of applicants. For this reason, prestige thinking is very important for all those who have made it to their position. They will usually go along with anything or try to go through a lot to keep their position and achieve their goal. In both cases, the institutions responsible for their teachers/trainers are responsible for the (young) dancers' health and, quite directly speaking, earn their daily bread from them. The rethinking of science of training, a redefinition of the dancing profession's status and responsibilities specifically and within society in general, the approach of dance medicine, and the focus on the professional handling of injuries and ill-health are absolutely necessary. A maximum use of injury-preventive measures long known in dance science is inevitable (and has been pending for too long). The enormous benefit of any injury preventive measure is that it always and "inevitably" leads to performance enhancement: Only a maximum of health can guarantee a maximum of performance.

Since "money" is an emotive word it can make many people look up, who would not have if we had just spoken the word "dancer": Injured and sick dancers cost money[81,82] and their "value" for the economy, to put it bluntly, decreases. It is essential to think about "alternative medicine for dancers" to avoid costs and reduce the loss for all parties involved as much as possible. As early as 1993, Garrick and Requa[83] outlined the costs and injury rates of a professional ballet company over 3 seasons: 309 injuries occurred in 104 dancers, resulting in a total of $ 398,396 in treatment costs for the insurance company and a staggering statistical mean of 2.97 injuries per dancer. Thus, on average, one injury accounted for $ 1,289. However, 4.2% of injuries alone created a cost of $ 5,000 per injury. 24 dancers alone (23.0% of those injured) sustained more than five injuries, accounting for 51.9% of all injuries. Feet (74 injuries, 23.9%), lumbar spine (71 injuries, 23.0%), and ankle (41 injuries, 13.3%) led the injury location ranks. Thus, **the injury statistics correspond to those of a professional sports team. In contrast to that, dance, since it is still treated as an art form only, does not receive nearly the same financial support and medical care** as, e.g., mass sports such as soccer, tennis, or skiing.

A similar picture was provided by Bronner et al. in 2003[84]: Bronner's team of dance scientists compared two seasons of a modern dance company with 42 dancers without dance medical interventions to the following three years, throughout which dancers and their management were directly provided with strict dance medical measures of injury prevention. The number of workers compensation cases was reduced from 81% to 17%. The days that dancers had to go on sick leave due to injury were reduced by 60%.

In 2001[85], comprehensive dance scientific management in a modern dance company resulted in a decline of 34% in total injury incidence, while workers compensation claims could be reduced by 66%, and the number of days lost to injuries by 56%. As such, enormous savings for the company in workers compensation premiums could be achieved again. But **above all, substantial burden of**

[81] Garrick JG, and Requa RK. *Ballet injuries: an analysis of epidemiology and financial outcome.* Am J Sports Med. 21. 586-590. 1993.
[82] Solomon R, Solomon J, Micheli LJ, and McGray E. *The "cost" of injuries in a professional ballet company: A five-year perspective.* Med Probl Perform Art. 11(4). 164-169. 1999.
[83] Garrick JG, and Requa RK. *Ballet injuries – an analysis of epidemiology and financial outcome.* Am J Sports Med. 21(4). 586-590. 1993.
[84] Bronner S, Ojofeitimi S, and Rose DJ. *Injuries in a modern dance company: effect of comprehensive management on injury incidence and time loss.* Am J Sports Med. 31(3).365-73. 2003.
[85] Ojofeitimi S, and Bronner S. *Injuries in a modern dance company effect of comprehensive management on injury incidence and cost.* J Dance Med Sci. 15(3). 116-122. 2011.

injury and their psychological correlates could be taken of the dancers' shoulders.

And in 2013, Allen et al.[86] implemented a prospective injury surveillance program in a professional ballet company over 3 years. Based on functional movement **screening** and injury history, dancers received **individual conditioning programs**, with the goal to decline injury incidence. Results showed substantial reductions for both genders: In male dancers, injury incidences (measured as year/1000hours of dancing) declined from year 1 with 4.76 injuries per 1000 hours, through year 2 with 2.40/1000 hours to year 3 with 2.22 injuries per 1000 hours of dancing. Female dancers could reduce injury incidence from 4.14 per 1000 hours in year 1, through 1.71/1000 hours in year 2 to 1.81/1000 hours in year 3. Injury incidence of both genders was thus reduced by more than half, "just" by implementing two major aspects of dance medicine and science: rigorous health and functional movement screenings (i.e., screening the dancers for health and training/dance technique weaknesses, with the aim to use the results for the design of individual conditioning programs, NOT to judge their abilities with any consequences for their work contracts and jobs) and individualized fitness training, built on the premise that dancers, as athletic artists, have the utmost need for targeted fitness training, because their fitness deficits obviously come with substantial injury risks.

Volume 3 of this series is dedicated to physiological aspects of dance medicine and science in dance practice, such as science of training, fitness, biomechanics etc. and will discuss screening for dancers as well as various aspects of training and fitness in theory and practice, thus providing extensive practical solutions and exercises.

These specific words and the many figures are deliberately placed at the beginning of this book to emphasize the need for a change in thinking. Although there are many studies available in dance medicine and dance science, the schools, companies, and dance professionals responsible for implementing the results for their dancers take too little to no notice of them. The number of injuries among dancers continues to rise, and little has changed in the dance profession's or teachers' reputation in society for decades. Invariably, the flimsy excuses for all those shortcomings are the **scarce finances and the alleged high cost of dance medicine**, which is why dance science continues to be ignored.

This introduction is not only intended to challenge the specter of physical and psychological injury among dancers in all clarity. Above all these words want to shed light on the financial but above all, the non-material losses that occur WITHOUT dance medicine for all those involved, i.e., the state, insurance companies, theaters, dance professionals, educators and trainers, and first and foremost the dancers.

Unvarnished addressing of shortcomings is frequent in this book, not only for the protection and support of dancers but also to protect the reputation of, defend and back up those who already really commit to dance medicine and science. Those who give their best (in financial and idealistic terms) to train, develop, and improve their own self-reflective work for the dancers entrusted to them exist in vast numbers.

Nevertheless, the reputation of dance teachers, trainers, and dance educationists is low in society. It has a negative connotation because of those who do not fulfill their responsibilities, as is the case in all professions, including institutions and policies in question. Dance medical interventions and a uniform prevention would drastically reduce many hidden costs (treatment and rehabilitation costs, insurances, costs for multiple castings and replacement for dancers and staff, replacement costumes, etc.), thus being a financial relief.

Dancers and teachers, to whom the world owes many beautiful or/and moving hours, deserve to have every support possible to stay physically, emotionally, psychologically, and mentally healthy in order to be able to present their incredible abilities without restriction, pain, or anxieties. Dance medicine and dance science provide all essential tools. Cooperating with and benefitting from what dance science can offer should be the overall goal of dance education and dance culture, audiences, media and all others involved.

---

[86] Allen N, Nevill AM, Brooks JH, Koutedakis Y, Wyon MA. *The effect of a comprehensive injury audit program on injury incidence in ballet: a 3-year prospective study.* Clin J Sport Med. 23(5). 373-378. 2013.

TO WHICH DANCE STYLES CAN DANCE MEDICINE BE APPLIED?

Dance Medicine can be applied to all styles, all dancers, all teachers, all levels of performance, and all ages. This series will provide thousands of references and publications, which show the high number of aspects, issues, and dance styles, dance medicine and science have addressed and covered.

Thinking about the development of dance over the last century, there has been a tremendous increase in demands on a dancer's performance and abilities. However, some may wonder whether there is still room for improvement without forcing dancers to expose their bodies to the highest risks and beyond anatomical, cognitive, and psychological limits without hesitation. Dance medicine makes every effort to provide solutions for injured or overworked dancers. Nevertheless, it is better to **prevent injuries and ill-health** in the first place **while simultaneously provide dancers with all possible tools, means, and knowledge to achieve maximum performance**. The most important aspect is that dance medicine and science have shown and are showing nonstop that **injury prevention and performance enhancement are interrelated**, killing two birds with one stone throughout all dance techniques and styles, as well as levels of expertise (vocational, professional, and amateur dancers).

Practice has shown that many teachers, trainers, and institutions such as schools, clubs, societies etc., claim to engage in dance medicine and science. However, their engagement often remains superficial, resulting in the belief that "dance medicine and science are fashionable but not very effective". Well, as with all things in life, things had better be done properly or not at all. Installing single aspects of dance medicine is an important step to start with. But when the overall goal is not to make sound changes with regard to basic principles for the sake of dancers' and teachers'/trainers' benefit, it is a drop in the ocean, resulting in the wrong idea that dance medicine is ineffective.

In order to be able to **take full advantage of dance medicine and science**, injury prevention together with performance enhancement must happen immediately and with the overall goal and willingness to make a number of in-depth changes, including letting go of outdated training traditions. For that it needs an open mind and a lot of knowledge in those who have or take the lead. In the best case, the implementation starts in the dance studio during education, at a time when the dancers' young minds are unbiased to grow up with healthy attitudes and their bodies are ready to meet correct dance technique from the very beginning, along with healthy nutrition, training, and many other safe habits. Professionals and adult dancers also need correct guidance from their trainers. And yet, mistakes committed during their own childhood and training can already affect their health at this point. For that reason, it is crucial to raise and educate children correctly on the basis of dance medicine and science early on, supporting their pathway to becoming dancers. Not only child dancers **rely on the knowledge of teachers** and their diligent guidance to healthy, reflected, holistic movement behavior, regardless of the dance style. Including dance medicine and science in all aspects of education and training of dancers is an education towards personal responsibility. Dancers should be allowed to learn why and how dance medicine can help them, and what they can and should do themselves to keep their instrument, their body, mind and soul, healthy. It is the only way to experience their desired profession for a long time, enjoying maximum performance and maximum health.

Of course, the respective dance techniques taught in the dance studio might differ tremendously in technique, equipment, training and environment, making a ballet dancer as unique as a b-boy. Still, all dance styles are performed by a human body. Thus, most of the scientific principles of biomechanics, motor control, motor learning, anatomy, physiology, pathology, psychology, and pedagogy equally apply to all dance styles. All related (at least basic) principles of dance medicine should be part of classes, training, and teachers' knowledge, if the best possible results in dancers want to be achieved – regardless of which dance style, level, gender, or age.

A critical element in dance medical dance pedagogy/teaching/training is equally crucial for all techniques and styles: the individuality of the dancer. **Recognizing, understanding, and acknowledging dancers' individuality** will be discussed in the following chapters and throughout this series as probably one of the most essential aspects of practical implementation of dance medicine and science.

Performance enhancing and injury preventive principles of dance medical dance pedagogy, teaching and training applies to all levels of expertise. Amateurs or recreational, vocational and professional dancers, novice (beginners) through intermediate to advanced levels, young dancers, adults, or older adults in leisure activities, up to accomplished dancers in their active careers – everybody including teachers, trainers, administrators, and any other involved in dance benefits from the dance medical achievements of the last decades.

Naturally, all aspects of dance medicine must be applied as such that they **meet the goals and needs** of the targeted group of dancers if they are supposed to be beneficial. Nevertheless, amateur, vocational, and professional dancers only have limited resources at their disposal – their bodies, mind and souls – and a more or less limited number of active years, depending on whether dance is a profession or a leisure activity. And dance medicine/science researches and supports all aspects of dance and therefore all levels of expertise with the goal to ensure safe and motivated dance practice.

Recurrently the question is discussed, who belongs to which group. Who is a professional, who is an amateur? Often the answer is that professionals are only those who get paid for dancing. Consequently, a dancer, who trains and performs for several hours five to seven times a week for several years, but (for various reasons) does not get paid or not get paid enough, is an amateur? On the other hand, a dancer, who trains three times a week for an hour and gets paid for various show acts and performances in the course of social or political events is a professional?

There is a wide range of dancers: Social dancers in clubs, dancers in private studios, or private ballet schools who train once or several times a week as a hobby or with the aim to prepare for vocational education; young dancers in federal vocational schools, students and dancers in university or other programs, dancers in unpaid groups or with short work contracts, freelance and employed company dancers. According to the group a dancer belongs to, the **task goals** are quite diverse, leading to specific needs in training. An amateur, who attends a few dance classes a week in a private studio does not qualify as a professional. And yet, time and again, exceptionally talented and hard-working young dancers emerge from private and "small" schools and become widely successful professionals. They are raised over many years by ambitious teachers and eventually successfully join a company, or make their living as professional freelance dancers. Thus, a school's size or reputation cannot be used as a criterium for the definition of professional or amateur either. Nor can or should (the implementation of) dance medicine and science be any criteria for such distinction: essential factors in dance and injury prevention such as good floors, the handling of footwear and clothing, the application of safety rules on and around the stage as well as in training rooms, but also the specific planning of training and the handling of basics such as warm-up and cool-down, stretching and the like, are equally important for professionals and amateurs. Thus, implementation of dance medicine does not serve as a reference point either.

The **amount of training and workload involved in reference to the goal** a dancer pursues should be the reference criteria, first and foremost, to ensure any dancer's health and wellbeing in the course of goal achievement. That, again, needs the expertise of the teacher, knowledgeable and experienced in evidence-based planning and conducting of dancers' training. **Training intensity, frequency, amount** and **duration, class structures**, **goal setting, physical** and **cognitive ability** as well as **mechanical loadability** must be precisely defined in constant reference to a realistic goal as well as the dancer's age and gender. These factors further determine the choice of methods and the targeted level of dance technique with regard to training loadability and time available. All aspects, again, **need precisely predefined goals,** which must be **realistic and achievable** to avoid injury but support individual development towards successful performance.

When training is planned and conducted appropriately, the mechanical load on the body will result in changes of all tissues involved. Tissues such as muscles, bones, tendons, ligaments, nerves, all organs, or blood, adapt to stress (e.g., training) and, in the best case, become increasingly stronger and resistant from training to training. Such biological adaptation is called **supercompensation or progressive overload**: After training and **in recovery time**, the body shrewdly adapts its tissues slightly more than what was needed and used in the previous training, in order to be on the safer side for any more or higher training load to follow. In the course of time (days and weeks of training), such constant over-adapting will result in an increase of the dancer's training status. To achieve such safe progress, teachers and trainers need a lot of knowledge in the fields of

science of training as well as **motor learning** and **motor development**. In the best case, the dancer's body can adjust to increasing workload over time, but has sufficient rest (i.e., sleep) and recovery time for all tissues to be ready for the next impact in due time. If recovery time and rest are insufficient, the dancer's body will suffer from overtraining, which, after a maximum of 4 weeks of acute **overtraining**, will result in lasting damage and become chronic.[87,88,89,90]

Volume 2 will discuss trainability and the difference between amateur and professional training from the perspective of motor learning, performance enhancement and injury prevention, while volume 3 addresses the issue with respect to science of training.

Amateur dancers – children, teenagers, and adults – differ significantly from vocational or professional dancers with respect to training load, motor learning, and goal setting. In recreational dancers, training frequency and intensity might not be enough for the body to be able to reach (higher levels of) positive supercompensation. Many recreational dancers only train for one or some hours per week, and such training impact will be more likely to ensure basic maintenance of health up to slight progress in training status – which is but the overall goal for dance as recreational activity, ensuring enjoyment and adherence. However, teachers and trainers in amateur classes have to be aware that some aspects of dance training and dance technique can never be achieved by recreational dancers and are therefore reserved for professional dance, because they depend on higher stages of motor learning as well as loadability, the ability of the body to adapt to training as a result of adequate amount of mechanical loading without being harmed. As much as overtraining or any other ill-health and injury have to be prevented in vocational and professional dancers through evidence-based planning of training, preparing the **training for amateurs** is not less demanding. Interestingly enough, way more dance teachers and trainers teaching amateurs are intensively studying and engaging in dance medicine, willing to train themselves to highest levels of knowledge for the benefit of their dancers, than those teaching/training vocational or professional dancers. Such responsible behavior is seen and appreciated and can serve as an example for all those who refuse.

While vocational and professional dancers train many hours a week, amateurs with one to a few training sessions have less time to learn and practice. To work faster or less thoroughly "to get it all done" might therefore lead to injuries as much as overtraining does in professionals. With fewer hours of training, **intensity as well as step/movement repertoire have to be planned accordingly** and can only be covered to a certain level. Amateurs should not use anything above this level because challenging and complicated steps, jumps, or turns need a certain amount of training, i.e., motor learning and physical adaptation, to prevent accidents but ensure motivation through goal achievement.

In vocational dancers the focus is on high numbers of repetitive movements to reach highest stages of motor learning, very often leading to monotony, which can lead to overwork as well as loss of motivation. With a focus on preparing the dancer for stage, performances are not the first and foremost focus in early professional education. However, in amateurs the **dream of stage** is mostly the dominating motivation, but can never be reached to the same extend as in vocational dancers. For teachers of young and adolescent amateur classes this aspect can be exceptionally demanding, because the teacher has to "perform a mental split" between what is possible and what is not, but dreamt of and fueled by the constant influence of social media, such as sensational(ly wrong) dance videos on Instagram & Co. In order to keep motivation high in amateur classes, teachers have to create a precise balance between dance technique training and preparation of choreographies and performances, often perceived as "the real dancing". At best, the **teacher communicates** to the dancer that it is essential for their enjoyment to train dance technique properly, but restrict it to movement repertoire, which is achievable and realistic for the sake of injury prevention and performance. As such, dancers will be able to reach higher stages of motor learning in basic dance technique and stay motivated, because the goal is realistic and results can be achieved and enjoyed. However, many

[87] Ackermann BJ. *Pain Across Artists' Lifespan.* Med Probl Perform Art. 33(1). 75-76. 2018.

[88] d'Hemecourt PA, and Luke A. *Sport-specific biomechanics of spinal injuries in aesthetic athletes (dancers, gymnasts, and figure skaters).* Clin Sports Med. 31(3). 397-408. 2012.

[89] O'Malley MJ, Hamilton WG, Munyak J, and DeFranco MJ. *Stress fractures at the base of the second metatarsal in ballet dancers.* Foot Ankle Int. 17(2). 89-94. 1996.

[90] Berriel GP, Costa RR, da Silva ES, Schons P, de Vargas GD, Peyré-Tartaruga LA, and Kruel LFM. *Stress and recovery perception, creatine kinase levels, and performance parameters of male volleyball athletes in a preseason for a championship.* Sports Med Open. 6(1). 26. 2020.

amateurs (or/and their parents) "dream bigger" in spite of the danger to sustain injuries or experience amotivation. Performing higher levels of repertoire might look impressive at first sight but too often than not is based on improper technique and can severely exceed anatomical, physical and cognitive capabilities. Such "tricks on stage" can become dangerous and are to be found in videos and clips on social media every day, but also common on stage and in stage competitions. Again, dance medical content knowledge in teachers is of utmost importance, to be able to reason with dancers and parents, but also in order to plan the training for amateurs as such, that their motivation can be high and (basic) dreams are fulfilled, while injuries are prevented.

Often people reason that injuries do not occur in amateurs, and that this distinguishes the professional from the amateur dancer (which in itself casts a very negative light on professional dance training!). This opinion must be refused, and a teacher with sufficient knowledge is capable of doing exactly that. Acute and overuse injuries can happen in amateurs as well. [91] Imbalances between training load and loadability due to lower numbers of training hours but high motivation in dancers and teachers can result in high degrees of over-confidence or over-motivation. [92, 93] Thus, chronic or overuse injuries can also be found in amateurs and do not constitute a distinguishing feature at all. The amateurs' "advantage" is probably that they can "just stop" dancing or take a break if the pain gets too bad, because dancing is first and foremost a hobby. Professionals who put many training hours and effort into their passion will find this more difficult. However, this thought by itself should already catch the attention of the reader: After all, why do dancers even have to get to the point where, due to physical or psychological discomfort, they only have one of two choices: give up or continue despite impairment?

Regarding **vocational** students, two further (dangerous) aspects enter the equation at this point: First, there is the additional argument that, after all, vocational dancers mostly had to go through rigorous years of training and **auditions** to be admitted to their education, which is why they understandably refuse to throw in the towel "easily" and are willing to fall silent about complaints for too long. (However, the thought that dancing is connected to pain and injury, which are therefore to be accepted, is also found to be engraved in the heads of amateurs and their teachers.) Second, not all schools cooperate with a dance medical specialist when it comes to aptitude tests in auditions, and even fewer engage in screening procedures. When young dancers suffer from first signs of complaints or become injured in early years of education, practice shows that many teachers and/or administrations are offhand about that, dismissing the issues as irrelevant, because dancers were admitted as well-suited for the education, which is why they cannot suffer any harm. However, just to have passed an audition, probably even with a dance medical specialist involved, does not guarantee any kind of invulnerability or justify any pressure in vocational training to work though pain. The rigorous aptitude tests and auditions in professional practice **do not protect** dancers **from** the **high injury rate** inherent in dance training.

Volume 3 of this series will address the importance of health-screening in dancers to support targeted planning and execution of training.

In both cases, the amateur and the professional dancer, and with no exception whatsoever, **dance technique must be taught individually, i.e., anatomically correct**. Repeatedly and improperly performed technique will lead to injuries due to compensatory movements resulting from wrong biomechanics. [94] The enormous pressure on young dancers in vocational schools, which is often justified by the lack of time and the short duration of their careers, must also be considered a significant factor in the high number of injuries, even among children and adolescents. Physical and mental adaptation through and to training takes time.

Especially teachers/trainers who work with professional and vocational dancers must not ignore this fact. Training for vocational and professional dancers is often rigorous,[95,96] based on ignorance towards the dancer's need for **recovery as essential component of training,**

[91] Lampe J, Groneberg DA, Ohlendorf D, and Wanke EM. *Pain in female dancers and dance teachers: Perception, assessment, and related behavior.* Scand J Med Sci Sports. 29(4). 623-632. 2019.

[92] Negus V, Hopper D, and Briffa NK. *Association between turnout and lower extremity injuries in classical ballet dancers.* J Orthop Sports Phys Ther. 35(5). 307-318. 2005.

[93] Steinberg N, Siev-Ner I, Peleg A, Dar G, Masharawi Y, Zeev A, and Hershkovitz I. *Injuries in female dancers aged 8 to 16 years. J Athl Training.* 48(1). 118-123. 2013.

[94] Koutedakis Y, Owolabi EO, and Apostolos M. *Dance biomechanics: a tool for controlling health, fitness, and training.* J Dance Med Sci. 12(3). 83-90. 2008.

[95] Twitchett E, Angioi M, Koutedakis Y, Wyon M. *The demands of a working day among female professional ballet dancers.* J Dance Med Sci. 14(4). 127-132. 2010.

[96] Kozai AC, Twitchett E, Morgan S, and Wyon MA. *Workload Intensity and Rest Periods in Professional Ballet: Connotations for Injury.* Int J Sports Med. 41(6). 373-379. 2020.

performance enhancement and injury prevention, resulting in already high numbers of injuries among young dancers.[97] Such evidence questions teachers, trainers, schools, and administrations, who are either unaware of such basic dance medical evidence due to their own lack of education and knowledge or ignore it in favor of old traditional training methods. Or they do not know how to make a change – but hesitate to ask dance medical professionals for help. Neither way is acceptable, because the dancer's health and wellbeing (ensuring their level of performance) is paramount.

Volume 3 of this series focuses on performance physiology, science of training, aspects of biomechanics, dance technique, and many more, presenting relevant information and solutions to meet this issue successfully. It will also discuss aspects such as warm-up, cool-down, stretching, or fitness training with respect to different levels of expertise, ages, and gender, stressing their importance for all dancers alike.

[97] Ekegren CL, Quested R, and Brodrick A. *Injuries in pre-professional ballet dancers: Incidence, characteristics and consequences.* J Sci Med Sport. 17(3). 271-275. 2014.

While dance medicine and science focus on injury prevention, performance enhancement, as well as health in and through dance, they cross roads with dance education and training, dance teaching, and dance pedagogy, who strive to **maximize a dancer's performance.** In order to maximize performance, health and wellbeing of the dancer are of utmost importance, because any ill-being will affect and thus decline performance. **Dance medicine enables dance education to focus on the dancer**: By knowing and acknowledging the anatomical, physiological, psychological, emotional and social principles underlying dance, mistakes and injuries can be prevented, while performance is free to reach its individual peak. That again **requires high levels of knowledge** in those who manage dancers, plan their training, and conduct their education as well as the education of teachers and trainers. The fusion of dance medicine and science with all fields of dance education and training can be regarded as the only solution to achieve that goal. **Such symbiosis can already be installed in early dance education, where the basis and awareness for safe dance practice is laid in children** (who will be the dancers and teachers, masters, choreographers of tomorrow!).[98]

Dancing and training as dancers, whether for vocational, professional or recreational purposes is part of most cultures, ages, and genders. While dance, as every form of physical activity, can lead to injuries and accidents, dance in general would be very healthy, supporting cognitive, physical, and psychological development in those engaging[99,100,101], the benefits of being physically active.[102,103] Hence, concerning the alleged harmfulness of dance education, dance medicine would basically disagree: Dance is anything but harmful when it is performed in an anatomical and physiological correct way, fostering the dancer's physiological, cognitive, and psychological development. To do so, internal and external factors and requirements have to be met, such as the training intensity and need for recovery, optimal flooring, footwear, but also the quality of the social environment, to only name a few and with many more discussed in this series. If all those factors are fulfilled, dance is not more harmful than any other professional high-performance or recreational activity monitored by sports medicine.

However, the idea that dance education and dancing is linked to suffering, sacrifice and pain still prevails. Measures of injury prevention are stressed and have been described, as introduced and cited on previous pages, with many more to follow. However, in spite of the growing body of research, dancers' pain and injuries have not seemed to decline within the last years.[104] It has been criticized recurrently that the extensive body of research provided is not implemented in dance practice, especially when environments are based on traditional approaches of dance education and training.[105,106] A few publications have directly addressed dancers and investigated, which reasons the dancers' perceive for their injuries or ill-health.[107,108,109,110,111] Such information is an important aspect to pursue for future installation of measures of injury prevention. **To prevent injuries the compliance and adherence of dancers (as well as teachers and trainers!) at best based on their knowledge is**

---

[98] Wilson M, and Deckert JL. *A screening program for dancers administered by dancers.* J Dance Med Sci. 13(3). 67-72. 2009.

[99] Coubard, OA, Ferrufino, L, Nonaka, T, Zelada, O, Bril, B, and Dietrich, G. *One month of contemporary dance modulates fractral posture in aging.* Frontiers in Aging Neuroscience. 6(17). 2014.

[100] Murcia C, Kreutz G, Clift S, and Bongard S. *Shall we dance? An exploration of the perceived benefits of dancing on well-being.* Arts & Health. 2. 149-163. 2010.

[101] Stark EA, Vuust P, and Kringelbach ML. *Music, dance, and other art forms: New insights into the links between hedonia (pleasure) and eudaimonia (well-being).* Prog Brain Res. 237. 129-152. 2018.

[102] Erickson, KI, Leckie, RL, and Weinstein, AM. *Physical activity, fitness, and gray matter volume.* Neurobiol Aging. 35(Suppl 2). 20-28. 2014.

[103] Stroth S, Reinhardt RK, Thöne J, Hille K, Schneider M, Härtel S, Weidemann W, Bös K, and Spitzer M. *Impact of aerobic exercise training on cognitive functions and affect associated to the COMT polymorphism in young adults.* Neurobiol Learn Mem. 94(3). 364-372. 2010.

[104] Kenny SJ, Whittaker JL, and Emery CA. *Risk factors for musculoskeletal injury in preprofessional dancers: a systematic review.* Br J Sports Med. 50(16). 997-1003. 2016.

[105] Wilmerding MV, and Krasnow D. *Dance pedagogy: Myth versus reality.* 3rd International Symposium on Performance Science. 283-289. 2011.

[106] Jenkins JB, Wyon M, and Nevill A. *Can turnout measurements be used to predict physiotherapist-reported injury rates in dancers?*. Med Probl Perform Art. 28(4). 230-235. 2013.

[107] Riding McCabe T, Ambegaonkar JP, Redding E, and Wyon M. *Fit to dance survey: a comparison with dancesport injuries.* Med Probl Perform Art. 29(2). 102-110. 2014.

[108] Brinson, Peter, and Fiona Dick. Fit to dance?: the report of the national inquiry into dancers' health and injury. London. Calouste Gulbenkian Foundation. 1996.

[109] Laws, Helen, Diane Parker, Joanna Apps, and Ian Bramley. Dance UK's Fit to Dance 2: Report of the Second National Inquiry into Dancers' Health and Injury in the UK. London. Newgate Press. 2005.

[110] Francisco R, Alarcão M, and Narciso I. *Aesthetic Sports as High-Risk Contexts for Eating Disorders – Young Elite Dancers and Gymnasts Perspectives.* The Spanish Journal of Psychology. 15(1). 2012.

[111] Dantas AG, Alonso DA, Sánchez-Miguel PA, and Del Río Sánchez C. *Factors Dancers Associate with their Body Dissatisfaction.* Body Image. 25. 40-47. 2018.

indispensable. [112, 113, 114, 115] First, interventions can specifically target the risk factors dancers have perceived and reported, indicating that the interventions will match exactly the environment and needs of the dancers. Second, asking them for the reasons they perceive for their injuries means to include their opinion, which supports their autonomy and gives them the feeling of being heard and personally supported. Consequently, and as the only chance for an intervention to be successful, the **adherence** to injury preventive interventions or **compliances** with necessary changes or measures will be sufficient enough to be effective. However, without the necessary and wise foresight, i.e., adherence and compliance of teachers and trainers, administrations etc., dancers very often do not get the chance to prevent their injuries and take necessary action.

Moreover, asking dancers for their perceived reasons for injuries and ill-health gives essential insight into the status quo of practical implementation of dance medicine and science in dance environments. **When dance medicine is implemented based on compliance of dancers and first and foremost those who manage and train them, injuries can be reduced, i.e., prevented successfully**![116] The teacher or trainer, their knowledge, methods of teaching, and the climate they create, also influencing their will to adhere to dance medical interventions, has been recurrently reported as (crucial) factor when it comes to prevention of injury or ill-health in all aspects of health and wellbeing of dancers.

Volume 2 and 3 discuss the role of the teacher, trainer, ballet master, artistic director, choreographer, or administrations in a number of different backgrounds and issues, such as motivational climate, fitness and science of training, or biomechanics.

For a very long time, and to a large extent still today, teaching dance was and is carried out by former dancers, who more or less voluntarily chose the profession of a dance teacher after their active career. However, especially in vocational and professional dance education and training, the teaching methods too often than not focus on dance technique only, due to a lack of knowledge and education in teachers and trainers. The focus on dance technique based on a high number of repetitive movements and, in the worst case, authoritative teacher/trainer behavior, comes with an extensive list of consequences.

A focus on **authoritative frontal teaching** primarily expects the student to learn from imitation, excluding those students from successful development who do not have a body that matches or at least closely resembles the teacher's. Those who are thus not fortunate enough to make progress through pure imitation and remain healthy at the same time must adapt their learning and training somehow, to get the maximum out of their individually and differently built bodies.

Frequently, this results in the dancer trying to or being forced to overcome their anatomical limitations through compensations somewhere along the kinetic chains of motion or by the targeted forcing of joints[117], to achieve their goals. If, in that very process, incipient **alarm signals** such as **physical** and **psychological pain** are ignored by both teachers and the affected dancers, significant damage can be done to the dancers' bodies, mind, and soul.

The cliché that dance (mostly ballet) is highly detrimental to health may have originated from this issue. In many countries, dance pedagogical education or related certification is not mandatory for dance teachers, and federal regulations are missing. As a result, many former dancers still believe that they are on top of their second career as teachers. However, **teaching and dancing are completely different professions**, and a lack of (willingness for) knowledge and education in teachers, trainers, ballet masters, and artistic directors is detrimental to dancers' health as well as performance.

---

[112] Shamlaye J, Tomšovský L, and Fulcher ML. *Attitudes, beliefs and factors influencing football coaches' adherence to the 11+ injury prevention programme.* BMJ Open Sport Exerc Med. 6(1):e000830. 2020.

[113] Silvers-Granelli H, Mandelbaum B, Adeniji O, Insler S, Bizzini M, Pohlig R, Junge A, Snyder-Mackler L, and Dvorak J. *Efficacy of the FIFA 11+ Injury Prevention Program in the Collegiate Male Soccer Player.* Am J Sports Med. 43(11). 2628-2637. 2015.

[114] Steffen K, Emery CA, Romiti M, Kang J, Bizzini M, Dvorak J, Finch CF, and Meeuwisse WH. *High adherence to a neuromuscular injury prevention programme (FIFA 11+) improves functional balance and reduces injury risk in Canadian youth female football players: a cluster randomised trial.* Br J Sports Med. 47(12). 794-802. 2013.

[115] Steffen K, Myklebust G, Olsen OE, Holme I, and Bahr R. *Preventing injuries in female youth football--a cluster-randomized controlled trial.* Scand J Med Sci Sports. 18(5). 605-614. 2008.

[116] Allen N, Nevill AM, Brooks JH, Koutedakis Y, Wyon MA. *The effect of a comprehensive injury audit program on injury incidence in ballet: a 3-year prospective study.* Clin J Sport Med. 23(5). 373-378. 2013.

[117] Kaufmann JE, Nelissen RGHH, Exner-Grave E, and Gademan MGJ. *Does forced or compensated turnout lead to musculoskeletal injuries in dancers? A systematic review on the complexity of causes.* J Biomech. 114. 110084. 2021.

How can we still have to face such issues in spite of all knowledge and scholarly protection and guidance that dance medicine and science provide? The answer is not easy, because it is dependent on many underlying aspects, which allow such shortcomings as unqualified teachers and trainers to prevail. Society, politics, and the resulting "dancer's identity" play essential roles.

Do dancers always have to be injured, in pain, and work through both?[118,119,120,121] Do injury and pain have to be part of the so-called **dance identity** or **dancer's identity**, probably even regarded as a sign that the dancer has worked with dedication, commitment, or "professionalism"? The paradox of the issue is, however, that professional and vocational dancers live in fear of injury throughout their career[122], while they silently (have to) accept their occurrence.

Moreover, such **misguided form of dance-identity** is already integrated in the education of the young, who grow up facing high numbers of injuries and have to deal with their consequences.[123,124,125] Making matters even worse, research has shown that such attitudes are even transferred into recreational dance, where dancers suffer from and work through pain and injuries as well.[126]

Professional and vocational dancers are at risk to lose contracts, jobs, or even their chance of education or career, when they are injured, which is why it is common to dance though injury and pain [127] – instead of implementing dance medicine and science to prevent all related issues in the first place, such as injury and pain as well as related stress, fear, suffering, denial, or consequences.

Where and why are we going wrong? We are living in the 21st century, in which dance medicine and science, sports medicine and all other related fields able to serve the dancer, can provide sufficient proof that many of dancers' injuries and a lot of other ill-health in the dance population could be prevented. Equally high-level evidence exists, which shows, how dancers' training of all levels and ages can be conducted as such, that peak performance is reached, based on the **individuality of the dancer**. Where and why are we going wrong?

It **needs those working closest with the dancer** to accept support from dance science and to implement dance medicine into dance practice: **teachers, trainers, pedagogues, artistic directors, ballet masters and choreographers**.

In 1997, Susan Ann Lee[128] wrote "The Artist as Teacher: A Psychological Perspective", an evidence-based report on the International Symposium on Career Transitions for Dancers in Switzerland. Dr Lee quoted the worries of personnel caring for dancers' health and overall wellbeing from panel discussions with regard to outdated training traditions and former dancers, who become teachers, ballet masters, or artistic directors without any education or content knowledge.

"How can we isolate these individuals so that they can do the least amount of damage?"

Still others commented, "we wish the individuals would leave or retire,"

and "we don't dare speak to them about their behavior out of respect for who they had been."

Further researchers have addressed the issue since 1997[129,130], showing that things have not changed much for many dancers in the world although so many people, on the other hand, fight hard to introduce changes.

---

[118] Wainwright SP, Williams C, and Turner BS. *Fractured identities: injury and the balletic body*. Health. 9(1). 49-66. 2005.

[119] Harrison C, and Ruddock-Hudson M. *Perceptions of Pain, Injury, and Transition-Retirement: The Experiences of Professional Dancers*. J Dance Med Sci. 21(2). 43-52. 2017.

[120] Turner BS, and Wainwright SP. *Corps de ballet: the case of the injured ballet dancer*. Sociol Health Illn. 25(4). 269-288. 2003.

[121] Jacobs CL, Cassidy JD, Côté P, Boyle E, Ramel E, Ammendolia C, Hartvigsen J, and Schwartz I. *Musculoskeletal Injury in Professional Dancers: Prevalence and Associated Factors: An International Cross-Sectional Study.* Clin J Sport Med. 27(2). 153-160. 2017.

[122] Kelman BB. *Occupational hazards in female ballet dancers. Advocate for a forgotten population.* AAOHN J. 48(9). 430-434. 2000.

[123] Jenkins JB, Wyon M, and Nevill A. *Can turnout measurements be used to predict physiotherapist-reported injury rates in dancers?* Med Probl Perform Art. 28(4). 230-235. 2013.

[124] Negus V, Hopper D, and Briffa NK. *Associations between turnout and lower extremity injuries in classical ballet dancers.* J Orthop Sports Phys Ther. 35(5). 307-318. 2005.

[125] Ekegren CL, Quested R, and Brodrick A. *Injuries in pre-professional ballet dancers: Incidence, characteristics and consequences.* J Sci Med Sport. 17(3). 271-275. 2014.

[126] Lampe J, Groneberg DA, Ohlendorf D, and Wanke EM. *Pain in female dancers and dance teachers: Perception, assessment, and related behavior.* Scand J Med Sci Sports. 29(4). 623-632. 2019.

[127] Vassallo AJ, Pappas E, Stamatakis E, Hiller CE. *Injury Fear, Stigma, and Reporting in Professional Dancers.* Saf Health Work. 10(3). 260-264. 2019.

[128] Lee, SA. The Artist as Teacher: A Psychological Perspective. Med Probl Perform Art. 12(2). 38-41. 1997.

[129] Lakes R. *The Messages behind the Methods: The Authoritarian Pedagogical Legacy in Western Concert Dance Technique Training and Rehearsals.* Arts Education Policy Review. 106. 3-20. 2005.

[130] Johnston D. *Private speech in ballet.* Research in Dance Education. 7. 3-14. 2006.

The following chapters as well as volume 2 and 3 of this series will discuss the consequences as well as the issue itself from various perspectives, e.g., with regard to teacher/master created motivational climate, feedback and communication, handling of pain, science of training and scheduling for dancers, as well as preventing automatizing faulty dance technique, among many others. Backgrounds will be explained and, above all, solutions offered.

More and more dancers (as well as physicians, parents etc.) are coming forward and demand dancers' right for a work and/or training environment, which does not harm them, encouraged by their own knowledge and interest in dance medicine and science. These dancers often stand in stark contrast to those people in higher positions who still too often lack knowledge needed for their second career as teachers or trainers. **Many teachers, trainers, ballet masters, directors etc. already actively and intensively engage in dance medicine and science, in order to support their dancers. Their reputation as well as the wellbeing of dancers suffer through those who refuse**.

Lee quoted, *"we don't dare speak to them about their behavior out of respect for who they had been."* It is not as easy as that, and many more factors are involved, such as lack of funding for programs implementing dance medicine in theatres, etc. However, decades of political correctness and fear of addressing grievances or shortcomings have not changed much, because, as quoted, everybody tried to stay polite and diplomatic. But is it right and fair against dancers to allow such people to proceed? Even worse, to pass on outdated traditions and support an education of misguided identity already in the young, resulting in many dancers who still believe it is an integrated part of their lives to be injured, in spite of learning (or secretly knowing) it better? As a teacher, ballet master, trainer, artistic director etc. a person has entered a new career path, which differs from that of a dancer. In their new career their tasks are to manage dancers' training, create their choreographies as well as their schedules, care for dancers. Out of respect to who they were, they are not addressed on the grievances they provoke, as cited above – while refusing to accept dance medical knowledge and the need for their own education and study? Is this respectful of dancers, who bear the consequences, while more and more already know themselves that this system is wrong? Where does (perceived) political correctness end and responsibility start? Trying to stay correct prevents us from asking such questions publicly, and science always aims to serve diplomatic and scholarly objectivity. But that also means to support such behavior, because the people in question count and live on exactly such correctness and respect – while they do not (need to) make an effort to change their (narcissistic and/or narrow-minded) behavior.

Respect is something somebody earns through their behavior. Former dancers who became ballet masters, directors, teachers, choreographers etc. may have been great dancers themselves, and for that they deserve all due respect. But they have made a transition in career. And the respect for their new career they still have to earn. For that matter, it is not a question of disrespect for their previous achievements when we ask the question why they do not invest their utmost to earn our respect for their new ones! We should start to ask the question, why they do not put their dancers' wellbeing first!

"To Jean Erdmann, who taught me to teach so that the individual artist in each of us could emerge without damage to the body or psyche."[131]

(Ruth Solomon's dedication to Jean Erdmann, 1990)

It is not enough to know and be sufficiently experienced in the dance technique one is teaching. Being a dancer and performing technique is something completely different than having to teach others and guide them in their own, individual goal achievement. Therefore, **not all former dancers are automatically good teachers, artistic directors, or trainers**. While someone may have been a ballerina, as a teacher, they may well fall far behind someone who has never received that title or even come close to it, but self-reflectively underwent comprehensive special training to be prepared for their second career as teacher.

For this person, teaching dance or dance pedagogy might be a vocation that comes with an intrinsic motivation for **knowledge** and **self-reflection**. It takes much more than dance technique and one's own dance experience to teach successfully, although, for sure, one's technique is essential. The assumption that all former, good dancers are naturally excellent teachers results in one of the biggest problems dance medicine and science have to deal with: frontal ("talk-and-chalk"-) teaching and a lack of knowledge to acknowledge a dancer's individuality.

All dancers to be educated or trained are individuals. Their bodies do not entirely resemble any other body in this world, not even the teacher's, even if some may appear similar. Thus, all dancers need individual attention in numerous areas. They all depend on the **teachers' awareness of and ability to recognize, understand, and acknowledge** their anatomical strengths, weaknesses, or limitations.

That in itself needs a lot of knowledge and experience, and even more is needed for the ability to plan dancers' training purposefully, based on prior analysis. Unless a teacher recognizes and acknowledges this individuality and knows how to identify and manage it, multiple and severe damage can be done to dancers' bodies and, of course, to their souls and minds. Dance medicine provides teachers and trainers with all possible knowledge and means to achieve that goal, and has globally taken root. However, if teachers/trainers still do not acknowledge the absolute necessity to study and use dance medicine, they simply do not pay dancers the respect they deserve.

In volume 2, the chapters on motivational climates and communication, and in volume 3, the chapters on screening and many chapters more provide information on how to recognize individuality and plan training accordingly.

The usefulness of teacher-oriented "chalk-and-talk-teaching" in dance (and all other disciplines) has been discussed in professional circles and publications intensively for decades. Regarding teachers as the center of dance education is founded on old traditions. The students try to follow their example and learning is based on imitation to a great extent, as already described above. When students cannot imitate the teacher, there are only a few further options: Frustration and giving up on the goal, or to attempt to adapt beyond the own body's capabilities. However, this attempt is bound to fail since any movement that violates one's anatomical-physiological abilities will sooner or later lead to injuries caused by compensating or forcing and thus leading to overuse.

It makes no difference whether this happens in amateur dance or professional training, in ballet, acrobatics, contemporary, or street styles. When dancers do not see (or are not shown!) any other possibility or are forced to work against their bodies to achieve their goals, it can permanently damage their musculoskeletal system. The disillusionment concerning their dreams and the bitter experience of failure and dropout can also damage their psyche.[132,133] However, does it even have to get to the point where students/dancers are left with only these two options: Giving up in favor of physical and mental health, or ignoring the body's alarm signals and ruining them to be able to realize their dream?

[131] Solomon, Ruth, Solomon, John, and Sandra Czerny Minton (eds.). Preventing Dance Injuries. Champaign (IL). Human Kinetics. 2005.

[132] Wagnsson S, Patriksson G, and Carlman P. *Causes and consequences of dropping out from organized youth sports.* Swedish J of Sports Res. 1. 26-54. 2013.

[133] Beck L, and Muia JA. *A Portrait of a Tragedy: Research Findings on the Dropout.* The High School J. 64(2). 1980.

Multiple alternatives exist, e.g., integrating aspects of motivational and teaching theories, such as Achievement-Goal-, Self-Determination-, or Motivational-Climate-Theory and many others, which are discussed and analyzed extensively with respect to dance and teaching dance in volume 2.

This is where **preventive dance medicine** should come into play first and foremost. It not only provides information on how the body functions in dance, which mechanisms and structures enable or inhibit which movement, or which training principles can enhance performance. It also explains how teachers can recognize dancers' individuality and support it in teaching and training. Such support seems complicated and demanding at first glance – and it still is at the second. First, it needs a lot of **content knowledge** (biomechanics, anatomy, science of training, psychology etc.), meaning that the teacher/trainer has to study. However, teachers in other disciplines such as math, sciences, languages etc., naturally have to study in order to be allowed to teach in schools, colleges etc. Why should dance be an exception of that rule, especially, when we have witnessed over decades that this concept based on a lack of education does not pay off? It, sure, needs more than the teacher's/trainer's/master's will to study, e.g., it needs **fair contracts** and **appropriate payment** for dancers (and teachers) so that they are able to invest in their own **education** as teachers during or after their active dance career. It also needs changes in politics and federal support, starting with the **legal acknowledgement of dance teachers as a profession**, which is still not the case in many countries, and subsequently, the introduction of **laws which regulate and supervise mandatory education** but also attract the economy, insurances etc. to invest in such educational programs, in dancers and teachers.

The following chapters will address injuries and the cost of injuries for all parties involved, showing the financial and economic benefits of the implementation of preventive dance medicine in dance environments.

The second aspect of recognizing dancers' individuality is that teachers and trainers must be willing to get to know dancers personally in a healthy, professional manner. If this is done based on mutual professional agreement, teachers do not need to fear any loss of authority. On the contrary, they can cooperate with the students and dancers to achieve peak performances. With content knowledge of dance medicine and science, teaching methods can be applied which foster empowering motivational climates and task-oriented goal-behavior in dancers and teachers, and thus autonomy, competence, and relatedness, i.e., the feeling that the teacher/trainer cares, that the dancer belongs and has a place to turn to with worries and concerns. This requires emotional intelligence, based on empathy, knowledge, and social skills from both sides, the dancers and the teachers. Such skills have to be learned.

Dance medicine does not admonish former dancers who want to share their knowledge as teachers and trainers. The point here is neither to judge teachers/trainers nor to doubt their good, positive attitude and that they undoubtedly have their dancers' best interest at heart. But in order to be able to achieve that very best it is necessary to have sufficient tools at hand. However, the high number of dancers' injuries shows that too many teachers, trainers, ballet masters etc. still lack such tools (i.e., knowledge). If such teachers then are unwilling to undergo sufficient education themselves, they are wrong in their profession, regardless of how good a dancer they had been.

One of the aspects involved in this dilemma is that new generations of teachers and trainers should understand that the focus of attention in dance education and training has to be the dancer, their performance and health. Acquiring such an open mindset may be a significant hurdle in dance training and pedagogy because, after all, dance as an art form is naturally also about a healthy amount of self-expression and career. But when someone wants to be a teacher, these are the very aspects that should not be the first and foremost focus of attention anymore. However, since many dancers themselves have struggled all their lives to be recognized for their achievements, it will, of course, not be easy for them to let go of their career and accept that the spotlight is on their dancers, once they change to being a teacher or trainer. Teachers are usually in their students' shadows, seeing them off, watching them fly away, and become famous in the best case. It is not easy for people who were used to being the center of attention themselves and having a career for which they gave everything to suddenly step back. What remains is usually a great deal of exhaustion, physical and usually also psychological pain.

The best teachers will still be those who have the strength and courage to put themselves second and who are willing to focus on their dancers with the aim to

make them better and healthier than the teachers ever were themselves. That is a significant thought and an even more significant step for former dancers to take. But this step is enough to earn them more respect and joy in their new profession than they could have ever gained by following the traditional, authoritative path.

Now, if former dancers take up the teaching profession out of passion, out of an inner calling to share their knowledge and serve dancers and their careers, they will feel the need to engage wholeheartedly in this new profession. If this is done self-reflectively, future teachers will find their way to dance medicine on their own, because they will want to adjust and be prepared. This is how and why so many teachers and trainers are already highly active (and highly welcome!) in the field of dance medicine and science. Dancers (and teachers in dance) could achieve a higher social (and financial) status through dance medicine and reach their deserved position as high-performance artistic athletes sooner or later. Especially dance teachers can and must actively promote this path and thus receive the respect they deserve from society themselves.

This series also dedicates itself to the **health of teachers and trainers, and how dance medicine can serve them specifically to achieve or restore high levels of motivation through an overall level of wellbeing**. In search for that, knowledge and information on how teachers can stay healthy in spite of all their enormous workload with regard to anatomy, science of training, or fitness in themselves is essential. Moreover, practical and theoretical information of how to improve dancers' training indirectly supports teachers and trainers as well.

The proverb "**knowledge is power**" is not unfounded: teachers who have content knowledge, will have enough tools at hand to improve their own performance and health, while they improve the performance and wellbeing of their dancers. That again will lead to intrinsic motivation and inspiration, both highly related to psychological and physiological wellbeing. Teachers, trainers, choreographers, ballet masters, or artistic directors as well as dancers will benefit if **dance** can gain a **higher status in society**, not least through dance medicine and science which will take dance education and dance training to higher levels.

For a long time, dance was thought of as purely physical activity. But anyone, who has danced knows that this view is too narrow and utterly outdated, especially since neuroscience knows that several areas in the brain responsible for all aspects of dancing constantly interact and are also responsible for functions such as decision making, emotions, memory and many more. Dance is more than "simple physical movement".[134,135]

Dance moves the body, soul, and mind of dancers (as well as teachers/trainers, and audiences) throughout all ages and levels of expertise, resulting in important benefits for many different aspects of health and wellbeing.[136, 137, 138, 139, 140] That is one reason why preventive programs such as "**Dance in Schools**" or "**Arts/Dance for Health**" are vital.[141,142,143] And dancers themselves can be counted among the most impressive people ever, being able to achieve **exceptional neurocognitive and physical goals and levels of performance**.[144]

How can this be achieved, and, generally speaking, what does this mean for teachers and dancers alike? **Which effects can dance have on those who dance?** What do dance teachers offer, if not mainly fitness through the acquisition of motor sequences?

Dance as a physical, cognitive, psychological, artistic, creative, and cultural concept (among many others) is beneficial to dancers far beyond sheer motor activity, when it is taught in a healthy way.[145] Naturally, the **effects of dance differ with regard to the goals**. When dance is performed as social activity with the overall goal to maintain or improve health and wellbeing it will affect body, mind and soul in another way than dance as high-performance activity affects the professional or vocational dancer. However, dance can promote **physical, cognitive, and psychological capacities**.[146,147] By developing one's motor-biological abilities, proper social dance training can positively affect dancers' overall health and wellbeing[148] – an outcome that should not be underestimated in times of increased life expectancy[149] but also increasing sedentary activities in all ages, leading to obesity or other aspects of ill-health.

As physical activity in general, dance enhances **metabolism**[150,151,152,153] and the **immune system**[154]. Not

[134] Adshead-Lansdale, Janet, and June Layson (eds.). Dance History – An Introduction (2nd edition). London. Routledge. 1994.

[135] Murci, Cynthia Quiroga. Tanzen: Subjektive und psychologische Wirkung [Dance: Subjective and psychological effects]. Dissertation. Frankfurt. Goethe-University Frankfurt/Main, Germany. 2010.

[136] Murcia C, Kreutz G, Clift S, and Bongard S. *Shall we dance? An exploration of the perceived benefits of dancing on well-being.* Arts & Health. 2. 149-163. 2010.

[137] Bennel K, Khan K, Matthews B, Cook E, Holzer K, McKay H, and Wark J. *Activity-associated differences in bone mineral are evident before puberty: A cross-sectional study of 130 female novice dancers and controls.* Pediatric Exercise Science. 12. 371-381. 2002.

[138] Coubard, OA, Ferrufino, L, Nonaka, T, Zelada, O, Bril, B, and Dietrich, G. *One month of contemporary dance modulates fractral posture in aging.* Frontiers in Aging Neuroscience. 6(17). 2014.

[139] Borhan A, Hewston P, Merom D, Kennedy C, Ioannidis G, Santesso N, Santaguida P, Thabane L, and Papaioannou A. Effects of dance on cognitive function among older adults: a protocol for systematic review and meta-analysis. Syst Rev. 7(1). 24. 2018.

[140] Kattenstroth JC, Kolankowska I, Kalisch T, and Dinse HR. *Superior sensory, motor, and cognitive performance in elderly individuals with multi-year dancing activities.* Front Aging Neurosci. 2. 31. 2010.

[141] Health Development Agency. *Arts for health: A review of good practice in community-based arts projects and initiatives which impact on health and wellbeing.* ISBN: 1-84279-016-1. Retrieved from www.hda-online.org.uk

[142] Burkhardt J, and Brennan C. *The effects of recreational dance interventions on the health and well-being of children and young people: A systematic review.* Arts & Health. 4. 1-14. 2012.

[143] Schroeder K, Ratcliffe SJ, Perez A, Earley D, Bowman C, and Lipman TH. *Dance for Health: An Intergenerational Program to Increase Access to Physical Activity.* J Pediatr Nurs. 37. 29-34. 2017.

[144] Bläsing B, Calvo-Merino B, Cross ES, Jola C, Honisch J, and Stevens CJ. *Neurocognitive control in dance perception and performance.* Acta Psychol (Amst). 139(2). 300-308. 2012.

[145] Gardner S, Komesaroff P, and Fensham R. *Dancing beyond exercise: Young people's experiences in dance classes.* J Youth Studies. 11. 701-709. 2008.

[146] Maraz A, Király O, Urbán R, Griffiths MD, Demetrovics Z. *Why Do You Dance? Development of the Dance Motivation Inventory (DMI).* PLoS ONE. 10(3): e0122866. 2015.

[147] Murrock CJ, and Graor CH. *Effects of dance on depression, physical function, and disability in underserved adults.* J Aging Phys Act. 22(3). 380-385. 2014.

[148] Guidetti L, Buzzachera CF, Emerenziani GP, Meucci M, Saavedra F, Gallotta MC, Baldari C. *Psychophysiological responses to Salsa dance.* PLoS One. 10(4):e0121465. 2015.

[149] Joung HJ, and Lee Y. *Effect of Creative Dance on Fitness, Functional Balance, and Mobility Control in the Elderly.* Gerontology. 65(5). 537-546. 2019.

[150] Na Ayudthaya WC, and Kritpet T. *Effects of Low Impact Aerobic Dance and Fitball Training on Bone Resorption and Health-Related Physical Fitness in Thai Working Women.* J Med Assoc Thai. 98 Suppl 8. 52-57. 2015.

[151] Williford HN, Scharff-Olson M, and Blessing DL. *The physiological effects of aerobic dance. A review.* Sports Med. 8(6). 335-345. 1989.

[152] Rodrigues-Krause J, Krause M, and Reischak-Oliveira A. *Dancing for Healthy Aging: Functional and Metabolic Perspectives.* Altern Ther Health Med. 25(1). 44-63. 2019.

[153] Araneta MR, Tanori D. *Benefits of Zumba Fitness® among sedentary adults with components of the metabolic syndrome: a pilot study.* J Sports Med Phys Fitness. 55(10). 1227-1233. 2015.

[154] Matthews CE, Ockene IS, Freedson PS, Rosal MC, Merriam PA, and Hebert JR. *Moderate to vigorous physical activity and risk of upper-respiratory tract infection.* Med Sci Sports Exerc. 34(8). 1242-1248. 2002.

only in professionals, dance trains and affects the **cardiovascular system** and **lung function**[155,156,157,158], however, in dance styles such as ballet or contemporary more in favor of anaerobic than aerobic contributions, which would but be essential for injury prevention and performance enhancement.[159,160]

Volume 3 of this series will discuss such aspects with reference to the practical design of dance classes, and how aerobic fitness can be supported in dance, especially in styles such as ballet, contemporary, or modern.

As such, one of the goals of evidence-based dance training is to **structure dance classes in a way that all aspects of fitness and health are met, thus serving the arts in the most efficient manner**. For instance, by particularly including the training of cognitive, psychological and physical stamina. Especially **aerobic endurance** is essential, boosting the **resistance to fatigue** and the **capacity for faster recovery** after training. Hence, endurance leads to **enhanced adaptation to training stimulus**. As such, the health and functionality of cardio-vascular, respiratory and immune systems is supported. That enhances overall wellbeing through prolonged ability to stay mentally and physically focused through ameliorated oxygen supply for muscles, other organs, and especially the brain.

Evidence-based dance training specifically targets **strength and strength endurance**, supporting health, posture, and inter- as well as intramuscular coordination. Strength training is of particular importance, because dance is naturally related to higher levels of **flexibility**, which are an integrating part of most dance techniques.

In order to allow **functional levels of flexibility**, stretching has to be combined with **targeted strength training**. As such, flexibility is of functional, i.e., operational, availability, because only the combination with specific strength training leads to high level of the already mentioned intra- and intermuscular coordination: the coordination within a muscle, i.e., its muscle cells with the assigned nerve cell(s); and the coordination between different muscles to allow functional kinetic chains of motion.

Such coordination is an underlying aspect of **postural and motor control**, which is essential in the **prevention of injuries** as well as overall **performance enhancement**. It forms the basis of motor development, motor learning and motor performance.

Coordination is basically always trained whenever somebody moves, and especially supported through evidence-based dance training due to its comprehensive repertoire of exercises targeting **proprioception** and **sensorimotor control**, the ability to control the own movement by engaging the body's sensory systems.

Volume 2 discusses proprioception and sensorimotor control with respect to neuropsychology, motor learning and related topics. Volume 3 builds on these aspects with specific information on evidence-based planning of training and provides a great number of related exercises for dancers and teachers/trainers.

Coordination and postural control influence **physical posture and appearance**, which can be linked to higher-levels of **self-esteem** and thus **self-efficacy**. Related to coordination, dance trains **spatial orientation** and fast **reaction times**, which are highly relevant in everyday life. The ability to react, which has been shown to be higher among athletes[161] than among those, who abstain from physical activity, is an essential component of preventing injuries in everyday life through enhanced levels of postural control.

Dance can unite and empower[162], having high impact on psychological aspects, such as **overcoming trauma** or pain, supporting self-esteem, **stress management** and

---

[155] Dahlström M. *Muscle characteristics, energy intake and expenditure in the dancer.* Phys Ther Rev. 2(4). 197-215. 1997.

[156] Metsios GS, Wyon M, Patel K, Allen N, Koutedakis Y. *Dancers' heart: Cardiac screening in elite dancers.* Eur J Sport Sci. 20(7). 920-925. 2020.

[157] Cohen JL, Gupta PK, Lichstein E, and Chadda KD. *The heart of a dancer: noninvasive cardiac evaluation of professional ballet dancers.* Am J Cardiol. 45(5). 959-65. 1980.

[158] Kaltsatou AC, Kouidi EI, Anifanti MA, Douka SI, and Deligiannis AP. *Functional and psychosocial effects of either a traditional dancing or a formal exercising training program in patients with chronic heart failure: a comparative randomized controlled study.* Clin Rehabil. 28(2). 128-138. 2014.

[159] Wyon MA, and Redding E. *Physiological monitoring of cardiorespiratory adaptations during rehearsal and performance of contemporary dance.* J Strength Cond Res. 19(3). 611-614. 2005.

[160] Wyon MA, Abt G, Redding E, Head A, and Sharp NC. *Oxygen uptake during modern dance class, rehearsal, and performance.* J Strength Cond Res. 18(3):646-649. 2004.

[161] Mouelhi Guizani S, Bouzaouach I, Tenenbaum G, Ben Kheder A, Feki Y, and Bouaziz M. *Simple and choice reaction times under varying levels of physical load in high skilled fencers.* J Sports Med Phys Fitness. 46(2). 344-351. 2006.

[162] Houston S. *Participation in Community Dance: A Road to Empowerment and Transformation?* New Theatre Quarterly. 21(2). 166-177. 2005.

resilience [163], which is why dance has already been regarded as healing[164] in ancient times and is successfully used as therapy to the present day.[165,166,167,168]

Cognitive skills such as **memory**, **attention** span and **concentration**, **verbal- and non-verbal communication** and **expression**, **empathy** and **emotional** as well as **social intelligence** and competence are fostered. The ability to memorize is essential for wellbeing and success, which is why all ages benefit from dance training, in which such cognitive development is specifically promoted.[169,170]

The ability for **relaxation** can be supported, which again enhances cognitive functions and psychological health.

The fusion of neurocognitive, psychological and physiological benefits supports the young in daily demands of social life, school, and education, adults in stress management juggling profession, family life and related issues, and older adults in the overall goal of preserving mobility, agility and quality of longevity.

Since dance, in addition to being related to other forms of art such as the **fine arts**, music, or **drama**, is usually accompanied by some form of music, it also cultivates a sense and "understanding" of **music** and **rhythm**. As such, dance promotes the ability to feel rhythm, differentiate, or anticipate. Dancers learn to adapt to auditory or any other forms of music/rhythm, or the movements of a partner through entrainment, i.e., **sensorimotor synchronization**.[171,172] Basically, such synchronization is a natural thing to occur, facilitating **social interaction**, **cooperation** and wellbeing through **positive emotional response** in those acting as well as observing the resulting entrainment, perceived as harmony. Examples would be parents cradling their child, gently swaying from side to side with a baby in their arms. The rhythm of the loving parents and the rhythm of the child naturally synchronize.[173, 174]

However, dance training takes this ability a big step further: it can promote the ability to **deliberately resist synchronizing** with others, which makes it possible to dance together while using different steps, **creating different rhythms**, or following various tempos, a sign for **enhanced motor control**.[175,176] To fulfil all these aspects, a dancer's nervous system learns to engage all senses and sensory organs, while their brains are able to test and develop different dynamical strategies, leading to enhanced **coupling of action** (dance, motion) **and perception** (of the motion, the execution, the environment, or the effect on the environment, etc.).[177]

Aside from all necessary aspects of motor control, learning, and performing, **emotions** and **affects** are involved in the **performance and interpretation of mental and physical motion**. Learning how to handle affects and emotions is an integrating aspect of social and emotional intelligence and empathy. Thus, dance can foster empathy, self-esteem through **perceived abilities**, enhancing related intelligence and competence. Such assets promote **communication skills**, with others, and with oneself, relating a dancer to their environment. That again is essential for **receiving and giving feedback**, further aspect of **communication**.

The development of a **healthy self-concept** through positive experiences of one's self in communication with the environment is further supported by the natural ways in which probably only dance can fuse physical motion with creativity, imagination, fantasy, rhythm, music and

[163] Buck R, and Snook B. *How might creative learning through dance support resilience?*, Journal of Human Behavior in the Social Environment. 30. 3. 289-305. 2020.

[164] Hanna JL. *The power of dance: health and healing.* J Altern Complement Med. 1(4). 323-31. 1995.

[165] Harris DA. *Dance/movement therapy approaches to fostering resilience and recovery among African adolescent torture survivors.* Torture. 17(2). 134-155. 2007.

[166] Ho R. *Effects of dance movement therapy on Chinese cancer patients: A pilot study in Hong Kong.* The Arts in Psychotherapy. 32. 337-345. 2005.

[167] Kiepe MS, Stockigt B, and Keil T. *Effects of dance therapy and ballroom dances on physical and mental illnesses: a systematic review.* Arts in Psychotherapy. 39(5). 404-411. 2012.

[168] Kosh S, Kunz T, Lykou S, and Cruz R. *Effects if dance movement therapy and dance on health-related psychological outcomes: A meta-analysis.* The Arts in Psychotherapy. 41. 46–64. 2013.

[169] Bläsing, Bettina, Puttke, Martin, and Thomas Schack. The Neurocognition of Dance. Mind, Movement and Motor Skills. New York. Psychology Press. 2010.

[170] Bläsing B. The dancer's memory: expertise and cognitive structures in dance. IN: B. Bläsing, M. Puttke, & T. Schack (Eds.), The Neurocognition of Dance: Mind, Movement and Motor Skills. New York.Psychology Press. 2010. p. 75-98.

[171] Jin X, Wang B, Lv Y, Lu Y, Chen J, and Zhou C. *Does dance training influence beat sensorimotor synchronization? Differences in finger-tapping sensorimotor synchronization between competitive ballroom dancers and nondancers.* Exp Brain Res. 237(3). 743-753. 2019.

[172] Brown S, Martinez MJ, and Parsons LM. *The neural basis of human dance.* Cereb Cortex. 16(8). 1157-1167. 2006.

[173] Phillips-Silver J, and Trainor LJ. *Feeling the beat: movement influences infant rhythm perception.* Science. 3. 308(5727). 1430. 2005.

[174] Zentner M, and Eerola T. *Rhythmic engagement with music in infancy.* Proc Natl Acad Sci. 107(13). 5768-5773. 2013.

[175] Miura A, Kudo K, and Nakazawa K. *Action-perception coordination dynamics of whole-body rhythmic movement in stance: a comparison study of street dancers and non-dancers.* Neurosci Lett. 544. 157-62. 201

[176] Miura A, Fujii S, Yamamoto Y, and Kudo K. *Motor control of rhythmic dance from a dynamical systems perspective: a review.* J Dance Med Sci. 19(1). 11-21. 2015.

[177] Miura A, Kudo K, and Nakazawa K. *Action-perception coordination dynamics of whole-body rhythmic movement in stance: a comparison study of street dancers and non-dancers.* Neurosci Lett. 544. 157-62. 2013.

social interaction.[178] That again supports learning on all levels and **promotes motor and cognitive development of all ages**.

When based on empowering motivational climates, dance can support the ability of constructive, healthy **self-reflection**, task-oriented ways of **goal setting** and achievement, and therefore the development of self-responsibility, an important aspect of **autonomy** leading to injury prevention and performance enhancement.

Coming full circle, the more the teacher/trainer can back dance education up with **targeted knowledge sharing**, the more (young) dancers can learn how to handle aspects of training, performance related behavior (e.g., training intensity, rest), or management of nutrition, injuries and so forth. Such **active knowledge in the dancer through shared and implemented content knowledge in the teacher/trainer** can lead to a healthy approach to and understanding of physical and mental appearance as well as performance. Resulting high levels of self-concept again affect **quality of motivation** as well as quality of movement, available energy resources, health, or mental and psychological attitudes.

Dance can override social, cultural, political, or other boundaries, for instance those related to language or differences between generations or ethnicities. It adds the aspect of body language and nonverbal communication. Resulting social interaction supports all aspects of wellbeing, particularly when consciously based on the development of character traits such as empathy, courtesy, mindfulness, courage and fairness (aspects of an empowering, task-oriented motivational climate). As such, very elevated, empowering dance classes can enhance abilities for communication, self-reflection, **conflict management**, **teamwork** and **cooperation** as well as **leadership skills**.

Looking at this list of aspects, goals, and possibilities in dancers' education and training, it may be clear how complex the profession of dance teachers or trainers actually is, and how much responsibility rests on them. Especially when teachers/trainers approach their profession with an awareness of all these aspects of dance, which they could deliberately address through targeted planning and teaching.

[178] Reddish P, Fischer R, and Bulbulia J. *Let's dance together: synchrony, shared intentionality and cooperation.* PLoS ONE. 8(8):e71182. 2013.

Dance medicine and science help to bear this responsibility successfully. This book as well as the other volumes discuss how to create such climates in the dance room, which promote all these aspects of health, motivation, inspiration and wellbeing beyond the obvious physical dance training and education.

Important is that when a teacher or trainer installs such comprehensive dance education or training, they are rewarded themselves: with their own injury prevention and performance enhancement, leading to their own high-level quality of motivation, health and wellbeing.[179]

[179] Roth G, Assor A, Kanat-Maymon Y, and Kaplan H. Autonomous Motivation for Teaching: How Self-Determined Teaching May Lead to Self-Determined Learning. J of Educ Psychol, Vol. 99(4), 761-774. 2007.

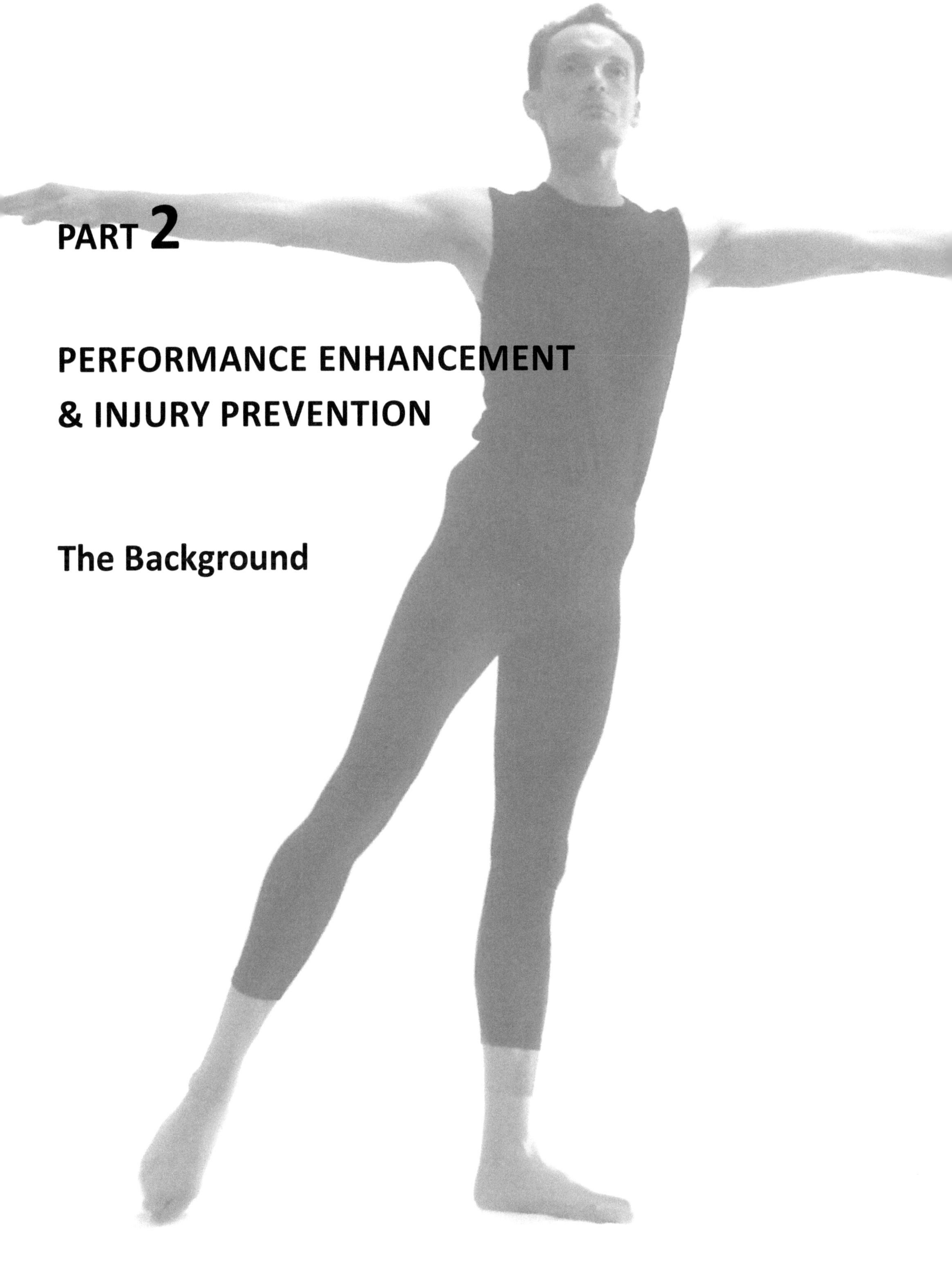

PART 2

PERFORMANCE ENHANCEMENT & INJURY PREVENTION

The Background

The upcoming chapters are meant to give an overview on injuries in dance. Related risks, causes, and mechanisms are explained. Acute injuries, those with a commonly known time and cause of onset, are compared to overuse injuries, which are a very complex issue, because many factors influence their etiology, while their time and cause of onset mostly are unclear. Hence, both injury mechanisms lead to different outcome and are linked to various interrelated factors. Only when underlying risk factors, which cause injuries, are clear, targeted injury prevention is possible. For that matter, risk factors are discussed from several perspectives: related to injury mechanism (acute or overuse), dance style, age, gender, (work) environment and motivational climates, knowledge and education of dancers, teachers, trainers, administrations, etc. It becomes clear that injuries have to be discussed in the context of different dance styles, where movement techniques, equipment such as shoes, and the way how training is being approached and conducted influence the etiology of injuries. However, age and gender are essential aspects as well.

Injuries, acute or chronic overtraining, and related factors already affect the youngest dancers, and thus can have severe long-term consequences, including pain, dysfunction, stress, anxiety, or dropout. Based on the introductory chapter, these factors as well as the consequences are discussed and a big focus is laid on the education of young vocational as well as recreational dancers in specific chapters. Injury prevention starts in the young, which is why dance pedagogy and teaching have to cooperate with dance medicine and science.

Volume 2 discusses neuropsychological aspects, such as pain, but for the better understanding a short overview of pain shall be provided here: Pain is a warning signal of the body, perceived by specialized nerve cells (nociceptors), which want to protect us from harm, e.g., injury. Two sides of pain have to be differentiated:

Performance pain (often called "positive pain") is a part of every athlete's life. It is the feeling that it is sometimes hard to get yourself going (which does not equal "going to dance through injury"!), motivate yourself for training, or to get over yourself with high loads of training at times. However, performance pain is never related to injury and has a totally different quality, i.e., how one perceives the pain: Performance pain can be that one needs a kickstart in the morning, that one has to overcome moderate tiredness or short break-downs of motivation, "bite through" demanding tasks or fights under adrenaline to present high-level performances. Performance pain can make somebody push limits in goal achievement. However, it is satisfying, not related to injury, mostly gone with (proper) warm-up and can be called an aspect of (healthy, empowering) discipline.

Injury pain (or often called "negative pain"), on the other hand, is the warning signal of the body that harm is on the verge to occur or has already occurred. Such a pain needs attention, diagnosis if applicable, and above all, healing time, when injuries have already occurred (among many other factors related to secondary injury prevention). **Injury pain must not be an integrating part of dancers' lives,** it is neither a sign for dedication nor professionalism or discipline. When ignored, it lays the fundament for overuse injuries and further severe consequences, as already described. The quality of injury pain is completely different from performance pain. Injury pain is sharp, hot, frightening, swelling, throbbing, pulsing, tearing, worrisome, often sudden. In case of overuse injury, it can be on-and-off, recurrent, probably already impacting the ability to dance, forcing to adjust dancing or use compensatory movements, coming in resting phases, lasting longer, never really gone.

At best, injuries are prevented before they happen, which is depending on comprehensive levels of content knowledge in teachers, trainers, but also dancers in the fields of dance medicine and science. Since the majority of dancers' injuries are overuse in nature, it becomes clear that too many people working in the dance sector are either not aware of this, do not know how to implement dance science, or are somehow hindered, not able to or willing to do it, for various reasons.

In any case, the provided information follows two different aims: First, to provide at least basics of content knowledge needed in dancers, teachers, trainers, or medical personnel working with dancers, and second, to show through exactly that, why the fusion between dance, teaching, dance medicine and science is crucial, when changes for the benefit of dancers and all involved want to be introduced to the dance world.

An **injury** is a form of harm or wound inflicted to the body by an intentional or unintentional force, which causes tissue damage leading to changes in functionality (the ability to function properly) or morphology (the appearance) of the affected person's tissues. Synonyms for injury can be "harm", "hurt", "trauma" or "lesion". Injuries happen to vocational and professional as well as amateur dancers of all levels, ages, and dance styles[180, 181], ranging from, e.g., 0.6 to 5.6 injuries per dancer in 1000 hours of dancing, according to prospective studies in styles such as ballet.[182]

An injury can be analyzed from several angles: On the one hand, from the **person who is affected**, thus bears the symptoms and/or any physical and psychological restrictions, and who must carry the various consequences in medical, legal, financial, and psychological terms. On the other hand, **injury can have financial, legal, and actuarial consequences for the people or institutions involved or/and responsible**. Thus, injury can be considered from a legal or economical point of view.[183,184,185]

Standardized injury definitions and uniform reporting guidelines are important, as recurrently stated in dance and sport science.[186, 187, 188, 189, 190] They are needed in scientific research and form the basis to meet the need of dancers and athletes with regard to injury prevention or insurance claims.[191] Several different definitions of injuries exist with regard to how they are recorded:

First, injuries can be defined by **diagnosis**, i.e., **medical attention injuries**, depending on medical assessment and therefore on tools to execute the diagnostic tests, such as x-ray, MRI, sonography etc. Second, injuries can be related to **time-loss**, i.e., days or time off dance participation due to restrictions through the injury sustained. Time-loss definitions have been broadly used in sports and dance science. However, such a definition disqualifies many overuse or chronic injuries from reporting, for which dancers do not have any time-loss to report, because they keep on training in spite of their pain.[192] Since, by far, the majority of injuries in dancers are overuse in nature, exclusive time-loss definitions are insufficient. They might result in underestimation of injury risk, prevalence or incidence.[193] Third, further definitions were proposed, such as **physical complaint injury** (i.e., dancer is able to dance but feels restricted and reports for triage), and **financial injury** (i.e., injury that requires financial expenses, also related to workers compensation or self-insurance).[194]

Thanks to dance medicine, there are numerous studies on injury in dance, discussing (among other):

- **etiology** (origin, development)
- **prevalence** (occurrence or number of injuries at a specific date/time of research)
- **incidence** (occurrence as development, i.e., number of new injuries occurring during a particular time period)
- **risk factors** (underlying factors, which could cause or raise the possibility that a dancer sustains an injury)

---

[180] Lampe J, Groneberg DA, Ohlendorf D, and Wanke EM. *Pain in female dancers and dance teachers: Perception, assessment, and related behavior.* Scand J Med Sci Sports. 29(4). 623-632. 2019.

[181] Steinberg N, Siev-Ner I, Peleg S, Dar G, Masharawi Y, Zeev A, and Hershkovitz I. *Extrinsic and intrinsic risk factors associated with injuries in young dancers aged 8-16 years.* J Sports Sci.30(5):485-495. 2012.

[182] Allen N, Nevill A, Brooks J, Koutedakis Y, Wyon M. *Ballet injuries: injury incidence and severity over 1 year.* J Orthop Sports Phys Ther. 42(9). 781-790. 2012.

[183] Kelman BB. *Occupational hazards in female ballet dancers. Advocate for a forgotten population.* AAOHN J. Off J Am Assoc Occup Health Nurses. 48(9). 430-434. 2000.

[184] Garrick JG, and RK Requa. *Ballet injuries – an analysis of epidemiology and financial outcome.* Am J Sports Med. 21(4). 586-590. 1993.

[185] Garrick JG. *Early identification of musculoskeletal complaints and injuries among female ballet students.* J Dance Med Sci. 3(2). 80-83. 1999.

[186] Liederbach M, Hagins M, Gamboa JM, and Welsh TM. *Technical report of the Standard Measures Consensus Initiative of the International Association for Dance Medicine and Science. Recommendations and implementation strategies for the assessment of reporting of dancer capacities, risk factors and injuries: steps toward consensus.* J Dance Med & Sci. 16(4). 139-153. 2012.

[187] Bronner S, Ojofeitimi S, and Mayers L. *Comprehensive surveillance of dance injuries: a proposal for uniform reporting guidelines for professional companies.* J Dance Med & Sci. 10(3). 69-80. 2006.

[188] Liederbach M, and Richardson M. *The importance of standardized injury reporting in dance.* J Dance Med Sci. 11(2). 45-48. 2007.

[189] van Mechelen W. *Sports injury surveillance systems. 'One size fits all'?* Sports Med. 24(3). 164-168. 1997.

[190] Fuller CW, Bahr R, Dick RW, Meeuwisse WH. *A framework for recording recurrences, reinjuries, and exacerbations in injury surveillance.* Clin J Sport Med. 17(3). 197-200. 2007.

[191] Clarsen B, Rønsen O, Myklebust G, Flørenes TW, and Bahr R. *The Oslo Sports Trauma Research Center questionnaire on health problems: a new approach to prospective monitoring of illness and injury in elite athletes.* Br J Sports Med. 48(9).754-760. 2014.

[192] Bahr R. *No injuries, but plenty of pain? On the methodology for recording overuse symptoms in sports.* Br J Sports Med. 43(13). 966-972. 2009.

[193] Clarsen B, Myklebust G, and Bahr R. *Development and validation of a new method for the registration of overuse injuries in sports injury epidemiology: the Oslo Sports Trauma Research Centre (OSTRC) overuse injury questionnaire.* Br J Sports Med. 47(8). 495-502. 2013.

[194] Bronner S, Ojofeitimi S, Mayers L. *Comprehensive surveillance of dance injuries: a proposal for uniform reporting guidelines for professional companies.* J Dance Med & Sci. 10(3). 69-80. 2006.

- **diagnosis** (determination of disease through medical assessment)
- **therapy** (treatment)
- **rehabilitation** (reintegration into everyday/dance life through specific training)

Since injuries are often multifactorial, they might depend on various extrinsic, exogenous, or external, and intrinsic, endogenous, or internal factors. As such, in the etiology and for the sake of the prevention of **injuries**, a distinction must be made between **age**[195], **gender**[196] as well as between **dance styles** and **dance techniques**, in which injury frequencies vary between **body parts** depending on the respective dance style, workload, level of expertise and so forth. Details on the respective **dance practice** (schedules, workload, styles in use) as well as any **injury history** of dancers are important.[197,198] Moreover, such a dance style-, gender- as well as age-specific **analysis of extrinsic and intrinsic factors** has to be based on a **profound understanding of the underlying mechanisms** (i.e., acute or overuse/chronic injuries), which could lead to or already led to an injury, to be able to successfully establish means of injury prevention.

Accidents can happen in any competitive sport, that is the nature of things. However, many injuries depend on the **mindfulness and knowledge of dance teachers, trainers, and the personnel surrounding the dancer, not to forget the dancers themselves.**[199] As such, many injuries in dancers, teachers, trainers and other could be avoided, if those responsible knew about underlying mechanisms and risk factors as well as their elimination.

The chapter on injury specifics in various dance styles will go into detail in that matter.

[195] Premelč J, Vučković G, James N, and Dimitriou L. *A Retrospective Investigation on Age and Gender Differences of Injuries in DanceSport.* Int J Environ Res Public Health. 16(21). 4164. 2019.

[196] Wanke EM, Mill H, Arendt M, und DA Groneberg. *Occupational accidents in professional dance with focus on gender differences.* J Occupational Med Toxicol. 8. 35-42. 2013.

[197] Moita JP, Gomes A, Xarez L, and Coelho C. *The role of prediagnostic data in injury epidemiology in preprofessional dancers.* Scand J Med Sci Sports. 29(4). 606-614. 2019.

[198] Angioi M, Maffulli GD, McCormack M, Morrissey D, Chan O, and Maffulli N. *Early signs of osteoarthritis in professional ballet dancers: a preliminary study.* Clin J Sport Med. 24(5). 435-437. 2014.

[199] Magida, Nontembiso. The cumulative incidence of musculoskeletal injuries among student dancers at Tshwane University of Technology. [Master-Thesis Physiotherapy at the Dept of Physiotherapy, University of the Western Cape. 2009.

With regard to injury mechanisms, two types of injuries have to be distinguished, namely acute (also called traumatic) from overuse (also called chronic).[200,201]

Acute injury:

- Accident
- Sudden sharp or blunt force trauma
- Course of events and time of onset known in most cases
- Can be multifactorial
- Mainly extrinsic/exogenous risk factors, among other:
  - Flooring
  - Partners
  - Sets, props, cables, stairs, lights
  - Schedules
- but also intrinsic/endogenous risk factors, among other:
  - Fatigue
  - Endurance and fitness deficits
  - Improper alignment
  - Faulty dance technique
  - Previous injury
  - Overuse injury

Acute injuries occur due to accidents and sudden impact of sharp or blunt forces. They differ significantly from chronic or overuse injuries, because it is **usually possible to specify the time of onset and course of events** that directly caused the damage. Such specifications are essential when it comes to insurance claims and worker compensations. Acute injuries can happen due to intrinsic/endogenous triggers, i.e., causes coming from dancers themselves, but are mainly connected to extrinsic/exogenous risk factors, i.e., external influences.[202,203,204] These can be multifactorial, including floors, partners, footwear, costume, clothing, jewelry, props, stage design, lighting, or stairs, as well as training and rehearsal schedules that leave no time for rest, food and water intake, warm-up or cool-down, or other forms of external pressure. Disregard of safety regulations, e.g., in technical gear and stage construction as well as in dress codes can also be a reason for acute injuries (costumes, training garments, shoes with open or loose ribbons etc.). Intrinsic or endogenous risk factors can be insufficient warm-up, fitness deficits, lack of concentration, fatigue, or malnutrition for instance leading to early onset of fatigue. Previous, repetitive/recurrent or overuse injuries can also bear severe risk for acute injuries.

In dance, as in all sportive activities, accidents can happen. As such, acute injuries are commonly regarded as inevitable in sports. However, although accidents recurrently happen in all disciplines, many of them can be avoided through rigorous implementation of information resulting from dance and sports medical knowledge in teachers, trainers as well as dancers themselves. Such knowledge leads to basic awareness for extrinsic and intrinsic risk factors and consequently to their elimination whenever possible.

Overuse injury:

- Imbalance between mechanical load (workload) and loadability
- Repeated/ongoing submaximal overload leads to tissue damage
- Multifactorial
- Multiple extrinsic/exogenous risk factors, among others:
  - Pressure from teachers, trainers, institutions, media
  - Motivational climates
  - Dancer's identity
  - Traditional training
- Multiple intrinsic/endogenous risk factors, among others:
  - Overtraining, fatigue
  - Same repetitive movements in technique classes
  - Erroneous dance technique
  - Compensating and forcing joints
  - Early specialization
    - Malnutrition

---

[200] Bronner S, Ojofeitimi S, and Mayers L. *Comprehensive surveillance of dance injuries: a proposal for uniform reporting guidelines for professional companies.* J Dance Med & Sci. 10(3). 69-80. 2006.

[201] Liederbach M, Hagins M, Gamboa JM, and Welsh TM. *Technical report of the Standard Measures Consensus Initiative of the International Association for Dance Medicine and Science. Recommendations and implementation strategies for the assessment of reporting of dancer capacities, risk factors and injuries: steps toward consensus.* J Dance Med & Sci. 16(4). 139-153. 2012.

[202] Wanke EM, Mill H, Wanke A, Davenport J, Koch F, and Groneberg DA. *Dance floors as injury risk: analysis and evaluation of acute injuries caused by dance floors in professional dance with regard to preventative aspects.* Med Probl Perform Art. 27(3). 137-142. 2012.

[203] Wanke EM, Mill H, Wanke A, Davenport J, Checcetti F, Koch F, and Groneberg DA. *Dance partner or dance floor?: exogenous factors resulting in accidents in professional dancers.* Med Probl Perform Art. 28(3). 131-136. 2013.

[204] Wanke EM, Arendt M, Mill H, Koch F, Davenport J, Fischer A, and Groneberg DA. *The theatrical stage as accident site in professional dance.* Med Probl Perform Art. 29(1). 32-36. 2014.

Overuse or chronic injuries occur due to re-injury, chronic injury and/or overuse. Overuse/chronic injuries develop over a more extended period of time, and **often cannot be retraced to their underlying cause and time of onset**. For that matter, overuse injuries are difficult to deal with when it comes to insurance and compensation claims.

Depending on the injury definition used in research, or in the understanding of the dancers, teachers and institutions involved, overuse injuries often are left undocumented or unattended. When time-loss or medical-diagnosis injury definitions are used, (beginning) overuse, for which dancers can neither report medical attention nor absence from training, often result in dancers or athletes having "no injuries but plenty of pain"[205]:

Many dancers (as well as teachers, trainers etc.) shrug beginning complaints off as minor injuries, thus accepting overtraining and overuse and leaving the injuries untreated. However, they more often than not result in severe and complex secondary or recurrent injuries. Examples are sore, hardened, or pulled muscles, which already are beginning to high-grade muscle injuries, but which are still regarded as simple sign of weakness in too many dancers. They have learned (!) to accept them as "part of dance", which has to be ignored in spite of the related pain and restrictions of performance. Such "minor complaints" can result in severe consequences, e.g., ruptured muscles and tendons, which would have needed immediate and sufficient time for recovery and rehabilitation but are often and severely underestimated.[206,207,208]

Consequently, overuse injuries can also be caused by a previous (acute or chronic) injury[209] that has not been adequately treated and/or cured. Then again, the resulting overuse injuries increase the risk for (further) acute injuries, resulting in secondary injuries from erroneous dance technique, training deficits, or compensation strategies. As such, ongoing and recurrent chronic injuries can **end in a vicious circle for a dancer** or athlete, which is hard to get out of again, but which is gradually tightening around the dancer, threating performance and wellbeing. Early identification as well as elimination of risk factors is paramount.[210]

Overuse injuries occur over a long period in which **submaximal mechanical loading** (i.e., training and work load) **repeatedly exceeds the tissues' loadability** (level that the affected tissue is capable of withstanding) for a variety of reasons. In other words: Chronic injury or overuse is not a maximal force impacting on the dancer's tissues, such as bones, muscles, tendons etc., but submaximal. Thus, the load a tissue perceives is ongoingly and repeatedly too much, but just not enough to result in sudden damage, as it would be the case in the maximal overload created by sudden impacting forces leading to acute injury.

Overuse injuries represent **the largest number of injuries** among dancers with multiple risk factors involved, one of them the underreporting of injury and pain due to various reasons.[211] They account for 65% to 95% of all dance injuries, compared to acute injuries[212,213] and are mainly sustained to the lower extremities and spine, with more than 50% of overuse injuries in the foot and ankle joints.[214,215,216,217]

Especially these injuries say a lot about dancers' lives, the disregard and ignoring of pain, and poorly trained dance teachers and trainers. So, not least, in terms of injury prevention, it is essential to include trainers and teachers in the education and training of dance medicine as well,

---

[205] Bahr R. *No injuries, but plenty of pain? On the methodology for recording overuse symptoms in sports.* Br J Sports Med. 43(13). 966-972. 2009.

[206] Askling C, Lund H, Saartok T, and Thorstensson A. *Self-reported hamstring injuries in student-dancers.* Scand J Med Sci Sports. 12(4).230-235. 2002.

[207] Askling C, Tengvar M, Saartok T, and Thorstensson A. *Sports related hamstring strains--two cases with different etiologies and injury sites.* Scand J Med Sci Sports. 10(5). 304-307. 2000.

[208] Askling CM, Tengvar M, Saartok T, and Thorstensson A. *Acute first-time hamstring strains during slow-speed stretching: clinical, magnetic resonance imaging, and recovery characteristics.* Am J Sports Med. 35(10). 1716-1724. 2007.

[209] von Rosen P, and Heijne A. *Previous and current injury and not training and competition factors were associated with future injury prevalence across a season in adolescent elite athletes.* Physiother Theory Pract. 18. 1-8. 2020.

[210] Garrick JG. *Early identification of musculoskeletal complaints and injuries among female ballet students.* J Dance Med Sci. 3(2). 80-83. 1999.

[211] Jacobs CL, Cassidy JD, Côté P, Boyle E, Ramel E, Ammendolia C, Hartvigsen J, and Schwartz I. *Musculoskeletal Injury in Professional Dancers: Prevalence and Associated Factors: An International Cross-Sectional Study.* Clin J Sport Med. 27(2). 153-160. 2017.

[212] Harkness Center for dance injuries. Newsletter 1(1). 2. 2005.

[213] Wanke EM, Mill H, Arendt M, und DA Groneberg. *Analyse und Evaluation akuter Verletzungen im professionellen Bühnentanz unter besonderer Berücksichtigung präventiver Aspekte.* Zbl Arbeitsmed. 62. 166–172. 2012.

[214] Denton J. *Overuse foot and ankle injuries in ballet.* Clin Podiatr Med Surg. 14(3). 525 – 532. 1997.

[215] Smith TO, Davies L, de Medici A, Hakim A, Haddad F, and Macgregor A. *Prevalence and profile of musculoskeletal injuries in ballet dancers: A systematic review and meta-analysis.* Phys Ther Sport. 19. 50-56. 2016.

[216] Hincapié CA, Morton EJ, and Cassidy JD. *Musculoskeletal injuries and pain in dancers: a systematic review.* Arch Phys Med Rehabil. 89(9). 1819-1829. 2008.

[217] Jacobs CL, Hincapié CA, Cassidy JD. *Musculoskeletal injuries and pain in dancers: a systematic review update.* J Dance Med Sci. 16(2). 74-84. 2012.

not just medical professionals in aftercare. [218] It is essential that the issue is approached scientifically, and that dancers, not least, are taken seriously with their symptoms and fears and learn to take them seriously themselves.[219]

As such, chronic injuries have an insidious beginning, often developing over many months or even years. They often result in one or several subsequent injury/injuries, which in further consequence often can no longer be assigned to a single cause. Risk factors for such repeating submaximal overload can be **incorrect dance technique** often paired with **disrespect for the dancer's anatomical, physiological or psychological individuality**, but also **insufficient flooring** on which the dancer has to perform ongoingly.[220,221,222] This is the reason why overuse injuries are so dangerous when not dealt with correctly and immediately: the dancer only seems to have some "minor complaints", tries to work through or is forced to work through them for various reasons, also discussed in the introductory chapters. Mostly, such minor complaints are paired with overtraining. That means that the dancer's body is already less capable of adapting and defending itself due to the overall consequences of overtraining, possibly also in combination with nutrition and fitness deficits. Thus, the primarily healthy tissue sooner or later has to succumb to the ongoing overload resulting in severe chronic injury.

The chapters on overtraining as well as primary and secondary injury prevention will discuss further related aspects.

Further risk factors for chronic injuries are the extremely **high number of working hours** and the **many repetitions** of the same and similar movements characterizing vocational and professional dancers' (daily) routines.[223] Such workload hardly occurs in such a concentrated form in any other sport.[224] Related to excessive workload, the predominant focus on **excessive technique training** to which many vocational and professional dancers must submit has to be reconsidered. Being a reason for overtraining due to extremely high numbers of repetitive motion, it can be held co-responsible for many of the overuse injuries, especially when ignorance of the dancer's anatomical individuality, faulty technique, or muscular imbalances, due to lateral bias in training, or fitness deficits are involved. [225,226,227,228] A strict exclusive focus on dance technique training in many styles also takes up time, which could be used to correct acute deficits in fitness or recovery.

A further risk factor is **early specialization** in a certain dance style or sport. Exclusive training regimes already in the young have shown to be associated with overuse injuries, burnout, and thus dropout.[229,230,231,232] Moreover it can be linked to a lack of content knowledge in teachers and trainers.[233]

Equally related to a lack of knowledge or ignorance are **the motivational climate** as well as any form of **external pressure** from teachers, trainers, artistic directors, choreographers, but also institutions, media, parents, and so forth. [234] Already nuances of disempowering teacher/master created climates can be related to injuries in dancers [235], due to focus on ego-involving

[218] Schoene LM. *What you should know about dance injuries*. Podiatry Today. 18(1). 2005.

[219] Turner BS, and Wainwright SP. *Corps de ballet: the case of the injured ballet dancer*. Sociol Health Illn. 25(4). 269-88. 2003.

[220] Kaufmann JE, Nelissen RGHH, Exner-Grave E, and Gademan MGJ. *Does forced or compensated turnout lead to musculoskeletal injuries in dancers? A systematic review on the complexity of causes.* J Biomech. 114. 110084. 2021.

[221] Arendt YD und F Kerschbaumer. *Injury and Overuse Pattern in Professional Ballet Dancers*. Z Ortho Unfallchirurgie. 141. 349-356-2003.

[222] Ahonen J. *Biomechanics of the foot in dance: a literature review.* J Dance Med Sci. 12(3). 99-108. 2008.

[223] Twitchett E, Angioi M, Koutedakis Y, and Wyon M. *The demands of a working day among female professional ballet dancers.* J Dance Med Sci. 14(4). 127-132. 2010.

[224] Ekegren C, Quested R, and A Brodrick. *Injuries in pre-professional ballet dancers: Incidence, characteristics, and consequences.* J Sci Med in Sports / Sports Med Australia. 17(3).271-275. 2014.

[225] Wanke EM, Schreiter J, Groneberg DA, Weisser B. *Muscular imbalances and balance capability in dance*. J Occup Med Toxicol. 3. 13:36. 2018.

[226] Chmelar RD, Schultz BB, Ruhling RO, Shepherd TA, Zupan MF, Fitt SS. *A Physiologic Profile Comparing Levels and Styles of Female Dancers.* Phys Sportsmed. 16(7). 87-96. 1988.

[227] Twitchett EA, Koutedakis Y, and Wyon MA. Physiological fitness and professional classical ballet performance: a brief review. J Strength Cond Res. 23(9). 2732-2740. 2009.

[228] Rietveld AB. *Dancers' and musicians' injuries.* Clin Rheumatol. 32(4). 425-434. 2013.

[229] LaPrade RF, Agel J, Baker J, Brenner JS, Cordasco FA, Côté J, Engebretsen L, Feeley BT, Gould D, Hainline B, Hewett T, Jayanthi N, Kocher MS, Myer GD, Nissen CW, Philippon MJ, and Provencher MT. AOSSM Early Sport Specialization Consensus Statement. Orthop J Sports Med. 4(4).2325967116644241. 2016.

[230] Matzkin E, and Garvey K. *Youth Sports Specialization: Does Practice Make Perfect?* NASN Sch Nurse. 34(2). 100-103. 2019.

[231] Scher A. *Branch Out.* Dance Magazine 94(6). 36-36. 2020.

[232] Valovich McLeod TC, Decoster LC, Loud KJ, Micheli LJ, Parker JT, Sandrey MA, White C. *National Athletic Trainers' Association position statement: prevention of pediatric overuse injuries.* J Athl Train. 46(2). 206-220. 2011.

[233] Post EG, Trigsted SM, Schaefer DA, Cadmus-Bertram LA, Watson AM, McGuine TA, Brooks MA, and Bell DR. *Knowledge, Attitudes, and Beliefs of Youth Sports Coaches Regarding Sport Volume Recommendations and Sport Specialization.* J Strength Cond Res. 34(10). 2911-2919. 2020.

[234] Bowling A. *Injuries to dancers: prevalence, treatment, and perceptions of causes.* BMJ. 298(6675). 731-734. 1989.

[235] Kaufmann JE, Nelissen RGHH, Appleton PR, Gademan MGJ. Teacher/master created motivational climate and musculoskeletal injuries in ballet dancers. Publ ahead of print.

atmospheres as well as controlling teacher behavior encouraging rivalry and social comparison.

Volume 2 of this series is dedicated to neuropsychological aspects in dance training and education. The roles of motivational climate, communication, as well as many related factors are among the publication's major points of focus. Theoretical background is analyzed shining an extensive spotlight on practical solutions.

Summing up the previously mentioned contributors to overuse injuries, the **dancer's identity**[236,237] as one of the major results but also underlying excuses for the survival of outdated training traditions must be regarded as substantial risk factor for overuse injuries. Many dancers learn to ignore injury pain as the body's warning signal from early education onwards. Such irresponsibility is being taught to dancers, and then passed on for generations and generations. While some of the many underlying reasons have been discussed, nonetheless, a lack of knowledge, ignorance, or the blaming on tradition or identity must never be allowed to serve as an excuse. Science has researched all factors involved.

For that matter, the conclusion remains the same: An enormous number of injuries that dancers must fight with could have been and can be avoided. This goal should be (made) a top priority for all those who work with dancers. It must be clear that injuries cause physical consequences for dancers and mostly come with significant psychological correlations.[238,239,240]

The following chapters will deal with the various factors underlying injury mechanisms. It is very important for many aspects that dancers are regarded as performing athletes. However, the precise specification of injury mechanisms especially for dance is a major reason why dance medicine had to branch out from sports medicine. **Understanding dance injuries and subsequently preventing or treating them means knowing about the lives of dancers**. For that, injuries and their etiology must be seen in direct relation to dancers' routines, the respective dance technique with its stylistic characteristics, as well as with an eye for dancers themselves and their individuality in every respect.[241] Just as the injury mechanisms of soccer players can only be explained to a minimal extent with those of skiers or swimmers and which is why it requires specialization in sports medicine, the injury mechanisms of dancers cannot be compared with other high-performance sports and therefore require the expertise of dance medicine. There is a need for medical, pedagogical, and scientific experts for the individual dance styles, who understand the essence of a technique and the respective dancers' lives. Only then can injury prevention truly be developed.

DEALING WITH ACUTE INJURIES & ACCIDENTS: FIRST AID

When an injury occurs due to overuse, improper technique, and/or an acute accident, the students or dancers must be granted recovery time as well as professional care by a physician and/or therapist. Moreover, institutions, teachers and trainers have to respect the instructions of medical personnel and immediately try to identify and eliminate risk factors underlying the dancer's injury. As such, re-injury can be prevented and, at best, (the same) risk factors, which might put other dancers at risk to sustain the same or other injuries can be identified and eliminated.

If it is an acute injury, i.e., an injury caused by a single accident, first aid[242], and accident protocols must be followed immediately by dance teachers/trainers. This requires training. Whether to request medical attention becomes apparent during first aid (e.g., dancer is passed-out, recurrently fainting, nauseous, cannot bear weight, severe wounds are open, etc.). **In cases of uncertainty regarding assessing the severity of the injury, *always* notify the physician/ambulance!** In case of an acute accident, it is neither the dance teachers' hysteria nor an admission of ignorance if they call the paramedics. On the contrary: They show their sense of responsibility:

[236] Wainwright SP, Williams C, and Turner BS. *Fractured identities: injury and the balletic body.* Health. 9(1). 49-66. 2005.
[237] Vassallo AJ, Pappas E, Stamatakis E, Hiller CE. *Injury Fear, Stigma, and Reporting in Professional Dancers.* Saf Health Work. 10(3). 260-264. 2019.
[238] Mainwaring L, Krasnow D, and G Kerr. *And the dance goes on – psychological impact of injury.* J Dance Med Sci. 5(4). 105-115. 2001.
[239] Mainwaring L, Kerr G, and Krasnow D. *Psychological correlates of dance injuries.* Med Probl Perform Art. 8. 3-6. 1993.
[240] Kelman BB. *Occupational hazards in female ballet dancers. Advocate for a forgotten population.* AAOHN J. Off J Am Assoc Occup Health Nurses. 48(9). 430-434. 2000.
[241] Campoy FA, Coelho LR, Bastos FN, Netto Júnior J, Vanderlei LC, Monteiro HL, Padovani CR, and Pastre CM. *Investigation of risk factors and characteristics of dance injuries.* Clin J Sport Med. 21(6). 493-498. 2011.
[242] IADMS, Sefcovic N, and Critchfield B. *First Aid for Dancers.* IADMS Resource Paper. 2010. https://iadms.site-ym.com/page/186

The primary care of acute/traumatic injuries within the first 48 hours after an accident are crucial and will determine about the course of healing and, above all, the chances of recovery.

When the ambulance is notified in minors' cases, the executive authority will intervene to clarify whether the injury was caused by someone else or by the victim. In most countries, that is a standard legal procedure that must be followed to protect minors and has nothing to do with distrusting trainers and teachers. The ambulance, according to regulations, notifies the police in such a case. If the persons responsible try to avoid this – for whatever reason – by not consulting medical help at all, they violate the law and put their dancers in considerable danger. Depending on the situation, in case of a dependent the dancer's parents have to be informed. Moreover, it might be necessary to inform teachers'/trainers' liability insurance and, if applicable, dancers' social and/or private insurances, again depending on the case.

Knowledge about first aid, as stated, is crucial. When it comes to an accident, tissues react to impacting forces and resulting wounds. Chemicals are engaged in the body, which are released into the blood and lead to a sequence of events, which is essential for and part of the first (as well as following) phase(s) of healing. Most importantly, immediate inflammatory responses (swelling, heating, reddening, changes of color) are a defense mechanism of the body, which should be controlled but must not be stopped entirely. Such inflammatory responses are essential to protect the body from infection by localizing and eliminating any injurious particles and are also meant to prevent further harm, because the swelling stabilizes the affected body part. One of the first and foremost chemical substances is histamine, which triggers vasodilation and increased vascular permeability, two aspects of the cascade of events resulting in the four (or five) cardinal signs of inflammation:

- **Redness** (Latin: rubor) is caused by the (vaso-) dilation, i.e., widening, of small blood vessels in the area of and around the injury to secure the necessity of increased blood flow to and from the site of damage. That enhances transportation of chemicals and support first phases of healing and reparation. Vasodilation comes with increased permeability of blood vessels to allow chemicals to enter and exit the blood vessels more effectively, i.e., faster, in order to reach the affected tissues. For that the blood vessels' walls have to become more permeable than they normally are. Under normal circumstances, they only allow water and salts to exit easily, but now there is a need to let fluids rich of protein, clotting factors, or antibodies to prevent infection pass through the vessels' walls. The enhanced permeability also results in leukocytes becoming able to exit from the blood stream into the affected tissues. Those white blood cells (e.g., phargocytes, neutrophils, monocytes, macrophages) are essential for immune defense of the body, being able to ingest tissue debris (e.g., from broken bone), produce antibodies and destroy infectious intruders, such as bacteria. As such, new cells can grow and damaged cells as well as debris are removed.
- **Heat** (Latin: calor) is the result from that increase of blood flow, which is experienced in peripheral body parts, for instance the skin. Fever, a bigger and "famous" sign of inflammation known to most people, would be an example for related inflammatory reactions to chemicals necessary to support immune defense and healing through an increase of temperature.
- **Swelling** (Latin: tumor) is the primary result of the accumulated fluids around the blood vessels triggered by the related chemicals. Migration of fluids is essential for the transportation of chemicals and cells towards the site of injury. And the resulting swelling, also called edema, is one of the reasons for the related pain.
- **Pain** (Latin: dolor) due to distortion (i.e., being twisted out of a normal position or shape) of tissues results from swelling. Mediating chemical substances, which are meant to start healing through disinfection, repairing fibers and cells (e.g., serotonin, prostaglandins, bradykinin) also trigger pain through respective specified nerve cells (nociceptors), which react to injury with increased sensitivity. Injury pain, as a natural response of the body to injury is supposed to restrict motion and motivate to rest and recover, in order to prevent further harm and allow time and chance for healing.
- **The loss of function** can be regarded as the fifth sign for inflammation and injury. Swelling as well as pain are the main reasons, why function is lost due to injury. As such the body wants to make sure that injured parts are allowed to rest and recover. A well-known sign for loss of function is also a criterium for the necessity of medical assistance, namely when the dancer is not able to bear weight on an affected limb. For instance, they cannot put weight onto their foot and leg after an ankle sprain etc.

Acute inflammation as the described first response to injury can last for several days and is a normal, important reaction. As such it must not be stopped completely but should be controlled as such that it does not get too much, impairing the clearing and repairing of damaged tissue and unwanted substances. During the first days of healing, cells capable of proliferation (repair or build new cells) will start to regenerate. Sometimes the body has to replace cells or parts of tissue, which results in the development of **scars** (fibrous or connective tissue used for replacement, which is eventually transformed into a dense collagenous area).

After the first day(s), depending on the severity of the injury and amount of damage to the tissues involved, acute inflammation should decline.

Mnemonics can help to memorize the rules of first aid. Since immediate first aid is of utmost importance to allow appropriate recovery in due time, dancers themselves as well as teachers, trainers, parents and all working with dancers benefit from memorizing two acronyms, which serve as these mnemonics or jingles:

P.R.I.C.E.D is the **list of rules for immediate application of first aid**, while **H.A.R.M. helps with long-term injury management**.

P. as in Protection: after an accident has occurred, immediately secure (protect) the injured dancer by removing additional risks or block any further danger. Be aware that this does not mean to drag the injured out of the room immediately, for injuries could be negatively affected by moving the dancer or a limb. Protection means to stop all others around from dancing to prevent further harm to the injured dancer as well as the others from sustaining any harm by tripping over etc. Address the dancer in calm voice and make yourself familiar with the extent of the accident: does the dancer respond, are open wounds to be found, is there a need to call for medical assistance (if so, send somebody for a phone, if possible, and stay with the injured. Make sure that a list with **emergency numbers** is available as is a **first aid kid**.)

R. as in Rest: the injured dancer has to stop dancing and the injured area should not be moved. Secure the injured body part as such that it cannot be moved (others falling over, or an elevated limb falling off a chair etc.). Be aware that shock, as a defense mechanism of the body to accidents, can lead to the dancer refusing to stop even with severe injuries.

I. as in Ice: apply cooling to the injured area. As a rule of thumb that should be done repeatedly for about 20 minutes every two hours to control the swelling. If wounds are open, cover them with appropriate material from the first aid kit first, before ice or other cooling is applied. Also make sure that when ice packs are applied, they are not to touch the skin directly because that will inflict further harm. Wrap them into cloths first. When there are no ice packs available, use a towel or other cloths with cold water to cool the injured area. Ice sprays and return to dancing is NOT what is meant with cooling injured body parts!

C. as in Compression: applying elastic compression bandages can help to control the swelling as well as to stabilize the injured body part. However, before the extent of the injury is not clear, refrain from bandaging with the aim to compress. Again, applied compression bandages do not mean that the injured dancer can go on dancing.

E. as in Elevation: another help to control the swelling as well as the related pain is to elevate the inured body part above the heart level. Make sure that the method of elevation is stable and a dancer's foot etc. cannot accidentally slide and drop from a stool, chair, or slip off a wall. When legs are elevated because the dancer is fainting (recurrently), call for medical assistance immediately.

D. as in Diagnosis: diagnosis is always done by medical professionals. It is NOT the teacher's/trainer's job to be a medical professional, which is neither a shortcoming nor a shame. In any case, better safe than sorry: call for help once too often that once too little.

The acronym **H.A.R.M.** helps to support recovery throughout the time of healing, **especially in the first days after onset of an acute injury**, while inflammatory processes are prevalent:

H. for Heat: Avoid any kind of exposure to heat, such as sun or hot baths. Heat speeds up circulation and will result in an increase of swelling and pain. As such, heat prolongs inflammation and therefor recovery time.

A. for Alcohol: Alcohol is a toxin to the body, which increases heat and swelling, and therefore again prolongs recovery time.

R. for Running or any other exercise: Exercising when injured or before the injury has recovered sufficiently can cause further harm, which is how chronic or overuse injuries develop. Exercising during phases of inflammation will increase body core temperature and therefore heat, resulting in more swelling and pain. After inflammation, appropriate exercise, such as maintenance of aerobic endurance, might be possible, but has to be done as such that the injured body part is not injured further or again.

M. for massage: massaging injured body parts can not only result in severe pain, but can inflict additional harm to the injury or result in increased swelling, even bleeding into neighboring tissues, which can lead to more swelling, including other areas.

Dancers very often suffer from **lesions of their skin**, for instance due to shoes rubbing and wounds becoming infectious through a lack of necessary hygiene or even in spite of treatment. Sometimes dancers use **inappropriate material**, such as tissues or paper towels, toilette paper or tapes and plasters directly applied onto wounded or previously wounded skin parts etc. to wrap wound toes with the aim to return to work (and into their shoes). Such injuries too often than not are shrugged off as minor things, because many dancers have to face them ongoingly. However, they are not minor injuries, because they can lead to further consequences, when not attended to correctly and immediately, for instance through disinfection (and proper healing). Skin lesions can lead to the formation of **pus** (called suppuration) as a reaction on inflammatory particles such as bacteria, which cannot be eliminated easily. The pus then is a viscous liquid consisting of these dead bacteria, debris, leaking fluids involved in the inflammatory process of the wounds, and dying white blood cells, who had intended to come to the rescue. Pus becomes enveloped in a membrane, called abscess, and depends on bursting open that it can be accessed by antibodies, disinfected and cured again. Initial first aid for such "minor" injuries therefore is as crucial as all first aid procedures are for all injuries: Repeated acute inflammation such as recurrently wounded toes can lead to chronic inflammation.

DEALING WITH OVERUSE & RECURRENT INJURIES: PREVENTIVE DANCE MEDICINE

In the case of **overuse** reactions that show themselves through **prolonged or/and recurring pain concerning a specific movement or posture**, an immediate analysis (environmental and dancer screening) of both the overuse reaction and its underlying cause (floors, footwear, dance technique, etc.) must be carried out. Results determine the consequences, for instance, what needs to be changed in the teaching, training, and/or dance technique, or the dancer's environment to prevent worse overuse reactions. Early identification of and response to overuse injuries is critical in preventing chronic injuries, as explained in the previous section.[243]

Ensuring that dance **injuries are reported and treated** is essential first and foremost for dancers themselves. In any case, an existing injury is the number one predictor of another, even worse injury, because the body can no longer rely on its injured structures, e.g., **proprioceptive abilities** are decreased in damaged tissues resulting in diminished postural control [244] and compensation strategies to avoid loading, which changes muscle activation.[245] However, dancers are used to relying on their bodies as instruments, as they have raised and trained them in countless hours of practice and work. If this body now suddenly changes due to injury and tissue damage, there is a high risk of (re-)injury in all movement sequences that previously might not have constituted any injury risk.

The impairment of dancers' proprioception (self-awareness and perception of one's position of joints in space), which accompanies any injury no matter how small, will be discussed in more detail in upcoming chapters. Volume 2 of the series discusses proprioception from neuroscientific point of view and provides many tools and exercises to train proprioceptive and sensorimotor abilities in dancers.

The risk of subsequent injuries is further aggravated by resulting compensations, i.e., postures and wrong alignment which are supposed to take strain off an injured body part, or joints, which are willed to compensate for an injured one, which cannot deliver its normal range of motion. Further problems can be pain leading to hardened muscles and myofascial (muscle-fascia) dysbalances in the body, again leading to unvoluntary compensations. These affect the dancer's technique and very often basic movements, which a dancer might have already taken for granted before and is depending on in (daily) training.

[243] Garrick JG. *Early identification of musculoskeletal complaints and injuries among female ballet students.* J Dance Med Sci. 3(2). 80-83. 1999.

[244] Lin CF, Lee IJ, Liao JH, Wu HW, and Su FC. *Comparison of postural stability between injured and uninjured ballet dancers.* Am J Sports Med. 39(6).1324-31.2011.

[245] Lee HH, Lin CW, Wu HW, Wu TC, and Lin CF. *Changes in biomechanics and muscle activation in injured ballet dancers during a jump-land task with turnout (Sissonne Fermée).* J Sports Sci. 30(7). 689-697. 2012.

In any case of injury, **the dancer needs to be self-responsible**. In order to do that, **dancers have to be provided with an environment, which allows them to be self-responsible**. That starts in early education, when they learn how to deal with pain and injury, and is further depending on the motivational climate, which determines their environment, and whether such a climate supports autonomy and competence, which is also related to self-esteem and therefore self-responsibility. Trainers, teachers, institutions, society, politics, insurance companies, and health insurance are asked to support that.

Time off and injury rehabilitation should no longer be seen as a disgrace and must never be a reason for exclusion from class or company resulting in financial nightmares for many professional dancers. That requires trainers and teachers who exemplify, teach, **demand,** and **examine** personal responsibility. If students or dancers of authoritarian trainers (have to) submit to their regiment in such a way that they (have to) continue to train even in case of injuries, be it out of fear of sanctions or/and out of misguided discipline, the alarmingly high number of dancers' injuries might prevail. Dancers must learn (through their trainers and teachers) that injuries take time to **heal**, chronic ones possibly even longer than acute ones, because more tissues might be affected and extensive damage might have occurred additionally to the original problem. Afterwards or already during this time, a fundamental revision of dance technique and planning of training are generally necessary, because a large part of injuries results from poor dance technique, insufficient preparation, poor fitness, or many other reasons, in vocational, professional as well as amateur dancers. Recognizing these and correcting them must be the highest priority for trainers.

But regardless of the cause, **injuries must be allowed heal** and all efforts should be invested to avoid them in future (in the same dancer as in all others). Healing takes time and must be allowed to be carried out thoroughly. Before dancers can be fully included in training again after recovery, **transition training** is essential to prevent immediate setbacks or backlashes due to re-injury. Only **after dancers had been medically cleared**, they are allowed to start transition training to train them back up for normal participation in training classes.

Transition training for dancers is addressed in volume 3 of the series, dedicated to science of training, among many other topics.

OVERTRAINING & INJURIES: EXCESSIVELY TRAINING WHILE INCREASINGLY UNDERPERFORMING

Dancers, as all athletes, constantly strive for performance enhancement. But teachers/trainers as well as dancers must never forget that **performance cannot be enhanced further than the health of a dancer allows**. As soon as training surpasses the individual capacity of a dancer to perform, their health (and after some time their performance) will be negatively affected.[246]

Specifically, **training is dependent on an individual balance between mechanical loading** (dancing, training) **and recovery** (doing nothing but rest, sleep, enjoy life, and give the body time to adapt to training stimulus). This assures physiological functionality of all tissues and organs. Such balance between controlled or progressive loading and recovery/adaptation time is called "**training**".

In order to achieve training effects, controlled overload has to happen, i.e., the dancer has to increase training load in a carefully planned manner over a period of time. This will result in physiological (healthy) reactions of all tissues, which adapt to the loading by reinforcing their structures in order to be able to withstand further loading, i.e., increasingly higher levels of training.

Such controlled overload is known as **progressive overload** (controlled overload over course of time), or **supercompensation**. In the long-term, only with sufficient rest training effects can occur as such that the dancer can make use of them, i.e., that they lead to performance enhancement. If this balance is disturbed, usually in favor of training load, the dancer's health and performance will suffer.

Such a situation is called overreaching, finally leading to a complex threat for health and wellbeing, called

[246] Kellmann, Michael. Enhancing Recovery. Under-recovery and overtraining: Different concepts - similar impact? Champain. Human Kinetics. 2002.

overtraining syndrome (OTS).[247,248] One of the first and foremost signs is that dancers are ongoingly and **extensively training while increasingly underperforming**, even after extended resting periods.

Volume 3 addresses overtraining in the context of science of training and the planning of schedules, while it is discussed with respect to injuries and ill-health in the following.

Overtraining can be acute, which refers to a short time of constant overloading, and which must not be longer than four weeks. Such states might be reached **before a première, competition, audition, or exam** and should be followed (or better accompanied) by sufficient recovery time: here, evidence-based scheduling (e.g., periodization[249,250]) becomes vital, which would mean that when rehearsal loads increase, training loads are reduced, and vice versa, with the constant goal to monitor a dancer's daily/weekly/monthly/seasonal load in order to prevent overtraining. However, when the status of acute overtraining exceeds four weeks because of insufficient scheduling, overtraining becomes chronic and can lead to severe long-term consequences, many of them irreversible.

Symptoms of overtraining are related to hormonal, metabolic, or psychological changes, depending on the impact on biochemical or immune-system-related processes.[251] These can be visible through changes in behavior, performance, ability to cope with stress and training per se. When allergies and diseases, which might produce the same symptoms, can be ruled out, symptoms associated with **acute overtraining** syndrome would be:

- Increased resting heart rate (HR_{rest}) of 5-10 beats per minute (bpm) more than under normal circumstances.
- High blood pressure
- Decreased heart rate variability (HRV): the heart adjusts it's beats to the needs of a person moving through life: for instance, it beats faster with increasing exercise but slows down after the exercising has stopped. When this variability, i.e., the ability to adjust immediately, becomes more static it is a sign for ill-health, among other.
- Reduced efficacy of the immune system, e.g., recurrent respiratory tract infections
- Elongated healing time of all injuries and wounds (including skin)
- Fatigue
- Reduced capacity for oxygen uptake
- High lactic acid values in muscles but low lactic acid values directly after training
- Muscle soreness leading to chronically hardened muscles
- Increase of muscle injury, e.g., delayed onset of muscle soreness (DOMS), strains, pulls
- Skin irritations
- Excessive perspiration
- Short of breath, increased frequency of or elaborate breathing
- Disability or problems to sleep
- Disability to relax (muscles, mind)
- Sighing, moaning, groaning
- Anxiety, feeling of irrational panic
- Depression

The symptoms of **chronic overtraining**, e.g., overtraining lasting for more than four weeks, are the same, but with

- Symptoms of the acute overtraining manifesting and becoming increasingly bothersome
- Hypothalamic oligomenorrhea (menstruation becomes irregular)
- Amenorrhea (menstruation stops or does never start)
- Loss of maximum power or strength
- Increased risks for allergies
- Chronic respiratory infections
- Inability to rest on days off
- Any forms of psychological burnout

Overtraining and the **etiology of injuries as well as diseases** are interconnected. **Overuse injuries** result from a dysbalance of repetitive submaximal mechanical overloading and loadability in tissues. That again is linked to a dysbalance of training and rest, which can lead to **repetitive micro traumata** (harm to cells and fibres of tissues on microscopic level) in muscles, joints, or bones, etc. Such recurrent injuries result in **high levels of inflammation** in the body, which are a natural reaction to injury, especially in the first phases of healing. However, when such inflammatory processes become excessive, the **stress** for the body increases. Stress results in reduced abilities to fend off disease and intruding bacteria or

[247] Koutedakis Y. *"Burnout" in Dance. The physiological viewpoint.* J Dance Med Sci. 4(4). 122-127. 2000.
[248] Stone MH, Keith RE, Kearney JT, Fleck SJ, Wilson GD, and Triplett NT. *Overtraining. A Review of the Signs, Symptoms and Possible Causes.* J Strength Cond Res. 5(1). 35-50. 1991.
[249] Wyon M. *Planning and preparation - the art of periodisation.* Dance UK News. 52. 10-13. 2004.
[250] Wyon M. *Preparing to perform: periodization and dance.* J Dance Med Sci. 14(2). 67-72. 2010.
[251] Mackinnon LT. *Immunity in athletes.* Int J Sports Med. 18 Suppl 1. 62-68. 1997.

viruses. Simultaneously the body lacks sufficient energy for tissues and cells to adapt to training load, because it has to battle inflammatory responses, consequences of low immune defence, and stress.[252,253] This vicious circle is discussed as the basis of the complexity of overtraining.[254] Such constant fighting against injuries and related inflammatory processes as well as recurrent exposure to infectious diseases can lead to extreme levels of exhaustion and fatigue. This in sum can result in overall ill-health, overuse as well as acute injuries, the latter resulting from e.g., fatigue and the disability of the dancer to concentrate.

Overtraining is often regarded as a mere physical overload, and with regard to dancers or athletes, mainly musculoskeletal injuries are discussed. However, the psychological and mental aspect of health is affected by overtraining as well, leading to neuro-psychological issues which can affect all aspects of a dancer's life. As with psychological burnout, dancers and athletes afflicted with overtraining syndrome have to face high levels of anxiety, stress, depression, sleeping problems, and other, leading to an inability to cope with even low levels of stress or physical loading. This, as stated above, can go so far – and is one of the leading signs for overtraining – that **even extensive periods of rest do not make a difference** to the poor overall state of affected dancers, because the body and mind are not able to "slow down" anymore.

When a dancer is afflicted with (chronic) overtraining, only extensive and targeted periods of rest and treatment can help. In case this is not taken, not allowed or ignored, the dancer may never recover[255,256,257], which is why overtraining can end careers, and that very often in the prime of a dancer's or athlete's professional life. Moreover, **overtraining does not only occur in professionals but also in children and adolescents, as well as in ambitious amateurs.**[258,259]

DEALING WITH INDIVIDUALITY & RESPONSIBILITY: EFFECTS ON TEACHERS/TRAINERS & DANCERS

Recognizing the individuality of dancers is an underlying theme of this entire series. It is also a top priority in terms of injury prevention. Many teachers argue that "coddling" dancers detracts them from their self-discipline and is therefore quite detrimental, especially to pupils. The answer to this can only be: In an empowering motivational climate, which fosters autonomy, task-orientation and self-concept in a dancer, very few dancers will show a lack of self-discipline and come up with problems that are none.

Suppose teachers have enough training in all subjects of dance medicine and pedagogy, they will be able to recognize whether a problem is significant or not. They will be able to open up to their students on a professional level without fearing a loss of authority. That will **encourage students or dancers to report pain or psychological stress**. In that case, teachers/trainers will **take this seriously** due to their high amount of content knowledge (and their own high level of self-concept!) and will be able to assess, whether help from medical professionals is needed. Due to their high levels of knowledge, they will also be willing to ask for and welcome such help.

Many things can be remedied or even better, be installed on a regular basis to avoid overuse injuries or overtraining in the first place, e.g.,

- executing health and environment screenings on a regular basis to prevent injuries
- taking time to screen dance technique and work with dancers individually and regularly
- installing a motivational climate, which fosters self-esteem, autonomy, relatedness and self-responsibility in dancers
- encouraging dancers to report any issue or complaint, based on the premise that the dancers

[252] Smith LL. *An alternate approach to assessing immune function related to URTI.* Int. Sports Med J. [online]. 4(3). 2003.

[253] Smith LL. *Overtraining, excessive exercise, and altered immune function: Is this a Th1- versus a Th2-lymphocyte response?* Sports Med. 33:347-364. 2003.

[254] Smith LL. *Tissue trauma: the underlying cause of overtraining syndrome?* J Strength Cond Res. 18(1). 185-93. 2004.

[255] Armstrong LE, and Vanheest JL. *The unknown mechanism of the overtraining syndrome.* Sports Med. 32. 185–209. 2002.

[256] Newsholme EA. *Biochemical mechanisms to explain immunosuppression in well-trained and overtrained athletes.* Int. J. Sports Med. 15. 142-147. 1994.

[257] Fry AC, and Kraemer WJ. *Resistance exercise overtraining and overreaching.* Sports Med. 23. 106-129. 1997.

[258] DiFiori JP, Benjamin HJ, Brenner J, Gregory A, Jayanthi N, Landry GL, and Luke A. *Overuse injuries and burnout in youth sports: a position statement from the American Medical Society for Sports Medicine.* Br J Sports Med. 48. 287-288. 2014.

[259] Brink MS, Nederhof E, Visscher C, Schmikli SL, and Lemmink KA. *Monitoring load, recovery, and performance in young elite soccer players.* J Strength Cond Res. 24(3). 597-603. 2010.

- do not become undisciplined but learn and demonstrate personal responsibility (as do the teachers/trainers who take the time to correct the problem!)
- performing an immediate and comprehensive analysis of risk factors (dance technique, environment) after complaint or injury

Taking such high levels of personal responsibility requires the **teacher's willingness for self-reflection**. Here many points from the introductory chapters on dance education and the following chapters on "dancers as teachers" play in too. The relationship between dancers (no matter what age) and teachers (no matter what degree of fame) should be characterized by respect and love for their respective tasks. Polite and constructive conversations about the dancer's problems, wishes, and concerns, as is the basis of empowering motivational climates have to be possible.

Suppose teachers notice that many of their dancers are struggling with, e.g., the same or related issues, or that a large number of overuse problems and pain are evident in their students/dancers, they should neither prohibit reporting it nor ignore the resulting consequence: If problems repeatedly occur in their classes, the teachers/trainers must seriously reflect on themselves. In doing so, they should not overlook deficits in their knowledge of dance pedagogy and medicine and tackle them without hesitation.

Nobody is perfect, but we all can strive for excellence. In the teacher's/trainer's case, the best scenario (and also the most effective solution) is when high levels of insatiable **intrinsic motivation for ongoing learning and improving** are leading to high levels of **perceived competency, self-efficacy, self-esteem** and thus the **ability of task-oriented self-reflection**. Such a teacher can put the focus on the dancers, their wellbeing and success, without having to suffer from low self-esteem, anxiety and overwhelming doubts. **Such a teacher/trainer will earn more respect and affection than any authoritative behavior could achieve**.

Volume 2 discusses motivational climate, communication, self-concept, and related aspects in theoretical as well as practical details. Moreover, part of this series on dance medicine and science is (recurrently) dedicated to the health and wellbeing of teachers and trainers themselves. Their behavior and the climate they create does not only affect their dancers. It is equally important for their own wellbeing and performance! As one of the most important people in a dancer's life, teachers and trainers deserve to be supported with regard to their own health, wellbeing and performance enhancement. They often come second, when the focus is exclusively on the dancer, thus this series also focuses on aspects, where (and how) they can support themselves by implementing dance medicine and science for their own benefit.

Many injuries could be prevented[260] through sufficient **science of training**, including health and dance-technique screenings, evidence-based scheduling, fitness training, or aspects such as (neuromuscular) **warm-up**[261] **and warm/cool-down**, able to meet basic **corrections of fitness deficits**. A few hours should be spent at the beginning of each school year or season to prepare together with the dancers, who can be guided towards autonomous handling of benefits such as warm-up already from a young age. Related aspects can be taught and should continually be monitored.

Volume 3 discusses theory and practice of warm-up as part of science of training in depth.

Supervision hours, in which teachers or trainers allow others to watch their work and give their feedback with regard to methods and content of teaching can be regarded as very important. Equally important, active **consultation hours** in which the teacher/trainer recurrently devotes time during the year to individually tackle dance technique deficiencies in dancers are a long-term solution. They should be established, because most individual technique- and training-related deficiencies cannot be solved during class only and take time. **Spending it on prevention, in turn, saves the time that the dancer would lose to injury.**

[260] Kaufmann JE, und A Kiselka. *Dance Medical Demands*. Dancer's Magazine. 2. 98-99. 2015.

[261] Kaufmann J-E, Nelissen RGHH, Stubbe JH, Gademan, MGJ. Neuromuscular warm up is associated with less overuse injuries in ballet dancers, compared to traditional ballet specific warm up routines. in press.

The chapter on primary and secondary injury prevention deals with this very important topic.

Specific and **targeted teacher/trainer education** in dance medicine and science as well as their own reading and study can support teachers and trainers with their own health and provide tools and guidance for their teaching and training. Medical professionals and other teachers/trainers can be invited for active consultation sessions, thereby providing dancers and teachers/trainers with their assistance and broaden their horizon.

AGE, SPECIALIZATION & SKILLS

A wide range of different factors are part of dancers' lives and thus possible causes of chronic and, to some extent, acute injuries: Gender specifics and style-dependent variability were already mentioned in the preceding and will further be discussed recurrently in various contexts. Age-related factors and overall physical, psychological and cognitive skills are further vital aspects.

Since (motor) development is a process starting before birth and ending with death, **age** is not only an issue at the end of a dancing career or in the context of training during childhood. The importance of putting **biological age** (the level of individual development of a person) first and **chronological age** (when a person is born) second will be discussed in upcoming chapters on childhood and adolescence. However, related to the discussion of age, the acknowledgment of the dancer's individual **level of skill** is essential for the design of training classes and the assignment of dancers of all ages to those classes. As much as age is used as an easy criterium of assignment, the individual level of expertise and skills should be the first and foremost criteria to decide, which class and training is suitable for whom, to prevent overtraining as well as boredom. This is not only essential in recreational dance, but also in vocational education.

Volume 2 of this series discusses details of motor development with respect to dance education and training.

Excessively intensive and early training can lead to young dancers not being able to cope with the demands placed upon them – neither physically, biomechanically, neuro-psychologically nor cognitively, possibly leading to injury, or loss of motivation and dropout. In sports and dance science this aspect is called specialization, or **early specialization**. It is highly related to the development of **overuse** injuries, **burnout and/or overtraining** (the reaction to overloading and overreaching) as well as **dropout**.[262,263,264,265]

Many parents as well as teachers and trainers consider early specialization in a single dance style as the only solution to train elite dancers.[266] However, there is sufficient evidence in dance and sports science that specialization before puberty has adverse effects. Even throughout adolescence, **versatility** and **diversification** are vital to support a dancer's health and wellbeing but also their commitment and motivation. Versatility and diversification in sports (e.g., training to become a dancer but allow other aspects of fitness and sport) and with respect to hobbies and privacy (allowing dancers to have interests other than dancing) are vital for the health as well as performance of ongoing (elite) dancers.

Additionally, only few teachers and trainers are aware that specialization, which comes along with various internal (the dancer) and external (teachers, trainers, parents, peers) aspects of (perfectionistic) striving and expectations, often leads to more than a recommended maximum of 8-9 months of training per year.[267] Many young dancers are sent to summer schools and workshops in their holidays, based on the misinformed assumption[268] of teachers/trainers/parents that there cannot be enough training, and holidays have detrimental

[262] Valovich McLeod TC, Decoster LC, Loud KJ, Micheli LJ, Parker JT, Sandrey MA, White C. *National Athletic Trainers' Association position statement: prevention of pediatric overuse injuries.* J Athl Train. 46(2). 206-220. 2011.

[263] Koutedakis Y. *"Burnout" in Dance. The physiological viewpoint.* J Dance Med Sci. 4(4). 122-127. 2000.

[264] Scher A. *Branch Out.* Dance Magazine 94(6). 36-36. 2020.

[265] LaPrade RF, Agel J, Baker J, Brenner JS, Cordasco FA, Côté J, Engebretsen L, Feeley BT, Gould D, Hainline B, Hewett T, Jayanthi N, Kocher MS, Myer GD, Nissen CW, Philippon MJ, and Provencher MT. *AOSSM Early Sport Specialization Consensus Statement.* Orthop J Sports Med. 4(4).2325967116644241. 2016.

[266] Matzkin E, and Garvey K. *Youth Sports Specialization: Does Practice Make Perfect?* NASN Sch Nurse. 34(2). 100-103. 2019.

[267] Post EG, Trigsted SM, Schaefer DA, Cadmus-Bertram LA, Watson AM, McGuine TA, Brooks MA, and Bell DR. *Knowledge, Attitudes, and Beliefs of Youth Sports Coaches Regarding Sport Volume Recommendations and Sport Specialization.* J Strength Cond Res. 34(10). 2911-2919. 2020.

[268] Padaki AS, Popkin CA, Hodgins JL, Kovacevic D, Lynch TS, Ahmad CS. *Factors That Drive Youth Specialization.* Sports Health. 9(6). 532-536. 2017.

effect on dancers' development and performance – while the contrary is the case![269]

Early specialization, success-oriented behavior and high expectations from others (parents, teachers, trainers, family, media, audiences) always are paired with high intensity or frequency of training already in the young dancer or athlete. As such, the likelihood to sustain injuries, experience overtraining and burnout as well as loss of motivation leading to dropping out is higher[270,271,272] than in dancers, who are allowed to be versatile, can rest, and have other aspects in life than just dance. Parents (and teachers), who had been in the same discipline can (unintentionally) exert more pressure on the young. Disillusion, performance plateaus, a lack of friends and privacy, among other, can lead to amotivation probably leading to dropout. [273] Early diversification, personal interest in the dancer or athlete and their wellbeing, as well as a positive relationship with the teacher can prevent overtraining, loss of motivation as well as dropout.[274]

Excessive training in early-to-late puberty, trying to **make up for years "lost" due to late dance initiation**, or teachers/trainers/parents, who are overly motivated to support a young talent can also lead to overtraining, injuries or loss of motivation. The first often affects young men, especially in vocational training, who might have started their professional training later than girls. In highly ambitious amateur dance, this problem of starting too late can also affect girls or women, who might want to fulfil dreams, which they could not enjoy in childhood. That is especially true when amateur classes are performance-oriented (competition, performance obligations). In any case, it is important to warn against so-called "**tricks**", as mentioned in the introductory chapters. **Technically inferior compensatory movements** are often used to quickly get children and young people to perform at a (superficially) high level. These movements soon appear to be effective on stage, or in training and rehearsal, but can lead to severe injuries.[275]

The teaching of proper and sufficient levels of dance technique is always based on children's individuality, cognitive and physical ability and refrains from superficial displays of crowd-pleasing maneuvers. Then again, **respecting individual levels of skill** in reference to biological age, i.e., individual levels of overall development, is crucial.

The latter, the special attention given to a **dancer regarded as specifically talented**, can affect both genders, and in all levels of expertise. In the best case, a teacher or trainer works with all dancers with an equal effort, allowing talents to identify themselves throughout a group or class, in order to avoid overtraining in a dancer regarded as specifically talented. In case the teacher/trainer really wants to focus on one dancer specifically, their knowledge and experience has to be sufficient enough to avoid overtraining in the dancer by preventing being overzealous in all parties involved, i.e., dancers, teacher/trainer, parents, media.

BALANCING ASPECTS OF DANCE TRAINING: FITNESS, BIOMECHANICAL ASPECTS & DIVERSITY

Regardless of style, the goal of evidence-based training and education should be a balance between the many facets of dance training. That will lead to diversity with regard to (motor) learning, dance technique and all aspects of fitness, to avoid deficits as well as overtraining. [276,277]

Some examples would be:

Avoiding monotony in classes and a loss of training stimulus due to habituation of the body as well as the brain.

[269] Koutedakis Y, Myszkewycz L, Soulas D, Papapostolou V, Sullivan I, and Sharp NC. *The effects of rest and subsequent training on selected physiological parameters in professional female classical dancers.* Int J Sports Med. 20(6). 379-383. 1999.

[270] Fraser-Thomas J, Côté J, and Deakin J. *Understanding dropout and prolonged engagement in adolescent competitive sport.* Psychology of Sport and Exercise. 9. 645-662. 2008.

[271] Fraser-Thomas J, Côté J, and Deakin J. *Examining adolescent sport dropout and prolonged engagement from a developmental perspective.* J Appl Sport Psychol. 20(3). 318–333. 2008.

[272] Wiersma L. *Risks and Benefits of Youth Sport Specialization: Perspectives and Recommendations.* Pediatric Exercise Science. 12. 13-22. 2000.

[273] Crane J, and Temple V. *A systematic review of dropout from organized sport among children and youth.* European Physical Education Review. 21. 114-131. 2014.

[274] Fraser-Thomas J, and Côté J. *Understanding Adolescents' Positive and Negative Developmental Experiences in Sport.* Sport Psychologist. 23. 2009.

[275] Ryan AJ, and RE Stephens. The dancer's guide to healthcare & a long career. Dance Books UK. 1988. p.102.

[276] Voigt L, Singh A, und Hohmann A. *Diversification in long-term athlete development. The perspective of expert youth coaches.* Sportwiss. 44. 134-152. 2014.

[277] Myer GD, Jayanthi N, DiFiori JP, Faigenbaum AD, Kiefer AW, Logerstedt D, Micheli LJ. *Sports Specialization, Part II: Alternative Solutions to Early Sport Specialization in Youth Athletes.* Sports Health. 8(1). 65-73. 2016.

Avoiding to introduce lateral bias, i.e., a "leg/arm/body side preferences", and training both sides of the body equally.

Combining the training of flexibility in dancers (stretching) with the necessary stabilization through targeted strength training (e.g., core stabilization) to avoid myofascial dysbalances, compensations and overstraining single structures in the individual kinetic chain of a dancer's motion.

Integrating exercises for proprioception and sensorimotor control. This supports postural control, which is essential with regard to reaction time, coordination, as well as alignment.

Training aerobic endurance, which is related to proper alignment as well as muscular endurance. Endurance prevents fatigue in dancers and supports faster recovery as well as increased ability to adapt to training stimulus.

Screening dance technique and a high focus on biomechanical correctness, such as proper alignment, is another, highly essential part of injury prevention, specifically the prevention of overuse injuries (e.g., avoiding any compensations for anatomical limitations through forcing of joints[278], evidence-based handling of hypermobility and hyperextended joints, faulty leg axes, or deficient positioning of arms, shoulders, head or spine). Biomechanics of dance allow for a lot of diversity in teaching that can result in a comprehensive and **holistic understanding of dance and dance technique** in the dancer. The teacher/trainer can include aspects of anatomy, physiology, motor learning, physics, history and many more.

While training is commonly related to action, rest and the ability to relax are also part of performance enhancement as well as injury prevention, beneficial to dancers of all dance styles and levels. They are related to psychological aspects such as performance anxiety or stage fright and associated with physiological topics, for instance the functionality of breathing or the pelvic floor.

Implementing specific aspects of training and teaching such as warm-up and warm-/cool-down, improvisation, breathing and relaxation techniques, theoretical aspects of dance (e.g., dance medicine and science, history, nutrition, music, fine arts) and any aspects that can complement training and lead towards diversity, will support the dancer's learning and development.

The more dancers are allowed to (physically, emotionally, cognitively) move "in all directions and with all means", the more they can avoid deficits and keep up the functionality of all tissues involved. **Mindful versatility, diversification, and a certain level of playfulness** also in vocational and professional dance are essential for injury prevention by enhancing motor skills and preventing loss of motivation and dropout, as described above.

Fitness as well as lateral bias in training, warm-up, biomechanics, alignment, flexibility and stretching, breathing and pelvic floor are discussed in volume 3 of the series in theory and with extensive practical solutions.

When working with dancers, the mentioned aspects must be respected based on the acknowledgement of dancers' individuality, as described recurrently. Respecting anatomical characteristics and limitations of dancers' physique that cannot be changed is as essential as allowing sufficient rest for sleep and recovery, **nutrition** intake, **water** balance, **screening** of health and technique, adapting **schedules** while **refraining from pressure** related to weight and appearance, training, performance, perception of pain and reporting of injuries

SHOES, CLOTHING, JEWELRY & HAIRSTYLE

Although shoes are an essential tool for the dancer to be able to perform [279] and an integrating aspect of the respective technique, research is relatively scarce. [280] Most dance shoes do not offer significant protection against the impact of ground reaction forces (pointe shoes, flamenco and tap shoes or high heels in musicals, dancesport and showdance, soft leather slippers, etc.).[281] That is especially important in the context of the high

[278] Kaufmann JE, Nelissen RGHH, Exner-Grave E, and Gademan MGJ. *Does forced or compensated turnout lead to musculoskeletal injuries in dancers? A systematic review on the complexity of causes.* J Biomech. 114. 110084. 2021.

[279] Perala HD, Wilson MA, and Dai B. *The Effect of Footwear on Free Moments During a Rotational Movement in Country Swing Dance.* J Dance Med Sci. 22(2). 84-90. 2018.

[280] Fong Yan A, Hiller C, Smith R, and Vanwanseele B. *Effect of footwear on dancers: a systematic review.* J Dance Med Sci.15(2). 86-92. 2011.

[281] Miller CD, Paulos LE, Parker RD, and Fishell M. *The ballet technique shoe: a preliminary study of eleven differently modified ballet technique shoes using force and pressure plates.* Foot Ankle. 11(2). 97-100. 1990.

focus on vertical and horizontal jumping activities and balance in dance, where footwear is considered to influence stability, postural control and thus injury risk.[282,283,284]

It is of utmost importance that dance shoes fit[285] the dancer, to offer the best protection and support they can. Further it is important that they are produced in a way, which supports the respective need in dance, for instance through evidence-based sole construction, or with respect to materials involved.[286]

Since they are essential for the dancer's performance, they have to be chosen with care. To find the right shoe is quite a science in dance, but it is essential to take **sufficient time for shoe fitting** and probably, at best, the dancer will find "the perfect shoe".

Volume 3 discusses pointe work and related topics, such as readiness, biomechanics, or movement analysis.

Shoes must be carefully selected to fit the shape of the foot and dancers' sizes and needs, where millimeters already can change the world for the performing dancer for the better or for the worse. The **length** of closed shoes is especially important to support the functionality of the feet's **longitudinal arches**. The shoe length must be chosen as such that dancers' toes can be extended freely are not forced to role inwards or claw (hammer toes) in plié (squats, knee bends), relévé (half and demi pointe; elevation onto the balls of the feet) or when rolling across the entire foot in walking, running etc.

It is recommended in fittings to perform pliés as well as relévés in the shoes, as this shows whether the dancer slides back and forth in them when they are too big or is forced to roll/claw the toes in stand and elevation. The dancer has to keep in mind that the shoe has to fit in standing and flat sole position and as well as motion, which is where the toes have to be able to extent freely.

Volume 3 discusses the habit of many dancers and teachers to use/recommend shoes a size smaller to make the foot look smaller or display a better arch. That however is dangerous, because it restricts the functionality of the arches of the feet and can therefore restrict dance technique and impair health.

The foot's **width** must also be taken into account not to restrict the forefoot's ability to roll. If the shoes are too narrow and tight, the foot cannot benefit from the functionality of its **transversal arch**, which acts like a spring whenever the foot leaves the floor. In order to do that, the width has to be sufficient enough that the transversal arch can flatten down when the foot is weight bearing and position itself with all toes and balls on the floor in a relaxed manner. When this functionality is impaired, the dancer's equilibrium (and health) might suffer.

A secure grip for the hindfoot (heel) must be provided in all dance shoes. Most styles incorporate elevation of the foot onto the ball (relévé, half or pointe) or incorporate heels into their technique (dancesport through flamenco). The more the heel rises off the floor and balance on the ball of the foot is needed, the more instable the ankle of the dancer will become, due to the anatomical construction and biomechanics of the talus bone, tibia and fibula. It is vital that dancers demonstrate sufficient strength and stability through **targeted training**, to manage such biomechanical challenges.

Volume 3 discusses the underlying anatomy, training and exercises.

It is equally important that shoes are secured with intact ribbons, elastics, or straps. Any damage to the shoe or its materials has to be mended immediately, or, if that is not possible, the shoes need to be exchanged.

The sole should support the foot and provide the necessary grip or slip, depending on the **dance style and floor**. When dancers are dancing on different floors, they might need different pairs of shoes for each floor condition, to avoid too much or too little friction. For that

[282] Walter HL, Docherty CL, and Schrader J. *Ground reaction forces in ballet dancers landing in flat shoes versus pointe shoes.* J Dance Med Sci. 15(2). 61-64.2011.

[283] McPherson AM, Schrader JW, and Docherty CL. *Ground Reaction Forces in Ballet Differences Resulting from Footwear and Jump Conditions.* J Dance Med Sci. 23(1). 34-39. 2019.

[284] Lobo da Costa PH, Azevedo Nora FG, Vieira MF, Bosch K, and Rosenbaum D. *Single leg balancing in ballet: effects of shoe conditions and poses.* Gait Posture. 37(3). 419-243. 2013.

[285] Cunningham BW, DiStefano AF, Kirjanov NA, Levine SE, and Schon LC. A comparative mechanical analysis of the pointe shoe toe box. An in vitro study. Am J Sports Med. 26(4). 555-561. 1998.

[286] Wyon MA, Cloak R, Lucas J, and Clarke F. *Effect of midsole thickness of dance shoes on dynamic postural stability.* Med Probl Perform Art. 28(4). 195-198. 2013.

matter it is of utmost **importance that dancers can test the floor** in general and especially in reference to their shoes, before they are to perform, are examined, are auditioning, or competing. It is the teacher's responsibility to educate dancers in that respect from an early age onwards already in order to reduce injury risk but also **performance anxiety** and extensive **stress** levels.

Equally important is that shoes are bought newly, and that they have been and will be selected, danced in, and maintained for and by the one dancer who bought them. Dancers only have a few tools, which support them in their work. Besides dancers' bodies, clothing and footwear are among the essential tools. Just as a body cannot be "worked in" through dance and passed on, the same cannot be done with shoes handed down to the next dancer, because they have been **bought to fit and worked in until they belong** to a specific body. Once they were used, they might not be able to support another dancer sufficiently.

A widespread habit, mostly underestimated and especially common in amateur dance, is to **pass on footwear** that is **no** longer needed or that has become too small from one dancer to another. With pointe shoes this is especially dangerous. Aside from hygienic aspects, many (inexperienced) dancers think that worn out/dead shoes, such as pointe shoes are easier to dance with, because they have become softer already. However, that is a misassumption and specifically dangerous. Dance science has shown the effect of **deterioration of pointe shoes** on foot and ankle **kinematics** (motion of joints or body parts without reference to the forces that move them) and **kinetics** (motion related to the forces which cause the movement) of professional ballet dancers.[287] In spite of their elite level of expertise, these dancers were significantly affected by the deterioration of their shoes, because it changed the stability and way their feet moved: the worn pointe shoes caused greater mid-foot flexion and ankle plantarflexion en pointe due to the reduced structural integrity of the shoe. That could increase injury risk. Another study investigated lower extremity biomechanics with respect to muscular activation.[288] Their results supported the association between **worn out/dead pointe shoes and injury risk**, showing that dancing with dead shoes is more demanding than with new ones, and that muscle activation patterns are changing along with changes of the shoe towards deterioration. These results transferred to inexperienced, amateur or younger dancers in general could even lead to more injury risk due to their lower experience and skill levels with respect to alignment or strength. Such results can be transferred to the practice of all dance styles. Worn out/dead shoes might not only lack the essential stability, but they also pose a risk factor with respect to their materials. Heels coming off during dancing, taps coming off the soundboard and rocketing into the hall, or soles, straps, elastics, ribbons or boxes breaking... the injury risk for dancers due to a loss of structural and functional integrity of shoes is high. And even if, luckily, the deterioration does not lead to accidents, the stress level of a dancer having to work in dead shoes can be enormous. As one of the most essential tools, dancers rely on their shoes. Any unreliability from that side can increase the dancer's anxiety or stage fright significantly, and can negatively affect the dancer's performance.

Clothing follows fashion trends in dance, and dancers understandably care about following these trends, not least because they wear them a lot (every day), often more than everyday clothes as far as professionals are concerned. Nevertheless, these clothes must be appropriate for the dance style and training requirements. Fripperies, extra decorations, loose ribbons or applications, or cuts that are too wide and long can pose an injury risk.

The mostly very tight-fitting training clothes of classical dancers offer hardly any **heat protection**. They are primarily made of mixed fabrics that do not support the body's temperature regulation and perspiration, although many companies already make essential efforts to meet the need of dancers. Therefore, vocational training schools should design their dress codes with care to support the dancer's daily body work by choosing appropriate fabric weaves and cuts.[289] Warming clothing for breaks and at the beginning of warm-ups and the end of cool-downs should be allowed, explained, and checked by the teacher. However, caution is advised when additional warming things are worn over feet in dance shoes. If, in addition to dance shoes, slippers, indoor footwear, oversized socks, casual leg warmers, oversized casual shoes, or warming dancer boots are put on, the feet lose their **grip on the floor**. Injuries from stumbling

[287] Bickle C, Deighan M, and Theis N. *The effect of pointe shoe deterioration on foot and ankle kinematics and kinetics in professional ballet dancers.* Hum Mov Sci. 60. 72-77. 2018.

[288] Aquino J, Amasay T, Shapiro S, Kuo YT, and Ambegaonkar JP. *Lower extremity biomechanics and muscle activity differ between 'new' and 'dead' pointe shoes in professional ballet dancers.* Sports Biomech. 31. 1-12. 2019.

[289] Pessenhofer H, Sauseng N, Kohle B, und G Schwaberger. *Einflüsse von textilen Materialien mit unterschiedlichen Sorptionseigenschaften auf Energiebereitstellung und Thermoregulation des Menschen.* [Influence of textile materials with various textures on energy supply and thermo regulation in humans]. Biomed Tech. 37(1). 235-238. 1992.

over uneven surfaces, slipping on steps or in sanitary facilities, getting tangled up in stage sets and floor elements, or sliding on dance floors are among frequent causes of injury. Warming clothing should be taken off after the warm-up. Hiding some dancers' supposed overweight with sweaters and pullovers should be addressed by teachers, especially if the dancers complete their training in sweaters that hinder their **thermoregulation** through the evaporation of sweat. If it is a legitimate body weight issue, it should be addressed separately. In any case, clothing that is too warm puts a significant strain on the heart and circulation.

Jewelry is a **no-go** for both dancers and trainers in the dance studio. The injury risk caused by necklaces, finger rings, and (dangling) earrings is too often underestimated. At the same time, teachers must be aware of their role model effect. The dance studio, the stage, and the rehearsal parquet should be a jewelry-free zone. Injuries of and provoked by dance teachers wearing jewelry can happen in moments of correction when trainers touch dancers or stand next to them. Jewelry that cannot or will not be removed must be taped over to prevent it from getting caught in cloths, hair etc. Care should be taken with all stud earrings, piercings, and finger rings. They may seem small and inconspicuous but can cause severe injuries through hooking and tearing.

Hair should be combed out of the face in all dance styles and handled in sensible manner. This applies even to indisputably "cool" dance styles such as urban styles or special requirements such as in contemporary dance. Loose hair can obstruct the dancers' and their partners' vision, injure eyes, and, when entangled with props or partners, cause whiplash injuries and low back pain that should not be underestimated. When performances depend on lose hair as part of the role's "outfit" or costume, and really cannot go without, it is essential that the dancer has sufficiently rehearsed with open hair. It is equally important that sets and props as well as choreography in such a case are designed as such that injuries can be prevented.

COSTUMES, LIGHT & SCENERY

Costumes should be tailored for dancers to ensure an optimal fit and thus do not negatively **affect** dance **performances**. However, this is often not possible for financial reasons, neither in professional nor in amateur dance. If costumes are tailored as ready-to-wear sizes or custom-tailored pieces are passed on, theater personnel and trainers/teachers must make sure that the costume fits the new dancer properly. Costumes that are too large, too small, or even defective are not only dangerous because they can hinder or constrict dancers, but they are also a significant source of distraction. Dancers distracted by dangling ribbons, loose applications, or unraveling seams are just as likely to be injured as those who are uncomfortable in their costumes because they make them feel "exposed". Similarly, costumes that are too tight and interfere with optimal movement and efficient breathing become a distraction and thus are dangerous for dancers.

Caution is also advised with "improvisations", not only concerning dancers and their partners. It is quite common for an inadequately fixed piece or even whole parts of a costume or prop to fall off. They might endanger the dancers and the audience when falling off while the dancers turn or jump and possibly hit the audience. Costumes or props that will lose parts, either unintentionally or intentionally (as an intended effect), can be detrimental to all those who must come on stage along with or after the one who lost them.

Decorative materials, feathers, needles, small pieces, rhinestones, and the like can turn stage and rehearsal floors into a "dangerous patch" and injure dancers. Spreading them around must be avoided at all costs. Since this is not always possible, and in case it is part of a production, the stage has to be cleaned as soon as the effect is over. These opportunities must not be left to chance but purposefully arranged and rehearsed. The same applies to liquids such as water or liquid colors ("blood") on stage. **Props** and **stage sets** can pose significant injury risk as well. First, they have to be secured that nothing can fall onto the dancer or into their way. Second, the increasing use of sometimes dangerous props such as ropes, knives, forks, and glass of all kinds in productions must be well thought through and managed by teachers and choreographers. If choreographers or teachers use such props, sets, or costumes, they are responsible for ensuring that their dancers' health can be guaranteed when using them. Intensive rehearsals and detailed examination of dangerous and any props or scene environment in general are crucial, that the dancers can familiarize themselves with their inherent dynamics and/or nature. The use of props, costume, or equipment that could physically or emotionally stress the dancers should be avoided. That includes choreographically attacking other roles with real knives or taping the mouth shut with gaffa tape, which has often been seen in recent years to express silence, powerlessness, "silent screams", oppression and the like. The creativity of choreographers and teachers is honored. Still, taping up mouths not only deprives dancers of the feeling of getting enough oxygen during their high performance (and thus poses a severe psychological threat). The adhesive's chemicals can also cause severe skin lesions, not only when the tape is torn off.

Lighting and **stage technology** must also be adapted to dancers, who are the most vulnerable element in the chain of all events. Lighting technology must be rehearsed and installed to support dancers while causing as little glare as possible. Dancers must withstand the bright light of numerous spotlights during the entire performance. Adding fancy lighting effects to this necessary illumination, often even using strobes that make it impossible for dancers to assess distances and depths, must be considered carefully. If it is crucial to the success of the production and choreographers' wishes, the lightning setup must be sufficiently rehearsed. It may not be changed afterward without rehearsing it again, involving the dancers.

Technical equipment such as spotlights, cables, brackets, beams, etc. must be checked for safety, best by professionals. They must be entirely **secured** and installed as such that they never affect dancers' performance. Under no circumstances may the expenses be the main focus.

Although theaters pay close attention to **fire safety** and similar regulations, dancers' safety must be considered in every situation as well. Makeshift solutions should be avoided. Even if **cables** are taped to the floor, they are dangerous for dancers who depend on their floors – onstage and backstage.

If it is not possible to avoid such solutions, they must be marked, communicated to the dancers and made visible with **reflective tape**. The same applies to the edges of stairs and ramps onstage and backstage. Adequate lighting has to be provided backstage as well as on stairs and in dressing rooms. Injuries occurring backstage due to lack of safety regulations are considered dance injuries because they happened in the work environment of dancers, just as those occurring on stage and in the dance studio.

WORK ENVIRONMENT: ON STAGE & BACKSTAGE

If the production involves children or adolescents, regardless of whether it is an amateur performance or a professional institution, the **trainer, teacher** or the **studio/school** is **responsible** for preparing the environment before the dancers come to rehearsals or performances. Backstage, on the stage, and around the stage, there is a permanent need for **tidiness** that children should be taught early. Costumes last longer if they are appropriately handled and must also be kept **tidy** by dancers themselves. Young dancers should have the chance to learn to **treat the outfits** they are provided with **respectfully and mindfully.** Moreover, such mindfulness prevents costumes or parts from rolling or lying around and, therefore, can be an essential aspect to prevent injuries, when things become hectic, what they mostly do. The stress related to the performance is already enough. Nobody needs dancers stumbling around, looking for lost items such as costumes or accessories.

Breaks must be allowed with appropriate frequency, because they are essential for dancers to recover, thus improving their performance. Schedules should include such breaks as integrating part of rehearsal plans to avoid that "there suddenly is no time left for breaks". Sufficient time for **eating** is important and dancers should always be allowed to drink water. The higher the physical exertion, temperature, and season, the more water dancers need. In principle, children and adolescents depend even more on regular and sufficient **water intake** than adults.

Central eating and drinking breaks should take place in separate rooms to avoid dirt from crumbs, paper, or water spills. Food leftovers, spilled liquids, and drinking bottles laying around or knocked over and rolling in the darkness are an immense danger in the hustle and bustle of stage activities. For this reason, a focus of education already in the little ones is mindful tidiness. The essential water bottles for quick drinking breaks must have a permanent location in the dance studio and theater, which is preferably not the fold of a curtain with the risk of knocking them over, but in a safe place to which the dancers have access.

Training in too cold or overheated rooms, open-air performances in the **cold**, rain, or even heat can be a challenge for dancers' health. Colds, strains, sprains, difficulties with the warm-up at low temperatures, heat strokes, dehydration, exhaustion, and heat cramps at **high temperatures** can be the result and must not be underestimated. When performances, shootings etc. are in exceptional places it is the institutions obligation to protect the dancers from all possible harm by providing sufficient places for retreat, breaks, changing, warm-up, warm/cool-down etc.

Air conditioning can lead to muscle injuries and colds when dancers are exposed to a constant draught while perspiring. At the same time, the heat generated by the dancers working, spotlights, curtains, and the audience's presence should not be underestimated. Hence, the use of air conditioning should neither be delayed nor overdosed but coordinated with the dancers, at best. They are the ones who must perform to a physical and mental maximum. Therefore, their well-being should be paramount. A possibility to open backdoors and ventilate in halls or theaters on hot evenings is also essential to avoid heat strokes and improve air quality. At **open-air** performances, rain-soaked stage floors are just as much of a hazard as those heated up by the sun. Burns in dance styles with floor work such as modern, jazz, street styles, gymnastics, acrobatics, or contemporary styles are typical injuries and can get worse when floors are exposed to sunlight. However, floor burns are not only related to open-air performances and floor coverings heated up by the sun but also to the quality and surface of the stages and the flooring in dance and rehearsal rooms.

FLOORS & SURFACE QUALITY

In general, the condition of floors on stages, in dance studios and training rooms is also part of health care for dancers, for professionals as much as amateurs. The **floor** is one of the few tools that dancers have at their disposal. It affects their performance and their health.[290,291,292,293,294,295] However, the lack of financial resources in dance as well as a lack of knowledge or/and ignorance often result in cutbacks on floors. According to a 2013[296] study, floors are the **second most frequent exogenous/extrinsic factor** for acute injuries in professional dancers (28.4%) after the partner (39.9%). Surface conditions (too slippery or too sticky) are the most frequent cause of accidents. However, it is not only the surfaces that can cause acute accidents. Texture, design, and the use of the wrong materials as floors and substructures can also lead to severe chronic injuries even among amateurs who train on them only twice a week. Floors that are too hard, such as PVC flooring directly on screed, particle boards on gymnasium floors or the popular floating touring stage elements made of steel with a PVC overlay, can lead to severe injuries. **Bursitis** and **tendonitis**, bruises on and sprains of the feet, spine, shoulders, and all other joints such as the hand, knee, and elbow (depending on dance style and technique) are commonplace in dance. Daily training, performances, and touring become painful and can result in long-term overuse problems if dancers have to perform in such conditions (repeatedly). **Stress fractures** constitute many chronic dance injuries that cannot always be attributed to inadequate technique only. Floors that are too hard and unsuspended can contribute.

Additionally, many dancers rehearse on floors that are different from those on which performances occur. That does not only bear severe injury risk, because dancers have to cope with a change of surfaces. Many dancers attempt to compensate for this discrepancy by adapting their dance technique. However, if during the final rehearsals or, in the most unprofessional case, already in front of the audience, dancers have to realize that the floor does not correspond to what they have rehearsed their parts on, not all adaptational changes (reinforced pliés, more powerful jumps) can be performed off the cuff. Therefore, in addition to **the injury risk**, floors always represent a **psychological burden** for dancers. Dancers work hard in their striving for excellence, and it can lead to severe anxiety if they are not be able to show their potential because of the flooring.[297] Floors can increase dancers' (daily) stress levels enormously, especially when they multiply stage fright and fear of failure. Leaving dancers in fear about whether or not they can successfully and healthily present their work only because of inadequate or unfamiliar floor conditions is incredibly unfair. Audiences and critics primarily attribute

[290] Wanke EM, Mill H, Wanke A, Davenport J, Koch F, and Groneberg DA. *Dance floors as injury risk: analysis and evaluation of acute injuries caused by dance floors in professional dance with regard to preventative aspects.* Med Probl Perform Art. 27(3). 137-142. 2012.
[291] Wanke EM, Arendt M, Mill H, and Groneberg DA. *Occupational accidents in professional dance with focus on gender differences.* J Occ Med Toxicol. 8. 35. 2013.
[292] Seals JG. *Dance Floors.* Med Probl Perform Art. 1(3). 81-84. 1986.
[293] Kelman BB. *Occupational hazards in female ballet dancers. Advocate for a forgotten population.* AAOHN J. 48(9). 430-443. 2000.
[294] Looseleaf V. *The silent partner.* Dance Magazine. 80(1). 88-93. 2006.
[295] Hackney J, Brummel S, Jungblut K, and Edge C. *The effect of sprung (suspended) floors on leg stiffness during grand jeté landings in ballet.* J Dance Med Sci. 15(3). 128-133. 2011.
[296] Wanke EM, Mill H, Wanke A, Davenport J, Checcetti F, Koch F, and Groneberg DA. *Dance partner or dance floors?: exogenous factors resulting in accidents in professional dancers.* Med Probl Perform Art. 28(3). 131-136. 2013.
[297] Ryan AJ, and RE Stephens. The dancer's guide to healthcare & a long career. Dance Books UK. 1988. p.117.

the ignominy of a botched performance to the dancer. Only few might "look behind the curtains" and ask themselves or the dancers, which work and performance conditions they so often have to encounter.

Not all dance floors are the same.[298] The demands they place on dancers are as varied as the dance styles and techniques, which are performed on them. Scientific research about dance style, **shock absorption** and **floor reaction forces**, surface texture, friction, and the like is conducted to provide dancers with the best possible support.[299,300] A smooth enough floor for dancesport may seem like an ice rink to a ballet dancer or acrobat. What is suitable for ballet dancers in pointe and soft shoes can lead to serious skin injuries and bruises in modern dancers, who perform barefoot and for whom turns and jumps on the knees are part of their daily repertoire.

Thus, the choice of **floor** and the **substructure** must always **meet the demands of the dance style** and should follow professional recommendation based on an analysis of the institution's needs and the dance style. That will guarantee not only an optimal choice of materials but also professional installation.

Joints of floor boards or podestas that have not been adequately closed or remain unbalanced in height can cause severe cuts and tears or even become tripping hazards. The same is valid for tapes that roll up, overlapping or flapping floor coverings and upturned edges, or subfloors that are so uneven that no overlay can cover dancers' feeling of a cross-country adventure. In addition to the quality of floors in dance studios, stage, and rehearsal rooms, it must also be considered that the **transition** to the **backstage area** and the corridors and stairwells must be **marked**.

Furthermore, surface quality of backstage areas should harmonize with the working surface on stage so that dancers do not run the risk of injuring themselves through a sudden change from non-slippery to slippery, or vice versa when walking/running off the stage.

Raked/inclined stages are a special challenge. Many stages provide floors with a slight inclination, especially in older theaters and halls which are used for multiple artistic purposes. As helpful as they are for acoustics with regard to singers and actors, they are enormously challenging to dance on. Many companies and dancers have to face them on tour and it is necessary to practice on them beforehand (without overworking the dancers, so appropriate scheduling is needed!). Raked stages significantly influence dancers' proprioception and affect turns and balance, jumping, and landing behavior. The dancers' **biomechanics change** when working on sloping surfaces and have been shown to **increase the risk of injury**.[301,302,303,304]

Furthermore, the color of the floor is an important aspect. Many choreographers fancy colors such as red or yellow for a complete stage floor – but for dancers, the color also changes their perception. The eye must learn to recalculate distances with new colors, especially when the floor runs uniformly across the entire stage in one **hue** without any (subtle) patterns. Takeoff in Pas de Deux and horizontal jumps can become extremely risky for dancers, especially if the floor also has a reflective surface as if the color was painted or varnished. Apart from the enormous risk of slipping, a reflective surface is always problematic because of the spotlights' glare. Dancers must contend with glaring light in many moments on stage, which must not be intensified by mirroring the light across a reflective floor covering. Dull, non-reflective surfaces are preferable here, as are muted colors, such as very dark gray or non-reflective, matte black, as well as cream and light gray, which allow dancers to assess depths three-dimensionally. Suppose it is necessary to use a color tone such as red, yellow, or the like, it is recommended to use floors without a uniform hue but mottled with, e.g., light gray to enable the dancers' eyes to calculate distances.

Training (not only when touring) or auditions often occur in incredible environments, ranging from drafty foyers where the counter serves as an ad hoc barre, to tiled floors in entrance halls and hotel lobbies lined with fitted carpets. That can also apply to show performances: Show groups of all dance genres often encounter unbelievable floors and stage conditions, sizes and shapes that make smaller show engagements very risky. Shows presented in different venues without a stage must have a **consistent floor**. Dance performers are too often exposed

[298] Foley M. *Dance Floors.* Fact Sheet Dance UK. No 6. 1998.
[299] Hopper LS, Alderson JA, Elliott BC, Ackland TR, and Fleming PR. *Dancer perceptions of quantified dance surface mechanical properties.* Proceedings of the Institution of Mechanical Engineers, Part P: J Sports Engineering Technology. 225. 65-73. 2011.
[300] Hopper LS, Alderson JA, Elliott BC, Ackland TR, and Fleming PR. *Do Dance Floor Force Reduction and Static Stiffness Represent Dynamic Floor Stiffness During Dance Landings?*Procedia Enineering. 72. 931-936. 2014.
[301] Hagins M, Pappas E, Kremenic I, Orishimo KF, and A Rundle. *The effect of an inclined landing surface on biomechanical variables during a jumping task.* Clinical biomechanics. 22(9). 1030-1036. 2007.
[302] Pappas E, Orishimo KF, Kremenic I, Liederbach M, Hagins M. *The effects of floor incline on lower extremity biomechanics during unilateral landing from a jump in dancers.* J Appl Biomech. 28(2).192-199. 2012.
[303] Pappas E, and M Hagins. *The effects of "raked" stages on standing posture in dancers.* J Dance Med Sci. 12(2). 54-58. 2008.
[304] Evans RW, Evans RI, Carvajal S. *Survey of injuries among West End performers.* Occup Environ Med. 55(9). 585-593. 1998.

to a mix of surfaces, ranging from carpets, flooring edges, parquet floors, and decorations or furniture protruding onto the dance floor when performing show acts. Company celebrations, anniversaries, openings, and the like can also lead to difficult challenges for amateur and professional performances if floor conditions and room size are not sufficiently clarified beforehand or are not sufficiently provided by the organizer. Dancers and especially the choreographers or teachers in charge should be aware of the injury risk and, if necessary, cancel a performance even at short notice when dancers' health is at stake.

Stage floors made of planks or loose boards can be found in many old theaters or improvised stages, where exams or performances of amateur dancers are held in rented theaters. These are dangerous for dancers of any style. In addition to the likelihood of tearing skin, leaving partly severe wood splinters, dancer could fall over floor planks that move against each other or entangle their shoes in gaps that are sometimes several millimeters wide. Such floors are also found in the professional area. Rarely onstage but very often backstage. However, the **backstage area, as recurrently mentioned, can also constitute injury risk**. Especially where there is little light available, sound floors and markings must be emphasized.

In addition to plank floors, gymnasium floors are often used in amateur dance and professional training. Here, parquet floors are just as problematic as particular foam-based floors that bend very much: Hard foam rubber flooring, which may be suitable for ball sports and the like, is usually very obstructive for dance because dancers must balance a lot. They need a surface that is **uniform and does not bend or sink in**. If the floor surface changes while oscillating (maintaining balance while moving), dancers will probably lose control. However, compensating for this by covering it with particle board is also inappropriate, even though it is still common, especially at dance festivals or various training or summer schools in many countries.

Stages consisting of platforms must be secured so that the individual platforms do not move against each other. The bumps at the t-joints have shown to cause cuts or become tripping hazards. Besides, freestanding stage platforms or suspended platforms must be secured at their outer edges. That includes visible **floor markings** and **surrounding guardrails**, to prevent falling when walking or running backward towards the back of the stage or the sides. Very often jet-black curtains that meet the often black floor from a great height surround such an open stage area. In that case, marking the edges of the stage and providing fall protection behind it, is all the more critical since dancers, commonly blinded by the stage lights, can no longer judge distances in an all-black environment.

Stairs leading up and down stages, like all stairs in staging areas, must be adequately **marked**, even if the surrounding area has a **safety light**. Dancers coming from the spotlights into darker surroundings are momentarily blind. Staircases are therefore a great danger and should be replaced with non-slippery (!) ramps.[305]

Dust and other types of **dirt**, which are part of everyday life in the theater and dance studio, are also worth mentioning. Dance floors must be carefully cleaned. Dancers have a right to not only present their performance without obstacles but also to stay clean. That applies to dust, wood splinters, oil from technical equipment, sweat, and other liquids. The usually very dusty theater environment can aggravate respiratory illnesses common among dancers and make stage floors slippery. Choreographic effects such as the sprinkling of dust, glitter, confetti, and the like and their immediate removal must be well planned and rehearsed. If effects are involved, the prevention of any hazard to dancers has to be the overall goal. Care must also be taken when rehearsing with socks or tights without footwear, as this leaves invisible but even more dangerous slippery spots on most floors.

In conclusion, it is the institution's, teachers' and/or choreographers' responsibility to review the dance environment regarding injury prevention, including surfaces on and around the dance floor, dance studio, and stage. Likewise, feedback from affected dancers must be heard when they report shortcomings, and dancers should always be encouraged to speak out.

- The basic rule of **only performing on floors** that have been **adequately tested and rehearsed on by the dancers beforehand**, should always be followed. The risk of injury increases when floors are unfamiliar.
- Floors that can be dismantled and transported quickly are recommended to allow dancers to move from training surface to stage floors seamlessly.

[305] Wanke EM. *Rahmenempfehlungen zur Prävention von Unfällen im professionellen Bühnentanz.* Unfallkasse Berlin Deutsche gesetzliche Unfallversicherung (ed.). München. 2009.

- If warm-up areas exist around stages, they should have at least the same surface as the stage to allow dancers to prepare in every way possible. If this is not possible, dancers must at least be able to rehearse on the stages adequately (rule 1).
- Stage floors must consist of uniform floor elements. Surface materials must not be mixed.
- The floor must meet the dance style and requirements in terms of its surface texture, grip or slipperiness, substructure and thus shock absorption, and installation.
- The floors should assist dancers, especially with respect to shock absorption considering the low support through dancers' footwear among most dance styles.

Incidences and prevalence, risks, types, and anatomical locations of injuries vary with respect to dance styles and their (motor) characteristics and demands.[306, 307, 308] Each dance style has specific advantages and disadvantages as well as technique- and equipment-dependent risks.

This introductory chapter will give an overview on general issues and injuries in dance, which more or less have a relevance for all dance styles.

Following that, a selection of the most common dance styles is going to be described in more detail. These chapters on dance style specifics all start off with a short summary of the injury panorama and/or risk factors in the very dance style.

After the summary, available (and sometimes selected, if more was on hand) scientific literature is quoted in order to give the reader an impression of what is allocatable, what has been conducted in research, and which general impression those studies give addressing the issues affecting a certain dance style. This goes uncommented as far as possible, in order to let the readers form their very own picture about the present situation in the respected dance style, issues researched, and results presented by the quoted literature.

Between 50% and 80% of all professional dancers suffer from overuse/chronic injuries at least once in their career, with over 65-90%, **overuse injuries account for the majority of all dance injuries.**[309,310,311]

Injuries in dancers are mainly found in the lower extremities and back/spine, which are the body parts exposed to the greatest loading due to the nature of dance in most styles. However, depending on the respective dance style and technique, the head, neck/cervical spine, and upper extremities are also affected.[312]

Aside from injuries to joints and ligaments, soft tissue injuries, e.g., injuries to muscles, including their tendons, are predominating.[313,314,315,316] Among the most prevalent are acute hamstring strains, commonly nicknamed "pulled muscles", especially in those styles which focus on high levels of joint range of motion (flexibility). In dancers and student dancers, such myotendofascial (muscle-tendon-connective-tissue) injuries often affect tendon more than muscle tissue, resulting in prolonged absence from dance, also because dancers keep on dancing through pain or severely underestimate recovery time and return to training too soon.[317,318,319]

With **dance technical demands constantly rising**, the burden on professional as well as vocational dancers is increasing with relation to **workload**, already in the young.[320, 321, 322, 323, 324, 325] Moreover, the number of performances, shows, and events is divided among fewer dancers due to increasing cost-cutting measures. That has

306 Harkness Center for dance injuries. *Injury Frequency*. Fact sheet. http://www.med.nyu.edu/sites/default/files/harkness/injuryrates_within_different_dance_disciplines.pdf [download am 11.4.14]

307 Noh YE, and Lee KY. *A comparison of the frequency and severity of injury among different styles and careers of dancers.* Paper presented at the Annual Research Conference, Victoria University, Australia. 2001.

308 Hald RD. *Dance injuries.* Primary Care. 19(2). 393-411. 1992.

309 Hincapié CA, Morton EJ, and Cassidy JD. *Musculoskeletal injuries and pain in dancers: a systematic review.* Arch Phys Med Rehabil. 89(9). 1819-1829. 2008.

310 Smith TO, Davies L, de Medici A, Hakim A, Haddad F, and Macgregor A. *Prevalence and profile of musculoskeletal injuries in ballet dancers: A systematic review and meta-analysis.* Phys Ther Sport. 19. 50-56. 2016.

311 Hamilton L, Hamilton WG, Meltzer JD, Marshall P, and Molnar M. Personality, stress, and injuries in professional ballet dancers. Am J Sports Med. 17(2). 263-267. 1989.

312 Nixon JE. *Injuries to the neck and upper extremities of dancers.* Clin Sports Med. 2(3).459-472. 1983.

313 Rietveld AB. *Dancers' and musicians' injuries.* Clin Rheumatol. 32(4). 425-434. 2013.

314 Solomon R, Micheli LJ, and Solomon J. *The „cost" of injuries in a professional ballet company.* Med Probl Perform Art. 10. 3-10. 1995.

315 Solomon R, Micheli LJ, Solomon j, and E McGray. *The „cost" of injuries in a professional ballet company: a five year perspective.* Med Probl Perform Art. 11(4). 164-169. 1999.

316 Hincapié CA, Morton EJ, and Cassidy JD. *Musculoskeletal injuries and pain in dancers: a systematic review.* Arch Phys Med Rehabil. 89(9). 1819-1829. 2008.

317 Askling C, Lund H, Saartok T, and Thorstensson A. *Self-reported hamstring injuries in student-dancers.* Scand J Med Sci Sports. 12(4).230-235. 2002.

318 Askling C, Tengvar M, Saartok T, and Thorstensson A. *Sports related hamstring strains--two cases with different etiologies and injury sites.* Scand J Med Sci Sports. 10(5). 304-307. 2000.

319 Askling CM, Tengvar M, Saartok T, and Thorstensson A. *Acute first-time hamstring strains during slow-speed stretching: clinical, magnetic resonance imaging, and recovery characteristics.* Am J Sports Med. 35(10). 1716-1724. 2007.

320 Twitchett E, Angioi M, Koutedakis Y, and Wyon M. *The demands of a working day among female professional ballet dancers.* J Dance Med Sci. 14(4). 127-132. 2010.

321 Kozai AC, Twitchett E, Morgan S, and Wyon MA. *Workload Intensity and Rest Periods in Professional Ballet: Connotations for Injury.* Int J Sports Med. 41(6). 373-379. 2020.

322 Volkova VG, Black AM, Kenny SJ. *Internal Training Load Measures in Elite Adolescent Ballet Dancers.* J Dance Med Sci. 24(4). 175-182. 2020.

323 Jeffries AC, Wallace L, and Coutts AJ. *Quantifying Training Loads in Contemporary Dance.* Int J Sports Physiol Perform. 12(6). 796-802. 2017.

324 Surgenor B, and Wyon M. *Measuring Training Load in Dance: The Construct Validity of Session-RPE.* Med Probl Perform Art. 34(1). 1-5. 2019.

325 Shaw JW, Springham M, Brown DD, Mattiussi AM, Pedlar CR, and Tallent J. *The Validity of the Session Rating of Perceived Exertion Method for Measuring Internal Training Load in Professional Classical Ballet Dancers.* Front Physiol. 11. 480. 2020.

drastically increased the number of acute accidents and work-related injuries in recent years. With injuries doubling since 1994, at least every other dancer is injured at least once per season.[326,327]

Toenail and skin problems of dancers of all styles are very common and equally commonly underestimated. From reactions to make-up, blisters and corns, calluses/hyperkerastosis and corneal cracks, to eczema and wounds – dancers must pay special attention to their skincare.[328] The skin must not be underestimated as it is the largest organ of our body with multiple responsibilities, among them protection against bacterial intruders.

Related is the general issue of **hygiene** with regard to shoes and their maintenance as well as hands when caring for wounds, and the wound care itself. Keeping floors, shoes, and clothing clean are one side of the medal. In order to care for wounds appropriately, **disinfecting hands before attending to wounds**, no matter how small, cleaning wounds themselves, and the **use of appropriate and sufficient wound care materials** is essential to prevent severe consequences, such as chronic inflammation or sepsis. Professional skincare for skin irritations and wounds of all kinds, must be a matter of course in the daily care of dancers. "Minor injuries" such as torn, broken, or even ingrown toenails and blisters, resulting in inflamed skin areas and wounds due to chafing shoes, must be treated immediately and professionally. Last but not least, and as already mentioned, **disinfection** is critical. Practice shows that a deficit in this regard due to a lack of appreciation of these "little things" can lead to dire health consequences, with which dancers often have to struggle for a very long time.

Repetitive injury[329,330,331,440] or increased risk to sustain new injury after a previous injury is also recurrently described as a risk factor. In dance students, a history of a previous lateral ankle sprain was associated with an increased risk of ankle sprain in the contralateral foot.[332] Injuries commonly leave a "weak spot", related to tissues which need sufficient time to heal and regain morphology and functionality, as well as the psychological and mental state of the dancer. Moreover, the impairment of proprioception and sensorimotor control after an injury could be a factor in the occurrence of repetitive or recurrent injury.

Related to science of training (or deficits in the planning of dancers' training and management of workload) **fatigue**[333,334,335] was discussed as a risk factor. It might specifically play a role in anterior cruciate ligament (ACL) injury[336] influencing the ability of the dancer to control dynamic alignment. Moreover, fatigue and exhaustion lay the groundwork for overtraining and/or burnout.

Repetitive movements[337,338,339] as well as the high number of partly overly acrobatic lifts in many dance styles can be further factors to increase injury risk.

Also related to fatigue, burnout and overtraining, **psychological issues**, e.g., stress and coping strategies, affect injury frequency as well as duration, as reported in several publications.[340,341,342,343] Not only are

[326] Wanke EM, Arendt M, Mill H, and Groneberg DA. *Occupational accidents in professional dance with focus on gender differences.* J Occupat Med Toxicol. 8. 35-42. 2013.

[327] Wanke EM. *Arbeitsbedingte Verletzungen und Erkrankungen.* IN: Exner-Grave, Elisabeth (ed.). Die medizinische Versorgung professioneller Tänzer. Stuttgart. Schattauer Verlag. 2008. p. 57.

[328] Vlahovic T,and H Palamarchuk. *Skin concerns in dancers.* IADMS presentation of the 16th annual meeting. Abstract 25. J Dance Med Sci. 11(1). 6. 2007.

[329] Dang Y, Koutedakis Y, and Wyon M. *Fit to Dance Survey: Elements of Lifestyle and Injury Incidence in Chinese Dancers.* Med Probl Perform Art. 35(1). 10-18. 2020.

[330] Ursej E, Sekulic D, Prus D, Gabrilo G, Zaletel P. *Investigating the Prevalence and Predictors of Injury Occurrence in Competitive Hip Hop Dancers: Prospective Analysis.* Int J Environ Res Public Health. 16(17). 3214. 2019.

[331] Steinberg N, Siev-Ner I, Peleg S, Dar G, Masharawi Y, Zeev A, and Hershkovitz I. *Injury patterns in young, non-professional dancers.* J Sports Sci. 29(1). 47-54. 2011.

[332] Hiller C, Refshauge K, Herbert R, and Kilbreath S. *Intrinsic Predictors of Lateral Ankle Sprain in Adolescent Dancers: A Prospective Cohort Study.* Clinical J Sport Med. 18. 44-48. 2008.

[333] Murgia C. *Overuse, tissue fatigue, and injuries.* J Dance Med Sci. 17(3). 92-100. 2013.

[334] Liederbach M Compagon JM. Psychological aspects of fatigue-related injuries in dancers. J Dance Med Sci. 5(4). 116-120. 2001.

[335] van Winden D, van Rijn RM, Savelsbergh G, Oudejans R, and Stubbe JH. *Characteristics and Extent of Mental Health Issues in Contemporary Dance Students.* Med Probl Perform Art.35(3). 121-129. 2020.

[336] Liederbach M, Dilgen FE, and Rose DJ. *Incidence of anterior cruciate ligament injuries among elite ballet and modern dancers: a 5-year prospective study.* Am J Sports Med. 36(9). 1779-1788. 2008.

[337] Costa MS, Ferreira AS, Orsini M, Silva EB, and Felicio LR. *Characteristics and prevalence of musculoskeletal injury in professional and non-professional ballet dancers.* Braz J Phys Ther. 20(2). 166-175. 2016.

[338] Swain CTV, Bradshaw EJ, Ekegren CL, and Whyte DG. *The Epidemiology of Low Back Pain and Injury in Dance: A Systematic Review.* J Orthop Sports Phys Ther. 49(4). 239-252. 2019.

[339] Nolton EC, and Ambegaonkar JP. *Recognizing and Managing Snapping Hip Syndrome in Dancers.* Med Probl Perform Art. 33(4). 286-291. 2018.

[340] Hamilton L, Hamilton WG, Meltzer JD, Marshall P, and Molnar M. Personality, stress, and injuries in professional ballet dancers. Am J Sports Med. 17(2). 263-267. 1989.

[341] Hincapié CA, Morton EJ, and Cassidy JD. *Musculoskeletal injuries and pain in dancers: a systematic review.* Arch Phys Med Rehabil. 89(9). 1819-1829. 2008.

[342] Jacobs CL, Hincapié CA, Cassidy JD. *Musculoskeletal injuries and pain in dancers: a systematic review update.* J Dance Med Sci. 16(2). 74-84. 2012.

[343] van Winden D, van Rijn RM, Savelsbergh G, Oudejans R, and Stubbe JH. *Characteristics and Extent of Mental Health Issues in Contemporary Dance Students.* Med Probl Perform Art.35(3). 121-129. 2020.

psychological issues a risk factor for injuries, but psychological correlates are also a severe consequence for all dancers, who sustained an injury.[344,345] While fear of injuries is understandably high in dancers, the misleading, tradition-steeped **"identity" in dance** might be one of the biggest risk factors, which is, however, still kept alive in the dance world[346,347,348]:

Pressure on dancers (as well as teachers to "produce" excellent dancers!) is high. This might be one of the factors manipulating dancers into **dancing through pain**, and that not only in styles such as classical ballet [349,413,425,441,515] while they perceive high levels of **shame** for their injuries. [350] Simultaneously, **lack of content knowledge** on dance medicine and science in teachers, trainers as well as dancers themselves leads to mistakes. Examples are the inability to differentiate between **injury pain and performance pain**[351,352], and then act accordingly, e.g., teach such important aspects already to the young, allow time for healing and rehabilitation of injuries. Any shortcomings in dealing with pain and injury and related aspects are detrimental to dancers' overall health and wellbeing, and they might also stand in the way of practical implementation of dance medicine and science in the dance world. Another, knowledge and education-related aspect is **erroneous dance technique** and **training deficiencies**, which constitute high risk factors for overuse as well as acute injuries.[353,354,355,356]

The most common extrinsic/exogenous **causes of injury** are partners, floors, and stage environment/props, as well as external pressure in all styles. [357,358] Recurrent intrinsic/endogenous factors are fatigue, a lack of or inadequate warm-up and cool-down, a lack of basic endurance and other fitness deficits, improper planning of training and erroneous technique with disregard of the dancer's underlying anatomical individuality as the basis of overuse injuries.[359,360,361,362]

Acute injuries are found in all dance styles, and are highly depending on the environment and technical demands of dancers and their respective style. In both genders and all dance styles, joint structures are particularly at risk. Furthermore, and as already mentioned in the context of repetitive movement, the large number of lifts in many dance styles is responsible for many acute injuries, such as concussion, bruises, contusions and injuries to the ribs, spine, shoulders and arms of both sexes. While muscle injuries are among the most common issues for men, women are specifically prone to suffer from ligament and joint related injuries, as upcoming chapters will detail.[363]

Gender specifics, age, stage of biological development, nutritional status and hormonal situation, aptitude, and the respective dance-specific vocabulary are further factors which must always be included for targeted injury prevention.[364] In 2014, a study on professional dancers[365] showed the relation between dance style and injury, investigating acute injuries with respect to five different

---

[344] Mainwaring L, Kerr G, and Krasnow D. *Psychological correlates of dance injuries*. Med probl perform Art. 8. 3-6. 1993.

[345] Mainwaring L, Krasnow D, and Kerr G. *And the dance goes on: Psychological impact of injury*. J Dance Med & Sci. 5(4). 105-115. 2001.

[346] Vassallo AJ, Pappas E, Stamatakis E, Hiller CE. *Injury Fear, Stigma, and Reporting in Professional Dancers.* Saf Health Work. 10(3). 260-264. 2019.

[347] Wainwright SP, Williams C, and Turner BS. *Fractured identities: injury and the balletic body*. Health. 9(1). 49-66. 2005.

[348] Kelman BB. *Occupational hazards in female ballet dancers. Advocate for a forgotten population*. AAOHN J. 48(9). 430-434. 2000.

[349] Jenkins JB, Wyon M, and Nevill A. *Can turnout measurements be used to predict physiotherapist-reported injury rates in dancers?* Med Probl Perform Art. 28(4). 230-235. 2013.

[350] Thomson P, and Jaque SV. *Exposing shame in dancers and athletes: shame, trauma, and dissociation in a nonclinical population.* J Trauma Dissociation. 14(4). 439-454. 2013.

[351] Anderson R, and Hanrahan SJ. *Dancing in pain: pain appraisal and coping in dancers.* J Dance Med Sci. 12(1). 9-16. 2008.

[352] Thomas H, and Tarr J. *Dancers' perceptions of pain and injury: positive and negative effects.* J Dance Med Sci. 13(2). 51-59. 2009.

[353] Arendt YD und F Kerschbaumer. *Injury and Overuse Pattern in Professional Ballet Dancers.* Z Ortho Unfallchirurgie. 141. 349-356-2003.

[354] Garrick JG, and Lewis SL. *Career hazards for the dancer.* Occup Med. 16(4). 609-618. 2001.

[355] Allen N, Nevill AM, Brooks JH, Koutedakis Y, Wyon MA. *The effect of a comprehensive injury audit program on injury incidence in ballet: a 3-year prospective study.* Clin J Sport Med. 23(5). 373-378. 2013.

[356] Kaufmann JE, Nelissen RGHH, Exner-Grave E, and Gademan MGJ. *Does forced or compensated turnout lead to musculoskeletal injuries in dancers? A systematic review on the complexity of causes.* J Biomech. 114. 110084. 2021.

[357] Wanke EM, Mill H, Wanke A, Davenport J, Koch F, and Groneberg DA. *Dance floors as injury risk: analysis and evaluation of acute injuries caused by dance floors in professional dance with regard to preventative aspects.* Med Probl Perform Art. 27(3). 137-142. 2012.

[358] Wanke EM, Mill H, Wanke A, Davenport J, Checcetti F, Koch F, and Groneberg DA. *Dance partner or dance floor?: exogenous factors resulting in accidents in professional dancers.* Med Probl Perform Art. 28(3). 131-136. 2013.

[359] Wyon MA, Abt G, Redding E, Head A, and Sharp NC. *Oxygen uptake during modern dance class, rehearsal, and performance.* J Strength Cond Res. 18(3). 646-649. 2004.

[360] Cahalan R, Purtill H, O'Sullivan K. *Biopsychosocial Factors Associated with Foot and Ankle Pain and Injury in Irish Dance: A Prospective Study.* Med Probl Perform Art. 32(2). 111-117. 2017.

[361] Cahalan R, Purtill H, O'Sullivan P, and O'Sullivan K. *A cross-sectional study of elite adult Irish dancers: biopsychosocial traits, pain, and injury.* J Dance Med Sci. 19(1). 31-43. 2015.

[362] Murgia C. *Overuse, tissue fatigue, and injuries.* J Dance Med Sci. 17(3). 92-100. 2013.

[363] Costa MS, Ferreira AS, Orsini M, Silva EB, and Felicio LR. *Characteristics and prevalence of musculoskeletal injury in professional and non-professional ballet dancers.* Braz J Phys Ther. 20(2). 166-175. 2016.

[364] Stensland SH, and J Sobal. *Dietary practices of ballet, jazz, and modern dancers.* Journal of the American Dietetic Association. 92. 319-324. 1992.

[365] Wanke EM, Mill H, Arendt M, Wanke A, Koch F, and Groneberg DA. *Occupational accidents in professional dancers with regard to different professional dance styles.* Work. 49(4). 597-606. 2014.

dance styles. 1339 dancers (658 females and 681 males) from six theatres, and 612 students (421 females and 191 males), from a State Ballet School were involved. Results showed that the lower extremities were the most frequently acutely injured anatomical region in all styles, but the more dancers moved away from classical ballet, the more acute head and neck injuries were sustained in modern styles. **Injury patterns and injured structures were related to dance styles**. While in classical ballet risk factors were mainly intrinsic, they became more extrinsic in more modern styles. The authors stressed the importance of dance-style specific injury prevention for interventions to be successful.

The **most common acute injuries in dance** are[366,367,368,369,370,371,372,373,374,375]

- Concussion
- Contusions
- Sprains
- Muscle strains ("pulled muscles")
- Muscle ruptures (tears)
- Joint blockages in the spine, especially the sacroiliac joint, or in the metatarsus
- Distortions (twisting) such as supination traumata (twisting the ankle)
- Ruptured ligaments
- Fractures (second or fifth metatarsal, kneecap, toes, articular processes of the vertebras)
- Meniscal tears
- Patellar luxation
- Herniated discs
- Labral tears
- Shoulder luxations

Chronic and overuse injuries affect children and adolescents in recreational as well as vocational training as they affect professional dancers of all styles. Most affected are the spine, hips, and the entire lower extremities, above all the knees, ankles, and feet. The main reasons or risk factors are a lack of knowledge in dance medicine and dance pedagogy among teachers, resulting in discrepancies with respect to science of training, motivational climate, and dance technique. Examples would be a lack of/insufficient warm-up, too much focus on flexibility with low muscular stabilization, deficient and erroneous dance technique accepted or remaining uncorrected in the dancer, poor scheduling, ill-handling of pain leading to chronic overuse and burnout. Ambition, early specialization, perfectionism, anatomical dispositions, and inadequate aptitude involve the dancers as well as their families and environment.[376,377,378,379,380,381,382,383]

Volume 3 provides additional information in words and pictures, especially with regard to movement analysis, dance technique and underlying biomechanics or anatomical limitations, offering an extensive body of practical exercises.

The **most common overuse injuries in dancers** are

- Low back pain/lumbosacral pain
- Myofascial imbalances
- Recurrent/chronic muscle soreness leading to chronically hardened muscles
- Iliopsoas syndrome
- Tightness of the iliotibial band
    - Anterior knee pain
- Thoracic hyperkyphosis
- Osteochondrosis
- Spondylarthritis
- Spondylosis

366 Scharff-Olson MR, Wiliford HN, and Brown JA. *Injuries associated with current dance-exercise-practices.* J Dance Med Sci. 3(4). 144-150. 1999.
367 Macintyre J, and Joy E. *Foot and ankle injuries in dance.* Clin Sports Med.19. 351-368. 2000.
368 Arendt YD and Kerschbaumer F. *Verletzungen und Überlastungserscheinungen im professionellen Ballett.* Z Ortho Unfallchirurgie. 141. 349-356- 2003.
369 Schon LC. *Foot and ankle problems in dancers.* Maryland Med J. 11. 267-269. 1993.
370 Schon LC, and Weinfeld SB. *Lower extremity musculoskeletal problems in dancers.* Curr Op Rheumatol. 8(2). 130-142. 1996.
371 Denton J. *Overuse foot and ankle injuries in ballet.* Clin Podiatr Med Surg. 14(3). 525-32. 1997.
372 Garrick JG, and Requa RK. Ballet injuries – *an analysis of epidemiology and financial outcome.* Am J Sports Med. 21(4). 586-590. 1993.
373 Milan KR. *Injury in ballet: an analysis of epidemiology and financial outcome.* Am J Sports Med. 21. 586-590. 1994.
374 Schoene LM. *What you should know about dance injuries.* Podiatry Today. 18(1). 2005.
375 Kern-Scott R, Peterson JR, Morgan P. Review of acetabular labral tears in dancers. J Dance Med Sci. 15(4). 149-156. 2011.
376 Rietveld AB. *Dancers' and musicians' injuries.* Clin Rheumatol. 32(4). 425-434. 2013.
377 Garrick JG, and Lewis SL. *Career hazards for the dancer.* Occup Med. 16(4). 609-618. 2001.
378 Kadel NJ. Foot and ankle injuries in dance. Phys Med Rehabil Clin N Am. 17(4). 813-826. 2006.
379 Kadel NJ, Teitz CC, and RA Kronmal. *Stress fractures in ballet dancers.* Am J Sports Med. 20. 445. 1992.
380 Wiesler ER, Hunter DM, Martin DF, Curl W, and H Hoen. *Ankle flexibility and injury patterns in dancers.* Am J Sports Med 24(6). 754-757. 1996.
381 Exner-Grave E. *Äußeres Umfeld.* IN: Simmel Liane. Tanzmedizin – Arbeitsplatz Tanz. Berlin. Unfallkasse Berlin. 2005.
382 Exner-Grave E. Dancing on the grave. Der Tänzer als Supersportler – gedopt und genmanipuliert? Tanzjournal. 5. 7-11. 2005.
383 Goertzen, Meinolf. Verletzungen und Überlastungsschäden im klassischen Ballett. Therapie, Rehabilitation und Prävention. Aachen. Verlag Unas. 1987.

- Spondylolisthesis
- Pelvic floor dysfunction (and related incontinence)
- Meniscal injuries
- Osteoarthritis
- Tibial Stress Syndrome (tibialis anterior and posterior muscle related)
- Stress fractures
  - Tibia
  - 2nd metatarsal, 5th metatarsal
  - Fibula
- Patella-maltracking; patella sub-/luxation
- Medial ankle pain and instability
  - Flexor hallucis longus tendonitis
  - Achilles tendonitis
  - Popliteus tendonitis
- Plantarfasciitis
- Metatarsalgia
- Sesamoiditis
- Bursitis
- Repetitive shoulder- and rotator cuff related injuries
  - Biceps brachialis caput longum tendonitis and related bursitis
  - Supraspinatus related tendonitis and bursitis
  - Recurrent shoulder luxation

CLASSICAL BALLET

Injury incidence in classical ballet is reported to be predominantly overuse, primarily affecting the lower extremities, followed by the lumbar spine, knee, and hip. [384], [385] Incidence is reported to be 0.62-5.6 injuries/1000 hours of dancing in professional and vocational dancers. [386] The knee, the upper ankle joint, and the foot in general are often acutely injured, with the upper ankle joint being particularly at risk in female ballet dancers.[387,388]

Among men, shoulder and cervical vertebrae injuries are also common due to partner work and lifting. The acute risk of injuring the lumbar spine in ballet is even higher for men than for women, while the hip joint can suffer acute injuries, e.g., labral tears, but mainly is affected by overuse injury.[389] In professional dancers more than in students, hip and groin injuries account for 17.2% of injuries. [390] In classical ballet, dance technique is particularly demanding due to turnout, pointe work, and excessive, increasingly acrobatic jumping and lifting.

Ballet might be the best researched dance style in dance science. Interestingly enough, practice shows that its tradition-steeped environment simultaneously might also make it the most resistant dance style with respect to the implementation of dance medicine for the sake of dancers' health, wellbeing and performance enhancement.

In 2016, a meta-analysis[391] reviewed nineteen studies on injuries and reported a sum of 7332 injuries in 2617 ballet dancers. As the most prevalent musculoskeletal disorders identified were hamstring strains (51%), ankle tendinopathies (19%) and generalized low back pain (14%).

A recent study[392] assessed self-reported injury and self-estimated functional inability due to pain in professional ballet dancers. The study reported a high point prevalence (the number of injuries documented at a specific point in time) of 54.8% (95% CI, 47.7-62.1) in the ballet dancers. Number of years dancing professionally (OR = 4.4, 95% CI, 1.6-12.3) and the rank of the dancer in the company (OR = 2.4, 95% CI, 1.2-4.8) were associated with injuries.

The study also stressed that around 15% of dancers did not report their injuries. As recurrently described, this aspect of dancers' identity is reported throughout

---

[384] Khan K, Brown J, and S Way. *Overuse injuries in classical ballet.* Sports Med. 19(5). 341-357. 1995.

[385] Smith TO, Davies L, de Medici A, Hakim A, Haddad F, and Macgregor A. *Prevalence and profile of musculoskeletal injuries in ballet dancers: A systematic review and meta-analysis.* Phys Ther Sport. 19. 50-56. 2016.

[386] Allen N, Nevill A, Brooks J, Koutedakis Y, and Wyon M. *Ballet injuries: injury incidence and severity over 1 year.* J Orthop Sports Phys Ther. 42(9). 781-790. 2012.

[387] Garrick JG, and RK Requa. *Ballet injuries – an analysis of epidemiology and financial outcome.* Am J Sports Med. 21(4). 586-590. 1993.

[388] Liederbach M. *Movement and function in dance.* IN: Brownstein Bruce, and Shaw Bronner. Evaluation, treatment, and outcomes on orthopaedic and sports physical therapy. New York. Churchill Livingstone Publ. 1997.

[389] Wanke EM. *Arbeitsbedingte Verletzungen und Erkrankungen.* IN: Exner-Grave, Elisabeth (ed.). Die medizinische Versorgung professioneller Tänzer. Stuttgart. Schattauer Verlag. 2008. p. 57-58.

[390] Trentacosta N, Sugimoto D, and Micheli LJ. *Hip and Groin Injuries in Dancers: A Systematic Review.* Sports Health. 9(5). 422-427. 2017.

[391] Smith TO, Davies L, de Medici A, Hakim A, Haddad F, and Macgregor A. *Prevalence and profile of musculoskeletal injuries in ballet dancers: A systematic review and meta-analysis.* Phys Ther Sport. 19. 50-56. 2016.

[392] Jacobs CL, Cassidy JD, Côté P, Boyle E, Ramel E, Ammendolia C, Hartvigsen J, and Schwartz I. *Musculoskeletal Injury in Professional Dancers: Prevalence and Associated Factors: An International Cross-Sectional Study.* Clin J Sport Med. 27(2). 153-160. 2017.

multiple documentations and research papers published on injury risk, prevalence and incidence in ballet dancers.

Many studies investigated professional ballet companies. In 2001, for instance, Nilsson et al.[393] performed a retro-/prospective longitudinal study, recording injury data in a Swedish professional ballet company over 5 consecutive years. 98 dancers sustained 390 injuries resulting in 0.6 injuries/1000 dance hours, predominantly overuse in nature. Long periods of sick leave (on average 2.3 weeks per injury) were needed and among those dancers employed for more than one year, 95% were injured during the study period.

The study further reported considerable differences with regard to gender, age, and injury mechanisms (acute or overuse), stressing the importance of including such risk factors into the planning of injury preventive measures: Male dancers sustained more acute injuries to the knee joint, most frequently soloists. Overuse injuries especially to the foot and ankle occurred more frequently to female dancers. Younger dancers more often suffered acute injuries, predominantly ankle sprains, but also sustained stress fractures.

In 2002, Byhring et al.[394] conducted a prospective study over nine weeks in the Norwegian National Ballet Company, assessing injuries, work situation and risk factors perceived by the dancers. In only nine weeks, 31 dancers of the 41 dancers experienced one injury or more, mainly to the foot and ankle, but only 22% acute. 75% of the injuries were soft tissue injuries of mild to moderate severity with 16% resulting in sick leaves. Risk factors perceived were related to training, organization and environment. 78% of the dancers experienced negative stress at work, and 64% reported that they had little influence on their work conditions, although the study could not statistically associate these factors with the injuries.

Injuries in amateurs as well as the young are an often-underestimated issue. In a 1984 study, amateur and open classes with varied dance technique levels had a lower injury rate in the upper ankle than recorded in professional dancers. However, in all other injury frequencies, they partially even exceeded the figures for professional dancers.[395]

In 2016, Costa et al. [396] investigated injuries in professional and non-professional ballet dancers using a questionnaire, partly confirming those results. Ankle sprains accounted for 69.8% of injuries in the professionals and 42.1% in non-professional dancers. The ankle joint was the most frequent anatomical injury location in both sexes among the professional dancers (67.6% female, 40.9% male). Ankle sprains occurred in 90% of all women's injuries, while 54.5% of the men's injuries were muscle injuries. **Pirouettes** were identified as the highest risk factor (67.9% of all injuries) in the professionals, while **repetitive movement** in the non-professional dancers accounted for 28.1% of all injuries.

The chapters on injury prevalence, incidence and risk in **children and adolescents will show the importance of practical implementation of dance science into dance education and training already in the young.** [397, 398] Injuries among children and adolescents in ballet show the danger of early specialization. Acute injuries are found in male ballet dancers mainly to the upper ankle, forearm, and wrist, followed by the foot, spine, lumbar and cervical spine, and head, indicating too early specialization in partnering and lifting. Girls in ballet primarily suffer from acute injuries to the upper ankle, knee, foot, forearm, wrist, spine, and neck/head, in descending order, stressing the prevention of early specialization also in girls with respect to pointework and training load.

As young dancers grow, joints and their associated structures, such as ligaments and bones, as well as the skin, followed by the musculature, are most affected. In adolescents and children, hypermobility, which is common in professional dance training, also increases the risk of injury.[399]

Improper or inappropriate introduction to pointe work in recreational dance is a further aspect of lack of practical

[393] Nilsson C, Leanderson J, Wykman A, and Strender LE. *The injury panorama in a Swedish professional ballet company.* Knee Surg Sports Traumatol Arthrosc. 9(4). 242-246. 2001.

[394] Byhring S, and Bø K. *Musculoskeletal injuries in the Norwegian National Ballet: a prospective cohort study.* Scand J Med Sci Sports. 12(6). 365-70. 2002.

[395] Quirk R. *Injuries in Classical ballet.* Austr Fam Physician 13. 802-804. 1984.

[396] Costa MS, Ferreira AS, Orsini M, Silva EB, and Felicio LR. *Characteristics and prevalence of musculoskeletal injury in professional and non-professional ballet dancers.* Braz J Phys Ther. 20(2). 166-175. 2016.

[397] Wanke EM. *Workrelated injuries and illness [Arbeitsbedingte Verletzungen und Erkrankungen.]* IN: Exner-Grave, Elisabeth (ed.). Die medizinische Versorgung professioneller Tänzer. Stuttgart. Schattauer Verlag. 2008. p. 63.

[398] Wanke EM. *Rahmenempfehlungen zur Prävention von Unfällen im professionellen Bühnentanz.* Deutsche gesetzliche Unfallversicherung und Unfallkasse Berlin (ed.), München. 2009.

[399] McCormack M, Briggs J, Hakim A, and R Grahame. *Joint laxity and the benign joint hypermobility syndrome in student and professional ballet dancers.* J Rheumatol. 31(1). 173-178. 2004.

implementation in dance medicine and science in teachers and trainers.[400]

While so many studies report and describe injuries and risk (factors) in ballet dancers, **prospective studies show the power of targeted injury prevention programs**. If they were just used and practically implemented, such outstanding work of dedicated researchers could effectively protect dancers from so much pain and overall correlates of injuries: In 2013[401], a team of researchers introduced an individualized conditioning program to professional ballet dancers over the course of three years. The program was based on thorough screening and planning of training, taking the dancers' history of injury, their workload and especially their individuality into account for evidence-based correction of fitness deficits. The researchers could show significant reduction of injuries through their individualized conditioning programs over the course of the three-year-period: For male ballet dancers, the incidence was reduced from 4.76 injuries per 1000 hours of dancing in the first year of documentation to 2.40 injuries/1000 hours in the second, and further 2.22/1000 hours in the third year of intervention. In female ballet dancers, injury incidence was cut down from 4.14 injuries per 1000 hours at the beginning of the intervention to the dashing number of 1.71 per 1000 hours in year two and 1.81/1000 hours in the third year.

MODERN DANCE

In modern dance, injuries are also affecting the lower extremities and spine in the first place. However, due to a lot of floor work, the upper extremity (shoulders, elbows, hands and wrists) is specifically at risk as well.

Many techniques include falls, jumps and turns on and onto the hands, elbows, shoulders and knees, with legs in parallel, external and internal rotation of the hip, which makes modern techniques particularly demanding for all the joints involved.[402,403,404,405,406,407]

Turnout is also one of the leading injury risks in those modern styles that use it, related to the list of overuse injuries.[408,409] A critical point in modern dancers could be that the use of turnout is too often underestimated. In these styles, many dancers have decided themselves to choose modern over classical ballet or had been deemed unsuitable for ballet training, not least because they lack external rotation of the hip and overall turnout capacities. However, turnout is used in modern dance techniques as well, even if commonly not as excessively as in ballet. This fact might lead to a reduced focus on sufficiently training technique and muscular endurance for turnout, resulting in specific risk for the dancers mentioned. Therefore, attention must be paid to technique and alignment.

As in classical ballet, most injuries in modern techniques occur due to **overuse** and the high number of **repetitive movements** in training.[410,411]

Weiss et al., 2008[412], assessed 184 professional modern dancers of various companies as well as freelancers in the USA (49 males, 135 females), to provide an overview on their work and health conditions. Mean age was 30.1 ±7.3 years, with professional experience of 8.9 ±7.2 years. Females started to dance earlier (aged 6.5 ±4.2 years)

---

[400] Nunes NM, Haddad JJ, Bartlett DJ, and KD Obright. *Musculoskeletal injuries among young, recreational, female dancers before and after dancing in pointe shoes.* Pediatr Phys Ther . 14(2).100-106. 2002.

[401] Allen N, Nevill AM, Brooks JH, Koutedakis Y, Wyon MA. *The effect of a comprehensive injury audit program on injury incidence in ballet: a 3-year prospective study.* Clin J Sport Med. 23(5). 373-378. 2013.

[402] Fuhrmann TL, Brayer A, Andrus N, and S McIntosh. *Injury Prevention for modern dancers: a pilot study of an educational intervention.* J Community Health. 35. 527-533. 2010.

[403] Sides SN, Ambegaonkar JP, Caswell SV. High incidence of shoulder injuries in collegiate modern dance students. Athl Ther Today. 14(4). 43-46. 2009.

[404] Weigert BJ, and Erickson M. *Incidence of injuries in female university-level modern dancers and the effectiveness of a screening program in altering injury patterns.* Med Probl Perform Art. 22(2). 52-57. 2007.

[405] Selina S, and W David. *Survey of injuries among professional modern dancers: Prevalence, Risk factors and Management.* Clin J Sports Med. 6(5). 437. 2006.

[406] White SB, Philpot A, Green A, and MG Bemben. Physiological Comparison Between Female University Ballet and Modern Dance Students. J Dance Med Sci. 8(1). 5-10. 2004.

[407] Angioi M, Metsios GS, Metsios G, Koutedakis Y, and MA Wyon. *Fitness in contemporary dance: a systematic review.* Int J Sports Med. 30(7). 475-484. 2009.

[408] VanMerkensteijn GG, and Edel Quin. *Assessment of compensated turnout characteristics and their relationship to injuries in university level modern dancers.* J Dance Med Sci. 19(2). 57-62. 2015.

[409]Cimelli SN, Curran SA. *Influence of turnout on foot posture and its relationship to overuse musculoskeletal injury in professional contemporary dancers: a preliminary investigation.* J Am Podiatr Med Assoc. 102(1). 25-33. 2012.

[410] Campoy FA, Coelho LR, Bastos FN, Netto Júnior J, Vanderlei LC, Monteiro HL, Padovani CR, and CM Pastre. *Investigation of risk factors and characteristics of dance injuries.* Clin J Sport Med. 21(6). 493-498. 2011.

[411] Bronner S, Ojofeitimi S, and DJ Rose. *Injuries in a modern dance company: effect of comprehensive management on injury incidence and time loss.* Am J Sports Med. 31(3).365-73. 2003.

[412] Weiss D, Shah S, and RJ Burchette. *A profile of the demographics and training characteristics of professional modern dancers.* J Dance Med Sci. 12(2). 2008.

compared to males (aged 15.6 ±6.2 years). 55% of females had started to dance with ballet, while the majority of males (51%) started with modern dance already ($p < 0.0001$). Per week, 8.3 ±6.0 hours were spent in class and 17.2 ±12.6 hours in rehearsal. 80% of the dancers took modern technique classes, studying between two and four modern techniques simultaneously, and 67% of the dancers also did ballet training. 8.2 ±6.6 hours per week were spent on additional training such as Pilates, yoga, or upper body weightlifting. With dancers wearing 12 different types of footwear for modern techniques alone, a high variety of footwear was used. Females performed for 23.3 ±14.0 weeks (range: 2-52 weeks) per year, males 20.4 ±3.9 weeks (range: 1-40). 54% received some type of insurance from their employer, while 23% purchased their own insurance, and 22% had insurance provided by their families. Only 16% of dancers reported that they had Workers' Compensation coverage.

In 2012[413], the team published a study on incidence, risk factors, and management of musculoskeletal injuries in those 184 professional modern dancers, based on a self-report questionnaire which additionally asked for in-depth details on the two most severe injuries in the previous 12 months. 82% had suffered between one and seven injuries, predominantly to the lower extremity and back (foot and ankle 40%, lower back 17%, knee 16%). Injury rate was 0.59 / 1000 hours of class and rehearsal. Most dancers did not miss any performances due to injury and many **returned to work before fully recovered**. For those who had to take sick leave, males returned to dancing after an average of 21 days, females after 18 days. 47% of those who sought medical assistance went to physicians, 41% to physiotherapists, and 34% to chiropractors. The majority of dancers adhered to the advice given in those consultations, namely 87% of males and 78% of females. Although the majority of injuries were work related, only a few were covered by Workers' Compensation insurance (12% of the most severe and 5% of the second severe). Through their study, Weiss, Shah and Burchette could show a similar picture as in many dancers of other dance styles.

In 2009, Sides et al.[414] investigated modern dancers in a university program reporting that 63.3% of dancers' injuries were observed in the lower extremities and the majority of sessions with a clinician dedicated to injury management was also related to the lower extremity (66.1%); however, 17.7% of injuries occurred to the upper extremity, of which 16.5% required medical assistance. 13.7% of the participants reported shoulder injuries, 2.0% injuries to the hand, wrist, and ribs, respectively, and 13.3% to the back.

As in ballet (and all other dance styles), **injury preventive measures could effectively protect the dancers from their injuries**. In 2018, Bronner et al.[415] published the results of a 15-years (!) prospective study monitoring two modern dance companies (30 and 12 dancers, respectively) with regard to injury risk and an extensive injury audit program. Data was collected by a physiotherapist in-house, and the 15 years were grouped into five 3-year-blocks (Block 1 to Block 5) to allow comparison. 69% of dancers reported work-related musculoskeletal injuries; 45% sustained at least one time-loss-injury. The first company, with greater annual work exposure, was 1.6-times more likely to sustain time-loss-injuries ($p = 0.016$, CI 1.095-2.422) and 5.6-times more likely to sustain time-loss overuse-injuries ($p = 0.003$, CI 1.812-17.327). Compared to the first-3-year-block (Block-1), work-related musculoskeletal injuries and time-loss-injuries decreased in Blocks-2, 3, and 5 ($p \leq 0.027$) and the ratio of time-loss overuse to acute injuries was reversed, with acute injuries accounting for over 80% of injuries by Block 5. Time-loss-injuries averaged 0.16 injuries/1000 hours, rates that are lower than commonly in ballet and sports. The decreased injury rates and **changes in injury patterns away from the dominance of overuse** (!) demonstrate the **efficacy of injury management and prevention programs**. These programs consisted of in-house comprehensive injury management involving injury recording based on triage, treatment, immediate referral to specialists when needed, and rehabilitation etc. Prevention services such as massages, strengthening, stretching, or cross training were available to all dancers with equal accessibility and at all times, including touring and performances. All help was provided to dancers on-site to avoid any stress through traveling. The program, installed and monitored by the senior researcher, even provided a specifically designed on-site physiotherapy room complete with treatment space, exercise equipment, whirlpool, ballet barre and sprung floor. Additionally, dancers received **individually designed training programs** according to their needs and based on

[413] Shah S, Weiss DS, and Burchette RJ. *Injuries in professional modern dancers: incidence, risk factors, and management.* J Dance Med Sci. 16(1). 17-25. 2012.

[414] Sides SN, Ambegaonkar JP, and Caswell SV. *High incidence of shoulder injuries in collegiate modern dance students.* Athl Ther Today. 14(4). 43-46. 2009.

[415] Bronner S, McBride C, and Gill A. *Musculoskeletal injuries in professional modern dancers: a prospective cohort study of 15 years.* J Sports Sci. 36(16). 1880-1888. 2018.

their screening results (compare to the study of Allen, Nevill, Brooks, Koutedakis and Wyon cited in the section on classical ballet!). Shaw Bronner[416], a former dancer dedicated to prevent injuries and enhance wellbeing in dancers as a scientist and physiotherapist, and her team presented an impressive study based on exceptional and hard work over years, which shows **how much can be done to support dancers and invest in their injury prevention and wellbeing**.

In 2011[417], similar positive effects with regard to injury prevention as well as cost reduction for a modern dance company were reported, analyzing injury and insurance data over eight years. **Comprehensive injury management resulted in a decline of total injury incidence** of 34%, 66% decrease in workers compensation claims, and 56% decrease in days lost to injuries, resulting in substantial overall savings (workers compensation) in a modern dance company.

As in other dance styles, **fitness deficits** in modern dancers can be associated with injury risk. A study[418] compared aerobic fitness levels in professional modern dancers to those of pre-professionals. The professionals showed higher levels of **cardiorespiratory capacities** than pre-professional dancers. However, the younger demonstrated improvement in **aerobic fitness** over time due to targeted intervention. The higher levels of aerobic capacities in professionals might be resulting from their performance demands. The study concluded that additional aerobic training is recommended for pre-professional modern dance students in order to prepare them for the demands of a professional career, which can be done efficiently through targeted wellness programs over time and will contribute to injury prevention.

CONTEMPORARY DANCE

In contemporary dancers, comparable to modern and ballet (and most dance styles), injuries mainly occur to the lower extremities (ankle and knee) as well as the lower back. Aside from musculoskeletal injuries, neuropsychological issues such as anxiety, stress, insufficient coping skills but also higher BMI could pose an injury and health risk. As in modern dance techniques, falls[419], slides, turns, or jumps onto knees, feet, arms, or shoulders could contribute to injury risk with regard to high contact forces.

In 45 first-year contemporary students of a dancer- and teacher-Bachelor-degree program[420] a prospective study assessed injury history of the lower extremities (questionnaire) and lower extremity kinematics and strength. The incidence of injuries to the lower extremities was 82.2%, of which 51.4% were substantial.

In students of Bachelor dance and Bachelor dance teacher programs engaging 130 contemporary dancers[421], over the course of one academic year 97% of the dancers reported at least one injury (including mental complaint) or other health problem. 58% of the injuries were substantial, leading to moderate up to severe reductions of training or/and performance load or the necessity of complete timeout from dancing. Injury incidence rate/1000 hours of dance exposure was 1.9 (95% CI 1.7 to 2.2). Ankle/foot (30%), lower back (17%) and knee (15%) were the most common sites of injury.

In the same cohort of contemporary dance students, mental health[422] was assessed, issues such as stress, anxiety, and (constant) tiredness. In one academic year, the incidence proportion of all reported mental health issues was 44.6% (with 58 dancers affected). For 29.2% of the students their mental health issue was the most severe health problem, with 39.4% regarded as substantial, i.e., issues leading to moderate, severe, or complete reductions in training volume or performance. General anxiety (20.0%), stress due to external factors (18.3%), and constant tiredness (16.7%) were the problems with the highest impact. More mental health

[416] https://www.alvinailey.org/school/ailey-school/shaw-bronner

[417] Ojofeitimi S, and Bronner S. *Injuries in a modern dance company effect of comprehensive management on injury incidence and cost.* J Dance Med Sci. 15(3). 116-122. 2011.

[418] Bronner S, Codman E, Hash-Campbell D, and Ojofeitimi S. *Differences in Preseason Aerobic Fitness Screening in Professional and Pre-professional Modern Dancers.* J Dance Med Sci. 20(1). 11-22. 2016.

[419] Van Ramshorst C, Choi WJ. *Characteristics of Contact Force and Muscle Activation During Choreographed Falls With 2 Common Landing Techniques in Contemporary Dance.* J Appl Biomech. 35(4). 256-262. 2019.

[420] van Seters C, van Rijn RM, van Middelkoop M, and Stubbe JH. *Risk Factors for Lower-Extremity Injuries Among Contemporary Dance Students.* Clin J Sport Med. 30(1). 60-66. 2020.

[421] van Winden DPAM, Van Rijn RM, Richardson A, Savelsbergh GJP, Oudejans RRD, and Stubbe JH. *Detailed injury epidemiology in contemporary dance: a 1-year prospective study of 134 students.* BMJ Open Sport Exerc Med. 5(1):e000453. 2019.

[422] van Winden D, van Rijn RM, Savelsbergh G, Oudejans R, and Stubbe JH. *Characteristics and Extent of Mental Health Issues in Contemporary Dance Students.* Med Probl Perform Art.35(3). 121-129. 2020.

issues were reported in dance-teacher-students (throughout all study years) and in second-year students from both educational programs. No gender differences were noted.

Coping, perfectionism and self-regulation also were investigated as potential risk factors for injuries in contemporary dancers.[423] Of 99 student-dancers, 48 (48.5%) reported at least one substantial injury. Coping skills (OR: 0.91; 95%CI 0.84-0.98), age (OR: 0.67; 95%CI 0.46-0.98), and BMI (OR: 1.38; 95%CI 1.05-1.80) were identified as significant risk factors. The study recommended to include **training of coping skills** into dancers' education in order to prevent injuries to contemporary dancers during careers, probably with a special focus on younger dancers and those with higher BMI.

A systematic review[424] investigated the association between injuries and 1) dancers' **transitioning to full-time training** as well as 2) their **transition to a professional company** in contemporary and ballet dancers. In transitioning ballet students, lower prevalence rates for time-loss injuries per dance exposure hour was found, whereas medical-attention injuries in contemporary and ballet students transitioning was higher. Dancers transitioning to a professional ballet company had higher time-loss injuries per exposure hour in relation to already established professionals. Transitioning professional contemporary dancers had lower rates of time-loss as well as medical-attention injuries. The study showed that phases of transition might come with higher risk for injuries.

In 21 professional contemporary dancers[425], the association between training load and symptoms of overuse injury was evaluated. Furthermore, any difference between the number of time-loss injuries and injuries causing significant symptoms not leading to decreased performance time was investigated. Dancers completed a questionnaire to quantify pain over 7 weeks. 251 symptoms of overuse injury were reported during study period, and 67% of the recorded time was danced with pain. While training load did not show to be associated with severity of pain, load in dancers with no overuse symptoms was significantly lower than in those who reported symptoms (p=0.02). No time-loss because of injury was reported during the study period, but this was probably due to the fact that two-third of the participants **danced with pain** during this 7-week period. Such studies again demonstrate the effect of misguided identity in dance: dancing through pain and injury in combination with too high workload contributes to the development of overuse injuries also in contemporary dance.

JAZZ DANCE, BROADWAY, REVUE & MUSICAL

For jazz, evidence on injury prevalence and incidence is scarce, not least because only few techniques exist and are explicitly known to dancers and teachers as jazz techniques.

Thus, in science, most studies mention jazz in combination with contemporary or modern, or jazz is, naturally, included in studies on "broadway", i.e., musical performers. In jazz[426], musical-, show-, theatrical- or broadway-dance, the foot and ankle joints are at maximum risk, followed by the lumbar spine, knee joints, and hip, comparable to classical ballet and modern.[427,428,429,430,431]

Skin lesions as common issue as well as higher injury risk in performance situations, compared to rehearsal and training, were identified as specifically relevant for this genre.[432]

[423] van Winden D, van Rijn RM, Savelsbergh GJP, Oudejans RRD, Stubbe JH. *Limited Coping Skills, Young Age, and High BMI Are Risk Factors for Injuries in Contemporary Dance: A 1-Year Prospective Study.* Front Psychol. 11. 1452. 2020.

[424] Fuller M, Moyle GM, Hunt AP, Minett GM. *Ballet and Contemporary Dance Injuries When Transitioning to Full-Time Training or Professional Level Dance: A Systematic Review.* J Dance Med Sci. 23(3). 112-125. 2019.

[425] Boeding JRE, Visser E, Meuffels DE, and de Vos RJ. *Is Training Load Associated with Symptoms of Overuse Injury in Dancers? A Prospective Observational Study.* J Dance Med Sci. 23(1). 11-16. 2019.

[426] DiPasquale S, Becker N, Green S, and Sauers K. *Self-Reported Injury and Management in a Liberal Arts College Dance Department.* Med Probl Perform Art. 30(4). 224-30. 2015.

[427] Evans RW, Ewans RI, Carjaval S, and S Perry. *A Survey of injuries among broadway performers.* Am J Pub Health. 86(1). 77-80. 1996.

[428] Evans RW, Evans RI, and S Carjaval. *Survey of injuries among west end performers.* Occup Environ Med. 55. 585-593. 1998.

[429] Washington EL. *Musculoskeletal injuries in theatrical dancers: site, frequency, and severity.* Am J Sports Med. 6. 75-98. 1978.

[430] Rovere GD, Webb LX, Gristina AG, and JM Vogel. *Musculoskeletal injuries in theatrical dance students.* Am J Sports Med. 11(4). 195-198. 1983.

[431] Bronner S, and B Brownstein. *Profile of dance injuries in a broadway show: A discussion of issues in dance medicine epidemiology.* J Orthop Sports Phys Ther. 26(2). 87-94. 1997.

[432] Wanke EM, Groneberg DA, and D Quarcoo. *Analysis and Evaluation of Acute Injuries in Musical Performers [Analyse und Evaluation von*

Turnout, as in modern dance, may constitute an injury risk factor. Since jazz dance in its basic, rhythmic forms is very common among children, especially in relation to musical and theatrical dance of related genres, children and adolescents recurrently sustain injuries from dance classes involving jazz techniques or their individual interpretation.[433]

The various forms of shoes in jazz could play a role in the etiology of injuries with respect to jump landings and shock absorption and also in the way children can develop jazz technique, because they might negatively influence their muscle activation patterns in legs and feet. [434,435,436]

In 2011, among five-hundred dancers (age 18.26 ±4.55 years) on a dance festival, the occurrence of injuries and their respective characteristics with reference to dance techniques were assessed via interview. [437] With 43 injuries (27.92%) to the thigh/leg reported for jazz and contemporary, jazz ranked between classical ballet, where dancers reported 92 ankle/foot injuries [28.75%] and 88 thigh/leg injuries [27.50%], and tap and folk, with 22 injuries [43.14] to the knee. Dynamic overload and excessive use were reported as the perceived causes in most cases. Age and body weight as well as duration of practice was statistically associated with jazz (and contemporary).

In a study[438] investigating paratendonitis of the foot and ankle in children and adolescents, 8-16 years of age, jazz dance was included in the dance styles the children performed on a recreational basis. Paratendonitis, also called tendovaginitis or tenosynitis, describes the inflammation of the fluid filled tendon-sheath, which protects a tendon from injury on specifically exposed or delicate positions, such as the run over bone ridges. 1082 young dancers were screened for dance technical errors, joint range of motion (ROM), body structure, as well as anatomical anomalies. 93 dancers (8.6%) showed paratendonitis of the foot/ankle. However, the study could neither identify causality nor link the injuries to specific dance styles, such as jazz, modern, or ballet, due to the recreational nature of the children's activities. Dance technique and increased hip ROM was discussed as possible risk factor in those with paratendonitis.

Including jazz dance in musical in 1996, a study on broadway performers[439] surveyed 313 performers of 23 Broadway companies. 55.5% of them were injured, resulting in a mean of 1.08 injuries per dancer. Lower extremity injuries were the most common, with 22.8% to ankle and feet, 15.7% to knees, 3.0% to the hip, and 20.3% were injuries to the lumbar spine. 62% of the performers believed that their injuries were preventable.

Surveying 269 West End performers of 12 dramas and 8 musicals in 1998[440] showed that 46% sustained at least one injury during the run of the productions (0.87 injuries per performer). While injuries to the lower extremities with 52.2% of all injuries were most common for dancers, actors mainly sustained injuries to neck and back (43.2%). Sprains and strains were the dominating diagnosis, and **sex**, a history of **previous injuries**, physically more **demanding roles** and **raked/inclined stages** were the underlying risk factors.

In 2019[441], again injuries in West End performers were recorded retrospectively with self-report over a 12-month period (2016 to 2017) based on an online injury surveillance questionnaire. Baseline demographics, injury location, diagnosis, severity, mechanism of injury, and external risk factors were documented. 47 performers (26 male, 21 female) responded, of which 65% reported at least one injury in the previous year. 50% of injuries affected the lower extremities with 37% diagnosed as muscle strains. The majority of injuries (53%) were sustained by men, although no sex differences were found regarding injury location ($\chi^2 = 2.296$, $p = 0.513$). 72% occurred during performance, and 1/3 were reported of having a gradual onset, interpretable as overuse injuries. However, **most dancers/performers worked through their injuries**, with little to no time-loss recorded.

---

akuten Verletzungen bei Musicaldarsteller/Innen]. Sportverletz Sportschaden. 25(3). 179-183. 2011.

[433] Roberts KJ, Nelson NG, and McKenzie L. *Dance-related injuries in children and adolescents treated in US emergency departments in 1991-2007.* J Phys Act Health. 10(2). 143-50. 2013.

[434] Fong Yan A, Hiller C, Sinclair PJ, and Smith RM. *Kinematic analysis of sautés in barefoot and shod conditions.* J Dance Med Sci. 18(4). 149-158. 2014.

[435] Fong Yan A, Smith RM, Hiller CE, and Sinclair PJ. *Impact attenuation properties of jazz shoes alter lower limb joint stiffness during jump landings.* J Sci Med Sport. 20(5). 464-468. 2017.

[436] Fong Yan A, Smith R, Vanwanseele B, Hiller C. *Mechanics of jazz shoes and their effect on pointing in child dancers.* J Appl Biomech. 28(3). 242-248. 2012.

[437] Campoy FA, Coelho LR, Bastos FN, Netto Júnior J, Vanderlei LC, Monteiro HL, Padovani CR, and Pastre CM. *Investigation of risk factors and characteristics of dance injuries.* Clin J Sport Med. 21(6). 493-498. 2011.

[438] Steinberg N, Hershkovitz I, Peleg S, Dar G, Masharawi Y, Siev-Ner I. *Paratenonitis of the foot and ankle in young female dancers.* Foot Ankle Int. 32(12). 1115-1121. 2011.

[439] Evans RW, Evans RI, Carvajal S. *A survey of injuries among broadway performers: types of injuries, treatments, and perceptions of performers.* Med Probl Perform Art. 11. 15-19. 1996.

[440] Evans RW, Evans RI, Carvajal S. *Survey of injuries among West End performers.* Occup Environ Med. 55(9). 585-593. 1998.

[441] James ASM, and Lazarczuk SL. *Epidemiology of Injuries in West End Performers.* J Dance Med Sci. 23(4). 139-144. 2019.

A further example showing similar results reported dancers' injuries in a Broadway show in 1997.[442] The majority of acute injuries affected legs, head, cervical spine, and upper extremities, and most of them were sustained to foot and ankle. With an overall injury rate of 40.0% compared with those of classical ballet companies injury rate was lower in this sample.

In a very detailed study injuries among musical dancers were documented over a twelve years period, confirming previous study results.[443] The lower extremity is most often acutely injured (61.6% in men and 58.2% in women), with the majority of acute injuries **(60.3%) occurring during ongoing performances**, 24.4% during rehearsals, and only 6.7% during training. **66.7% of the accidents have exogenous and clearly identifiable causes**, most notably the dance partner with 17.9%, props with 15.4%, and the dance floor with 11.6%. Gender specifics and accident frequency in the evening were also recorded. **Skin lesions** were noted as common injuries, comparable to contemporary dance and dancesport.

In 2014, acute injuries in **Revue** dancers were investigated.[444] In revue, dancing, singing, musical and recital sequences are presented, based on a variety of different dance styles and mainly high numbers of performances (> 250/10 months). Although Revue can be considered an individual artistic genre, it is partly linked to musical and thus should be mentioned here. The assessment was based on work accident reports of the German Social Accident Insurance Institution Berlin (UKB), and included 440 revue dancers (183 males and 257 females). Within one season, the dancers sustained 0.22 acute injuries/1000 hours, which equals one out of three females and one out of two males, resulting in an incidence rate of 0.44 for males and 0.31 for females. The lower limbs followed by the spine were the anatomical locations mostly affected. 75.1% of the accidents happened on stage, 69% during performances, and 81.7% within the first three hours of work. In Revue dancers, the partner as well as the dance floors were noted as the most important extrinsic factor, with no differences in sex.

IRISH DANCE

Irish dance, in its enormously demanding biomechanical complexity, especially stresses the knees, foot, ankle and spine in elite and professional dancers but also affects the rest of the dancer's body.[445,446] The higher a dancer's level, the higher the injury rates.[447,448] Irish dance includes Irish Step as well as presentation of traditional and national dancers. For that, Irish dancers present two types of shoes: Ghillies are soft leather shoes worn by females, slightly comparable to soft ballet slippers. Reels are the male equivalent, mostly having fiberglass heels incorporated, while the shoes resemble the hard shoes more than soft slippers. Ghillies and Reels support the part of Irish dance, which presents dances independent of foot percussion ("Irish Step") presenting light, high jumping. The hard version of Irish shoes (often nicknamed "Heavies") is supposed to make percussive sounds, and for that purpose has bulky (mainly) fiberglass support under the balls of the shoes as well as heels.

The weight of the shoes, the technique with crossed legs, erect back, arms aligned with the torso, and the enormous jumping demands make Irish dancers mainly prone to injuries of the lower extremities (94.9%), especially foot/ankle and knee, as well as lumbar spine, sacrum, sacroiliac joints, and pelvis (5.1%). Most dancers, especially those of higher technical levels, suffer many injuries, a lot of them being affected by several at the same time (79.7%). The majority of injuries are again chronic (80%), triggered by overuse, causing intense muscle and joint pain in the affected dancers.[449,450] Stress fractures, especially to the sesamoid bones of the foot,

[442] Bronner S, and B Brownstein. *Profile of dance injuries in a broadway show: A discussion of issues in dance medicine epidemiology*. J Ortho Sports Phys Ther. 26(2). 87-94. 1997.
[443] Wanke EM, Groneberg DA, and D Quarcoo. *Analysis and Evaluation of Acute Injuries in Musical Performers [Analyse und Evaluation von akuten Verletzungen bei Musicaldarsteller/Innen]*. Sportverletz Sportschaden. 25(3). 179-183. 2011.
[444] Wanke EM, Arendt M, Mill H, Koch F, Wanke A, and Groneberg DA. *Traumatic injuries in revue dancers.* J Dance Med Sci. 18(1). 22-8. 2014.
[445] Cahalan R, Purtill H, O'Sullivan P, and O'Sullivan K. *A cross-sectional study of elite adult Irish dancers: biopsychosocial traits, pain, and injury.* J Dance Med Sci. 19(1). 31-43. 2015.
[446] Cahalan R, Purtill H, O'Sullivan K. *Biopsychosocial Factors Associated with Foot and Ankle Pain and Injury in Irish Dance: A Prospective Study.* Med Probl Perform Art. 32(2). 111-117. 2017.
[447] Eustergerling M, and C Emery. *Risk factors for injuries in competitive Irish dancers enrolled in dance schools in Calgary, Canada.* Med Probl Perform Art. 30(1). 26-29. 2015.
[448] Cahalan R, Purtill H, O'Sullivan P, and K O'Sullivan. *Foot and ankle pain and injuries in elite adult Irish dancers.* Med Probl Perform Art. 29(4). 198-206. 2014.
[449] Stein CJ, Tyson KD, Johnson VM, Popoli DM, d'Hemecourt PA, and LJ Micheli. *Injuries in Irish dance.* J Dance Med Sci. 17(4). 159-164. 2013.
[450] Cahalan R, Purtill H, O'Sullivan P, and K O'Sullivan. *Foot and ankle pain and injuries in elite adult Irish dancers.* Med Probl Perform Art. 29(4). 198-206. 2014.

are among the most common injuries in Irish dance, followed by problems with the patellofemoral joint as well as the patellar cartilage, not least because of the predominant asymmetry in this style and the bruises and sprains caused by the ground reaction forces impacting on foot and leg.[451,452,453]

In a study published in 2010[454], the forces within the muscles and contact forces at the joints of the dancers were calculated, using force plates mounted on sprung floor and 3D motion analysis. Analysis showed that the "rock step" produced **maximum ground reaction force 4.5 times the dancer's body weight**; Calf muscles connected to the Achilles tendon experienced a maximum force comparable to their maximal isometric strength and the **contact force at the ankle joint was 14 times body weight**, of which the majority of the force was due to muscle contraction. The study concluded that such high forces constitute injury risk. For the dancers' health and performance, appropriate footwear and monitoring of training load is essential in Irish dance.

In order to assess plantar loading[455], elite Irish dancers with 9.2 ±2.1 years of experience in Irish dance completed one bar of a set phrase in each of three shoes: Irish dance soft shoe, hard shoe, and a dance trainer. Maximum force, maximum pressure, and impulse (at 100Hz using a Pedar insole pressure sensor system) were analyzed for the whole foot, forefoot, and rearfoot. Significant differences between shoe types were observed in impulse ($p < 0.01$) and maximum pressure ($p < 0.01$), with the trainer exhibiting lower values than the other shoes. With regard to loading on the different regions, differences were also found between shoes, with forefoot values highest in the soft shoe. The footwear choice had a significant effect on the measured kinetics [motion with respect to forces acting upon the dancer]: The trainer had lower kinetic values than the soft shoe, making it a safer (i.e., less injurious) choice for training.

Supporting this conclusion, prevalence of overuse injuries in the right ankle was assessed in 18 performing Irish dancers[456] (8 male, 10 female) through questionnaires. Results showed that only three ankles could be considered radiologically normal, while 14 showed Achilles tendinopathies (mostly at point of tendon insertion), 7 plantar fasciitis, 2 bone oedemas, and 2 calcaneocuboid joint degenerations. MRI patterns did not always correlate with clinical scores, indicating that many injuries were sub-clinical. Dancers with pain were functionally impaired.

Next to ankle and foot injuries, the knees are severely affected by overuse injuries. In addition to the problem of overuse injuries, Irish dancing, as so many other dance styles, show **specific burden for child and adolescent dancers** due to an enormous focus on early, specialized skill acquisition. In 2014[457], a study retrospectively investigated adolescent (< 19 years) Irish dancers, who presented to a sports medicine or orthopedic clinic with knee injuries, partially or directly related to Irish dance, between January 1, 2000 and December 31, 2010. 67 young Irish dancers showed 86 knee injuries. 50.7% of these patients received more than one diagnosis during these visits. **Overuse injuries accounted for 90.7%, with duration to triage ranging from less than 1 week to over 1 year.** In contrast, dancers with traumatic injuries came significantly earlier. 53.5% were patellar tracking disorders (patellofemoral syndrome, hypermobile patella, and patellar subluxation). The study stressed that targeted prevention programs could potentially eliminate a large portion of knee pain and injury experienced by young Irish dancers.

Injuries of 69 female Irish dancers (age 8-23 years) were recorded at an academic sports medicine center from June 2002 to September 2009, stemming from a single Irish Dance Company. The 69 dancers sustained 217 injuries, mainly to the lower extremities (94.9%), the lumbosacral spine and pelvis (5.1%). 79.7% of the dancers had multiple injuries, with **numbers increasing along with increasing level of expertise**. A trend was noted towards younger dancers with already high skill levels, indicating the **danger of early specialization for children**. Among the injuries reported were stress fractures (29.9%), patellofemoral pain syndrome (11.1%), Sever condition [also known as apophysitis of the calcaneus, which is an inflammation of the growth plate in the calcaneus/heel bone of children, mainly during growth spurts] (6.0%), ankle sprains (5.1%), posterior tibialis

451 Noon M, Hoch AZ, McNamara L, and J Schimke. *Injury patterns in female Irish dancers.* PM R. 2(11).1030-1034. 2010.
452 Cromie S, Greenwood JG, JF McCullagh. *Does Irish-dance training influence lower-limb asymmetry?* Laterality. 12(6). 500-506. 2007.
453 Beasley MA, Stracciolini A, Tyson KD, and CJ Stein. *Knee injury patterns in young irish dancers.* Med Probl Perform Art. 29(2).70-73. 2014.
454 Shippen JM, and May B. *Calculation of muscle loading and joint contact forces during the rock step in Irish dance.* J Dance Med Sci. 14(1). 11-8. 2010.
455 Trégouët P, and F Merland F. *The effects of different shoes on plantar forces in Irish dance.* J Dance Med Sci. 17(1). 41-46. 2013.
456 Walls RJ, Brennan SA, Hodnett P, O'Byrne JM, Eustace SJ, and Stephens MM. *Overuse ankle injuries in professional Irish dancers.* Foot Ankle Surg. 16(1). 45-9. 2010.
457 Beasley MA, Stracciolini A, Tyson KD, and Stein CJ. *Knee injury patterns in young irish dancers.* Med Probl Perform Art. 29(2).70-73. 2014.

tendonitis (4.6%), and plantar fasciitis (4.6%). The sesamoid bones were mostly affected by stress fractures (27.7% of all stress fractures and 8.3% of total injuries).

Again with respect to injuries in the young, a study[458] documented pain and injury incidence in 37 elite adolescent Irish dancers and assessed potentially associated biopsychosocial risk factors. Baseline questionnaires recorded information on health and lifestyle (dance practice, general health, sleep, eating habits, passion for dance and other) as well as any episode of pain or injury over the previous 12 months, dividing the dancers in a "more-pain" (n = 17) and "less-pain" (n = 20) group. Through a screening, balance, fitness, flexibility, endurance, and functional movement was evaluated. 84% reported at least one location of pain/injury, with foot and ankle most commonly affected. Factors significantly associated with pain and injury included having an unusual number of troublesome body parts (p = 0.002), often or always dancing in pain (p = 0.033), and high levels of anger or hostility (p = 0.045). The study highlighted the injury risk for young dancers, stressing aspects such as inappropriate technique progression, unique choreographic features, and an overly arduous calendar of competitive events.

These results were supported by other studies, investigating Irish dance. The high number of studies investigating the genre does not only show its popularity, but can also be regarded as a sign of its complexity, artistically as well as with regard to injury risks. Comparable to styles such as classical ballet or breakdance, Irish dance has increasingly attracted the interest of research within the last 10-15 years.

In 2015[459], three of five Irish dance schools in Calgary participated in a retrospective survey study, documenting injuries within one year. 36 dancers completed the questionnaires, of which 26 (IP = 72.2%; 95% CI 54.8-85.8%) reported at least one Irish dance-related injury in the past year. Altogether, 60 injuries were reported with the majority (57%) affecting foot and ankle. Elite level dancers (OR 6.33; 95%CI 1.27-31.57) and dancers over 18 years of age (OR 24.43; 95% CI 2.60-229.56) were at greater risk of injury in the past year than non-elite and younger dancers.

[458] Cahalan R, Bargary N, and O'Sullivan K. *Pain and Injury in Elite Adolescent Irish Dancers: A Cross-Sectional Study*. J Dance Med Sci. 22(2). 91-99. 2018.

[459] Eustergerling M, and Emery C. *Risk factors for injuries in competitive Irish dancers enrolled in dance schools in Calgary, Canada.* Med Probl Perform Art. 30(1). 26-29. 2015.

A study compared biopsychosocial characteristics[460] of 29 healthy to 53 dancers, who declared their foot and ankle as most troublesome anatomical area. Several factors were statistically linked to pain and injury in the foot and ankle in professional, competitive, and student adult Irish dancers: female gender (p = 0.004), greater gastrocnemius flexibility (p = 0.021), better single leg balance (p = 0.019), and a higher number of endurance jumps (p = 0.009). In general, the injured dancers reported more severe levels of day-to-day pain (p = 0.038), greater burden of daily pain (p = 0.005), more subjective health complaints (p = 0.024), more psychological complaints (p = 0.030), and a higher number of bodily locations experiencing pain and injury (p = 0.025).

104 elite and competitive Irish dancers[445] engaged in a survey, self-reporting an injury rate of 76.9% over the previous 5 years, resulting in a mean of 1.49 injuries per dancer sustained to all body parts. On average, 126.1 days were lost annually to injury. 84 were subjected to a physical screening of lower limb flexibility involving balance and endurance tests, a battery of functional tests, and anthropometric, biomechanical, and anatomical assessments. 33 (31.7%) were classified as significantly injured and 71 (68.3%) as not significantly injured. Factors associated with being significantly-injured were female sex (p = 0.036), higher number of subjective general health (p = 0.001) and psychological (p = 0.036) complaints, low mood (p = 0.01), heightened catastrophizing (p = 0.047), and failure to always complete a warm-up (p = 0.006).

In a prospective study [446], 85 elite adult Irish dancers were followed up prospectively each month for 1 year to evaluate foot and ankle pain/injury rates and potential risk factors (after their baseline-screening for biopsychosocial factors). 28 (25 females, 3 males) were in the foot-and-ankle-pain/injury group, 21 (14 females, 7 males) in the "not-injured"-group. Factors statistically associated with the injured dancers were: failing to always perform a warm-up (p = 0.042), lower levels of energy (p = 0.013), and more bothersome pain (p = 0.021). Subjects also scored worse on two dimensions of the Athletic Coping Skills Inventory: i.e., coping with adversity (p = 0.035) and goal setting and mental preparation (p = 0.009).

[460] Cahalan R, Purtill H, O'Sullivan P, and O'Sullivan K. *Foot and ankle pain and injuries in elite adult Irish dancers.* Med Probl Perform Art. 29(4). 198-206. 2014.

Folk and character dance ranging from Anatolian[461] to Belly[462] dance, is a very broad field in dance, given the many nations of the world whose national dances are adapted for stage. Hence, the demands dancers have to face differ with respect to biomechanics and therefore result in different injuries. Moreover, comparable to jazz dance or flamenco, folk dances are often summed up with other styles such as contemporary or tap dance in scientific publications, which makes it hard to report clear results. Many folk- and character dances incorporate virtuous jumping and turning techniques, which can also include turnout/en dehors, resulting in high impact forces for knees and ankles. It was described that muscles stabilizing and moving the knee, such as the musculus popliteus, as well as cruciate ligaments or menisci are prone to injuries through repetitive rotational strains.[463] The danger to the knee was demonstrated in several studies.

A total of 377 injuries (75.40%) in the previous 12 months were reported by 500 dancers (409 women and 91 men, mean age 18.26 ±4.55 years) participating in the 26th Dance Festival of Joinville (Brazil).[464] With 22 injuries (43.14%) to the knee, tap and folk dance ranked third among the most affected anatomical locations. Dynamic overload and excessive use were perceived as the most important causes, and body height was associated with injuries in tap and folk dance.

In a very recent study[444], acute knee injuries to an Anatolian Folk-Dance group, "Fire of Anatolia", were reported. The group, consisting of 82 dancers, 37 males and 45 females (45.1% and 54.9%, respectively) show a mean age of 27.96 ±5.05 years (range: 18-38 years) and are specialize in Caucasian dances, where jumps into, from and in deep squats ("grand pliés") as well as single leg twists pose a significant risk to the knee. During a 10-year period, 9 injuries required surgical treatment (3 meniscus tears, 4 anterior cruciate ligament tears, 1 posterior cruciate ligament tear, 1 patellar dislocation). A second study presented the overuse injuries of the company.[465] 70 overuse injuries were documented in 25 dancers, many with multiple injuries. With 68% of all cases, the majority was sustained to the knee. Other anatomical locations affected were the thigh in 24%, lumbar region in 24%, feet in 20%, shoulder in 16%, and hip in 12%. No ankle injuries were found, in contrast to styles such as ballet, modern or Irish dance.

In an MRI-based retrospective study[466], professional folk dancers were checked on anatomical liabilities and their effect on the musculotendinous unit of the popliteus muscle. 32 MRI scans of members of a professional folk-dance group (mean age 30.2±7.9 years, range 18-38) revealed popliteal tendinitis in 5 dancers (5 knees). The researchers found that the affected dancers had higher popliteus sulcus depth (PSD) and a higher ratio of PSD/lateral condyle width (LCW), which can be related to popliteal tendinitis due to extensive practice incorporating rotational strains on the knee.

With regard to injury prevention, a discrepancy between training and performance in terms of **anaerobic and aerobic endurance capacity**[467] also increases the risk of injury in folk dance due to fatigue and exhaustion, as all fitness deficits in all other dance styles. Comparable to similar assessments[468], 9 female championship Highland dancers (age 14.2 ±1.47 years) were assessed on the physiological effects of performance in their genre. The purpose of the study was to consider whether traditional training methods (class and rehearsal) provided the dancer with sufficient training stimulus to be well-prepared for stage. During a competition, heart rate and blood lactate concentrations were measured before and after three dances, and heart rate was documented

[461] Aksu N, Akgonul B, Aksu T, Atansay V, Kara AN. Traumatic knee injury patterns in Anatolian folk dancers: a case series and literature review. Int J Occup Med Environ Health. 32(5). 585-593. 2019.

[462] Milner SC, Gray A, and Bussey M. *A Retrospective Study Investigating Injury Incidence and Factors Associated with Injury Among Belly Dancers.* J Dance Med Sci. 23(1). 26-33. 2019.

[463] Aumann EK, Aksu T, Atansay V, Kara AN, and Aksu N. *Relationship of Popliteus Sulcus Depth and Tibiofemoral Rotational Alignment with Popliteus Tendinitis in Professional Folk Dancers Exposed to Turnout Positions: An MRI Analysis.* Med Probl Perform Art. 34(3). 141-146. 2019.

[464] Campoy FA, Coelho LR, Bastos FN, Netto Júnior J, Vanderlei LC, Monteiro HL, Padovani CR, and Pastre CM. *Investigation of risk factors and characteristics of dance injuries.* Clin J Sport Med. 21(6). 493-498. 2011.

[465] Aksu N, Atansay V, Aksu T, Damla Kara Ş, Koçulu S, Karalök I. Overuse Injuries in Professional Anatolian Folk Dancers: A Descriptive Study Verified with MRI. Med Probl Perform Art. 2017 Sep;32(3):152-158.

[466] Aumann EK, Aksu T, Atansay V, Kara AN, and Aksu N. *Relationship of Popliteus Sulcus Depth and Tibiofemoral Rotational Alignment with Popliteus Tendinitis in Professional Folk Dancers Exposed to Turnout Positions: An MRI Analysis.* Med Probl Perform Art. 34(3). 141-146. 2019.

[467] Baillie Y, Wyon M, and A Head. *Highland dance: heart-rate and blood lactate differences between competition and class.* Int J Sports Physiol Perform. 2(4). 371-376. 2007.

[468] Wyon MA, Abt G, Redding E, Head A, and Sharp NC. *Oxygen uptake during modern dance class, rehearsal, and performance.* J Strength Cond Res. 18(3). 646-649. 2004.

rehearsing the same three dances. Results were comparable to cited studies from other dance styles which show that training classes do not sufficiently prepare the dancers for the demands of competition or performance with regard to oxygen uptake and heart rate (aerobic and anaerobic energy systems).

Oriental dance and belly dance are very under-researched fields, but one study investigated injury risk and underlying factors in belly dancers[445] over a 12-month retrospective period in New Zealand, based on a questionnaire. 109 female dancers were included (mean age 44.3 years; dancing for an average of 3.0 hours per week). Recorded injury rate was 37% with 40 injuries in 109 dancers and an injury incidence proportion of 24.8%. 27 dancers reported at least one injury, resulting in a dance exposure of 1.69/1000 dance hours. Lower limb injuries were the most common, followed by trunk injuries. Factors associated with a decreased risk of injury were age, total dance hours/week, and participation in a non-dance exercise regimen of any kind. Performing regularly was associated with an increased injury rate. The authors concluded that belly dancing can be injurious and future interventions are recommended.

FLAMENCO

Comparable to Irish and Tap dance, the characteristic, highly percussive zapateado (foot work) of Flamenco exposes dancers to high impact forces. The shoes of both, male and female dancers, have heels, and they as well as the tips of the soles under the toes are traditionally nailed to allow for the characteristic foot percussions.

Although flamenco is a widely accepted dance style, research on injuries and health in flamenco dancers is very rare.[469] Given that the foot is the main instrument, the flamenco dancer is predisposed to podiatic (foot-related) pathologic (ill, not-physiological) disorders and deformities, such as metatarsal pain, sesamoiditis, hyperkerastosis, hallux abducto valgus, a particularly high prevalence of hypermobility of the first ray, claw toe, and varus fifth toe.[470,471,472] However, the constant vibrations created by the impacting forces as well as the expressive but demanding posture and dynamics of upper body, neck and head, are associated with high loading in the pelvis as well as neck and back, although that might be more related to myofascial overloading than to the spine or intervertebral discs (degenerative diskopathy).[473,474]

In 1988[475], a pilot study recorded foot pressures, hip and knee vibrations in 10 female Flamenco dancers using the electrodynogram and skin-mounted accelerometers. A health questionnaire was distributed to 29 dancers. Foot pressures and acceleration data showed the high impact on the dancers' body with the hip joint (hips and knees are mostly in slight flexion in flamenco) absorbing most of the impact. Clinical findings based on a screening of the dancers showed calluses, among other, which were correlating with the pressure distribution. Identified urogenital disorders, back and neck pain, may result from the vibrations generated by the footwork.

Examining self-reported injuries of professional and student flamenco dancers[476] with respect to the impact of zapateado, injury patterns of student flamenco dancers were compared to those of professional flamenco dancers based on a questionnaire comprising 80 dancers. Professionals reported higher numbers than student dancers. 45% of student's injuries were sustained to the foot, compared to 17% in the professionals, who additionally reported 23% of ankle injuries. The knee accounted for 15% in students and 30% in professionals, the back for 20% in both groups and the neck for 5% in students and 7% in professionals. "Other injuries" (15% and 3%, respectively) were noted.

---

[469] Forczek W, Baena-Chicón I, and Vargas-Macías A. *Movement concepts approach in studies on flamenco dancing: A systematic review.* Eur J Sport Sci. 17(9). 1161-1176. 2017.

[470] Castillo-López JM, Vargas-Macías A, Domínguez-Maldonado G, Lafuente-Sotillos G, Ramos-Ortega J, Palomo-Toucedo IC, Reina-Bueno M, and Munuera-Martínez PV. *Metatarsal pain and plantar hyperkeratosis in the forefeet of female professional flamenco dancers.* Med Probl Perform Art. 29(4). 193-197. 2014.

[471] Castillo-López JM, Munuera-Martínez PV, Algaba-Guisado C, Reina-Bueno M, Salti-Pozo N, and Vargas-Macías A. *Pathologic Disorders of the Foot in Professional Female Flamenco Dancers.* J Am Podiatr Med Assoc. 106(1). 54-59. 2016.

[472] Shybut TB, Rose DJ, and Strongwater AM. *Second metatarsal physeal arrest in an adolescent flamenco dancer: a case report.* Foot Ankle Int. 29(8). 859-862. 2008.

[473] Capel A, Medina FS, Medina D, and Gómez S. *Magnetic resonance study of lumbar disks in female dancers.* Am J Sports Med. 37(6). 1208-1213. 2009.

[474] Bejjani FJ. *Occupational biomechanics of athletes and dancers: a comparative approach.* Clin Podiatr Med Surg. 4(3). 671-711. 1987.

[475] Bejjani FJ, Halpern N, Pio A, Dominguez R, Voloshin A, and Frankel VH. *Musculoskeletal demands on flamenco dancers: a clinical and biomechanical study.* Foot Ankle. 8(5). 254-263. 1988.

[476] Pederson E, and Wilmerding E. *Injury profiles of student and professional flamenco dancers.* J Dance Med Sci. 2. 108-114. 1998.

The relationship between frequency of metatarsal pain and hyperkeratosis (calluses) on the plantar forefoot was investigated.[457] The 44 female professional flamenco dancers trained and danced a minimum of 25 hours per week. Heel hight of the shoes as well as plantar pressures were measured on a pressure platform (barefoot and with usual dance shoes) and pain was recorded. 80.7% of the dancers experienced metatarsal pain during dancing, and 84.1% presented with plantar hyperkeratosis. In 67.04% of the feet studied the two disorders coincided. Loading points did not show an increase of pressure on the metatarsals through a change in weight distribution in shoes (52.4% loading in the rearfoot and 47.6% in the forefoot) versus barefoot (59.5% in the rearfoot and 40.5% in the forefoot). Thus, the metatarsal pain as well as the hyperkeratosis may be caused by repetitive micro traumata due to Flamenco's percussive nature.

TAP DANCE

Comparable to Flamenco and Irish Dance/Step, American tap dancers are particularly prone to foot and ankle injuries due to the repetitive, percussive rhythmic stomping and beating movements. As in Flamenco with the nailed heels and toe-balls of the shoes, tap dance presents plates ("taps") under the shoes, which enable the dancer to create the rhythmic sounds of their dance style. Tap dance shows potential for sprains, bruises, and, due to the relatively heavy but not cushioned footwear, basic overload reactions of the foot, lower leg, knee, and spine. [477, 478, 479, 480, 481] Due to its unique hip-led leg technique, tap dance also puts a lot of strain on the dancer's knee, especially the original American Tap.

One study documented acute and overuse injuries in tap dancers: 90 female and 14 male tap dancers of advanced and master classes in a New York Tap Dance Festival were investigated using a survey.[482] Their mean age was 34 ±14 years (range: 15 to 75 years) and they reported an average of 21 ±13 years of tap experience (range: 1 to 60 years). Including 5 ±6.5 hours/week in dance classes, 1.5 ±1.75 hours of strength and 3.25 ±0.75 hours of aerobic training, they spent an average of 40% of their work/school time performing or teaching. 90% reported that they concentrated on tap dancing as a dance style. 41% did not report any injuries attributable to dance activities. 34% reported one, 16% two, 4% three, and 3% four injuries. One dancer reported 6 injuries, and another 7. The 14 affected male dancers reported 9 injuries (0.64 injuries/dancer) while the 90 females reported 87 injuries (0.97 injuries/dancer). 75% were acute injuries. "Major" injuries (16% of all injuries) reported were: 4 acute fractures, 3 stress fractures, 3 meniscal tears in 2 subjects, 2 disc ruptures, 1 patella dislocation, 1 anterior cruciate ligament tear, 1 rib cartilage separation. "Minor" injuries noted were: 50 joint sprains (foot, ankle, knee, hip, back, and neck), 4 hamstring and calf muscle strains, 11 Achilles and hip tendinopathies and bursitis, patella tendinopathy, and foot contusion. Overuse injuries reported were shin splints, stress fractures, Morton neuroma, compartment syndrome, bursitis and tendonitis. This study concluded that injury numbers are moderate to low in tap compared to other dance styles.

In order to investigate related impact as well as joint forces and moments in tap dance, a further study gave an overview of peak kinetic and kinematic data.[464] Six professional tap dancers performed four tap sequences on a force platform, monitored with a five-camera motion analysis system. Relatively low impacting forces and moments were noted in the study, which might explain the claimed lower injury incidence in tap dancers reported in the previous study. But the author team concluded that the very complex topic needs further study of underlying factors.

[477] Mayers L, Bronner S, Agraharasamakulam S, Ojofeitimi S. *Lower extremity kinetics in tap dance*. J Dance Med Sci. 14(1). 3-10. 2010.
[478] Mayers L, Judelson BS, and S Bronner. *The prevalence of injury among tap dancers*. J Dance Med Sci. 7(4). 121-125. 2003.
[479] Wanke EM. *Arbeitsbedingte Verletzungen und Erkrankungen*. IN: Exner-Grave, Elisabeth (ed.). Die medizinische Versorgung professioneller Tänzer. Stuttgart. Schattauer Verlag. 2008. p. 57-58.
[480] Campoy FA, Coelho LR, Bastos FN, Netto Júnior J, Vanderlei LC, Monteiro HL, Padovani CR, and CM Pastre. *Investigation of risk factors and characteristics of dance injuries*. Clin J Sport Med. 21(6). 493-498. 2011.
[481] Pederson E, and E Wilmerding. *Injury profiles of student and professional flamenco dancers*. J Dance Med Sci. 2. 108-114. 1998.
[482] Mayers L, Judelson BS, and S Bronner. *The prevalence of injury among tap dancers*. J Dance Med Sci. 7(4). 121-125. 2003.

Dancesport[483,484,485,486], also called ballroom dancing in its non-competitive form, demands a lot of energy from dancers and shows a correspondingly high number of injuries in professionals[487,488], though lower in seniors.[489] The overuse of forefoot and midfoot as well as lower back, the spine, especially cervical and lumbar spine, and knee joint are the locations commonly affected. The strain on neck and thorax can lead to severe impairment due to frequent lateral rotation and hyperextension of the cervical spine as part of dance technique. [490] Acute and chronic injuries of the cervical spine and the shoulder area, as well as the ankles, foot, and lumbar spine, represent a problem for women. Simultaneously, both partners, like most dancers of other styles, suffer from skin problems that must not be underestimated. As reasons are discussed the enormous need for make-up, a lack of water during training and competitions or a lack of warm-up and re-warm-up after standing periods.

In 2013, a review[491] investigated available literature on injuries in competitive dancesport dancers. An eight-database search resulted in 34 articles related to all aspects of dance sport, including biomechanics, substance use, or psychology. The review reported common injuries affecting the neck, shoulder, spine, knee, lower leg, and foot. With regard to energy expenditure, Dancesport shows high to very high intensities, mean heart rates of 175.2 ±10.7 bpm among males, and 178.6 ±8.6 bpm among females. Both aerobic and anaerobic energy systems are employed. Alpha-beta and heart rate variability intervention techniques are reported to successfully enhance performance.

To retrospectively quantify incidence of injuries and to identify the nature of injuries as well as potential risk factors of injury to dancers of dancesport, a study[492] used a questionnaire at the 2004 South African national championships. The overall incidence of injury was 0.99/1000 hours without statistically significant difference between males (0.49/1000 hours) and females (1.45/1000 hours). With 80%, acute injuries occurred more frequently in males and with 54.5% chronic injuries occurred more frequently in females. The ankle, foot and toe (39.5%), followed by back and neck (23.3%) were the most frequently injured anatomical locations. Males showed a relatively even distribution of injuries ($p > 0.05$), whereas a statistically significant difference ($p < 0.05$) was observed among females, with muscle spasms (24%) and blisters (21%) the most frequent injuries. The study concluded that dancers need to learn to seek medical help when injured and are advised to include fitness training into their routines.

Latin American Formation is a group of Ballroom dancers performing together. In 2014, a study[493] investigated 52 male and 48 female formation dancers of the German professional top-level league. Results showed similarities with injuries in individual partner dances, although gender specific dance technique was reflected in the injuries. An anonymized retrospective approach was used. In the 100 dancers, 409 injuries resulting in 4.1 injuries per dancer were reported. 80.4 % were acute injuries and 19.5 % overuse complaints. 2/3 were caused by extrinsic and 1/3 by intrinsic causes. 69.3% of men and 77.6% of women sustained at least one acute injury, with 97.9% of the injuries occurring during training. With 64.5% in men and 71.2% in women, the lower extremities were affected the most. Upper extremity (male: 21.2% and female 17.6%) and spine/torso (male 12.0% and female 8.5%) followed. Pulled muscles and blockages were mostly reported by males and contusions and pulled muscles by females. Chondropathy and osteoarthritis were the most frequently reported overuse injuries.

---

[483] Foscht, Claudia. Charakterisierung der körperlichen Merkmale von Amateurtänzern/-tänzerinnen der Lateinamerikanischen Tänzer und Standardtänze und darausfolgende Konsequenzen für die Trainingspraxis. Unveröffentlichte Dissertation Karl-Franzens-Universität Graz. 1995.

[484] Smyers Evanson A, Myrer JW, Eggett DL, Mitchell UH, and Johnson AW. *Multifidus Muscle Size and Symmetry in Ballroom Dancers with and without Low Back Pain.* Int J Sports Med. 39(8). 630-635. 2018.

[485] Wanke EM. *Akute Verletzungen und chronische Sportschäden.* IN: Wanke, Eileen M. TanzSportMedizin. Handbuch für Tänzer, Trainer, Therapeuten und Ärzte. Köln. Sportverlag Strauß. 2011. p. 229-254.

[486] Tsien CL, and E Trepman. *Internal Rotation Knee Injury During Ballroom Dance. A Case Report.* J Dance Med Sci. 5(3). 82-92. 2001.

[487] Premelč J, Vučković G, James N, and Dimitriou L. *A Retrospective Investigation on Age and Gender Differences of Injuries in DanceSport.* Int J Environ Res Public Health. 16(21). 4164. 2019.

[488] Wanke, Eileen M. TanzSportMedizin. Handbuch für Tänzer, Trainer, Therapeuten und Ärzte. Köln. Sportverlag Strauß. 2011.

[489] Wanke EM, Borchardt M, Fischer A, and Groneberg DA. *Verletzungen im Senioren-Turniertanzsport [Injury profile in competitive senior ballroom dancers].* Sportverletz Sportschaden. 28(4). 204-10. 2014.

[490] Tsung P, and GJ Mulford. *Ballroom dancing and cervical radiculopathy: A case report.* Arch Phys Med Rehabil. 79. 1306-1308. 1988.

[491] McCabe TR, Wyon M, Ambegaonkar JP, and Riding E. *A Bibliographic Review of Medicine and Science Research in DanceSport.* Med Probl Perform Art. 28(2). 70-79. 2013.

[492] Kuisis SM, Camacho T, Krüger E, and AL Camacho. *Self-reported incidence of injuries among ballroom dancers.* African J Physical, Health Education, Recreation Dance. 18(Suppl 1). 107–119. 2011.

[493] Wanke EM, Fischer T, Pieper HG, and Groneberg DA. *Dance sport: injury profile in Latin American formation dancing [Tanzsport: Verletzungsmuster im Lateinamerikanischen Formationstanz].* Sportverletz Sportschaden. 28(3). 132-138. 2014

Aside from injuries to feet and ankle, the neck as well as the knees bear a lot of mechanical loading. This loading comes with the intensive dance technical but asymmetrical presentation of torso and head, and the dance technically necessary repetitive locking and internal rotation of the knee.

In 2014, a study described the consequences of this hyperextension and left rotation of the head and neck for the female upper extremities.[494] An online survey aimed to document extension neck injuries in 127 female Dancesport competitors. 25% reported that they are affected, and 68% of these injuries occurred at competitions. Younger dancers (mean age 20 ±4.8 years) were significantly ($p < 0.003$) more likely to suffer from extension neck injuries than older dancers (mean age 34 ±12.9 years).

In a case report[495], cervical radiculopathy in a female dancer was described. Radiculopathy refers to symptoms such as tingling, chronic and acute pain, weakness in the related area, "needle piercing", or numbness produced by a pinched nerve root in the spinal column. The report described an international ballroom dancer who developed a left C7 radiculopathy (i.e., of the 7th cervical vertebra) as the result the repetitive hyperextension combined with lateral rotation of the neck and head documented through MRI and electrodiagnostic testing. Although her neck pain and cervical radicular symptoms declined in severity with treatment, she still suffered 4 1/2 months later.

Another common problem, as already mentioned, can be the internal rotation of the knee/leg resulting in tendinopathy of the myotendinous unit of the popliteus muscle in the back of the knee, an issue also found in folk dance. A dancer[496] sustained a strain to the popliteus tendon (without lateral meniscus tear) during the execution of the syncopated spin, a dance figure involving internal rotation of the leg. Transient locking and pain at the posterolateral aspect (on the back-outside of the) knee showed posterolateral joint line tenderness and pain in active external rotation of the flexed knee. Magnetic resonance imaging exhibited effusion around the popliteus tendon and activity had to be limited, leading to the recovery of the patient in the course of several weeks.

Stress and anxiety in dancesport and ballroom were described as high due to its competitive nature. A study[497] compared experienced ballroom dancers and healthy controls. The aim was to investigate anecdotally reported higher susceptibility for disease in competitive dancers. Blood and saliva samples were used to assess diurnal cortisol and alpha-amylase output as well as inflammatory parameters interleukin-6 and C-reactive protein. Diurnal cortisol and alpha-amylase output were lower in dancers while higher levels in interleukin-6 but not in C-reactive protein were shown. Reduced activity in stress systems and higher peripheral inflammation along with more self-reported physical complaints indicate that ballroom dance is a chronic stressor, leading to functional consequences, which might be related to ill-health. Dancers reported to be more anxious and reported more physical health complaints than controls.

URBAN STYLES: HIP HOP, BREAKDANCE & CO

As shortly addressed in the introductory chapters it is challenging for dance medicine to support those dancers, who work with techniques without primarily established movement repertoire and teachers. Urban styles, for instance, are based primarily on individual creations of moves and permanent evolution of dancers and choreographers in movement and style. They often lack teaching systems and methods. That makes conducting dance studies, evaluating the limited data available as well as dance medical interventions in the field difficult.

In urban styles, the injury situation is quite delicate, which is why they are mentioned at the end of the list to give them special attention. A study published in 2012 described the following: 312 Hip Hop dancers of all levels and event types (battles, dance festivals, clubs, show acts) were analyzed for six months.[498] The dancers were

[494] McCabe T, Ambegaonkar J, Wyon M, and Redding E. *Extension Neck Injury in Female DanceSport Competitors.* International Journal of Athletic Therapy and Training. 19. 32-36. 2014.

[495] Tsung P, and GJ Mulford. *Ballroom dancing and cervical radiculopathy: A case report.* Arch Phys Med Rehabil. 79. 1306-1308. 1988.

[496] Tsien CL, and Trepman E. *Internal Rotation Knee Injury During Ballroom Dance. A Case Report.* J Dance Med Sci. 5(3). 82-92. 2001.

[497] Berndt C, Strahler J, Kirschbaum C, and Rohleder N. *Lower stress system activity and higher peripheral inflammation in competitive ballroom dancers.* Biol Psychol. 91(3). 357-364. 2012.

[498] Ojofeitimi S, Bronner S, and H Woo. *Injury incidence in hip hop dance.* Scand J Med Sci Sports. 22. 347-355. 2012.

all older than 13 years and were divided into three disciplines: **breakers, poppers/lockers,** and **new stylers/new schoolers**. The results confirm the challenge for dance medicine mentioned: 738 injuries were recorded in 232 dancers, of which 506 (in 205 dancers) led to severe limitation and extensive time-loss for the dancers. Multiple and repetitive injuries per year were recorded for each dancer. The lower extremities accounted for 52% of the injury frequency and the upper extremities for 32%. The injury frequency for breakers was much higher than that for popping/locking and new style dancers indicating the importance of injury surveillance and dance medical approach to training and teaching. Education concerning warm-up and cool-down, basics in dance medicine, and the use of injury-preventive equipment such as joint protectors, suitable footwear, and the evaluation of floors are essential in this regard. However, style-specific warm-up or the use of functional floors and other equipment is often missing due to the impulsiveness typical for these styles.

In a prospective study over three months [499], injury occurrence and potential predictors were evaluated in 129 competitive hip hop dancers (114 females), age: 17.95 ±4.15 years- Predictors analyzed were sociodemographic factors, sport-related factors, previous injury status, anthropometric and body build indices, and dynamic balance performance (Star Excursion Balance Test-SEBT). Injury occurrence was prospectively observed once a week, using the Oslo Sports Trauma Research Center Overuse Injury Questionnaire (OSTRC). 101 injuries occurred within the 3 months (equated annual injury incidence 312%), with a mean of 0.78 injuries per dancer (95% CI 0.61-0.97), females 0.76 (95% CI 0.60-0.95) and males 0.93 (95% CI 0.75-1.13). 17% sustained multiple injuries and 49% of all injuries were time-loss injuries. With 42% the most frequently injured location was the knee followed by the back (32%) and ankle (15%). Previous injury was a strong predictor of injury occurrence (Odds Ratio: 3.76, 95% CI 1.87-4.59). Better scores on the Star Excursion Balance Test were correlating with lower injury risk, irrespective of gender and previous injury status. Anthropometric and body build variables did not influence injury occurrence. The authors advised dancers and trainers to be informed about the certain protective effects of dynamic balance on the prevention of musculoskeletal injury in hip hop in order to assure safe and effective practices. In other words, the practical implementation of dance medicine was stressed.

Especially injuries to breakdancers have been well researched with studies from the 1980/90s[500,501,502,503,504] starting to report the danger of this virtuous, acrobatic discipline for bones[505,506,507] and joints[508,509,510,511] with related tissues[512], blood vessels[513], and organs.[514,515] The highly acrobatic breakdancing/b-boying can be considered to be a high-risk dance style.

Two studies published in 2009 investigated injuries and risk factors in breakdancers. 40 professionals and 104 amateurs were asked about their injuries using a questionnaire. [516] 1665 injuries and 206 overuse syndromes resulting from 380 588 hours of training were reported in those 144 dancers. Professionals reported significantly more injuries and overuse syndromes with more injuries to the wrist, knee, hip/thigh, ankle/foot, and elbow, in descending order. With regard to the time lost per injury and the time lost per overuse syndrome, no difference was noted between amateurs and professionals. Pain occurred most frequently in the region of the wrist, spine, shoulder, and ankle. The

[499] Ursej E, Sekulic D, Prus D, Gabrilo G, and Zaletel P. *Investigating the Prevalence and Predictors of Injury Occurrence in Competitive Hip Hop Dancers: Prospective Analysis.* Int J Environ Res Public Health. 16(17). 3214. 2019.
[500] Goscienski PJ, and L Luevanos. *Injury caused by 'break dancing'.* JAMA. 252(24). 3367. 1984.
[501] Dorey RS, and V Mayne. *Break-dancing injuries.* Med J Aust. 144(11). 610-611. 1986.
[502] Leung AK. *Hazards of break dancing.* NY State J Med. 84(12). 592. 1984.
[503] Norman RA, and MA Grodin. *Injuries from break dancing.* Am Fam Physician.30(4). 109-112. 1984.
[504] Sharma V, Knapp JK, Wasserman GS, Walsh I, and CJ Hoover. *Injuries associated with break dancing.* Pediatr Emerg Care. 2(1):21-22. 1986.
[505] Chen YH, Kuo CL, Lin LC, Wang SJ, and Lee CH. *Stress fracture of the ulna in a break-dancer.* J Sports Sci Med. 7(4). 556-559. 2008
[506] Cho CH, Song KS, Min BW, Bae KC, Lee KJ, and SH Kim. *Scaphoid nonunion in break-dancers: a report of 3 cases.* Orthopedics. 32(7). 526. 2009.
[507] Dieden JD. *Break dancer's fracture of the fifth metatarsal.* West J Med. 142(1). 101. 1985.
[508] Gerber SD, Griffin PP, and BP Simmons. *Break dancer's wrist.* J Pediatr Orthop. 6(1). 98-99. 1986.
[509] Khoury JJ, Loberant N, and J Jerushalmi. *Shoulder pain in a young break-dancer evaluated with bone scintigraphy.* Clin Nucl Med. 34(12). 916-917. 2009.
[510] McBride DQ, Lehman LP, and JR Mangiardi. Break-dancing neck. N Engl J Med. 312(3). 186. 1985.
[511] Winkler AR, Barnes JC, and JA Ogden. *Break dance hip: chronic avulsion of the anterior superior iliac spine.* Pediatr Radiol. 17(6). 501-502. 1987.
[512] Broome HE, and RB Heppenstall. *'Break dancers' bursitis'.* JAMA. 253(6). 777. 1985.
[513] Schneider F, Milesi I, Haesler E, Wicky S, Schnyder P, and A Denys. *Break-dance: an unusual cause of hammer syndrome.* Cardiovasc Intervent Radiol. 25(4). 330-331. 2002.
[514] Balfour-Lynn IM. *Break dancer's lung.* Arch Dis Child. 86(3). 224. 2002.
[515] Joondeph BC, Spigelman AV, and JS Pulido. *Ocular trauma from break dancing.* Arch Ophthalmol. 104(2). 176-177. 1986.
[516] Kauther MD, Wedemeyer C, Wegner A, Kauther KM, and von Knoch M. *Breakdance injuries and overuse syndromes in amateurs and professionals.* Am J Sports Med. 37(4).797-802. 2009.

injuries led to a time-loss of 10970.6 training days although even with severe injuries, **dancers interrupted their training only for limited periods** of time. A negative correlation between protective gear and injuries or frequency of pain could not be shown, indicating the enormous injury risk and the importance of implementing evidence-based training routines or screening, which might thus be more efficient than protective gear.

Of 23 professional and 19 amateur breakdancers in the second study[517], 40 (95.2%) had musculoskeletal injuries at more than one site, as another epidemiologic study reported 2009. The mean number of injury sites per dancer was 4.60 and reported anatomical locations included wrist (69.0%), finger (61.9%), knee (61.9%), shoulder (52.4%), lumbar spine (50.0%), elbow (42.9%), cervical spine (38.1%), ankle (38.1%), foot (28.6%) and hip (16.7%). The most common diagnoses were sprains, strains and tendonitis. Of the 42 dancers, 13 (31%) had fractures or dislocations. **Only eight (19.1%) learned break-dancing under supervised instruction**, 17 (40.5%) used protective devices and 28 (66.7%) performed warm-up exercises before dancing. There were differences in age, length of dance career, amount of dance training, mean number of injury sites and the presence of supervised training between professionals and amateurs. The authors concluded that careful screening, instruction and supervised training of break-dancers will help to prevent injuries.

Another aspect, which might be underestimated is the effect of excessive volumes/decibels of music used in Urban Styles (and other dance styles!) on the auditory system of dancers as well as audiences. [518,519,520]

Head spinning, a move in which the dancers spin on the top of their head, counts among the most famous moves in breakdancing/b-boying but comes with a high risk of fractures, dislocations, spinal cord injuries and hair loss[521] in breakdancers. [522] In 2014, a study described the underlying biomechanics and risk factors due to reversed body loading for the cervical spine.[523] 25 participants with "headspin" ability (age 16-34 years) were interviewed and biomechanically tested with respect to their cervical spine, history of neck pain, cervical range of motion and torque. Compared to 25 participants without any cervical spine problems they reported better subjective fitness, more cervical complaints, higher pain intensity, a longer history of neck pain, a 2-2.5 times higher rate of neck pain, and worse scores on the Neck Disability Index compared to the control group (increased cervical flexion and cervical torque in all planes; the cervical range of motion showed a negative correlation with Neck Disability Index, pain intensity and history of neck pain.)

The "Cone-Head" or "Headspin-Hole" has been reported repeatedly in breakdancers. A very recent study [524] described the "Cone Head" as a painless lump on the vertex of the skull in breakers through MRI assessment. Magnetic resonance imaging in a 38-year old breakdancer revealed a cone-shaped deformity on the vertex of the skull with deep scalp thickening adjacent to the outer-table cortex. The loss of hair due to the friction of the head-spinning dancer with the floor led to the name "Headspin Hole". The lump and hair loss are a secondary injury resulting from chronic inflammation. In a study[525] interviewing 106 breakdancers, 60.4% suffered from overuse injuries of the scalp due to headspins. Hair loss was found in 31.1%, painless avulsions on the head in 23.6%, and inflammation of the scalp in 36.8%.

Head-spinning can lead to serious injuries in amateurs as well, who overestimate their own abilities or teachers/trainers, who lack knowledge and responsibility. A case report[526] described a 27-year-old in New York ending up with a spontaneous intracerebral hematoma (a hematoma in the brain) from head-spinning without sufficient experience and under influence of alcohol. Although such incidences might be the exception, injuries from breakdancing in recreationals (amateurs) occur frequently, as cited above.

---

[517] Cho CH, Song KS, Min BW, Lee SM, Chang HW, and DS Eum. *Musculoskeletal injuries in break-dancers*. Injury. 40(11). 1207-1211. 2009.

[518] Breinbauer HA, AnabalÃµn JL, Gutierrez D, Carcamo R, Olivares C, and Caro J. *Output Capabilities of Personal Music Players and Assessment of preferred Listening Levels of Test Subjects: Outlining Recommendations for preventing music-induced hearing loss.* Laryngoscope. 122(11). 2549-2556. 2012.

[519] Barlow C. Evidence of noise-induced hearing loss in young people studying popular music. Med Probl Perform Art. 26(2). 96-101. 2011.

[520] Müller T. *In weniger als drei Minuten mit Hip-Hop zum Hörschaden.* Springermedizin.de. 31.10.2012.

[521] Monselise A, Chan LJ, and J Shapiro. *Break dancing: a new risk factor for scarring hair loss.* J Cutan Med Surg. 15(3). 177.179. 2011.

[522] Byun HS, Cantos EL, and PP Patel. *Severe cervical injury due to break dancing.* A case report. Orthopedics. 9(4). 550-551. 1986.

[523] Kauther MD, Piotrowski M, Hussmann B, Lendemans S, Wedemeyer C, and Jaeger M. *Cervical biomechanics and neck pain of "head-spinning" breakdancers.* Int J Sports Med. 35(5). 412-417. 2014.

[524] Korczynski M, Nguyen A, Snyder T. *The "Cone-Head" sign: Magnetic resonance image findings of the "Headspin Hole", an overuse injury found in breakdancers.* Radiol Case Rep. 15(5). 489-491. 2020.

[525] Kauther MD, Wedemeyer C, Kauther KM, Weidle PA, Wegner A und von Knoch M. *Breakdancer's "Headspin Hole" – first description of a common overuse syndrome.* Sportverletz Sportschaden. 23(1). 52-53. 2009.

[526] Lee KC, and Clough C. *Intracerebral hemorrhage after break dancing.* N Engl J Med.323(9). 615-616. 1990.

Training habits and musculoskeletal injuries of the previous 12 months in 46 male and 16 female recreational breakers were documented in 2015[527] to evaluate the effects of training habits and sex on injury rates. 4.02 injuries/1000h without gender difference were noted, above all to the knees (23.4%) and wrist (15.3%). Females sustained more finger injuries and less shoulder injuries than males. In addition, of all the factors evaluated, only the amount of time spent dancing correlated with injury rate. No correlation was noted for warm-up, stretching, strength training, protective equipment, move types and supervision. The study concluded that injury preventive interventions should focus on protecting specific body parts and improving training quality and recovery.

[527] Joka T, Clarke ND, Cohen DD, Delextrat A. *Etiology of musculoskeletal injuries in amateur breakdancers*. J Sports Med Phys Fitness. 55(10). 1174-1183. 2015.

Since the focus of this book and series is not exclusively on the dancer, it is of utmost importance that teachers, trainers and choreographers of all styles study and implement dance medicine and science into their own practice for their own benefit. Given the enormous workload of their profession, it is rarely asked how trainers and dance teachers feel while they teach, rehearse and manage between 25 and sometimes more than 60-80 hours (!) per week, often still in advanced age. Hence, this series also wants to shine a huge spotlight on their wellbeing.

In 1997, Monica Dahlström compared physical effort in teachers and students during dance training as well as students when they were teaching themselves.[528] In 11 dance teachers (age: 39 ±7 years) and 11 dance students (age: 24 ±2 years) maximal heart rate (maximal cycle ergometer test) was measured before, and maximal oxygen uptake (VO_2max) was estimated from the heart rate during a submaximal test with correction for the individual maximal heart rate. During the training, heart rate, blood lactate concentration, and fluid loss were recorded. Effort during sessions was expressed as the percentage of the individual's maximal heart rate. VO_2max did not show to be different between the groups, and the average heart rate was 70% of the maximal heart rate in teachers, students and also when students taught. The study shows how high the physical effort of dance teaching is and that teachers, who most often are not actively dancing anymore, still have the same physical effort to manage as their dancers. Dance teachers **who teach amateurs, children, and adolescents** are **particularly stressed in their profession** because they permanently need to demonstrate and dance themselves, in contrast to teaching students in vocational training or professional dancers. It also has to be taken into account that teachers are usually (a lot) older than their protégés and have already had an active career, which may have left them with injuries or at least signs of wear and tear, but certainly with a high level of exhaustion in their new profession.

In 2012 and 2015, a team led by Eileen M. Wanke, whose work significantly contributes to dance medicine worldwide, further investigated the aspect. Wanke et al. confirmed the **high demands placed on dance teachers**, which are dance style-specific and depend on the students' age and level. The team further documented the fact that in many countries the profession of dance teachers is not protected by law, which means that legal regulations for their support but also for mandatory teacher education are often missing. In the study, mental and physical workload was investigated in 133 professional dance pedagogues via online questionnaire.[529] Although the workload depended on dance style, age of students and level of classes, the majority of dance teachers thought their level of physical and mental workload to be almost as high as that of their dancers, confirming Dahlström's study from 1997. More than 60% of the teachers also reported that they valued the influence of their occupation on their own health aspects such as self-realization (78.2%), the health of their musculoskeletal system (66.9%), and social aspects (61.7%). However, 58.6% perceived their workload as hazardous for their musculoskeletal system and 50.4% perceived financial insecurity as burden. A majority, 65.4% males and 63.9% females, expressed their interest in education on injury prevention and management of workload.

A study evaluating occupational accidents in 41 professional full-time employed dance teachers[530] was based on data from work accident reports, accident records as well as case records of the State Accident Insurance Berlin (UKB) of 17 males and 24 females (aged 35-59 years). 46.6% of the accidents were related to the teachers' profession, and the injury pattern was similar between sexes. 47.1% of the acute injuries happened to men and 54.2% to women. As with dancers, the lower extremities were a common injury location. Correlation between time of day and heightening injury risk was found. 67.9% of the accidents could be related to a clearly definable external cause, while 32.1% were multifactorial.

2020, a study[531] investigated the cardiovascular load in 21 dance teachers (teaching vocational and recreational dancers) with respect to the **essential role of aerobic**

[528] Dahlström M. *Physical Effort During Dance Training A Comparison Between Teachers and Students.* J Dance Med Sci. 1(4). 143-148. 1997.
[529] Wanke EM, Schmidt M, Leslie-Spinks J, Fischer A, and DA Groneberg. *Physical and mental workloads in professional dance teachers.* Med Probl Perform Art. 30(1). 54-60. 2015.
[530] Wanke EM, Quarrcoo D, Uibel S und DA Groneberg. *Work accidents in professional full-time dance teachers. Evaluation of dance pedagogic as an example [Arbeitsunfälle bei Bewegung vermittelnden, angestellten Lehrkräften].* Trauma Berufskrankh. 14. 46-50. 2011.
[531] Wanke EM, Schmidt M, Oremek G, and Groneberg DA. *Work related cardiovascular load in professional dance teachers - a pilot study.* J Occup Med Toxicol. 15. 7. 2020.

endurance for injury prevention. Heart rate was measured during ballet, jazz/modern and pre-school dance classes and maximum heart rate (HRmax) was assessed spiroergometically. Additionally, the team documented how the teachers themselves perceived their load directly after class. In the 18 female and 3 male teachers (age 48.2 ±9.3) the average heart rate ranged between 56.7% ±7.4% in ballet and 63.6% ±9.8% in pre-school classes as ratio of the individual HRmax, but no differences between styles with regard to minimum, medium and maximum teaching loads were found. The perceived load ratings of the teachers were 11.4 ±2.1 on the BORG scale, correlating with the mean and maximum cardiovascular loads for all dance units ($r = 0.376$, $p = 0.037$ and $r = 0.441$, $p = 0.013$) and for the mean loads in jazz/modern ($r = 0.558$, $p = 0.044$). Such loads do not train aerobic endurance and can thus not support injury prevention.

Published 2021, another study [532] investigated pain intensity in dance teachers retrospectively over 3 months employing an online survey. Of the 166 teachers participating, 143 reported to be in pain and were included in the analysis. Lower extremities, head and trunk showed the highest pain intensities. Functional impairment, biomechanical exposure and pain at rest were the three factors significantly related to pain intensity ($R2 = 0.22$, $F (3, 106) = 10.04$, $p < 0.001$) and can be explained by the demands of practice as a teacher.

Training and caring for dancers require physical, mental and emotional stamina, strength, and concentration and can come with physical and mental strain, especially when the teacher has to manage an extensive work load and probably suffers from pain and injury. Teaching mostly includes an enormous amount of preparation and administration, which is rarely to be seen from the outside. It must be added to the active and visible working hours mentioned above. In addition to the workload, it involves maintaining a healthy relationship with the dancers within a professional framework, requiring **social and emotional competence**.

Volume 2 presents the neuropsychological background of dancing and teaching and includes practical guidance, how aspects such as motivational climate, communication and feedback can enhance performance, health, and wellbeing in teachers and dancers.

Reflective[533] teachers try to keep dancers healthy while they guide them towards their individual goal, which consumes **high amounts of resources** in every respect: physically, psychologically, idealistically, and financially. Those **dance teachers** and **trainers have to invest cognitive, financial and time resources** into their own education and study, and spend a lot of time preparing for and reflecting on their classes. Trying to put dance medicine into practice every day and with all available means for their dancers' benefit needs high levels of **psychological, cognitive, and physical performance**. As such, dance teachers contribute to health and wellbeing in dancers of all levels and styles, ages and genders and thus support governments and medical administrations in their caring for their people.

Dance teachers deserve as much respect from society and politics as all other responsible jobs, for instance, they deserve legal anchoring of their profession. Dance medicine and science see and acknowledge the burden placed on teachers and trainers and try to protect them. Therefore, throughout this book series, recommendations and support for teachers/trainers/choreographers will be presented with respect to the various topics discussed, while a whole volume of the series is specifically dedicated to teachers' performance enhancement and health.

[532] Wanke E, Haenel J, Schoettker-Koeniger T, and Groneberg D. *Determinants of Pain Intensity in Physical Education Teachers Focusing on Dance Teachers: A Cross-Sectional Study.* Int J Environ Res Publ Health. 18(4). 2193. 2021.

[533] Andersson N. *Making space for assessment: dance teachers´ experience of learning and teaching prerequisites.* Res in Dance Educ. 19(3). 274-293. 2018.

The following chapters aim to give an overview on children and adolescents in dance. On the one hand, how children can benefit for life from dance classes. On the other hand, the chapters want to shine a special light on injury etiology (i.e., development) and related risk factors, which always are age-dependent, by presenting an overview of existing literature from dance medicine and science.

As this series wants to stress, it is essential for everybody (teachers, trainers, parents, dancers themselves, physicians, medical professionals...) to actively use publications provided by dance medicine and science to gain insight into how to work with (young) dancers, how to enhance performance and how to prevent injuries.

In case you might not have the experience how to find, read and use scholarly literature yet, do not hesitate to read into the chapters on how to deal with exactly these issues in part 4 at the end of this book. They provide the most basic first steps and are written for everyone who wants to get started. Dance medicine and science have everybody at heart who wants to (start to) engage!

If training stimuli are set physiological-individually focused, and continuously increased, the body begins to adapt to this gradually increasing loading. This is called training, the basis of which is the body's ability for biological adaptation, as discussed in the introductory chapters. This situation is even more delicate for children and adolescents than it already is for adult dancers. **Their tissues are not yet fully loadable and are busy daily with their own natural biological adaptation aside from any training, called growth**. That alone is high performance in the young. When training – perhaps even with the goal to become an elite dancer – wants to be focused on in the years of adolescence, **evidence-based structuring of loading and environment is paramount to avoid harming the dancer-to-be**.

Growth is individual and happens in phases interrupted by times of spurts, which demand a lot from the little body and mind. Such growth spurts, of which two are huge, are individual but recognizable for a dance medically well-trained teacher. In girls they commonly happen slightly earlier than in boys, especially the second growth spurt. Girls and boys have their **first growth spurt** after they started with elementary school, between the age of 5 and 8 years.

The **second growth spurt** marks the onset of **puberty**, and is found between 9 and 13 years in girls and 10 and 15 in boys. Puberty, as part of **adolescence** lasts between 3 and 5 years. Growth ends in girls around the age of 15 and the boys between 16 and 17. The spurts are marked by an increase of limb lengths, i.e., arms and legs grow faster than the spine, which is why the phases of spurts commonly are marked with slight clumsiness in children, where long extremities need to be coordinated with the slowly growing rest of the body. Growth spurts can come with increased appetite, because so much change needs energy, but also with increased fatigue.

It is critical that the teacher reacts to these moments and has enough knowledge to adjust training, and perhaps even more knowledge to replace certain aspects of physically very demanding training with more cognitive input, in order to bridge a young dancer over the most vulnerable times of growth spurt, how the upcoming chapters will show.

BENEFITING FROM CHILD DANCE CLASSES FOR LIFE

Dance, just like any sport, is vital for children and promotes healthy (motor) development. [534] Targeted training several times a week is recommended to best guide children in their physical, mental, and emotional development going through adolescence. Children who take part in three to four dance training sessions per week mostly meet the training requirements recommended for children to prevent civilization diseases such as obesity, related cardiovascular disorders, or osteoporosis. [535,536] Dance is a sport which serves all fitness aspects, especially

[534] Burkhardt J, and Brennan C. *The effects of recreational dance interventions on the health and well-being of children and young people: A systematic review.* Arts & Health. 4. 1-14. 2012.

[535] Sallis JF, and Patrick K. *Physical activity guidelines for adolescents.* Paediatric Exercise Science. Nr 6. 302-314. 1994.

[536] Boreham CAG, and Twisk J. *Physical activity, sports participation, and risk factors in adolescents.* Medicine and Science in Sports and Exercise. 29(6). 788-793. 1997.

if it is taught in a targeted, evidence-based manner, e.g., includes targeted strength and aerobic endurance training.[537, 538] Children who attend continuous, professional dance training playfully work on endurance, strength, flexibility, coordination, postural control, agility and power. Such training is beneficial for their everyday life[539], because it supports injury prevention and promotes overall cognitive and motor development. These children are ahead of their sedentary peers, both in sports and cognitive abilities.[540,541]

Stamina, strength, or flexibility cannot be accumulated in childhood and are not naturally transferred or retained through adolescence to adulthood when somebody stops dancing during or after adolescence. However, (evidence-based) dancing in young years nonetheless lays a lot of groundwork for a healthy adult life. **High quality motivation** once perceived within dance classes as a child might echo throughout adulthood and encourage a person to keep on dancing for recreational pleasure – or has even made somebody become a professional dancer. However, **advanced sensorimotor abilities**, once acquired, help when reaching an advanced age and can prevent injuries. Osteoporosis, which mostly affects women after menopause, depends partially on exercise and dietary habits in childhood and adolescence.[542] **Bone mineral density** (BMD) peaks between the ages of 20 and 30, and the years of puberty with their hormonal changes are the most significant contribution to the **peak bone mass**, the highest individually achievable value of bone mineral density.[543] The higher the quality-amount-ratio of exercise and nutrition adolescents have enjoyed during childhood, the higher their bone mineral density will be by the time it reaches its peak. Thus, dance and targeted exercise in childhood can be an important factor to prevent diseases such as osteoporosis.

The **dance teacher or trainer, dance studios and schools hence contribute extensively to health and wellbeing in the general population** by providing dance classes and courses. The higher their knowledge and dedication to dance medicine and science, the more they all provide environments in which children and adolescents can grow up with an overall support of their cognitive, mental, psychological, physical and motor development. More and more dancers and teachers become aware of the benefits, dance medicine and science can offer and consciously design dance classes as such that they specifically target essential aspects in the lives of children and adolescents, from which they benefit for a lifetime.

Summarizing, continuous and targeted dance training promotes cognitive and motor development from childhood to older adulthood, providing training of motor learning skills, the development of imagination, creativity, spatial perception, and psychological aspects such as emotional and social intelligence, self-esteem, self-confidence, and a healthy form of discipline (better called motivation).[544]

Volume 2 discusses underlying neuropsychological aspects of (motor) development in details, while Volume 3 is dedicated to biomechanical aspects and science of training, thus targeting the physical aspects of dance.

---

537 Hoekstra T, Boreham CA, Murray LJ, and JW Twisk. *Associations between aerobic and muscular fitness and cardiovascular disease risk: the Northern Ireland young hearts study.* J Physical Act Health. 5(6). 815-29. 2008.

538 Padfield JA, Eisenman PA, Luetkemeier MJ, and SS Fitt. *Physiological profiles of performing and recreational early adolescent female dancers.* Paediatric Exercise Science. 5. 51-59. 1993.

539 Gardner S, Komesaroff P, and Fensham R. *Dancing beyond exercise: Young people's experiences in dance classes.* J Youth Studies. 11. 701-709. 2008.

540 Shephard RJ. *Physical activity and child health.* Sports Med. 1. 205-233. 1984.

541 Kulinna PH, Stylianou M, Dyson B, Banville D, Dryden C, Colby R. *The Effect of an Authentic Acute Physical Education Session of Dance on Elementary Students' Selective Attention.* Biomed Res Int. 8790283. 2018.

542 Janz KF, Thomas DQ, Ford MA, and SM Williams. *Top 10 research questions related to physical activity and bone health in children and adolescents.* Research quarterly for exercise and sport. 86(1):5-12. 2015.

543 Khan KM, Bennell KL, and Crichton KJ. *Childhood ballet classes, not adult ballet training predicts adult hipbone density in former dancers.* Medicine and Science in Sports and Exercise. No.29. 1997.

544 Hecht, Thom. Emotionally Intelligent Ballet Training: Facilitating Emotional Intelligence in Vocational Dance Training. Saarbrücken. Verlag Dr Müller. 2007.

Several studies have described injury risk, characteristics, incidences, prevalence and risk factors among young dancers and some will be presented in the following to provide a scholarly background.

Summarizing, the **most important facts** are:[545,546,547,548]

- Adolescent dancers are confronted with high injury risk, incidence, prevalence, and pain
- Vocational as well as recreational[549]
- **Injury incidence** has been reported between 0.62 and 5.6 injuries per 1000 hours of dancing
- And increases with age[550] with special vulnerability in phases of growth spurts
- **Injury risk** was high, and is considered higher than in other youth sports, e.g., 76% in vocational ballet[551]
- But advanced levels of experience and skill level might decrease risk[552]
- Early onset of menarche decreased injury risk[553] which is why it is so important to prevent female athletic triad
- Early **identification**[554] of injury etiology, injury risk, risk factors and their elimination are stressed

Identified **risk factors** are different for acute and overuse injuries:

- As in adults, prevention of **acute injuries** is gender-, dance-style-, and age-dependent
- External risk factors are the environment (floors, stairs, props, sets, shoes, schedules...)
- As well as partners, pressure from teachers, peers, parents or media
- **Acute injuries** in adolescents are often multifactorial, i.e., not only dependent on external factors, which is why many risk factors commonly related to **overuse injuries** can also play a role in the etiology of acute injuries:
- Lack of evidence-based warm-up, such as neuromuscular warm-up
- Poor scheduling
- Fatigue
- Jump training was identified as the motor action most responsible for the gradual etiology of overuse injury[555]
- Overtraining, i.e., too high a workload, too sudden an increase of loading, and early specialization
- Tradition, "dancer's identity", and lack of knowledge in dancers, teachers and trainers
- Ill-handling of injury pain as warning system
- Confusing injury and performance pain leading to dancers dancing through pain
- Faulty dance technique and biomechanics
- Compensating for or forcing beyond anatomical limitations
- Hyper-flexibility in combination with a lack of sufficiently stabilizing strength
- Lower back pain
- Repetitive or previous injuries[556]
- Poor coping skills with regard to psychological stress
- Perfectionistic tendencies, ambition, obsession (in dancers as well as teachers or parents)

[545] Gamboa JM, Roberts LA, Maring J, and Fergus A. *Injury patterns in elite preprofessional ballet dancers and the utility of screening programs to identify risk characteristics.* J Orthop Sports Phys Ther. 38(3). 126-36. 2008.
[546] Luke A, Kinney S, D'Hemecourt P, Baum J, Owen M, and Micheli L. *Determinants of Injuries in Young Dancers.* Med Probl Perform Art. 17. 105-112. 2002
[547] Caine D, Goodwin BJ, Caine CG, and Bergeron G. *Epidemiological Review of Injury in Pre-Professional Ballet Dancers.* J Dance Med Sci. 19(4). 140-148. 2015.
[548] Wanke EM, Mill H, and Groneberg DA. *Ballet as high-performance activity: health risks exemplified by acute injuries in dance students [Ballett als Leistungssport – Gesundheitliche Gefährdungen am Beispiel akuter Verletzungen bei Tanzschülern].* Sportverletzung Sportschaden. 26(3). 164-170. 2012.
[549] Lampe J, Groneberg DA, Ohlendorf D, and Wanke EM. *Pain in female dancers and dance teachers: Perception, assessment, and related behavior.* Scand J Med Sci Sports. 29(4). 623-632. 2019.
[550] Leanderson C, Leanderson J, Wykman A, Strender LE, Johansson SE, and Sundquist K. *Musculoskeletal injuries in young ballet dancers.* Knee Surg Sports Traumatol Arthrosc. 19(9). 1531-1535. 2011.
[551] Ekegren CL, Quested R, and Brodrick A. *Injuries in pre-professional ballet dancers: Incidence, characteristics and consequences.* J Sci Med Sport. 17(3). 271-275. 2014.
[552] Caine D, Bergeron G, Goodwin BJ, Thomas J, Caine CG, Steinfeld S, Dyck K, and André S. *A Survey of Injuries Affecting Pre-Professional Ballet Dancers.* J Dance Med Sci. 20(3). 115-126. 2016.
[553] Steinberg N, Siev-Ner I, Peleg S, Dar G, Masharawi Y, Zeev A, and Hershkovitz I. *Extrinsic and intrinsic risk factors associated with injuries in young dancers aged 8-16 years.* J Sports Sci. 30(5). 485-495. 2012.
[554] Garrick JG. *Early identification of musculoskeletal complaints and injuries among female ballet students.* J Dance Med Sci. 3(2). 80-83. 1999.
[555] Moita JP, Gomes A, Xarez L, and Coelho C. *The role of prediagnostic data in injury epidemiology in preprofessional dancers.* Scand J Med Sci Sports. 29(4). 606-614. 2019.
[556] Kenny SJ, Whittaker JL, and Emery CA. *Risk factors for musculoskeletal injury in preprofessional dancers: a systematic review.* Br J Sports Med. 50(16). 997-1003. 2016.

The many risk factors are mirrored in a very often **high number of different diagnoses** in children[557,558]:

- Ankle/foot, lower back and the knee joint are the most affected anatomical regions
  - Important is that the most frequently affected body areas change depending on the age of the dancer[559]
  - Although injury risk and rates are high in all stages of puberty
  - With children in **earlier puberty** the back, foot, ankle and knee are specifically at risk and injuries are more bone related
  - With children in **middle and late puberty** upper extremity, spine, hip, knee, foot and ankle face increased risk, and injuries are bone- as well as soft tissue related
- The majority of injuries are overuse in nature

Dance injuries in childhood and adolescence, with the critical age being found primarily in early to middle puberty, are based on the fact that the adolescent body is more vulnerable than in other stages of growth.[560] However, this is also the time where many dancers face an increase of training frequency and intensity, in amateur and professional training, and the demands placed on young dancers are suddenly much higher than they were in childhood.[561,562] This sudden **increase in training intensity, frequency and duration** can negatively affect the biomechanical changes that occur during the second growth spurt of the young student.

Children are known to be "flexible" in all respects. While flexibility/stretching must not be overstressed in children, a playful approach to dance and training can always expect to meet an open mind in children as well as a softer, adjustable body with respect to its tissues compared to adolescents. However, when children reach puberty, the **second growth spurt** leads to significant changes. Limbs start growing in length, leading to a **discrepancy between growth of bones** (e.g., tibia, fibula and femur) and **adjustability of muscle-tendon-units**: bones are growing faster than muscles and tendons can adjust to, which is why young dancers in early puberty become stiffer.[563] Many find their already achieved levels of dance technique suddenly unreliable. Shock absorption is reduced, postural control and equilibrium are impaired, and dysbalances among growing tissue result in increased **injury risk**. Aside from the psychological impact (confusion, anxiety, frustration, loss of motivation) the onset of puberty can be related to a loss of flexibility, high levels of fatigue, growth pain (aching muscles due to the faster growing bones), loss of balance and strength, and hence, temporary loss of dance technique.

While male dancers experience sudden increase in strength and power due to the impact of testosterone, girls do not experience such impressive changes in physical abilities but may have their efforts to accept changes in appearance and body shape, the onset of the menarche and possible related pain, especially in professional dance settings with high training loads. All these changes, additionally to joint stiffness, fatigue and possible inability to concentrate, lead to a **temporary loss of neuromuscular and thus motor control**, which makes young dancers specifically prone to injury. Related performance plateaus or even setbacks can be a significant burden for young dancers. Depending on the **motivational climate** the young dancer is embedded in and which is highly related to dance medical knowledge of teachers and trainers[564,565], young dancers can find themselves supported by a caring teacher or pushed relentlessly through such "weak moments" – which is one of the foundations for overuse injuries in general but also acute injuries related to age, gender and dance-style.

With respect to teacher-responsibility, one also has to keep in mind that young dancers want to work and are eager to follow a teacher/trainer, who pushes through phases of growth spurt. It is up to the teacher and trainer to recognize such phases and to deal with the situation as such that the growing dancer is protected and guided away from possible perfectionistic concerns leading to

---

[557] Steinberg N, Siev-Ner I, Peleg S, Dar G, Masharawi Y, Zeev A, and Hershkovitz I. *Injuries in female dancers aged 8 to 16 years.* J Athl Train. 48(1). 118-123. 2013.

[558] Yin AX, Sugimoto D, Martin DJ, and Stracciolini A. *Pediatric Dance Injuries: A Cross-Sectional Epidemiological Study.* PM R. 8(4). 348-355. 2016.

[559] Stracciolini A, Yin AX, and Sugimoto D. *Etiology and body area of injuries in young female dancers presenting to sports medicine clinic: A comparison by age group.* Phys Sportsmed. 43(4). 342-347. 2015.

[560] Caine D, Goodwin BJ, Caine CG, and Bergeron G. *Epidemiological Review of Injury in Pre-Professional Ballet Dancers.* J Dance Med Sci. 19(4). 140-148. 2015.

[561] Albert H. *Dance-related injuries in young people on the increase.* J Phys Act Health. 10. 143-150. 2013.

[562] Luke AC, Kinney SA, D'Hemecourt PA, Baum J, Owen M, and LJ Micheli. *Determinants of injuries in young dancers.* Med Probl Perform Art.17(3). 105-112. 2002.

[563] Storm JM, Wolman R, Bakker EWP, and Wyon MA. *The Relationship Between Range of Motion and Injuries in Adolescent Dancers and Sportspersons: A Systematic Review.* Front Psychol. 9:287. 2018.

[564] Mitchell SB, Haase AM, Malina RM, and Cumming SP. *The role of puberty in the making and breaking of young ballet dancers: Perspectives of dance teachers.* J of adolescence. 47. 81-89. 2016.

[565] Garcia-Dantas A, Alonso DA, Sánchez-Miguel PA, and Del Río Sánchez C. *Factors Dancers Associate with their Body Dissatisfaction.* Body Image. 25. 40-47. 2018.

(the will to engage in) intensified training towards evidence-based science of training. These times are a fine line to tread like walking on a tightrope. Many respond that generally children's injury regeneration is rapid. However, this must not be used as a carte blanche to simply take the chances.[566,567,568]

A descriptive epidemiological study[569] on the incidence of musculoskeletal injuries in pre-professional dancers was published in 2017 based on records of the University of North Carolina School of the Arts (UNCSA) from Fall 2009 to Spring 2015. An injury was defined as any event that made a dancer report at the UNCSA Student Health Services and caused the dancer to modify or curtail dance activity for at least 1 day. 1014 injuries were sustained by 480 dancers, mostly to the lower extremities and the majority a **result of overuse**. As in studies by Wanke et al., among others, and discussed in the previous chapters, this study stressed the importance that **prevention of acute injury needs to be sex- and dance style-specific**. No differences were observed in overuse injury rates by sex or style, suggesting that **overuse prevention strategies are generally essential**.

Approximately 113,084 children and adolescents between 3(!) to 19 years were treated in US emergency departments for dance-related injuries between 1991-2007, reported in a retrospective analysis based on data from the National Electronic Injury Surveillance System. [570] Ballet, jazz, tap, and modern accounted for 55.0% of those injuries. Adolescents between 15-19 years of age constituted 40.4% of cases, with the majority of injuries (58.1%) occurring to the lower extremities. With 52.4%, sprains or strains were the most common injury while falls (as in "accident", not modern dance technique) were the most common mechanism of injury (44.8%). The study showed that dance-related injuries have distinct injury patterns and mechanisms which **differ by dance-styles and age**, with **injury risk increasing in adolescence**.

A similar analysis[571] built upon 806 dancers, 10-18 years of age, who answered a survey, documenting injuries of young dancers attending Centres for Advanced Training (CAT), UK. 347 of the 806 dancers reported an injury. Results showed that the total hours of practice per week increased significantly with increasing age. Injury incidence/1000 hours within the age group of **early puberty (11-12 years)** were significantly **higher compared to dancers in middle and later puberty (13-18)**, corresponding with the **second growth spurt** of children in early puberty. However, **adolescent dancers per se are exposed to high injury risk**, confirming reports mentioned above. Foot and ankle, and lower extremities in general, were most commonly affected, and muscle injuries were the most common type of injury. Total months in CAT training (OR=1.044, 95% CI 1.014-1.075) and hours of practice per week (OR=1.282, 95% CI 1.068-1.539) were found to be significantly associated with injuries.

In 2012, Wanke et al. stressed the importance of relinquishing too early specialization in vocational ballet in favor of evidence-based and broadly-oriented training for young dancers.[572] Her team examined 1000 cases of acute dance injuries in a study with vocational students. The picture painted by the study is intended not only to highlight **the alarmingly high acute injury rate among children and adolescents** but also to serve as a guide on how prevention of acute injuries can be targeted, namely (again) gender-specific and cause-focused. The report could show that **one out of three young ballet dancers were acutely injured at least once a year**, while one out of ten accidents were classified as severe with age- and gender-dependent differences as well as time-period-related accumulations. Injury rates were already comparable to professional dancers' in those children. However, children's bodies are not comparable to adults, and should especially not suffer from so many injuries. The lower extremity was the most frequently injured localization (67.8%; male 57.6%; female 73.0%) and the upper extremity with 15.6% (male 21.7%, female 11.9%), the spine with 7.4% (male 9.4%, female 6.8%), and head and trunk with 9.1% (male 11.3%, female 8.1%) also were frequently affected by injuries. Ligaments and joints were the most frequently acutely injured body structures (69.5%) and contusions (23%), distorsions (33%) and muscular strains (20%) the most frequent types of injuries. Upper ankle injuries were more common in

---

[566] Sharma P, Luscombe KL, and N Maffulli. *Sports injuries in children.* Trauma. 5. 245-259. 2003.

[567] Maffulli N, and AD Baxter-Jones. *Common skeletal injuries in young athletes.* Sports Med. 19. 137-149. 1995.

[568] Rang, Mercer. Children's Fractures. Philadelphia. JB Lippincott Publisher. 1983.

[569] Yau RK, Golightly YM, Richardson DB, Runfola CD, Waller AE, and Marshall SW. *Potential Predictors of Injury Among Pre-Professional Ballet and Contemporary Dancers.* J Dance Med Sci. 21(2). 53-63. 2017.

[570] Roberts KJ, Nelson NG, and McKenzie L. *Dance-related injuries in children and adolescents treated in US emergency departments in 1991-2007.* J Phys Act Health. 10(2). 143-150. 2013.

[571] Steinberg N, Aujla I, Zeev A, Redding E. *Injuries among talented young dancers: findings from the U.K. Centres for Advanced Training.* Int J Sports Med. 35(3). 238-244. 2014.

[572] Wanke EM, Mill H, and Groneberg DA. *Ballet as high-performance activity: health risks exemplified by acute injuries in dance students [Ballett als Leistungssport – Gesundheitliche Gefährdungen am Beispiel akuter Verletzungen bei Tanzschülern].* Sportverletzung Sportschaden. 26(3). 164-170. 2012.

female ballet students (41%) than in their male counterparts (30.6%). The situation is similar for the knee joint. Not least, lifts more often cause forearm and wrist injuries in male students (male 15.4% and female 8.1%), head and neck injuries (male 9.4%, female 6.2%), spine (9.4%) and shoulder injuries (male 6.3%, female 3.8%). Interestingly enough, the study could show that **acute injuries** in young are often **multifactorial** (70%; females71.6 %; males 64.5%) instead of based on extrinsic factors only (30%; females 28.4%; males 35.5%), as is the case in many adult dancers, indicating the complexity of injury etiology and risk in children and adolescents. "Corridors and stairs" with 8.8% and 13.7% in females and males, respectively, followed by "human being" (partner, classmate, or dancers themselves) with 7.5% and 13.2% and the "dance floor" with 7.5% and 5.7% were the main **external factors for accidents. Only half of the students stopped the training immediately after an accident, while the others continued to train with the injury**. Practice consistently paints similar pictures in numerous vocational training schools, showing how many teachers/institutions ignore or do not have sufficient knowledge on dance medicine and science (yet).[573,574]

Ekegren et al., 2014[575], presented a similar picture in a prospective epidemiological study on 266 vocational ballet dancers from three elite pre-professional ballet schools, who were followed prospectively over one school year. In the 112 male and 154 female young dancers, aged 15-19 years, injury incidence was 1.42 injuries per dancer and **injury risk 76%** to sustain an injury within the 1-year period. The rate of injury was 1.38/1000 hours of dance and 1.87/1000 dance exposures (i.e., not necessarily 60 minutes per exposure). **Joints were the most commonly injured structures and the ankle was the most commonly injured anatomical location. The majority of injuries were overuse injuries**, and time-loss was the highest for bone related injuries such as stress fractures as well as injuries to the knee. The study also noted that injury risk and rate increased through dancers' three years of education, and while injury rates were similar to those of other child athletes, ballet dancers had a higher injury risk, attributable to the high training load.

Picking a 5% random probability sample of young patients of a sports medical clinic in a pediatric (i.e., children's) medical center, a cross-sectional study [576] evaluated characteristics of dance injuries from January 1st, 2000 until December 31st, 2009. The 171 female and 10 male dancers were 14.8 ±2.0 years old and 222 injuries were diagnosed in this total of 181 children. **46 different diagnoses were recorded**, most of them to the lower extremities and led by tendopathies, patellofemoral pain syndromes, apophysitis, ankle impingement syndrome, and hip labral tears. Classification by injury type showed that **joints were the body structures most likely to be injured, followed by soft tissues, bones, ligaments and cartilages, and growth plates**. The most frequent joint injury was patellofemoral pain syndrome. The most frequent soft tissue injury was tendonitis or other tendinopathies. The most common skeletal injury was lumbar spondylolysis, a stress fracture of the pars interarticularis (the articulating parts of a vertebra, which form a joint with the vertebrae above or below). The most common physeal injury was apophysitis, a painful inflammation of the (area of the) growth plate, often where a muscle or tendon attaches. Many dancers needed surgery, and were mainly further treated with physical therapy. The study concluded that **child dancers significantly suffer from partly rare injuries, often with long-term consequences**.

The same team of authors presented an essential analysis of injuries by age group[577], stressing **the importance to differentiate between early, middle and late stages of puberty in primary and secondary injury prevention** measures: The females were stratified (i.e., grouped) by age, resulting in two groups of < 12-year-old and ≥ 12-year-old dancers. Anatomical **location, injury type and etiology were analyzed age-specifically**. Throughout puberty, injuries to the ankle/foot slightly declined, while soft tissue injuries as well as injuries to thigh, hip, spine and upper extremities increased. For both groups, the majority of injuries was due to overuse (< 12 years: 86.7%; ≥ 12 years old: 82.1%, Fisher's Exact: p = 1.00). For an overview of the study's results:

---

[573] Jenkins JB, Wyon M, and Nevill A. *Can turnout measurements be used to predict physiotherapist-reported injury rates in dancers?* Med Probl Perform Art. 28(4). 230-235. 2013.

[574] Negus V, Hopper D, and Briffa NK. *Associations between turnout and lower extremity injuries in classical ballet dancers.* J Orthop Sports Phys Ther. 35(5). 307-318. 2005.

[575] Ekegren CL, Quested R, and Brodrick A. *Injuries in pre-professional ballet dancers: Incidence, characteristics and consequences.* J Sci Med Sport. 17(3). 271-275. 2014.

[576] Yin AX, Sugimoto D, Martin DJ, and Stracciolini A. *Pediatric Dance Injuries: A Cross-Sectional Epidemiological Study.* PM R. 8(4). 348-355. 2016.

[577] Stracciolini A, Yin AX, and Sugimoto D. *Etiology and body area of injuries in young female dancers presenting to sports medicine clinic: A comparison by age group.* Phys Sportsmed. 43(4). 342-347. 2015.

The younger age group was

- mainly affected by injuries to the foot/ankle, lower leg, and knee (93.3%)
- and injuries to the thigh and hip, spine, and upper extremity (6.7%) were less frequent
- 2/3 of their injuries were bony

The older group, in contrary,

- had a larger injury proportion to the thigh, hip, spine and upper extremities (32.7%) Fisher's Exact: $p = 0.04$
- while ankle/foot, lower leg, and knee was highly affected as well (67.3%)
- their injuries were half bony (51.3%) and half soft tissue related (48.7%), Fisher's Exact: $p = 0.29$

Although many studies are done with vocational dancers, injuries also affect amateurs/recreational pediatric dancers. Steinberg et al., 2013[578], analyzed injuries of 569 female dancers ranging between 8 and 16 years of age. **61 types of current injuries** were classified into 4 major categories, namely back injuries, injuries to the knee, foot and ankle tendinopathies, and other injuries. 42.4% of the dancers had sustained at least one previous injury, **stressing the problem of repetitive injuries already in the young**. The knee was most likely to be affected (40.4%), followed by other injuries (23.4%). Frequency of back injuries and tendopathies decreased with age, while knee injuries increased. Scoliosis, age, and joint range of motion (hip external rotation ability) were identified as predictive variables for back injuries. Injury types were associated with angles of ankle plantar flexion, hip external rotation, hip abduction, and knee flexion (see below). The study warned of overload through stretching/flexibility training and exercises stressing the back, especially in children under 10 years of age, concurrent with similar research. The team further specialized [579] that some factors were positively and negatively associated with injuries:

- **Range of motion**: for instance, dancers with hyper-hip-abduction-ability were more prone to foot or ankle tendinopathies than dancers with hypo-range-of-motion.
- Dancers with **anatomical anomalies** such as scoliosis showed a higher rate of injuries than non-scoliotic dancers.
- **Erroneous dance technique** such as hyperpronation of the foot or hyperlordosis in turnout was correlating with injuries.
- **Dance discipline and specialization**, such as too early start with pointe work in classical ballet was associated with more injuries.
- And **an early onset of menarche decreased the risk** for an injury.

The very common patella-femoral-pain-syndrome in young dancers[580] was linked to hyper-hip-abduction (OR = 0.906) and lower back and hamstring flexibility (OR = 3.542) in 10 to 11-year-olds. In dancers 12-14 years of age, hyper-ankle-dorsiflexion (OR = 0.888), hind foot-varum (OR = 0.260), and mobility of patella (OR = 2.666) showed to be related. Scoliosis (OR = 5.209), limited ankle plantar-flexion (OR = 1.060), and limited hip internal rotation (OR = 1.063) was linked to injuries in late puberty with dancers ranging from 15 to 16 years of age. **Such studies show the importance of content knowledge in teachers and trainers, who can incorporate related information into training and planning of classes with relation to their different age groups.**

Conclusive with cited other reports of recreational dancers, advancing age and increasing dance load and exposure increased injury prevalence[581]: 1 out of 10 girls in the 8-year cohort of female dancers (1.05 injuries/1000 hours) compared to 1 out of 3 girls in the 14-year cohort (1.25 injuries/1000 hours) was affected by injuries. The study concluded that young, non-professional dancers are at high risk for injury, especially dancers who already had previous injury were at higher risk for re-injury.

Some further aspects are important to mention: Too high a focus on flexibility training, especially when paired with low levels of muscular ability to stabilize joint range of motion, and the habit of teachers and schools to select those young dancers with (tendencies for) trained or genetic hypermobility has shown to be related to injury risk. [582] In this respect it is especially important for teachers/trainers as well as dancers to understand, that

[578] Steinberg N, Siev-Ner I, Peleg S, Dar G, Masharawi Y, Zeev A, and Hershkovitz I. *Injuries in female dancers aged 8 to 16 years.* J Athl Train. 48(1). 118-123. 2013.

[579] Steinberg N, Siev-Ner I, Peleg S, Dar G, Masharawi Y, Zeev A, and Hershkovitz I. *Extrinsic and intrinsic risk factors associated with injuries in young dancers aged 8-16 years.* J Sports Sci. 30(5). 485-495. 2012.

[580] Steinberg N, Tenenbaum S, Hershkovitz I, Zeev A, and Siev-Ner I. *Lower extremity and spine characteristics in young dancers with and without patellofemoral pain.* Res Sports Med. 25(2). 166-180. 2017.

[581] Steinberg N, Siev-Ner I, Peleg S, Dar G, Masharawi Y, Zeev A, and Hershkovitz I. *Injury patterns in young, non-professional dancers.* J Sports Sci. 29(1). 47-54. 2011.

[582] McCormack M, Briggs J, Hakim A, and Grahame R. *Joint laxity and the benign joint hypermobility syndrome in student and professional ballet dancers.* J Rheumatol. 31(1). 173-178. 2004.

joint range of motion is first and foremost determined by **passive anatomical predispositions**, i.e., the way individual shapes of bones genetically define a dancers joint range of motion. Such individuality must neither be targeted by the effort to change or overcome individual limitations through various exercises considered to be stretching,[583] nor "solved" by compensating for limited joint ROM in one joint by forcing other joints in order to achieve ideal dance technique.[584]

Volume 3 provides extensive information on stretching for dancers as well as warm-up and further related aspects.

Altered lumbopelvic control was associated with injuries and pain, such as lower back pain, which is very common in dancers.[585] Insufficient neuromuscular control of the lower spine-pelvis region is related to flexibility and the way dancers train flexibility, as well as fitness deficits, especially core stability, and dance technique (such as hyperlordosis as compensation strategy in turnout). Supporting previously mentioned aspects, it is vital that young dancers already learn and **understand the importance of correct dance technique and targeted fitness training**. As such, they depend on evidence-based guidance and teaching skills of their trainers and teachers. Essential within this background, scoliosis has also been identified to increase injury risk in dancers[586,587] and is an aspect in lumbopelvic control and core stabilization, which is not always influenceable by training.

Furthermore, Kenny et al. [588] stressed the **importance of injury definition** in research as well as documentation and management of injuries in schools, companies as well as clinical settings. **Time-loss and medical attention-definitions have shown to severely underestimate burden in adolescent, pre-professional dancers** (as they do with adult dancers and all other athletes[589,590]). The team investigated 85 full-time preprofessional ballet dancers (of which 77 female) with a median age of 15 years (range 11-19 years), and 60 contemporary dancers (of which 58 female) with a median age of 19 years (range 17-30 years), using a weekly questionnaire based on 3 different injury definitions: 1. Time-loss, defined as inability to complete one or more classes/rehearsals/performances for one or more days beyond onset. 2. Medical attention, indicating that professional help was needed. 3. Any complaint definition, allowing dancers to report complaints, which were not regarded as injury yet, but which could already have the potential to become an overuse injury if not reported and managed. Injury prevalence ranged between 9.4% for time-loss injuries and 82.4% for "any complaint". Injury incidence rates showed to be between 0.1 for time-loss and 4.9 for "any complaint" per 1000 hours. Time-loss and medical-attention injury definitions underestimate the injury burden in (preprofessional) dancers and many complaints which already constitute the gradual onset of overuse injuries will be overlooked.

Another important aspect highlighted in dance medicine and science and a recurrent topic of this series is **content knowledge in teachers/trainers but also physicians and medical personnel**. [591,592,593] As described, the majority of injuries in (young) dancers is overuse in nature, clearly showing a related **lack of teachers' knowledge in science of training**, i.e., how training has to be planned as such that overtraining and overuse can be prevented. Moreover, the status of erroneous dance technique as injury risk factor also mirrors severe deficits in knowledge on dance technique and methods of teaching in many teachers and trainers. That further leads to the misguided education in the young to disregard anatomical limitations as well as pain (and intuition) for the sake of

---

583 Steinberg N, Hershkovitz I, Peleg S, Dar G, Masharawi Y, Heim M, and Siev-Ner I. *Range of joint movement in female dancers and nondancers aged 8 to 16 years: anatomical and clinical implications.* Am J Sports Med. 34(5). 814-823. 2006.

584 Kaufmann JE, Nelissen RGHH, Exner-Grave E, and Gademan MGJ. *Does forced or compensated turnout lead to musculoskeletal injuries in dancers? A systematic review on the complexity of causes.* J Biomech. 114. 110084. 2021.

585 Roussel NA, Nijs J, Mottram S, Van Moorsel A, Truijen S, and Stassijns G. *Altered lumbopelvic movement control but not generalized joint hypermobility is associated with increased injury in dancers. A prospective study.* Man Ther. 14(6). 630-635. 2009.

586 Steinberg N, Siev-Ner I, Peleg S, Dar G, Masharawi Y, Zeev A, and Hershkovitz I. *Extrinsic and intrinsic risk factors associated with injuries in young dancers aged 8-16 years.* J Sports Sci. 30(5). 485-495. 2012.

587 Steinberg N, Tenenbaum S, Hershkovitz I, Zeev A, and Siev-Ner I. *Lower extremity and spine characteristics in young dancers with and without patellofemoral pain.* Res Sports Med. 25(2). 166-180. 2017.

588 Kenny SJ, Palacios-Derflingher L, Whittaker JL, and Emery CA. *The Influence of Injury Definition on Injury Burden in Preprofessional Ballet and Contemporary Dancers.* J Orthop Sports Phys Ther. 48(3). 185-193. 2018.

589 Bahr R. *No injuries, but plenty of pain? On the methodology for recording overuse symptoms in sports.* Br J Sports Med. 43(13). 966-972. 2009.

590 Clarsen B, Myklebust G, and Bahr R. *Development and validation of a new method for the registration of overuse injuries in sports injury epidemiology: the Oslo Sports Trauma Research Centre (OSTRC) overuse injury questionnaire.* Br J Sports Med. 47(8). 495-502. 2013.

591 Khan K, Brown J, Way S, Vass N, Crichton K, Alexander R, Baxter A, Butler M, and Wark J. *Overuse injuries in classical ballet.* Sports Med. 19(5). 341-357. 1995.

592 Rietveld B, and van de Wiel A. *Dance, art and top performance sport with specific injuries [Article in Dutch: Dans: kunst en topsport met specifieke letsels].* Ned Tijdschr Geneeskd. 155(51). A4283. 2011.

593 Wilson JC, Quinn BJ, Stratton CW, Southwick H, and MacDonald JP. *Athletes Doing Arabesques: Important Considerations in the Care of Young Dancers.* Curr Sports Med Rep. 14(6). 448-454. 2015.

superficial dance technical achievements. With respect to medical personnel, specific knowledge in **medical professionals** is needed because dancers' injuries have shown to be dance-style and -life specific, and professionals need to understand both, when they want to help (young) dancers with injury management but also prevention. Overuse injuries, for instance, develop in direct relation to a specific dance technique, and must therefore also be evaluated and treated in precisely this context, which requires a lot of knowledge about dance medicine from the attending physician or therapist. Not least, for this reason, dance medicine worldwide is always striving to sensitize healthcare professionals to dance concerns and train them for dance-medical, style-specific treatment and rehabilitation. If the injury is treated outside of the context of dance medicine and without direct relation to the dancer and their dance class, functional limitations and irreversible damage can be left behind. Just as adult dancers' rehabilitation requires precise dance-specific procedures after the treatment of an injury, so does the treatment of a child dancer's injury.[594,595,596,597]

Moreover, it is important that medical professionals are aware that dance is a high performance artistic-activity and a profession/study or at least highly beloved leisure activity. Thus, the advice to just stop dancing in case of injury is detrimental to dancers' health and trust in a physician. Reactions like that have recurrently shown a lack of knowledge of dance medicine and science in medical personnel. Both, teachers/trainers and medical personnel are essential for overall health and wellbeing of dancers of all ages, genders and styles.

Summarizing, primary [598] as well as secondary **injury prevention** has to start already in the young, including

- profound teacher/trainer education and knowledge
- dance specific knowledge in proactive clinicians and medical professionals
- cooperation between teachers/trainers and medical personnel with dedication from both sides
- also with regard to secondary injury prevention (diagnostics, treatment, rehabilitation etc.)
- identification and elimination of risk factors
- recurrent dancer screenings
- targeted training (dance technique, fitness, nutrition etc.) in dancers
- and dance medical content knowledge for dancers themselves
- creating an understanding for dance medicine and injury preventive behavior already in the young
- including the installation of environments through teachers and institutions, which allow to learn and live such behavior

EARLY SPECIALIZATION: THE WRONG IDEA ABOUT HOW TO BECOME A PROFESSIONAL

The risk of clustered acute and chronic injuries in dance rises – as in any (competitive) sport – with early specialization leading to increased training effort, load and ambition. Such injury risk can affect young amateur dancers, but is a very specific risk for young vocational dancers.

Especially in dance and not only among styles such as classical ballet, many believe, dancers can only become professionals, when they start earliest with intensive training. Furthermore, the common belief is that a dancer has to specialize as early as possible in their preferred dance style, because this is the only chance to reach elite level. And (a lack of knowledge in) teachers, trainers, and parents as significant others in the lives of children and adolescents have to be regarded as specific (driving) factors in this misguided assumption.[599] However, the multiple stressors introduced to the lives of children and adolescents through early specialization are more likely to adversely affect young dancers' chances to reach elite status.

Specialization before (early to middle of) puberty does not support the goal of achieving elite status, in the contrary: A (sudden) increase in **training intensity** for children and adolescents striving for elite status has shown to be significantly **related to (overuse) injury risk,**

[594] Outerbridge ER, and Micheli LJ. *Overuse injuries in the young athlete.* Clin Sports Med. 14. 503-516. 1995.

[595] Caine D, diFiori J, and Maffulli N. *Physeal injuries in children's and youth sports: reasons for concern.* Br J Sports Med. 40. 749-760. 2006.

[596] Brenner JS. *Overuse injuries, overtraining, and burnout in child and adolescent athletes.* Pediatrics. 119. 1242-1245. 2007.

[597] Dalton S. *Overuse injuries in adolescent athletes.* Sports Med. 13. 58-70. 1992.

[598] Wilson JC, Quinn BJ, Stratton CW, Southwick H, and MacDonald JP. *Athletes Doing Arabesques: Important Considerations in the Care of Young Dancers.* Curr Sports Med Rep. 14(6). 448-454. 2015.

[599] Padaki AS, Popkin CA, Hodgins JL, Kovacevic D, Lynch TS, Ahmad CS. *Factors That Drive Youth Specialization.* Sports Health. 9(6). 532-536. 2017.

overtraining, burnout and dropout.[600,601,602,603,604] The increasing intensity of training in many child athletes and dancers is associated with a decline in physical and psychological function, motivation, and overall health through greater stress levels, increase of perfectionistic tendencies and concerns, social isolation, poor academic performance, increase of anxieties, insufficient sleep, decreased family time, burnout and the physiological as well as psychological burden and correlates of injuries and overtraining.[605] The upcoming paragraphs will show the risk for children related to higher training intensity and early specialization which peaks significantly in certain stages of development, e.g., growth spurts and puberty.

Further chapters on adolescence in dance in this book as well as volume 2 and 3 will provide information about how to prevent early specialization and risk of injury and overtraining with special focus on puberty.

THE SILENT DANGER OF REPETITIVE MICRO-TRAUMATA FOR GROWING STRUCTURES

Acute dance and sports injuries are relatively easy to recognize, because time of onset as well as cause of injury are usually known: A particular traumatic incident, e.g., falling, results in an injury. Usually, teachers, trainers, parents or/and caretakers are involved, at least by being or becoming informed. However, practice shows that and how many acute injuries to dancers are concealed or shrugged off and can remain untreated, especially when dancers (have to) keep on dancing through/with them, as repeatedly cited above. Such behavior is one of the many causes for repetitive injuries and may sooner or later result in overuse injuries.

Chronic or overuse injuries are a **commonly underestimated** (and therefore even greater) burden for all athletes, because in contrary to acute or traumatic injuries, their clear point of onset as well as the underlying causes are too often than not unknown. While they develop gradually, dancers very often **suffer silently from ongoing and/or recurrent pain, restrictions, fear and stress**, resulting from the anxiety as natural psychological correlate of pain and injury. Moreover, overuse injuries are based on overuse, as their name states, which is why they manifest gradually based on **repetitive, submaximal overloading (i.e., overusing) of tissue**. This repeated (i.e., repetitive) overloading is just never strong enough (i.e., submaximal) to inflict acute harm, which is why it is often shrugged off and denied, with the dancer/teacher expecting pain and related issues to just disappear when successfully ignored long enough. **Denial, silent prayer, or ignorance are but the worst ways to deal with such gradually increasing issues and pain.** Many dancers who do not stop adopt **compensatory strategies** to prevaricate further harm or escape pain. This can lead to secondary damage in other body parts due to the compensation, which mostly leads to a **change in biomechanics** away from the ideal, i.e., individually best and economic motion pattern in a motor goal pursuit. And the **"dance identity"** based on **harmful misinterpretation of discipline**, in which **complaints are regarded as weakness resulting in shame**[606], lays the foundation of many cases, which might have easily been prevented with **knowledge and awareness.** If these first moments of alarm are overlooked without targeted action, such as identifying and eliminating underlying causes, these issues will manifest themselves through **repetitive micro-traumata (repeating smallest injuries)**, which eventually result in severe and complex chronic damage.

For that matter, overuse injuries are often really not caused by one factor only anymore but have progressing, multifactorial underlying reasons, which makes it even harder for dancers and teachers to identify and eliminate risk factors later. Especially when injuries are chronic already, identified underlying risk factors such as faulty dance technique cannot easily be corrected for the dancer to go on with the problem solved. When the

600 Valovich McLeod TC, Decoster LC, Loud KJ, Micheli LJ, Parker JT, Sandrey MA, and White C. *National Athletic Trainers' Association position statement: prevention of pediatric overuse injuries*. J Athl Train. 46(2). 206-220. 2011.

601 Scher A. *Branch Out*. Dance Magazine 94(6). 36-36. 2020.

602 LaPrade RF, Agel J, Baker J, Brenner JS, Cordasco FA, Côté J, Engebretsen L, Feeley BT, Gould D, Hainline B, Hewett T, Jayanthi N, Kocher MS, Myer GD, Nissen CW, Philippon MJ, and Provencher MT. *AOSSM Early Sport Specialization Consensus Statement*. Orthop J Sports Med. 4(4).2325967116644241. 2016.

603 Matzkin E, and Garvey K. *Youth Sports Specialization: Does Practice Make Perfect?* NASN Sch Nurse. 34(2). 100-103. 2019.

604 Post EG, Struminger AH, Hibberd EE. Sport specialization is associated with upper-extremity overuse injury in high school baseball players. J Shoulder Elbow Surg. 29(9). 1775-1782. 2020.

605 Brenner JS, LaBotz M, Sugimoto D, and Stracciolini A. *The Psychosocial Implications of Sport Specialization in Pediatric Athletes*. J Athl Train. 54(10). 1021-1029. 2019.

606 Thomson P, and Jaque SV. *Exposing shame in dancers and athletes: shame, trauma, and dissociation in a nonclinical population*. J Trauma Dissociation. 14(4). 439-454. 2013.

dancer is affected by overuse injury already, correcting technique might have to wait because the dancer needs diagnosis, treatment, rehabilitation, medical clearance, transition training… Too often these aspects are erroneously associated with "time-lost" for the dancer – which is why they too often than not are denied or neglected. However, overuse injuries are comparable to going to the dentist's or orthodontist's: when it needs to be faced then it is essential to do exactly that. Otherwise matters can only get worse.

The chapters on primary and secondary injury prevention discusses this topic and explains, why injury prevention is never a time-loss, but is exactly the opposite: it prevents time-loss due to injury and so many other losses coming along with injury.

Overuse injuries are not necessarily depending on level of experience. They can happen in amateur, vocational, and professional dance, **when dance technical errors are not corrected or consciously welcomed**, in order to achieve a dance technical goal, come what may. They also happen in all levels of expertise **when training is not planned as such that the dancer can build on progressive overloading** (supercompensation), but has to deal with ongoing or repeated submaximal overloading.

The **dancer's knowledge**[607,608] on dance medical basics such as the **difference between injury and performance pain**, or the **clever way to speak out** in any case of complaint is as essential as content knowledge is in teachers and trainers. Training dancers is not only to get and keep them going, i.e., dancing. **It is guiding them towards a mutually predefined goal in a constant search for *their* individual pathway towards goal achievement.** Along that way, the teacher's wisdom is essential[609,610,611] and will be shown through their decisions and actions. This starts with

- creating an empowering motivational climate and
- allowing, or better encouraging, the dancer to immediately speak out in case of any, even small ill-feeling or complaint
- taking all necessary and appropriate action to identify and eliminate risk factors together
- involving asking other specialists for help when needed to reach that goal
- having the trained ability to identify and acknowledge a dancer's physical, cognitive, and psychological individuality
- correcting and teaching dance technique within **the dancer's range of individuality**
- **understanding the difference between a child dancer and an adult**
- having enough knowledge to identify incorrect technique
- planning training based on dance scientific evidence

The ability to identify incorrect technique and conduct evidence-based training might be regarded as the natural basis of every teaching personnel. However, many teachers have no other tool at hand than their own dance technique and the memory of what they themselves have learnt from their teachers.[612,613] Dance medicine and reports on dancers' injuries constantly show that this is not even close to being enough. **Planning of training is as high a science as is correcting and teaching appropriate, i.e., individual dance technique.**

While talent as well as calling in teachers and trainers are essential, knowledge only comes with intensive study and targeted education, and not even the greatest dancer is born with dance medical/pedagogical wisdom. While in amateurs and lower levels of skills one might argue that incorrect dance technique is easily identifiable and correctable (which stands to be discussed), in higher and highest skill levels erroneous technique might be barely recognizable in highly complex motion. In any case, it needs a trained eye to identify faulty individual motor patterns and then, first and foremost be able and willing to correct them, even when that means in most of all cases that the teacher has to **find many other ways to help the dancer achieve their own goal in their own time and with their own individual means**. A dance-medically trained pedagogical eye is decisive when injuries want to be prevented.

---

607 Tosi M, Maslyanskaya S, Dodson NA, and Coupey SM. *The Female Athlete Triad: A Comparison of Knowledge and Risk in Adolescent and Young Adult Figure Skaters, Dancers, and Runners.* J Pediatr Adolesc Gynecol. 32(2). 165-169. 2019.

608 Kotler DH, Lynch M, Cushman D, Hu J, and Garner J. *Dancers' Perceived and Actual Knowledge of Anatomy.* J Dance Med Sci. 21(2). 76-81. 2017.

609 Stracciolini A, Yin AX, and D Sugimoto. *Etiology and body area of injuries in young female dancers presenting to sports medicine clinic: A comparison by age group.* Phys Sportsmed. 8. 1-6. 2015. Published online.

610 Howse J. *The importance of good teaching in injury prevention.* Med Probl Perform Art. 9(2). 1994.

611 Post EG, Trigsted SM, Schaefer DA, Cadmus-Bertram LA, Watson AM, McGuine TA, Brooks MA, and Bell DR. *Knowledge, Attitudes, and Beliefs of Youth Sports Coaches Regarding Sport Volume Recommendations and Sport Specialization.* J Strength Cond Res. 34(10). 2911-2919. 2020.

612 Howse J. *The importance of good teaching in injury prevention.* Med Probl Perform Art. 9(2). 1994.

613 Lee SA. *The Artist as Teacher: A Psychological Perspective.* Medical Problems of Performing Artists. 12(2). 38-41. 1997.

When young dancers feel pain, it is often attributed to growth, the heavy school bag, poor posture, performance pressure, and mental overload, or other things, but rarely to dance classes and training elements, especially in vocational training. In amateur classes pain is attributed to dance elements more frequently, but there children and adolescents usually stop dancing when the pain does not stop, leading to the cliché that "dance hurts and is very harmful". In any way, those who struggle their way through their pain can suffer severe damage leading to **long-term risk and consequences.**

The danger of ignoring repetitive micro-traumata resulting in overuse is high in children[614,615] and highly underestimated, based on so many underlying causes such as dance identity, knowledge, traditions etc. The nature of overuse injuries with their gradual onset based on all those reasons so often makes dancers and teachers ignore complaints over long periods, report too late, and sometimes even receive unhelpful clinical support, when medical professionals do not possess knowledge on dance medicine and science. Very often underlying reasons are unclear, making treatment and therapy difficult and the risk for further harm high.[616,617,618] Hence, primary prevention has to be the overall goal of all parties involved. For that, dancers need help and guidance.

A CHILD DANCER IS NOT AN ADULT DANCER: GROWTH & TRANSITION PHASES

One very important aspect is that the teacher/trainer is aware that **child/adolescent dancers are not adult dancers yet**, and that they need different things and need to do things differently than their grown-up colleagues. Repeatedly or excessively overstraining the growing child's or adolescent's body can cause other or more severe damage than in adults. Keeping in mind that it is the goal of a young dancer to *become* a dancer one day, with so many years of education and a whole career still to master, it must be clear that this goal can only be achieved successfully, when the child's body, mind and soul are allowed to stay healthy.

Even though many people irresponsibly argue that injuries heal and are part of dance, injuries always leave scars. Be it related to connective tissue healing actual physical wounds and leaving a weak spot behind, or the (often worse) psychological consequence of injury, leaving already young children with stress and anxiety levels, which might affect them for life and predispose them for further injuries. **Dance must stop to be "naturally" equated with pain and injury**. This is the first and foremost step to tackle the problem of (overuse) injury, because then any excuses for not preventing them in dancers of all ages go up in smoke.

Comparing children to adults, the bone metabolism in children and adolescents focuses primarily on the development and growth of a functional skeleton, which is not ready yet. Hence it cannot take the same load as in adults, while it also needs extra specific care such as adequate nutrition and more sleep. Every age in our ongoing (motor) development has its advantages. However, not only in phases of growth or transition, children's bodies have numerous and constantly changing weak points due to the permanent remodeling of cells, such as bones growing (i.e., ossifying) in length and width.[619,620,621,622]

Repeatedly and ongoingly, dance medicine has invoked teachers and trainers to become aware of the responsibility of their profession, especially when it comes to those injuries in children and adolescents, which were caused by a clear lack of education, knowledge – and, as sad as it is to say, responsibility.[623,624]

---

614 Garrick JG, and SL Lewis. *Carreer hazards for the dancer.* Occup Med. 16(4). 609-618 (iv). 2001.

615 O'Neill DB, and LJ Micheli. *Overuse injuries in the young athlete.* Clin Sports Med. 7. 591-610. 1988.

616 DiFiori JP. *Overuse Injuries in Children and Adolescents.* Phys Sportsmed. 27(1). 75-89. 1999.

617 Maffulli N, and E Pintore. *Intensive training in young athletes.* Br J Sports Med. 24. 237-239. 1990.

618 Niemeyer P, Weinberg A, Schmitt H, Kreuz PC, Ewerbeck V, and P Kasten. *Stress fractures in adolescent competitive athletes with open physis.* Knee Surg Sports Traumatol Arthrosc. 14. 771-777. 2006.

619 Ogden John A. Skeletal injury in the Child. New York. Springer-Verlag. 2000.

620 Flachsmann R, Broom ND, Hardy AE. *Why is the adolescent joint particularly susceptible to osteochondral shear fracture?* Clin Orthop Relat Res. 212-221. 2000.

621 Bright RW, Burstein AH, and SM Elmore. *Epiphyseal-plate cartilage. A biomechanical and histological analysis of failure modes.* J Bone Joint Surg Am. 56. 688-703. 1974.

622 Fuller M, Moyle GM, Hunt AP, Minett GM. *Ballet and Contemporary Dance Injuries When Transitioning to Full-Time Training or Professional Level Dance: A Systematic Review.* J Dance Med Sci. 23(3). 112-125. 2019.

623 Shah S. *Premature Growth Plate Closure in a Ballet Dancer en Pointe.* Clin J Sport Med. 27(5). 69-71. 2017.

624 Tosi M, Maslyanskaya S, Dodson NA, and Coupey SM. *The Female Athlete Triad: A Comparison of Knowledge and Risk in Adolescent and Young Adult Figure Skaters, Dancers, and Runners.* J Pediatr Adolesc Gynecol. 32(2). 165-169. 2019.

Again, in order to be able to be responsible, knowledge is essential.

Injuries to children's **joints**[625,626,627], **bones**[628,629,630,631,632] and **epiphyseal plates** (cartilage growth plate in the bone, allowing the bone to increase in length) can severely affect growth and result in lifelong damage.[633,634,635,636,637] Stress fractures resulting from chronic overuse in dancers and athletes become more common.[638,639,640,641] The **high number of adolescents**[642,643] is particularly shocking because it reflects an **education away from natural body awareness, mindfulness and intuition in dancers**, who should actually be (learning how to be) in harmony with their bodies as their sole instruments.[644]

However, education already teaches the young to suppress pain, ignore its warning signals, and deny the natural response to pain and developing injury, which would be crying out and seeking help. Instead of this, young dancers often spend long, silent periods of time in pain and distress, followed by the necessity of long healing time. Overuse entails a structural change of the bone and cell health introducing a change of its metabolism which can even result in altered biomechanics, when the dancer has to compensate for pain or instability. Such changes as well as the pain perceived affect the dancer's physique and technique. This includes poor alignment, myofascial dysbalances, instability, muscle weakness or limited joint mobility (just because dancers are usually very flexible, it does not mean that each of their joints can enjoy its physiological range of motion, when affected or restricted by pain or injury!).[645]

The same applies to the child's muscles, tendons, and organs. They are not built for the same strain as those of an adult, but need to be carefully guided on their way to progressively "grow into" the demands of professional dance, like children grow into their clothes too. They do not fit into adult clothes from early age onwards either.

Training for children and adolescents needs to be planned for each individual age with care, has to acknowledge biological before chronological age, and requires a lot of knowledge to achieve the **essential balance between necessary progressive loading (training) and loadability of individual growing structures**. Furthermore, training professional dancers is something utterly different than educating children and adolescents to become dancers. This aspect is also important to keep in mind when it comes to **phases of transition**: Children who embark on vocational dance education need specific help, because a sudden increase of training load comes with injury risk. Same goes for adolescents transitioning into professional careers from vocational schools. Comparable to growth spurts, such transition phases again need high levels of content knowledge in teachers and trainers, to sufficiently and gradually (i.e., early enough) prepare young dancers for such important and demanding moments.

---

625 Steinberg N, Tenenbaum S, Stern M, Zeev A, and Siev-Ner I. *Patellofemoral pain, body morphology and alignment in female pubertal dancers: One-year follow-up.* J Sports Sci. 37(15). 1690-1698. 2019.

626 Steinberg N, Tenenbaum S, Waddington G, Adams R, Zakin G, Zeev A, and Siev-Ner I. *Unilateral and bilateral patellofemoral pain in young female dancers: Associated factors.* J Sports Sci. 38(7). 719-730. 2020.

627 Steinberg N, Tenenbaum S, Itzhak SN, and Aviva Z. *Can young dancers skip/recover from patellofemoral pain? A two-year follow-up.* Res Sports Med. 28(3). 459-467. 2020.

628 Albisetti W, Perugia D, De Bartolomeo O, Tagliabue L, Camerucci E, and Calori GM. *Stress fractures of the base of the metatarsal bones in young trainee ballet dancers.* Int Orthop. 34(1). 51-55. 2010.

629 Kadel NJ, Teitz CC, Kronmal RA. Stress fractures in ballet dancers. Am J Sports Med. 20(4). 445-449. 1992.

630 Nussbaum AR, Treves ST, and Micheli L. *Bone stress lesions in ballet dancers: scintigraphic assessment.* AJR Am J Roentgenol. 150(4). 851-855. 1988.

631 Sobrino FJ, Guillén P. *Overuse Injuries in Professional Ballet: Influence of Age and Years of Professional Practice.* Orthop J Sports Med. 5(6):2325967117712704. 2017.

632 Reid DC. *Prevention of hip and knee injuries in ballet dancers.* Sports Med. 6(5). 295-307. 1988.

633 Siev-Ner I, Stern MD, Tenenbaum S, Blankstein A, Zeev A, and Steinberg N. *Ultrasonography findings and physical examination outcomes in dancers with and without patellofemoral pain.* Phys Sportsmed. 46(1). 48-55. 2018.

634 Gerber SD, Griffin PP, and Simmons BP. *Break dancer's wrist.* J Pediatr Orthop. 6(1). 98-99. 1986.

635 Winkler AR, Barnes JC, and Ogden JA. *Break dance hip: chronic avulsion of the anterior superior iliac spine.* Pediatr Radiol. 17(6). 501-502. 1987.

636 Kasper JC, Gerhardt MB, and Mandelbaum BR. *Stress injury leading to slipped capital femoral epiphysis in a competitive adolescent tennis player: a case report.* Clin J Sport Med. 17(1). 72-74. 2007.

637 Hellmich HJ, Krieg AH. Epiphyseolysis capitis femoris – Ätiologie und Pathogenese [Slipped capital femoral epiphysis-etiology and pathogenesis]. Orthopaede. 48(8). 644-650. 2019.

638 Bennel K, Matheson G, Meeuwisse W. *Risk factors for stress fractures.* Sports Med. 28. 91-122. 1999.

639 O'Malley MJ, Hamilton WG, and J Munyak. *Stress fractures at the base of the second metatarsal in ballet dancers.* Foot Ankle Int. 17. 89-94. 1996.

640 Micheli LJ, Sohn RS, and R Solomon. *Stress fractures of the second metatarsal involving Lisfranc's joint in ballet dancers.* J Bone Joint Surg Am. 67. 1372-1375. 1985.

641 Stuart J, David B, and P Brukner. *Stress fractures: pathophysiology, epidemiology, and risk factors.* Curr Osteoporos Rep. 4. 103-109. 2006.

642 Milgrom C, Finestone A, and N Shlamkovitch. *Youth is a risk factor for stress fracture. A study of 783 infantry recruits.* J Bone Joint Surg Br. 76(1).20-22. 1994.

643 Dubravcic-Simunjak S, Pecina M, Kuipers H, et al. *The incidence of injuries in elite junior figure skaters.* Am J Sports Med.31(4). 511-517. 2003.

644 Motta-Valencia K. *Dance-related injury.* Phys Med Rehabil Clin N Am. 17(3). 697-723. 2006.

645 Pecina Marco M, and Ivan Bojanic. Overuse injuries of the musculoskeletal system. 2nd ed. Boca Raton. CRC Press. 2003. p. 316-319.

In 1999, James G. Garrick researched the etiology of injuries in female adolescent dancers and stressed the importance of early identification of chronic injuries ad their risk factors in dance.[646]

Over a period of 20 months, he observed 54 vocational ballet dancers of a pre-professional school, who were granted easy access to professional medical attention. These consultations were widely used. Out of 54 students between the age of 12 and 19, 38 reported as many as 194 complaints and injuries. The reports were compared to 1353 injuries of a similar age group, who had sought help in a sports and dance medical clinic. This comparison showed that reported incidence rates were the same. Garrick concluded that the complaints reported by the 38 vocational students were early manifestations of overuse injuries, with which they would later seek help in a clinic.

He stressed the importance of dance medical interventions and targeted measures of injury prevention early enough to prevent young dancers from having to reach the moment of severe injury, with which they end in a clinic. Such measures include education of dancers and teachers on handling of early onset of complaints to avoid later, harmful consequences. Most importantly, installation of **easy access medical care** is needed, which young dancers can contact unaffected by school and teachers to prevent overuse injuries.

Garrick further emphasized the importance of using dance medical research results to **continuously screen teachers** and their **classes**, how they teach **dance technique** and how teachers handle students' individuality and development within dance education. Furthermore, he provided an answer to the concern of numerous teachers that taking the dancers' complaints seriously could lead to effeminacy, fearing the "softening" and disciplinary neglect of the (young) dancers:

The (young) dancer's pain and worries must always be taken seriously and handled professionally. Suppose it turns out that it was a false alarm – all the better. However, the figures of dance medicine show that the dancers are serious about their pain. How much has changed since Garrick's efforts in 1999?

The chapters on motivational climate and emotional intelligence in Volume 2 will discuss the importance of the atmosphere and environment which teachers and trainers create, and their association with psychological and physiological injury – or their prevention.

When it comes to (young) dancers' training, teachers, trainers and schools should cooperate with dance medical specialists and, above all, give students the possibility to contact them, whenever needed, which must not have negative consequences for their training or relationship to their teachers.

Additionally, teachers need to be self-reflective enough to critically look at their own classes and methods, especially when dancers in their classes suffer from complaints and overuse. Furthermore, when physicians or therapists give advice and orders with regard to dancers' injuries and their management, their realization must be top priority for all teachers and institutions.

Studies on children and adolescents in dance, their risk of injury, and the prevalence of injury (incidences) are provided by dance medicine in large numbers for both amateurs and professionals, as described above. Here, however, the question arises whether dance teachers and trainers recognize the data, critically reflect their teaching methods and therefore change them or not.[647,648]

With the risk in professionals being 90% to sustain an injury at least once in their career [649] and the injury risk in children as high as 76%[650] **the focus must immediately be put on a change in dance education for children and adolescents to protect the dancer's health in future!** That, again, needs education of teachers and trainers.

[646] Garrick JG. *Early identification of musculoskeletal complaints and injuries among female ballet students.* J Dance Med Sci. 3(2). 80-83. 1999.

[647] Wilmerding MV, and Krasnow D. *Dance pedagogy: Myth versus reality. 3rd International Symposium on Performance Science.* 283-289. 2011.

[648] Kretschmann R, Mathis-Mansury EH, and E Bronner. *Global perspectives on dance pedagogy – research and practice. Congress on Research in Dance (CORD) Special Conference, 25.-27.6.2009, Leicester, UK.* Sportwiss. 40. 224-226. 2010.

[649] Schoene L. *Biomechanical evaluation of dancers and assessment of their risk of injury.* J Am Pod Med Assoc. 1. 75-80. 2007.

[650] Ekegren CL, Quested R, and Brodrick A. *Injuries in pre-professional ballet dancers: Incidence, characteristics and consequences.* J Sci Med Sport. 17(3). 271-275. 2014.

Transition, as a time of change or passage, is a topic very often associated with anxiety or even regarded as threat. One the one hand, because transition phases often are directly connected to insecurity, involuntary changes a dancer has to succumb to, or even injury. On the other hand, because every transition is a walking out of a (more or less) comfort zone into a new unknown stage of life. However, regarding it from a neuropsychological point of view, transitions happen to us every day, or even every second: With every input our nervous system receives, evaluates and stores, with every experience we make in every minute of our lives, we change from the person we had been to a "new" version of our present self. As such, we experience constant transitions due to our nervous system's ability for neuroplasticity: the ability to (re-) connect nerves through their synapses (contact endings) according to our focus of attention, experiences, and learning, which results in new behavior, voluntarily or involuntarily, consciously and unconsciously.

> *Volume 2 of this series discusses such related neuropsychological aspects of learning and development with regard to dance and dance education.*

Hence, transition *"results in a change in assumptions about oneself and the world and thus requires a corresponding change in one's behavior and relationships."*[651] Our traits, states, our self-concept (self-esteem, self-efficacy), the dancer's **perception of their own identity and competence**, feelings of **relatedness** and **autonomy**, overall health, awareness for the transition, **voluntariness**, and thus the way teachers and trainers can guide a dancer towards and through such phases are essential aspects for transition. The dancer, their teachers and the environment involved will decide, how a dancer can experience the transition: As something they approach consciously, voluntarily, mindfully, and guided. Or as something that suddenly came upon them, making transitions an involuntary and often extrinsically determined issue, which can result in long-term scars and consequences (e.g., depression, fear, anxiety, burnout, dropout, psychological and physiological ill-health, injury, conflicts, financial burden etc.). [652,653]

Transition has been researched in depth throughout the last 10 to 15 years in athletes and dancers.[654,655,656,657] However, such research is mainly dedicated to the transition of athletes and dancers from their active, (semi-)professional career into retirement or a second career path. Approaches such as the **Holistic Athletic Career Transition Model**[658] provide in-depth discussion on aspects related to career transition in athletes and their (motor) development.

But aside from such a very important crossroads in a dancer's life, there are several other phases of transition, which provide the dancer with **chances** or expose them to **particularly high injury risk**, depending on how such transitions are approached, experienced, and above all, prepared for. Moreover, this last phase of transition in a dancer's life is highly dependent on the handling of all transitions and related experiences beforehand.

The following chapter will thus briefly address the most important transition phases in a dancer's life, which all come along with physical, psychological, cognitive/mental, biopsychosocial, and often also financial changes for the dancer:

- Transition I: from child dance class to vocational or recreational education
- Transition II: from vocational to professional environment
- Transition III: from professional to retirement/2nd career
- Transition IVa: from vacation into season/schoolyear
- Transition IVb: within a season/school year

651 Schlossberg NK. *A model for analyzing human adaptation to transition.* The Counseling Psychol. 9(2). 2-18. 1981. p.5.

652 Taylor J, and Ogilvie BC. *Career termination among athletes.* IN: Singer, R.N., Hausenblas, H.E., and C.M. Janelle (Eds.). Handbook of Sport Psychology. New York. Wiley. 672-691. 2001.

653 Warringer K, and Lavallee D. *The retirement experiences of female gymnasts: Self identity and the physiological self.* J Apll Sport Psychol. 20. 301-317. 2008.

654 Lavallee D, Grove R, and Gordon S. *The Causes of Career Termination from Sport and their Relationship to Post-Retirement Adjustment Among Elite-Amateur Athletes in Australia.* Australian Psychologist. 32. 131-135. 1997.

655 Harrison C, and Ruddock-Hudson M. *Perceptions of Pain, Injury, and Transition-Retirement: The Experiences of Professional Dancers.* J Dance Med Sci. 21(2). 43-52. 2017.

656 Tekavc J, Wylleman P, and Erpič S.*.Perceptions of dual career development among elite level swimmers and basketball players.* Psychol Sport Exerc. 21. 2015.

657 Wylleman P. *A developmental and holistic perspective on transitioning out of elite sport.* IN: Anshel, M..H. (Ed.), APA Handbook of Sport and Exercise Psychology Vol 1. Sport Psychology. American Psychological Association (APA). 2019.

658 Wylleman P, and Rosier N. *A holistic perspective on the development of elite athletes.* IN: Raab, M., Wylleman, P., Seiler, R., Elbe, A.-M., and A. Hatzigeorgiardis (Eds.). Sport and Exercise Psychology Research: from Theory to Practice. Oxford. Elsevier. 2016. 270-288.

- Transition V: transition training from rehabilitation back to performing

Through the eyes of dance medicine and dance-medical dance pedagogy, each of these transition phases has its own challenges, chances, and risks. They involve different age group, different environments, and thus, have different goals. However, each one can be supported by dance medicine and science as such that they become chances, open new doors, and help develop a healthy, confident, autonomous identity in a dancer.

TRANSITION I: FROM CHILD DANCE CLASS TO VOCATIONAL OR RECREATIONAL EDUCATION

As previous chapters have stated, child dance classes should be the same for all children, no matter whether they choose to take up a vocational or recreational approach afterwards. In the age groups of 3 to approximately 10 years, dance is meant to support children's overall development. Hence, it is best aiming at supporting a child's intrinsic motivation, curiosity, and thus, development. From 10 years onwards, children often already have to make their decision between going on professionally and into vocational education, or deciding for recreational pathways, which can also be found to be very ambitious at times.

Characteristic for this transition would be the extrinsic influence and management. Often one hears that "the child decides for a vocational path" – but children are not yet able to make such informed decisions on their own. Their dreams might be here, but neither their brain's frontal lobe nor their level of experience is sufficiently developed to really make such a decision. Moreover, they do not have the legal or financial chances to make such choices. Hence, it is mostly the adults involved, who make the decision for and in the name of the child. First, by allowing and supporting the one or the other goal (i.e., vocational or recreational dance education), and second, by taking charge of the legal and financial steps, which are involved.

In vocational more than in recreational dance, children often have to undergo extensive auditions, which are a first big step towards vocational education. In the best case, such auditions are prepared for on the long-run, involving knowledgeable teachers in closest cooperation with child and parents. However, the serious side of life commences with the child taking up vocational (or particularly ambitious recreational) training and education. Such school years usually start in early autumn, after the child hopefully had an extensive summer break, being physically and psychologically recovered and ready for education. Then the success of the transition depends on the school, and how the transfer from child dance to intensive education is approached. As mentioned in the chapter on injury risk in children and adolescents, the danger is twofold: first, a **sudden increase of training frequency, duration, and intensity**, and second, **early specialization in dance style and technique** have been identified as specific risk factors for (overuse) injury, burnout, and dropout in the young.[659,660,661] Motivation usually is high, in children, parents, and teachers. While the first two have high expectations, the teacher also has to carry a lot of pressure aside from their responsibility: **teachers are supposed to deliver "perfect" dancers, and such pressure must not be underestimated**. Teachers, especially in vocational schools, are part of an institution and its administration, and rarely are able to make their own decisions with regard to scheduling, science of training and other related, vital aspects for the child's healthy development and transition.

Hence, **it is essential that the institution provides the environment for teachers and young dancers to work and cooperate based on dance medicine and science**. Scheduling, training, rehearsals, motivational climate, approaches to technique, nutrition and so many aspects already discussed in this book, have to be managed and provided from the top of the organizational pyramid. At best, such administration is based on periodization and thus, teamwork, involving all teachers, administrators, parents and children alike. As such, this transition can be planned accordingly. First weeks and months (and years!) can be based on specific, evidence-based scheduling (periodization), allowing the child to experience a smooth transition lasting for several months, which allows to

[659] Valovich McLeod TC, Decoster LC, Loud KJ, Micheli LJ, Parker JT, Sandrey MA, and White C. *National Athletic Trainers' Association position statement: prevention of pediatric overuse injuries.* J Athl Train. 46(2). 206-220. 2011.

[660] Steinberg N, Siev-Ner I, Peleg S, Dar G, Masharawi Y, Zeev A, and Hershkovitz I. *Extrinsic and intrinsic risk factors associated with injuries in young dancers aged 8-16 years.* J Sports Sci. 30(5). 485-495. 2012.

[661] LaPrade RF, Agel J, Baker J, Brenner JS, Cordasco FA, Côté J, Engebretsen L, Feeley BT, Gould D, Hainline B, Hewett T, Jayanthi N, Kocher MS, Myer GD, Nissen CW, Philippon MJ, and Provencher MT. *AOSSM Early Sport Specialization Consensus Statement.* Orthop J Sports Med. 4(4).2325967116644241. 2016.

adjust physically, mentally and psychologically to the new life and goals. These months lay the groundwork for the years to come, and have to be planned with a view for the long-run. Such a long-term perspective needs **periodization**, because training and goals have to be coordinated in micro-, meso-, and macro-cycles, each of these blocks related to what was done before, what is done presently, and both together laying the groundwork for what will be done and expected of dancer and teacher in the future.

The **cooperation between all adults involved** is the most essential aspect in this first big transition of a dancer: their knowledge and will for teamwork will decide, how the child can transition, which experiences are made, how their physical and psychological development will unfold – which form of identity starts to form in the young dancer. One must never forget that the decision for transition was made mostly for the child, even when in accordance with them. Hence, the process of goal setting and achieving of the adults for the dancer will provide the child with all tools for a future career. In such a moment, chances are high to educate a child towards strong and healthy body, mind, and soul, which again will decide over their future chances and health.

Regarding **age group**, the decision for the first great transition of a dancer happens between first and second growth spurt, around the age of 10. As related in previous chapters, this is an age characterized by highest forms of intrinsic motivation. The child is not in a growth spurt anymore, settled in the second half of elementary education, but also not affected by puberty yet. However, the child is still a child, and as discussed, motivation needs knowledgeable, responsible guidance from teachers (and parents). The child will do whatever told, trusting those who guide, not able to rely on their own wisdom and foresight.

As soon as the child has entered the transition, many changes outside of the dance environment will also affect the dance and overall development of the child: change of school means an important transition, coming along with changes in relationships, schedules, daily behavior and load. It is a natural way that parents become second, while school environments come first on the child's inner ranking, with the teacher becoming the most important significant other. At best, **pre-vocational schools and vocational schools cooperate**, which would ensure the child's best for the moment of transition. However, family still is essential for the child's health and wellbeing. And while all focus lies on the transition and the dance education to embark on, family life and the mindful safety of parents' love and guidance must never come second, no matter how high the motivation for dance.

Goals for this transition involve dance technical and training-related groundwork, which has to be laid. Early specialization has to be avoided, depending on periodized curricula, at best involving the child through appropriate teaching of early dance medical basics[662]: For instance, explaining and practicing training, warm-up and warm/cool-down as well as eating behavior, stretching, handling of pain, etc. The motivational climate a school and a teacher create in combination with the mentioned curricula will decide, how the child can experience the transition. Either as a loss of childhood privilege and an abrupt transition into the seriousness of life, or as the beginning of a journey towards highest levels of dancer's identity full of self-determination and thus, physical and psychological wellbeing. Open communication and teamwork involving the child will pay off for the upcoming years and future transitions, which are directly related to this very first one and the years to follow.

Children going through (ambitious) recreational education have a different approach to many aspects. As discussed in previous chapters, it is important to bridge the dream of stage with sufficient training stimulus and dance technical basics. Again, early specialization as well as a sudden increase of or blocked intensive training have to be avoided (e.g., early pointe work, etc.), when preparing for recreational experiences of stage. At best, decisions are made with the child, explaining background and goal setting. As with vocational education, risk factors have to be identified and eliminated as early as possible. Here, again, is no difference between dance medical dance pedagogy for vocational or recreational dance.

In recreational dance, many young dancers stop dancing when they change from elementary school to higher education, or when or shortly after they entered puberty. That again is a form of transition, namely, the decision to break up with the dream of stage, sometimes forever. For many young this is not a voluntary decision, with parents trying to reduce the load of changing school and involved changes of daily behavior and tasks. It is important that the teacher in the dance school or club does not take such a decision personally. They are hardly ever meant to be a negative feedback for the teacher and their dance training. However, it is hard for a teacher (as it is for the child!) to let go in moments of such great development,

[662] Wilson M, and Deckert JL. *A screening program for dancers administered by dancers.* J Dance Med Sci. 13(3). 67-72. 2009.

which these years usually are, as described above. Again, the way a teacher and school can handle such a usually life-changing experience and decision, will lay the groundwork for a lot in the recreational dancer as well: Many will return to dance later, and if in adulthood, if the teacher manages to provide a heartfelt, empowering farewell. Seeing such a child off from dance class personally, and with best wishes and the sentence that they are always welcome to return, can make a huge difference for the child, who has to say good bye. A teacher, who takes such a decision personally and probably acts accordingly, namely affronted, might leave a permanent hurting or stain connected to the memory of dance class in the child. This "small" moment of farewell might lay the essential groundwork for a child ever returning to dance in later years. In any case, it decides how positive or negative a child experiences the usually hard decision to say good bye to dance. As all experiences, it will influence future decisions, self-esteem, and identity also in recreational and amateur dancers.

TRANSITION II: FROM VOCATIONAL TO PROFESSIONAL ENVIRONMENT

It is rare that dancers are specifically prepared for their transition from vocational to professional dance environment. As previous chapters have described, the handling of puberty and the curricula available and implemented will decide, how such a transition will be experienced by the young dancer. Although vocational educations mostly are very strict and rigorous, school nonetheless means a more secure environment, compared to the transition to independent, professional, and adult life as a dancer.

Vocational educations sometimes provide direct transition of a dancer from school into a company. Others terminate a vocational education and are not transferred into a (often related) company. For them, the search for a job will start. Both ways of transition come with specific risks. While the first is characterized by a sudden change in daily schedules and an increase in training, rehearsal and performance load, the latter can often leave the dancer facing a void, starting off in a frantic search for auditions and jobs. While the young dancer entering a company faces highest workloads, the freelancer very often finds themselves suddenly without training facilities, schedules, and teacher/trainer/administrator guidance. Both can be related to mental, psychological and physical risks, including injury, burnout, stress, anxiety, or depression.

At best, such transfers are prepared specifically and in direct communication and thus cooperation with the dancer. Included in the periodized curriculum of the vocational institution, years of pubertal climaxes as well as the months directly before the termination of the education should include the mental, psychological, and physical preparation of the dancer for the upcoming transition. This also involves the design of the summer break after ending of school, as will be discussed in the following. Direct and open communication is essential, involving financial, insurance- and other legal information, the dancer will need for their future pathways after education. The more a young dancer can be prepared before transition to professional life (starting already with the first transition into vocational education!), the fitter the dancer will be to manage such transitions.

Again, the creation of a healthy dancer's identity is essential throughout vocational education and puberty, because it will decide how the dancer themselves can influence their own transition to a professional career: If the curricula included dance medical lectures, vocational orientation and career guidance, and have fostered empowering climates resulting in high levels of self-concept and autonomy, the young dancer will be able to make informed decisions with regard to their own health, wellbeing and safety.

Characteristics of this transition between vocational and professional dancing can be the change in lifestyle, coming from the school environment into the life in a company or the search for a job as a freelancer. Both come along with a change in training behavior and training load. And very often, especially when not particularly prepared, this transition suddenly confronts the dancer with their own financial and legal responsibility. While this is always a huge step in the life of every person, for dancers as well as other athletes, it often happens very young. Many young dancers are ready with school and directly enter their professional life with the age of 17 to 19, an age in which many young coming from apprenticeship or even high school just start to gain orientation in their new life as an adult. Dancers, having decided for a career at the age of 10 to 12, have to face adult and professional life early. Such "sudden" impact of financial, legal, and training burden can be overwhelming. Injury risk increases[663], especially since transitions are always related to a need of change in behavior such as training habits, daily routines, relationships, traits, states, and, last but not least, the support a dancer perceives and receives from teachers, peers, school, company, and family.

With regard to **age**, the transition usually affects dancers between 17 years and their early twenties. Late puberty should be behind them, and a solid first state of identity will be the result of the years of puberty at the end of adolescence. At best, such identity is connected to a more or less clear picture of future goals and chances. At least, such identity should be based on highest possible levels of self-concept, supporting the young dancer in making informed decisions. Again, this identity should include the clear awareness of the end of the active career. At best, living in the moment with clear aims and motivated task-goals for the upcoming years of a dancer should already be paired with thoughts for a second career. Or at least, keeping an open mind for the matter.

This chapter again shows, how much a young dancer is dependent on teachers'/trainers'/administrators' knowledge and dance medical guidance in moments of transition. Dancers have to learn how to be self-responsible based on dance medicine and science. In moments of transition, it will take stress off them, and allow them, for instance, to plan and execute their own training as freelancer between transition and jobs, or between jobs. As a company dancer, such dancers will know what is best for them and proactively support an empowering motivational climate in a company, even when young. Dance medical dance pedagogy experienced on highest level in their education will now decide, how the dancer deals with training, pain, injury, maturity, communication, motivation, and self-determination. New demands of professional as well as private life, new routines, new environments, new extrinsic and intrinsic risk factors will have to be faced. At best without anxiety, albeit with excitement. The life as professional dancer will more often than not be governed by traditional environments and hierarchies, which will restrict the dancer's chance to be self-determined in all aspects. However, the higher the knowledge about dance medicine in such a young dancer, the more they will know how to deal with such environments.

As there are transition agencies and centers for dancers in their transitioning from active career to second path or retirement, such centers are also needed for young dancers transitioning into professional lives. Particularly, when vocational schools do not offer dance medical, evidence-based curricula, including most of the important knowledge beforehand and during puberty. Although it is already late to start to prepare young dancers for their transition when they already find themselves in the middle of it, as long as vocational schools do not change their curricula towards described evidence-based dance medical dance pedagogy, such centers will be second best to support young dancers facing their transition. In case vocational schools offer evidence-based curricula, they will themselves include appropriate measures into their periodized scheduling to prepare the dancer for this transfer. At the very best, they release a self-determined (freelance) dancer and additionally cooperate with the company, they send the dancer into, if it is not a freelancer.

TRANSITION III: FROM PROFESSIONAL LIFE TO RETIREMENT OR 2ND CAREER

As stated in the introduction, a lot of research is dedicated to the transition of athletes' active career into retirement or second career path. In 2017[664], a study investigated 20 professional dancers and their experiences of career transition, showing that many were not adequately prepared for the end of career as well as the transition, rendering the transition and post-career life a challenge. Dancers had arrived from a career with high levels of persistent pain and injury, and not all career transitions were voluntary.

Before, in 1996, Brinson and Dick presented the Fit to Dance[665], UK, survey, in which they have already addressed shortcomings with regard to dancers' transition, speaking of forced retirements and

[663] Fuller M, Moyle GM, Hunt AP, Minett GM. *Ballet and Contemporary Dance Injuries When Transitioning to Full-Time Training or Professional Level Dance: A Systematic Review.* J Dance Med Sci. 23(3). 112-125. 2019.

[664] Harrison C, and Ruddock-Hudson M. *Perceptions of Pain, Injury, and Transition-Retirement: The Experiences of Professional Dancers.* J Dance Med Sci. 21(2). 43-52. 2017.

[665] Brinson Peter, and Fiona Dick. *Fit to dance?: the report of the national inquiry into dancers' health and injury.* London. Calouste Gulbenkian Foundation. 1996.

unnecessarily complex challenges in dancers' careers paired with significant levels of ill-health. Such shortcomings first stem from a lack of medical and educational support of dancers, as discussed in other chapters, and second, from resulting low morale and disempowering climates perceived by the dancers.

Characteristics of this transition phase would be that dancers need an awareness for the moment to come, grounded in the education and motivational climate they received and experienced during education. Such education – or a lack of it – will determine, whether the dancer can deal with the end of career with a mindful approach, or is caught in the middle of desperately denying the moment. That again will determine, whether the dancer has already made plans and set goals for the future, or even already started to prepare for the transition, for instance by taking up special training for a future career path. Here, many dancers are caught without preparation or goals. Moreover, many dancers find themselves with insufficient or unfinished scholarly education, which makes it even harder to enter second-career educational programs after or during transition. This can lead to severe psychological, mental as well as physiological consequences with regard to health and wellbeing. Anxiety, depression, burnout, pain, and injury are correlates of such an **unprepared transition**. Since becoming a dance teacher in many countries is not legally regulated, many dancers engage in teaching after their active career (was) terminated. The issues related to such decisions, especially when paired with a lack of dance-medical/pedagogical education have been sufficiently related. However, such moments do not only bear consequences for the young dancer, who is confronted with a teacher without education but possible high levels of stress, anxiety, and low self-concept. Such consequences influence the former-dancer and teacher-in-spe themselves. The stress levels of having to teach without knowledge while facing troubles to cope with career termination and transition must be incredible and can add to pain, injury, anxiety, and depression in many dance teachers. Research with athletes including dancers/teachers has described the burden of such unprepared transitions into retirement or second career. They involve mental health problems, loneliness, depression and fear, a **lack of goal setting (ability)**, as well as pain and injury, which can multiply the rest.[666,667,668,669]

Special challenges involved are the **levels of preparedness**, health and ill-health, **voluntariness**, perspectives, financial situation, private life and social support, as well as trait and state of the dancer in the moment of and the way through transition. Regarding the **age** group, this transition is delicate, because it can occur to dancers of all ages. Directly related to the aspect of voluntariness, many dancers have to transition out of an active career already at a young age, forced by injuries, or also forced through other extrinsic factors. The previous chapters have highlighted the importance of school curricula, which support all forms of transition and address related issues before they become any. **Coping skills** are best trained before the transition, where they can be replaced by **conscious awareness and mindful approach**. Such changes in curricula would then result in dancers, who are not only aware of the career end, but also plan on a long-run, already starting in school and/or during active career: new goals have to be set, which needs an overview of existing possibilities as well as a certain level of identity and self-concept, enabling the dancer to know about their own ideas, strengths, weaknesses, motivation, talents, and thus future wishes and chances for a second career. Involving dance medicine and science in curricula already provides the young dancer with a broad array of ideas and motivations for future career paths, while it takes the stress away through the knowledge that dance can always be a career, one just has to know how.

Curricula supporting empowered dancer's identity during education allow for privacy and social development, time for hobbies and "looking outside of the dance box". That will be of highest benefit when it comes to moments of transition, for instance by increasing the chance that the dancer is embedded in a solid social environment, the building of which was supported during their education and career. With high levels of self-concept, a dancer will be more open for changes. Then again, such an open mindset reduces angst and enables a dancer to face the transition and set new goals for achievement with joy and motivation, supporting the dancer's social and emotional intelligence, competence, and thus chances.

---

[666] Lampe J, Groneberg DA, Ohlendorf D, and Wanke EM. *Pain in female dancers and dance teachers: Perception, assessment, and related behavior.* Scand J Med Sci Sports. 29(4). 623-632. 2019.

[667] Gouttebarge V, Jonkers R, Moen M, Verhagen E, Wylleman P, and Kerkhoffs G. *The prevalence and risk indicators of symptoms of common mental disorders among current and former Dutch elite athletes.* J Sports Sci. 35(21). 2148-2156. 2017.

[668] Wylleman P, Rosier N, and Knop, P. *Transitional challenges and elite athletes' mental health.* IN: Baker J., Safi, P., and J. Fraser-Thomas (Eds). Health and elite sport. Is high performance sport a healthy pursuit?. 99-116. 2015.

[669] Taylor J, and Ogilvie BC. *Career termination among athletes.* IN: Singer, R.N., Hausenblas, H.E., and C.M. Janelle (Eds.). Handbook of Sport Psychology. New York. Wiley. 672-691. 2001.

Transitions from summer holidays, which have been highlighted in their importance for dancers[670], as well as smaller transitions within seasons or school years are often underestimated. Commonly because they are not identified as such. However, albeit small, they have a vital influence on the dancer's health and wellbeing, particularly with regard to burnout, overtraining, injury, and the underlying adaptation to training stimuli. Such phases of transition are directly associated with periodization [671] in dancers' work and school environment. Naturally, they affect all ages and levels of expertise and an understanding of their essence should therefore be included into dancers' education (and implemented from administrations) from early dance education onwards to avoid burnout and overtraining.

Volume 3 of this series addresses periodization and related aspects.

When summer vacations are planned, the dancer should (be allowed to) learn to enjoy holidays and phases of recovery from training, i.e., break of dancing. At best, summer breaks are planned as a natural part of season or school training plans. Educating the dancer in that matter also implies to **plan, instruct and address the return to dance season or school year**. Evidence-based training plans can be made for dancers, which will instruct in details, how the dancer can start training up for an upcoming season/schoolyear, and also, when to start. The dancer needs guidance in the planning of training, e.g., which exercises to use, how to assemble them and when or how to train with regard to intensity and frequency. Moreover, it is essential for the **dancer's conscious enjoyment of summer holidays** to know when to pick up training again. It has to be clear that until this very day, the dancer is to be on holidays, i.e., time off training. Such planning of the summer takes the burden off dancers, who feel that they would need a total break from dancing, but very often do not dare to allow themselves such breaks. As a consequence, dancers try to stay in training throughout the summer months, which is contra indicative of what the actually aim for. Having a clear plan for summer means to know when to take time off and when to return to training. Planning for summer can be used (among many other examples) to show the dancer that rest and recovery are an integrating part of training. Again, the education and communication in dancers' early education counts. This includes, first, the trust in the teacher to know what they are doing, when they advise total time-off. Second, it needs the motivational climate which advocates taking breaks, particularly because taking breaks in traditional environments is still regarded as lack of discipline instead of vital, integrating aspects of training.

Volume 3 discusses such training plans and provides examples.

Comparable to the planning of summer holidays, the **structuring of school year or season** should also be based on conscious goal setting and scheduling. At best, **periodization** is used and all administrators, teachers, and trainers are involved, while decisions are communicated openly to the dancer. In practice, however, such periodization is hardly ever set forth. Instead, dancers in vocational, recreational, as well as professional environments are commonly presented with their schedules weekly, and goals are rarely planned so professionally that they can be based on periodized structuring of short-, medium-, and long-term goal setting and achievement.

Structuring seasons or school years would involve to map out the days, weeks, and months coming up to dancers and teachers/trainers. Only such planning can support the **transitions within season or schoolyear**:

- The dancer transitions from vacation back into year or season. Here it is important to plan beforehand,
  - if and how a dancer can train up for this transition, and
  - how school or company have to structure the first weeks of training on site.
  - Periodized, training gradually increases and is reduced as soon as rehearsal time starts:
- Which is the next small transition, from training focus into rehearsal focus. Here it becomes

[670] Koutedakis Y, Myszkewycz L, Soulas D, Papapostolou V, Sullivan I, and Sharp NC. *The effects of rest and subsequent training on selected physiological parameters in professional female classical dancers.* Int J Sports Med. 20(6). 379-383. 1999.

[671] Wyon M. *Preparing to perform: periodization and dance.* J Dance Med Sci. 14(2). 67-72. 2010.

visible already how often this aspect is neglected, when rehearsals start immediately after a dancer has returned from summer. Very often the dancer is not ready for rehearsing yet with regard to training status. Additionally, training load should not be as comprehensive during rehearsal times as it is without rehearsal focus. At best, again, the dancer receives enough time to train back up with the trainer/teacher, based on their own summer-season/year preparatory training before rehearsal times start.

- Comparably, rehearsal load is being reduced, as soon as the dancer transitions into performances/exam periods.
- Additionally, the amount of dance technique training is adapted to the respective rehearsal or performance/exam phases the dancer has to cope with.

It becomes visible, how directly these small phases of transition are linked to periodization and thus evidence-based science of training. However, they decide, how well the dancer is protected against overtraining and injury.

TRANSITION V: TRANSITION-TRAINING FROM REHABILITATION BACK TO PERFORMING

The first chapter of the next part of this book will discuss primary and secondary injury prevention. The latter refers to a dancer, who has sustained an injury and needs medical assistance, treatment, and/or recovery time. Transition-training is a specific form of training planned for the dancer, who wants to return to "normal" training and dancing/working after an injury. Following treatment and rehabilitation the dancer needs **specific exercises** to make them fit again for every-day training load and challenges of dancing. Very often, dancers do not only underestimate recovery time (or even dance through injury and pain without any timeout for healing!) but they also return to training immediately after recovery, without having any transition-training. That comes with high risk of re-injury.

Transition-training is supposed to restore optimal morphology and function of tissues in the body, comparable to rehabilitation, but additionally takes it a step further: it is meant to train the dancer back into their very dance technique and restore (or, in many, provide for the first time) dance-related aspects needed for an injury-free future. Among such aspects are proprioception and sensorimotor training to support proper alignment and biomechanics; dance technique checks and possible corrections; aerobic endurance training and strength specifically preparing for upcoming productions or/and dance style. At best, transition-training involves the dancer as such that they can understand the underlying reason of exercises, in order to apply them in future for their own injury prevention and performance enhancement, for instance, embedded in warm-up.

Volume 3 discusses transition-training and gives examples.

PART 3

PERFORMANCE ENHANCEMENT & INJURY PREVENTION

The Implementation

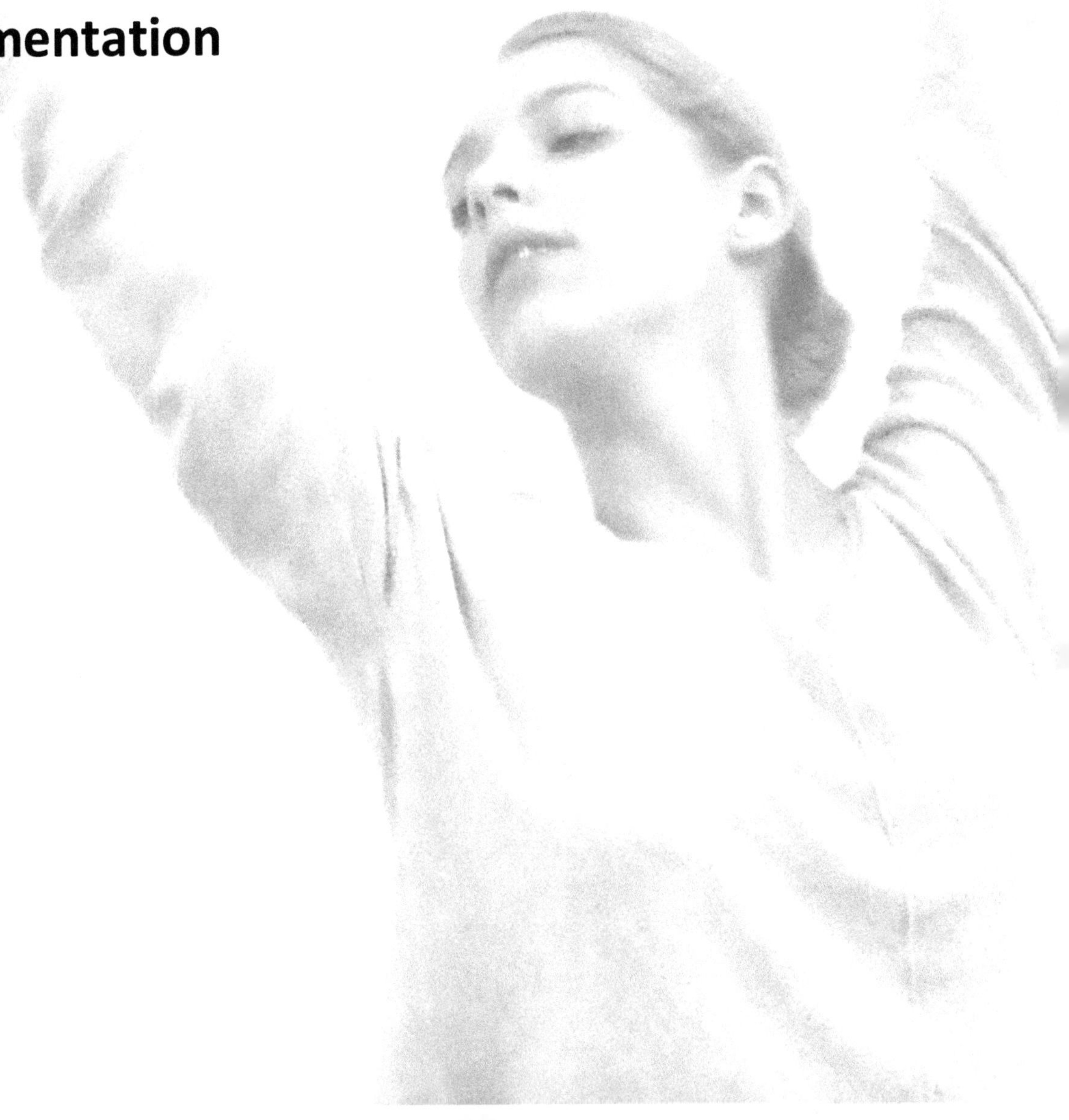

PART 3 PERFORMANCE ENHANCEMENT & INJURY PREVENTION – THE IMPLEMENTATION

Part 3 is discussing the practical relevance of the previously provided information. With a focus on children and the very important aspect of adolescence in general and puberty in particular, the goals of injury prevention in dance are discussed. The overall goal is to install functional, targeted, high levels of primary injury prevention in all fields of dance and dance pedagogy. Primary prevention is the implementation of all measures, which prevent injuries from happening in the first place. All other aspects of injury prevention, such as secondary or tertiary prevention can only be applied to the already injured dancer. Although not all injuries, especially accidents, can be prevented in dance as high-performance athletic art, the main goal of the symbiosis discussed in this series is to strive for primary injury prevention with every breath we all, dancers, teachers, trainers, clinicians, parents, consultants, administrators, take for the sake of the dancer.

Hence, part 3 starts with a comparison between primary and secondary injury prevention, showing the physical, psychological, cognitive, financial, and social burden of injury in comparison to the implementation of means of primary prevention. Further chapters address childhood and adolescence in dance, how (motor) development can be supported through dance medical dance pedagogy and what happens, if such an effort is not made. Often forgotten aspects of injury prevention as well as performance enhancement, such as nutrition, smoking, or communication and motivational climate are shortly reviewed or addressed. They provide the groundwork for the further volumes of this series, praise the self-reflective, educated, knowledgeable and dedicated dance pedagogue, teacher, or trainer, who is the conductor on the dancer's way to health, wellbeing, individual performance peaks, and injury prevention.

The chapters on Athletic Triads relate the association between dancer's identity, aspects of beauty and esthetics, planning of training, energy availability and long-term health consequences for the dancer to the reader. The chapter will explain, how bone health is related to nutrition, when an unnaturally low energy availability leads to low percentage of fat, introducing a shortage of estrogen as well as lower levels of leptin in the blood, resulting in hormonal dysbalances and impaired bone health, making the dancer prone for osteopenia and osteoporosis.

Moreover, in the last three years, efforts have been made to research the Female Athletic Triad as a Male Athletic Triad, showing the consequences of low energy availability through overtraining and unprofessional scheduling as well as the focus on esthetics for dancers of both genders.

The prevention of overuse is the control of use!
(Itzhak Siev-Ner)

Recurrently means and interventions of injury prevention are rejected by companies or schools with the argument that it takes too much time, effort, or money to implement such measures or that they are not needed. While the first is wrong and has been discussed, the second is nothing less than utterly irresponsible, as long as there are still dancers present who have pain, who possibly already suffer from injuries, or who also might benefit from the preventive screening of technique or fitness deficits, which is mostly the case. The following presents a comparison between primary and secondary injury prevention with respect to investing resources.

Primary injury prevention aims to prevent any injuries or ill-health before they occur. To be efficient, preventive measures have to target the specific needs of the respective field (dance) or discipline (dance style) and their associated risk factors. Thanks to dance medicine and science, many of these risk factors have been identified, and ongoing research is dedicated to inventing and testing the efficacy of preventive measures.[672]

Secondary injury prevention tries to reduce the impact of a disease or injury that has already occurred, such as physiological, psychological, financial, or legal consequences. However, in case of secondary injury prevention, an injury has already happened to a dancer and as such will always leave physical or psychological weaknesses, if not long-term damages. In case an injury results in ill-health with lasting effects, there is only **tertiary prevention** left as mitigating measure, to moderate effects and ease ramifications.

Figure 1 should serve as a comparison of basic aspects of primary versus secondary injury prevention in dancers. The graphic lists only basic resources which are needed for either form of prevention. Written in *italics*, the additional efforts of secondary injury prevention, which also need additional physiological, psychological, cognitive, financial, administrative (etc.) resources, are highlighted.

It is clear that an injury always leads to consequences such as medical assessment, treatment, therapy, rehabilitation and so forth. As such, the "introduction" to secondary injury prevention (medical assessment, therapy, rehabilitation, clearance, transition) already is a long list in itself, before the dancer can even start to return to training. Some fitness deficits might be correctable during recovery and rehabilitation, depending on the location and severity of the injury. Aerobic endurance through cycling or swimming, specific strength training and the like are likely to be part of therapy and rehabilitation, and, with medical clearance, are highly recommended to stay fit in spite of an injury during recovery time and promote healing through targeted exercising. Working with motor imagery, i.e., mental training, and integrating videos recorded prior to injury for analysis of dance technique is a valuable asset to **use timeout effectively** by dancers as well as teachers and trainers. So is dance medical education, gathering information, checking nutrition habits (healthy and balanced nutrition is essential for healing!).

After rehabilitation and therapy, and given the **medical clearance**, transition training can begin. However, here (at the latest) many problems start. In most cases (not only of overuse injury) correction of erroneous dance technique is essential, but the dancer might not be able to train fully. However, working on de-programming erroneous technique and practicing correct movement patterns is dependent on extensive practice and repetitive exercise (motor learning) – and can therefore not be tackled until the dancer is fully recovered, medically cleared, and has successfully been trained up through transition training.

Volume 2, dedicated to neuro-psychological aspects of dance, education and training, also discusses related aspects of motor imagery, motor learning, and the problem of automatizing erroneous movement and what it means to correct such faulty movement patterns for the dancer.

[672] Solomon, Ruth, and John Solomon. Dance Medicine & Science Bibliography, 7th Edition. International Association for Dance Medicine & Science. 2017.

Primary Injury Prevention

- Identification & elimination of risk factors
    - recurrent health screenings
        - used for correction of fitness deficits
        - used for correction of nutrition deficits
    - recurrent dance technique screenings
    - constant environment screening (floors, etc.)
- Acknowledgement of dancer's individuality
- Education for trainers & teachers
    - content knowledge in dance medicine & science
        - evidence-based/science of teaching
        - evidence-based/science of training
        - handling of pain & injury
        - installing empowering motivational climates
            - many more
- Education for dancers
    - handling of pain & injury, nutrition etc.
    - science of training for dancers
    - programs to foster self-determination
        - many more
- Re-consideration of audition or aptitude procedures
- Actively including specialists of dance medicine and science into all aspects

Secondary Injury Prevention

- *Medical assessment*
- *Diagnosis*
- *Treatment, therapy*
- *Break, time-loss, or restriction*
- *Involvement of insurances*
- *Rehabilitation*
- *Medical clearance*
- *Transition training & prevention of re-injury*
- Identification & elimination of risk factors
    - health & dance technique screening
        - *after recovery and transition*
    - used for correction of fitness deficits
        - *if possible during recovery*
        - *after recovery*
    - used for correction of nutrition deficits
        - *immediately*
    - environment screening (floors, etc.)
- *In-action-identification & correction of dance technical errors*
    - *passively/mentally during rehabilitation; imagery, video-analysis*
    - *actively after rehabilitation and transition*
    - *neuromotor-deprogramming of faulty technique*
    - *re-learning correct movement patterns*
    - *practicing newly learned movement patterns*
    - *automatizing newly learned movement patterns*
- Future acknowledgement of dancer's individuality
- Education for trainers & teachers
    - content knowledge in dance medicine & science
        - evidence-based/science of teaching
        - evidence-based/science of training
        - handling of pain & injury
        - installing empowering motivational climates
            - many more
- Education for dancers
    - handling of pain & injury, nutrition etc.
    - science of training for dancers
    - programs to foster self-determination
        - many more
- Re-consideration of audition or aptitude procedures
- Actively including specialists of dance medicine and science into all aspects

Figure 1: Comparison primary and secondary preventive resources (image: Courtesy of the Academy for Dance Pedagogy & Dance Medicine, Austria)

Very often dancers return to training too early and unprepared, neither having completely healed an injury nor having been trained up sufficiently through transition training. Such mistakes lay the groundwork for re-injury and chronic injury. And probably equally often dancers do not (get the chance to) heal their injuries at all: Discussing the benefits of primary injury prevention versus secondary possibilities with an artistic director of a world-renowned ballet company last year, he answered: "This is too much. It's easier when dancers don't complain about their injuries, then we don't need to waste our time and money with all that diagnosing and therapies. I need my dancers dancing, not complaining."

Most children start dancing at an early age. The children's early dance education is essential for their later development and perhaps professional career. However, through the eyes of dance medicine, not first and foremost with respect to performance, but how children learn to deal with dance, performance, risks, and goals from an early age, which will positively affect all aspects of performance enhancement and injury prevention. It will define their future **quality of health, wellbeing, success, and motivation**.

Childhood and (motor) development is characterized by permanent **learning**, underlying adaptational changes, visible through performance. All that is a **self-organizational process**. At best, the child is allowed to go through life with **curiosity** and **interest**, is mentally, psychologically and physically supported and can feel **related.** [673] The time between the age of 10 and 17, sometimes even earlier in girls, brings along the quickest and most intensive changes in the course of the second growth spurt and puberty. When children receive intensive dance education, **the most essential years of education meet the most vital ones in their development**. It is not surprising that their maturation impacts their dance development, and vice versa. In this respect, the idea "I don't teach professionals, I only teach children and adolescents, for that you don't need to know much" is a sign for a severe lack of knowledge because it must be just the other way round: Teaching children and adolescents requires more expertise than teaching any other age group. In children and adolescents, foundations are laid for all aspects of future (dance) life:

- Motivation and goal orientation (task-oriented or ego-oriented behavior)[674]
- Goal setting, planning and joyful, conscious achievement
- Self-determination (feelings of competence, autonomy, relatedness)[675]
- Perceived competence: what are my strengths and my weaknesses
- Self-concept: Who am I and how do I perceive myself within my environment?
  - self-image, self-esteem, ideal self[676]
- Future sense of identity
- Maturity and social / emotional intelligence (e.g., allowing to be outspoken to stand up for the own wellbeing)
- Coping skills (e.g., with stress, conflicts, challenges etc.)
- Dance technique inevitably linked to the very own individuality
- Handling of training and a natural idea of load-rest-ratio
- Handling of pain and injury
- ...to name a few...

Volume 2 focuses on most of the above-mentioned points and relates motivational, educational, and communicational theories relevant for dancing and teaching to the development of a (young) dancer as well as the success and wellbeing of a teacher/trainer.

LAYING THE GROUNDWORK: VOCATIONAL & RECREATIONAL ASPECTS

The years up to the age of ten should be the same for all children or at least similar: **playful dance engagement** with **healthy, correct "physical, emotional and cognitive movement" in an empowering motivational climate** is paramount. Foundations must be laid, both in terms of physical movement and the child's cognitive and psychological abilities. The difference between amateur and professional training is not yet relevant. And in no way must any earlier differentiation be determined by how much **fun** a child has **when dancing**. For children and their healthy development, fun, interest and curiosity are the best factors for learning, because they lead to **high quality motivation**. No hard discipline and drill can beat

[673] Spitzer, Manfred. Lernen – Gehirnforschung und die Schule des Lebens. [Learning – Neuroscience and Lifelong Learning] Heidelberg. Spektrum Akad.Verlag. 2006.

[674] Nicholls JG. *Achievement motivation: Conceptions of ability, subjective experience, task choice, and performance. PSYCHOLOGICAL REVIEW. 91*(3). 328-346. 1984.

[675] Deci EL, and Ryan RM. Self-Determination Theory: A Macrotheory of Human Motivation, Development, and Health. Canadian Psychology. 49(3). 182-185.

[676] Rogers CM, Smith MD, and Coleman JM. *Social comparison in the classroom: The relationship between academic achievement and self-concept.* J Edu Psychol. 70(1). 50-57. 1978.

that with respect to successful learning transfer and high performance as the visible outcome.

Another aspect is the acknowledgment of the **child's individuality**: From earliest dance education onwards, the dancer's very own body is unique and has to be **acknowledged, e.g., recognized and accepted**, and every aspect of training and education should be based on that individuality to avoid ill-being but achieve a maximum of performance and wellbeing. With respect to teachers and trainers, practice shows that a major discrepancy between teachers in vocational schools and teachers of so-called amateur classes or "private ballet/dance studios" can be found related to the aspect of individuality. Commonly, more dance teachers and trainers from amateur and recreational dance than from vocational schools participate in special education in the field of dance medicine and science. However, they do not need the special training more than their colleagues teaching in vocational programs do. On the contrary. But many of them have shown to be more open, self-reflective, and courageous (i.e., responsible) to rethink their own teaching style, see the child as an individual, and break with old traditions of ballet and dance education to enhance and ensure their dancers' wellbeing. They might also be **supported by** their **(heads of) schools, studios and institutions**, which might be more open to science and "the outside world" than traditional vocational schools very often show to be.

No matter whether the child aims to become a professional one day or not, dance is supposed to be related to fun, enjoyment and curiosity based on the acknowledgement of the dancer's individual uniqueness. That does not mean that every dancer has to be raised in single classes, one-to-one with the teacher. It means that **through sufficient dance medical knowledge and training, a teacher is quick to recognize individuality in dance technique and other** needs and demands, and can guide a dancer individually within a class of other individuals who have their individuality acknowledged the same way.

As early as around the age of ten years, most start to make a difference between vocational and recreational (amateur) training. However, previous chapters have shown how dangerous early specialization is with regard to injuries, burnout, dropout, and overall well- or ill-being of a child. When preparing a child for a professional career, all the foundations for their later life (from dance technique to self-concept) must be laid with evidence-based, individual **accuracy** in the early years of puberty. In vocational settings, training loads very often increase significantly and too fast, when children enter the pre-professional programs. The training becomes very monotonous and is meant to follow strict rules to support motor learning. Due to the focus on dance technique and commonly high numbers of training hours, the dancer reaches higher stages of motor learning more quickly, which is the overall goal of vocational education aiming to reach highest stages of motor learning and the **autonomy of movement**.

Volume 2 discusses the stages of motor learning[677,678] with respect to educational aspects in dance settings.

The aim in **vocational** training is to lay a fundamental dance technical basis which is essential for a future profession and aims to reach high levels of **variable, automated availability of the learned**. In the first years of vocational training, great rehearsals or performances are rare so that the child is not distracted from their training. In **recreational** dance the opposite can be found, with a focus on performing and the dream of stage, but commonly less on dance technique due to a lack of available time for practice. That again, is a form of early specialization in recreational dance, with the focus on performance, often paired with too little basis of dance technique and science of training. If not based on dance medicine and science to guide the child in a specific, pre-defined task-goal oriented manner, these two opposing approaches are equally dangerous. The introductory chapters have discussed the matter.

In addition to all the striving for artistic-athletic excellence in dance education, one crucial point is too often overlooked: **Behind these disciplined, willing young dancers hides a child's soul. A young person is easily influenced[679], especially since they look up to their teachers, who are usually the dancer's role model – whether they are fit for that or not.**[680] This child has a dream, and although the teacher/trainer is not solely responsible to protect this dream and ensure its achievement, it is their task to be aware of the trust the dancer (and related others) have in them. Children are willing to submit to enormous discipline and partly far-

[677] Fitts, P.M. & Posner, M.I. Human Performance. Belmont. Brooks/Cole. 1987.

[678] Fitts, P.M. Perceptual motor skill learning. In: Welton, A.W. Categories of Human Learning. NY. Academic Press. p. 243-255. 1964.

[679] Stark A, and Newton M. *A dancer's well-being: The influence of the social psychological climate during adolescence.* Psychology of Sport and Exercise. 15. 356-363.

[680] Lee SA. *The Artist as Teacher: A Psychological Perspective.* Medical Problems of Performing Artists. 12(2). 38-41. 1997.

reaching sacrifices, especially in vocational education. They voluntarily give up a large part of their childhood (as their teachers used to do!) and many aspects that other children of their age may take for granted and enjoy. The dream of the stage is a fire in the child's soul. This (hopefully intrinsic) motivation, allows them to go through a strenuous education focused on dance. **Tribute paid to all teachers who can support this individual, intrinsic, i.e., high quality motivation and turn it into a fire of high levels of self-concept and autonomy, without putting the flame out.** To do so, they must have recognized that dance education and dance medicine/science must go hand in hand.[681]

Only a healthy, strong self-esteem in an un-injured body and soul can make (young) dancers fit for the requirements they will face in their extremely demanding profession. The type of dance training that bases on authoritative teacher behavior, drill and discipline will keep the child's sense of self-esteem and self-efficacy on a modest scale.[682,683] However, educating children must always and exclusively have one focus only: the child must be allowed to gain a healthy level of both to ensure their wellbeing, autonomy and success. As such, children are prepared for the high numbers of stressors they have to deal with in their professional (dance) life.

The **physical, psychological**, and **cognitive development** of a child needs to be looked at **individually** and is significantly influenced by subjective experiences, family, and social environment. Therefore, a child's performance depends on various factors. It must always be evaluated in connection with their biological age, i.e., their individual developmental stage. In a class with children chronologically of the same age, one child will differ significantly from the other in their development. Teachers and trainers must consciously learn to distinguish between **chronological**, **biological**, and **psycho-social age** in a child's individual development. Ignoring biological individuality or dance medicine in dance education can lead to overuse, overstrain and injuries already in the young (as well as in the teacher).

Volume 2 and 3 give practical ideas, approaches and exercises, how classes with children and adolescents can be designed based on dance/sports medicine and science, always relating these examples to evidence provided by these disciplines.

PHASES OF ADOLESCENT DEVELOPMENT: AN OVERVIEW

The **development** of a child[684] into an adult can be divided into **phases**[685]:

- **infancy** from birth to the end of the first year of life
- **early childhood** from the first to the sixth year of life
- **childhood** from school age to about ten years
- **puberty**, which is to be considered gender-dependent and individual between the age of ten and 18. Puberty in itself can be divided in three underlying phases, which will be discussed in a special chapter below.

Each phase has its vulnerabilities and strengths. And each next phase can only be reached, when all necessary aspects in the development are ready to make the next step. These aspects are called limiting factors: A child will only start to stand up, when all aspects are ready to be able to tackle this next step: neurological (e.g., nerve-muscle coordination, balance, motor control), psychological (e.g., motivational aspects, the inspiration to do the next step), physiological (e.g., the strength needed in muscles, tendons, ligaments, bones), etc. When one of these factors is lacking, every so-called early support or fostering to put the child onto its legs will not be successful, because the body signals its lack of readiness. If teachers know about child development, e.g., limiting factors, and so many other aspects involved they will achieve the best result for all persons involved through their dance class.

---

681 Molnar M. Dance and development in children and adolescents. J Dance Med Sci. 3(2). 1999.

682 Garcia-Dantas A, Caracuel JC. Interacciones entre estilo docente y motivacion del alumnado en un conservatorio profesional de danza. [Interactions between teaching style and students´ motivation in a professional dance conservatoire.] Proceedings of Congreso Andaluz de Psicologia del Deporte. Sevilla, Spain, 17-19 de Noviembre de 2011.

683 Garcia-Dantas A, Caracuel JC. *Factores que influyen en el abandono en los conservatorios de danza. [Factors that influence on the dance conservatoires dropping out.]* RIPED. 6(1). 79-97. 2011.

684 Haywood, Kathleen M, and Nancy Getchell. Life span motor development (6th edition). Champaign. Human Kinetics. 2014.

685 Exner-Grave E. *Entwicklungsphasen vom Kind zum Erwachsenen unter Berücksichtigung der unteren Extremitäten (UE).* IN: Exner-Grave, Elisabeth (ed.). Tanzmedizin. Die medizinische Versorgung professioneller Tänzer. Stuttgart. SchattauerVerlag. 2008. 29-32.

From **early childhood** onwards, toddlers, who are coming from the bowed legs of an infant, show a change in leg axis from bowed to knocked knees when they start to stand and walk. The so-called "in-toe walking", which most **children** show until about school age, is a result of related changes in the growing body's length and axis ratios.[686,687] The child usually shows slight knock-knees, can also have a flat and sickling (planovalgus) foot when standing, which they can compensate (eliminate) when raising up onto the balls of their feet (relévé). Their leg, abdominal, and back muscles must first adapt to the growth and the necessary motor control as well as strength must be developed anew with each change. This is why hyperlordosis and round bellies are a natural thing in the very young. The **teacher can start to create an awareness for correct posture** and active engagement of muscles such as the abdominals, but has to be prepared that children will forget to do that actively themselves. The **knock-knee** and the flat foot during this early **pre-school phase must not be corrected** by working on **turnout** of the legs. The child's hip joints as well as all bones related to the leg axes are in a remodeling phase and tend to continuously rotate the leg inwards during this time. Again, the teacher can create a sense of awareness, explaining healthy behavior such as the common concept to keep the knee cap vertically aligned with the toes. But, in case basic approaches to dance technique are integrated already at this young age, the feet must not turn further outwards than the hip can allow, even if the first position hardly differs from the sixth. And such approaches have to be designed as **playful experience, not dance technical exercising**.

Children in preschool or kinder garden develop their sense of dance best through such playful engagement, as with most aspects of their lives. The **motivation** kindled in the child by playing and their **curiosity** significantly **promotes** the self-organizational **process of (motor) learning**. Simultaneously, the child's imagination and cognitive and emotional intelligence are best promoted by a child-friendly approach to the art of dance, focusing on the versatility of movement and music. Limiting factors have to be considered, e.g., that many children practice a movement preferably to one side only first, that unilaterality comes before the child can manage contralateral motion, or might need their time to process such complex motions as gallop or skipping. Pressure or intensive practice are not helpful, because the child will only do the next step when it is ready to do exactly that. The more freedom children can experience in that matter the "faster" they will develop. The teacher can show and provide a broad versatility of motions and exercises, but will achieve better progress when the **focus is on exploring dance**, and the child has the freedom to **find their own ideal because of individual approach to motor task achievement**. Specific training of dance technique such as the turnout can and must wait, because they are highly depending on the phase of development a child is going through, e.g., the angles and torsions of bones and resulting range of motion in joints.

In (early) childhood, children can suffer from **growing pain** and sometimes great fatigue. Both are not an indicator that dance class is bad for them or that the teacher made a mistake. It only means that growth needs a lot of energy, which is why they need more sleep and are very hungry during phases of growth. And growing pain, experienced by approximately 1/3 of children in childhood is a commonly bilateral lower-extremity non-inflammatory nocturnal pain, for which the cause is basically unclear.[688,689,690] But common notions regard a discrepancy between faster bone growth and slower soft tissue growth as a main reason. However, the transition from bowed legs in infancy to the toddler's knock-knees is characterized by a tremendous strain on the growing muscles, tendons and ligaments, which have to adapt to bipedality while growing in length. The legs' inner sides can react with pulling pain due to the knock-knee position after intense physical activity. Nevertheless, moderate exercise, healthy nutrition, plenty of drinking, and sufficient sleep are the best "therapy" to respond to the pain in the knees and lower legs in healthy children. Exercise helps the body grow by boosting metabolism and ensuring sufficient stability in the tissues through **appropriate loading**.

In **childhood** or early school age, approximately from the age of six to ten, the child experiences the **first significant growth spurt**, which primarily affects the **longitudinal growth** of the **extremities**. The bones grow particularly fast, and muscles, tendons, and ligaments have difficulty keeping up. For some time, the child seems lanky and clumsy. During this time, **coordination** and **mobility** training in dance is most important, again without forcing

[686] Westhoff B, Jäger M and Krauspe R. Axes of the legs in childhood What is pathologic? [Kindliche Beinachsen. Was ist pathologisch?]. Orthopäde. 36. 485-500. 2007.

[687] Cordier W and Katthagen BD. *Femoral torsional deformities [Femorale Torsionsfehler]*. Orthopäde. 29. 795-801. 2000.

[688] Lehman PJ, and Carl RL. *Growing Pains*. Sports Health. 9(2). 132-138. 2017..

[689] Pavone V, Vescio A, Valenti F, Sapienza M, Sessa G, and Testa G. *Growing pains: What do we know about etiology? A systematic review.* World J Orthop. 10(4). 192-205. 2019..

[690] Lowe RM, and Hashkes PJ. *Growing pains: a noninflammatory pain syndrome of early childhood.* Nat Clin Pract Rheumatol. 4(10). 542-549. 2008.

the child into relentless stretching routines or dance technical drills. The knock-knee should now grow into a straight leg alignment. The planovalgus foot should also be compensated by sufficiently strong foot muscles in normal stance and gait. Both can specifically be supported by the knowledgeable dance teacher, who teaches awareness for proper postural control, whole body alignment and correct use of leg axes through targeted use of exercises.

The **late childhood**, basically the last year/two years of elementary school, which lasts from the age of 9 or 10 until the onset of puberty, builds on the gains of previous years and dance classes. In those years, children show to be especially attentive and can make significant steps forward in their dancing. **Power** and **endurance** are particularly trainable here and complement the physical development of flexibility and finetuning of coordination until the onset of puberty. In **boys**, puberty focuses on **developing strength**, while girls experience an impressive development of their **fine coordination** in dance. Targeted **aerobic endurance** training should be gently increased and included in the classes from early childhood. It creates a fundamental basis for **resistance to fatigue**, better **physical and cognitive stamina**, as well as **faster recovery** after training. As such it is a major aspect for injury prevention in puberty and young adulthood.

The extraordinarily **high developmental capacity of mobility, flexibility and coordination, speed, and endurance in childhood shows how vital evidence-based early dance education is for a healthy and injury-free adult life.** It is the foundation for healthy exercise and the formation of all the motor skills that adults need to maintain their physical and mental fitness. The healthy, individual development of the child must not be restricted or disturbed in any way. Neither should children be forced to perform nor should they be dissuaded from following the path of their natural, individual cognitive, emotional and physical development based on curiosity and motivation. In the subsequent years of puberty some children might focus their attention onto a professional career. Times will show, whether the **quality of motivation in the dancer through the teacher created motivational climate** are high enough (additionally to all extrinsic and intrinsic factors influencing a child in such a decision) to keep on engaging and see through such a strenuous pathway. However, whether professional or amateur, puberty can be the biggest challenge for a young dancer during their training – and with that, for their teachers.

But when the teacher/trainer can draw from dance medicine and science, they can also turn those years to some of the best in a young dancer's life, in which the most essential steps towards a successful career are laid and which have the potency to protect and guide a dancer throughout their future with a maximum of performance through a maximum of health.

PUBERTY AS A SPECIAL CHALLENGE

Young people involved in competitive sports need special attention regarding dance medicine.[691] Puberty is part of adolescence, and might be regarded as the most challenging and therefore most important bridge from childhood into adult life. Depending on the levels of physical and cognitive stress in the young dancer, individual changes in the endocrine system (hormone system) lead to different adaptational reactions in the young dancer.

On the one hand, they are very **individual** in their time of **onset**, and adolescents of the same age within a class can and will differ very much from each other in their development, which makes planning of training a big challenge for teachers and schools. On the other hand, competitive sports- and dance-related factors that influence successful training and performance are **predominantly genetically determined** and increasingly come into play through puberty:

Innate neuromuscular abilities such as flexibility, the dominant type of muscle fiber, but also high psychological stability, willingness to perform, motivation and trainability, which are enormously important for the career as a dancer, are partly genetically determined.

However, to a great extent many of them also depend on environmental factors such as teachers, nutrition, science of training, family and social environment as well as the motivational climate in the dance setting.

[691] Hebestreit Helge, and Oded Bar-Or (eds.). The Young Athlete (Encyclopedia of Sports Medicine). Oxford Blackwell Publishers. 2007.

In puberty, neurophysiological processes lead to **changes in the hormonal balance** of the young person with the overall goal of sexual maturity. The years of **puberty** represent a critical and essential time for adolescents. Significant **changes** in **physique** and **metabolism** take place. However, these changes also have numerous **psychological consequences.**[692]

In the **second** or pubertal **growth spurt**, the hormone system changes from child to adult and sexual hormones come into play. The result is a severe change of **body proportions**, **weight** as well as emotional states and interests. For many adolescents, puberty comes with a temporary **loss of control** over their bodies, a control that they had previously worked hard on to achieve in dance training. This loss of control can be a great shock and setback.

The **risk of injury** also **increases significantly**, because the adolescent dancer temporarily loses neuromuscular control over their "new" and continuously changing body.[693] During this time, it is crucial that the teacher immediately recognizes the occurring changes and **adapts training** and environment to correspond to the adolescent's development and needs. That applies to amateur dance as well as to professional training. During adolescence, the dancer is very vulnerable, while, especially in early stages, some adolescents might (pretend to) feel invincible.

Puberty reveals the hormonal and, thus, psycho-physical differences between young male and female dancers. Due to their fundamentally different physique, young women have disadvantages in body strength, which, together with their hormone status, possibly entail lower levels of performance and resilience of the musculoskeletal system. At the same time women have advantages over men in terms of functionality and performance of organs up to menopause, making women more efficient than men for a longer time to come after puberty. However, sometimes very pronounced periodic hormonal imbalances not only at the beginning of puberty can negatively affect female performance, which is why dancers need a lot of care during puberty, for instance to avoid the very dangerous female athletic triad.

While hormonal changes influence the dancer and thus their performance in education, high physical performance also influences hormonal regulation, and can reduce or interrupt it entirely, depending on the complexity of the training load and the energy supply from their diet.[694]

The growth spurts of puberty can be related to frustration for the young dancers. An identity crisis, the search for coordination, social confirmation, self-esteem and perspectives, while revolting against existing relationships and authorities are part of the adolescent's natural development on their way to adulthood. Professional dance education comes with the risk that adolescents will not experience phases of puberty in due extent due to their dogged training and disciplined lifestyle. In vocational training, there is rarely time for **teenage rebellion** against authorities such as teachers or parents. Usually, young dancers do not even think about it because of the enormous discipline that their training demands. However, this may only be an advantage in the short run because rebelling, testing boundaries, falling in and out of love for the first time with unattainable role models or older stars (as a secure test-run), and the like are part of **creating identity**. As a result of not experiencing the search for who they are, as it is often the case with adolescents in vocational training, children retreat into their shells. They **hide behind** the daily **discipline,** an **unnatural self-image,** and significant emotional and, therefore, cognitive and motor **insecurity.**[695]

Not forging identity can and will catch up with the dancers at the latest at the end of their active career, when they have to say goodbye to their beloved profession and look for a new way of life and second career path. Suppose, the teacher or the institution uses the growth spurts to show the adolescents how dance, medicine and science provides career opportunities after an active career, young dancers **think about** their **interests** regarding a second career early on and also, hopefully, have interests other than dance already in puberty. Thus, **stress** provoked by highly physical activity is **reduced** in the adolescent at a time full of physical and mental changes, and much of their later stress before the end of their career is precautionarily eliminated right away by

692 IAMDS. Education Committee. The challenge of the adolescent dancer. International Association for Dance Medicine and Science. 2000.

693 Storm JM, Wolman R, Bakker EWP, and Wyon MA. *The Relationship Between Range of Motion and Injuries in Adolescent Dancers and Sportspersons: A Systematic Review.* Front Psychol. 9:287. 2018.

694 Constantini NW, Dubnov G, and CM Lebrun. *The menstrual cycle and sport performance.* Clin Sports Med 24. 51-82. 2005.

695 Robson BE. *Adolescent development: How dancers compare with the typical teenager.* Med Probl Perform Art. 16(3). 109-114. 2001.

consciously looking into and discussing the future with an open mind.[696,697,698]

The chapter on nutrition as vital aspect of injury prevention and performance enhancement discusses this issue in detail.

Going through adolescence[699,700] can be divided into three main phases, namely early, middle, and late puberty/adolescence and is characterized by major differences between non-dancing population, recreational, and vocational dancers.[701,702]

Early puberty is determined by the second growth spurt. Children become lanky and the growth of limbs has to be coordinated, possibly leading to many temporary setbacks or performance plateaus in young dancers. Frequent weight changes mostly effect girls, especially since many dance styles put such a high focus on abnormal levels of thinness and low BMI. Weight changes, hair, skin and facial markers as well as the increase in limb length are **main signs** that the child has entered puberty and sex hormones have taken the reins. The fact that dancers around the age of 12 are neurologically mature, does rarely contribute to their self-esteem, because their inexperience can lead to major social discrepancies, which increase their levels of self-consciousness. Coping with hormone-related changes in overall appearance, possible changes in skin and hair and overall appearance, growing pain, high levels of fatigue, joint stiffness and reduction in flexibility due to growth, and perceived (or teacher produced)[703] weight issues add to these levels of self-consciousness.

Social life and interests other than dance, including rebellion against authorities (parents, teachers), might distract many young in recreational classes, while students of vocational schools may not get the chance to experience these aspects in their full extent.

Many pre-professional dancers fall silent over their feelings in turmoil, which is why this early dancer's identity is often called "silent bodies in the making". In vocational and recreational settings, first crushes should have their room in early puberty and are mainly targeted at people out of reach of the young dancer. Such distant admiration allows to experience first feelings of love from a safe distance, because mostly the person adored is out of reach (a star of the company or other, a teacher etc.), which is nature's contribution to the safety of the adolescent within these first "run-throughs".

Middle puberty shows the differences between sexes. **After the growth spurt has overcome its peak**, boys significantly gain strength, while menstruation starts in the girls – provided that the girl is healthy and allowed to meet the high energy demands of dance with sufficient nutrition intake and resting periods (to avoid eating disorders or even female athletic triad). While boys gain muscles due to testosterone kicks, girls change from a child's body to female shapes. Mostly, boys cherish their new appearance, at least with regard to muscle mass, chest circumference, and strength, which finally makes them feel ahead of girls, while female young dancers might not experience such excruciating changes but feel uneasy about their mood swings and developing female form. During those years many young dancers start to smoke, especially in vocational education. First, because smoking is a way of rebellion, which "is allowed", given the fact that most other aspects are suppressed in vocational settings (!). Second, because it (supposedly) helps to cope with stress and dieting, especially in girls. And third, because already young dancers realize that they have more breaks when they can claim that they need them as smokers.

Not enough that so many aspects of early and middle puberty are a contradiction in terms. Many adolescents might find themselves on top of the world with feelings of invincibility and self-centered world-view, knowing that all grown-ups around them do not know things as well as they do. And that adults have basically become weird all of a sudden anyway… However, on the other side of the-top-of-the-world, very high levels of fatigue and easy exhaustion make them (feel) specifically vulnerable and "weak". Such contradictory discrepancies are hard to deal with for teachers (and parents) in recreational dancers, but are mainly locked up behind highest training demands in vocational settings. The first is nature's way, and although exhausting for parents,

[696] Hamilton LH. *Psychological Profile of the adolescent dancer.* J Dance Med Sci. 3(2). 48-50. 1999.
[697] Hamilton LH, Bristow E, and MJ Byars. *College programs for professional ballet dancers: The Impact on Career Transition.* J Dance Med Sci. 6(1). 20-23. 2002.
[698] Lee SA. *Is it the last dance?: Ballet dancers at age 30.* Med Probl Perform Art. 3(1). 1988.
[699] IADMS. Education Committee. *The challenge of the adolescent dancer.* The International Association for Dance Medicine and Science. 2000.
[700] Stace JM. *The Physiological Development of the Adolescent Dancer.* J Dance Med Sci. 3(2). 59-65. 1999.
[701] Padfield JA, Eisenman PA, Luetkemeier, MJ, and Fitt SS. *Physiological profiles of performing and recreational early adolescent female dancers.* Paediatric Exercise Science. 5. 51-59. 1993.
[702] Robson B. *Adolescent Development: How Dancers Compare with the Typical Teenager.* Med Probl Perform Art. 16. 109-114. 2001.
[703] Garcia-Dantas A, Alonso DA, Sánchez-Miguel PA, and Del Río Sánchez C. *Factors Dancers Associate with their Body Dissatisfaction.* Body Image. 25. 40-47. 2018.

teachers and trainers alike, they constitute a healthy aspect of adolescent development. The second, vocational, way can lead to low levels of self-concept, hence self-confidence, self-responsibility, and low levels of forged identity.

In **late puberty** and final phases of adolescence, the young dancers start "finding their middle". Boys have finally become men, have grown into new perceptions of hygiene and pride in their appearance. They also start to differ from girls with respect to cardio-pulmonic capacities, growing bigger hearts and higher lung capacities. Girls have lower levels of hemoglobin, due to a lack of male levels of testosterone, which comes with a disadvantage, compared to boys, with regard to metabolism and oxygen supply/usability. However, hormones start to find their balanced levels, resulting in the young dancer becoming calmer, more centered with respect to social life, authorities, and education. At best, the end of puberty is marked by final forging of early identity, leading to the young having their own opinions, attitudes, cherishing friendships and family life, and starting to think of the future, including choice of profession. As discussed above, in vocational dance these aspects might again remain neglected, and outlooks into the future already start to be characterized by the fear of injury and anxiety leading to denial in many, when it comes to the thought about the inevitable end of the dancing career. It depends on the teachers and institution to make changes to the better (see below), and pave the way through puberty as such that young vocational dancers are blessed to have the chance to forge their identity in a way that comes closest possible to non-dancing adolescents or recreational dancers.

BALANCING NEEDS, DEMANDS, PERFORMANCE ENHANCEMENT & INJURY PREVENTION

Early specialization and overtraining must but be avoided in any case and all phases and ages, which is why it needs to be considered to reduce the enormous **number of technique classes** in the most significant phases of growth.

It is possible to mentally support adolescent dancers by reducing excessive technical training in favor of an additional focus on anatomy, physiology, proprioceptive, sensorimotor and targeted strength as well as endurance training, dance history, music classes, etc. Art, an insight into dance medical professions, therapy, and choreography, can also be promoted here. All these aspects appear to be time-lost to so many teachers. But dance medicine and science know that they are not.

On the contrary, such additional focus in education which widens the cognitive as well as physical horizon of a young dancer, significantly contributes to performance enhancement and injury prevention. First, because excessive dance technique training can be reduced to an evidence-based, sensible amount preventing injuries and overtraining, and second, because such education supports the development and perception of their own identity in dancers. **Thinking about the future and professions related to dance** early enough in their education before they reach the (often most dreaded) **end of their active career**, takes a lot of stress off (young) dancers' hearts, minds and souls and supports the development of a determined yet open mindset and goal setting.

Very often the question arises, **how acknowledging the individuality of the dancers, supporting the development of identity and prevention of injury can be achieved while excellent dancers are supposed to be "produced"**. Even more since onset of puberty, growth spurts and related needs are so individual that a teacher will hardly ever find a class in which all dancers can be found in the same stage of development. The answer to this is twofold:

First, it is basically of highest importance to **rethink the structures of vocational education** in dancers towards a **remodeling of curricula**, due to the enormously high injury risk and incidence in young dancers. Part of this remodeling is **targeted teachers' education**, which guarantees that evidence-based curricula are not only composed but also realized in practice. Such curricula should be based on **health and dance technique screening** of dancers, teaching **screenings of teachers**, and principles of **periodization**, which per se already dictate monitored loading, controlled use of dance technique training, versatility, teamwork among teachers and administration for the dancers' benefit, and inclusion of individualized interventions based on the results of the health and dance technique screenings (fitness training, nutrition workshops, implementation of classes related to dance medical knowledge for dancers etc.).

Second, when teachers are wise and educated in dance medicine, science and dance pedagogy, they have learned about how to teach, which possibilities exist to support pedagogical methods, such as the principles underlying motivation and goal achievement relevant for teaching and guiding.

Practical implementation of, for instance, achievement-goal- and self-determination-theories offer so many possibilities how to teach classes (thus, also dance) fostering autonomy, competence, and relatedness in dancers through task-focused goal orientation embedded in an empowering motivational climate. Many of these possibilities are based on grouping of dancers, self-based studies in which dancers have to work on exercises themselves and find their own task-solutions, and other possibilities related to the factors of timing or focusing.

All aspects of dance-relevant topics can be implemented (dance medicine and science, arts, music, drama, ...) for groups of dancers working themselves and presenting their findings afterwards (or in another class), while others are working with the teacher on other aspects, ... They all aim to achieve high levels of self-concept and self-efficacy in dancers, fostering autonomy and perceived ability/competence. And they all move away from frontal, chalk-and-talk-teaching. Implementing such solutions kills more than two birds with one stone:

They create self-responsible dancers with higher levels of own content knowledge and efficacy, dance technique and condition based on individuality and supported by health, thus reaching a maximum of performance and so forth. And they can be used to monitor workload, group and teach dancers according to their needs (such as growth spurts), without losing anything, but in contrary, gaining such a lot.

Volume 2 discusses many of these aspects and approaches with relevance to dance and provides practical examples how to implement them.

Such exemplary approach is hardly anywhere ever put into practice. Few trainers and institutions push forward and courageously set examples by making enormous efforts to introduce even more enormous changes to dance education. They see that young dancers' overall health during puberty (and anyway) is responsible for better performances of future professional dancers in the long run. Too many others, on the other hand, fail to meet their responsibility and to live up to the trust placed into them, arguing with the **alleged loss of time and effeminacy**, which has always been considered the best **excuse** for disciplining young dancers and hiding a lack of knowledge and will to change. However, as injury reports show, this way does not pay off – at least not for the dancers. Since they and their maximum wellbeing have to be the focus of attention of all people involved, it is time to make a change! "A tree must be bent while it is young" – must not be equated to the "making and breaking of young dancers".[704] The seeds that are sowed in childhood and adolescence in dance will be reaped when these children are adults, latest. Guiding and protecting that little tree, who has decided to train hardest for a profession at such an early age where peers mostly do not even think of or know what to do in their professional future, has to be the highest calling of every teacher. **The tools for that are provided by dance medicine and science, complementing (and defining new, higher, science-based levels of) dance pedagogy**.

ASPECTS OF GENDER DIFFERENCES & GROWTH

When puberty starts, the differences between the two sexes come into effect. When **boys** go through the **second growth spurt** they grow faster in height, and after that their muscle mass increases significantly. This can make balancing and jumping harder, as the adolescent cannot yet handle the enormous and, above all, rapid muscle growth. At the same time, the kick of testosterone makes many young boys hyperactive, who develop a new motivation for increased training intensities and frequencies, which should be controlled and only supported by the (inspired!) teacher to a certain amount.

One or two short but effective **strength training sessions** per week are needed to targeted muscular strength, strength endurance, postural control and coordination. It is recommended to combine such sessions with a **special focus on proprioceptive and sensorimotor training**, to support the newly needed abilities for neuromuscular control.

The teacher also has to keep in mind that motivated young males are often found to work excessively on their dashing new jumping abilities. However, jumping[705] was identified as most important motor activity with respect

[704] Mitchell SB, Haase AM, Malina RM, and Cumming SP. *The role of puberty in the making and breaking of young ballet dancers: Perspectives of dance teachers.* J of adolescence. 47. 81-89. 2016.

[705] Moita JP, Gomes A, Xarez L, and Coelho C. *The role of prediagnostic data in injury epidemiology in preprofessional dancers.* Scand J Med Sci Sports. 29(4). 606-614. 2019.

to overuse injuries, and must not be overdone in young dancers during such phases of growth and adaptation. While muscle mass increases, stretchability dramatically decreases. Boys need to **stretch more** to get the flexibility needed in dance and prevent muscular imbalances. However, even if stretchability decreases and the focus is on strength training, adolescents should **under no circumstance** be put under **pressure when stretching**. Dangling weights off their extremities in stretching positions or putting somebody's body weight, for instance the teacher's, on the stretching adolescent can lead to severe injuries (in male as well as in female dancers!). The **hormone boosts** soften the **growth plates** in the last growth spurt, and the young dancer's body becomes **very vulnerable**.

An example for such severe injuries is the SCFE, i.e., slipped capital femoral epiphysis.[706,707,708] It is a fracture of the epiphyseal plate in the head of the growing femur, a hip disorder, which mainly affects pubescent males and usually on one side.[709] It can be recognized by a sudden, mostly unilateral extensive increase of turnout in the hip joint and can be attributed to the use of **force during stretching**, to **too much technical training** in phases of growth spurts, as well as to **wrong dance technique**, e.g., **forcing of turnout**. Plates of hyaline cartilage are found in the areas of the bone where longitudinal growth takes place in the still developing skeleton. These areas soften on phases of increased growth, especially when the sexual hormones in puberty come into play, which initiate the second major growth spurt. With the end of puberty, the growth plates in the bones ossify, and the process of growing comes to a standstill, thus reducing the risk of injury again. An injury like SCFE can, depending on the severity, mean complicated operations and, in the worst case, the end of training for the young dancer.

The hormonal softening of the growth plates in the last growth spurt makes the young dancer's body very vulnerable and can also affect **girls** exposed to **pointe work too early or/and too extensively,** which can also be found in recreational training.[710,711,712,713] Not the age of the girl who wants to start with pointe work is the first and foremost evaluation criteria for readiness, but the **training level**. To dance on pointe, several training sessions per week focused on dance technique, strength, proprioceptive and sensorimotor control are necessary to prepare the young dancer's body before the dancer is to be put on pointe. Amateurs who only train one or two times a week do not have enough physical strength and preparation to train on pointe. In this case, the teacher must say no in favor of the child, even if parents and children are usually very persistent. Girls should be allowed to try it and step in the shoes for a few minutes, probably repeat some exercises sufficiently secured by the barre. But still, continuous training on pointe must be sufficiently prepared and requires an already high physical level of dance technique, strength and experience to avoid injuries.

For **girls**, **puberty** brings about the very **unpopular increase in body fat** on hips and thighs, which **should not be negatively commented on or even tried to be stopped or prevented entirely**, as mentioned above and discussed in the chapter on nutrition in the following. The shoulders remain relatively narrow compared to the hips – the body fat percentage increases. If young dancers after puberty at the age of about 20-29 years are compared to males with respect to body fat percentage, in men a ratio of 7-11% is called "thin/underweight", in girls a percentage of 18-25%.[714] This substantial difference is intended to show how important (and natural) it is that young women, including female dancers, do not (have to) prevent their pubescent physical development by starving, which is usually precisely the opposite in vocational training. Especially girls run the risk of eating disorders if they are forced to drastically reduce or keep the fat percentage low despite the natural need to gain fat. Compared to the average population, the **incidence** of **eating disorders** such as bulimia or anorexia nervosa in young dancers is **high**, up to 25% compared to 2% among the rest of the population. [715] In puberty, the adolescent woman in competitive sports is particularly at risk of hindering her natural development and increasing the fat percentage

---

[706] Castillo C, and Mendez M. *Slipped Capital Femoral Epiphysis: A Review for Pediatricians*. Pediatr Ann. 47(9). 377-380. 2018.

[707] Zilkens C, Bittersohl B, Westhoff B und R Krauspe. *Epiphysiolysis Capitis Femoris*. Monatsschr Kinderheilkd. 162. 996-1003. 2014.

[708] Exner-Grave, Elisabeth (ed.). Tanzmedizin. Die medizinische Versorgung professioneller Tänzer. Stuttgart New York. Schattauer Verlag 2008.

[709] Caine D, diFiori J, and N Maffulli. *Physeal injuries in children's and youth sports: reasons for concern*. Br J Sports Med. 40. 749-760. 2006.

[710] Meck C, Hess RA, Helldobler R, and J Roh. *Pre-Pointe Evaluation Components Used by Dance Schools. J Dance Med Sci. 8(2). 37-42. 2004.*

[711] Guggenheim C. A survey of elite professional ballet schools regarding the initiation of pointe work in children. Med Probl Perform Art. 9(1). 15-17. 1994.

[712] Nunes NM, Haddad JJ, Bartlett DJ, and KD Obright. *Musculoskeletal injuries among young, recreational, female dancers before and after dancing in pointe shoes*. Pediatr Phys Ther. 14(2). 100-106. 2002.

[713] Barringer Janice, and Sarah Schlesinger. The Pointe Book: Shoes, Training and Technique. Pennington. Princeton Books Co. 2012.

[714] Koutedakis Y, and NC Graig Sharp. The fit and healthy dancer. Chichester. John Wiley & sons. 1999. p. 272.

[715] Koutedakis Y, and NC Graig Sharp. The fit and healthy dancer. Chichester. John Wiley & sons. 1999. p. 280.

by starving. The next chapter will examine that in more detail.

Due to frequent hormonal imbalances and vegetative changes caused by the onset of the menstrual cycle in the adolescent girl, a **late menarche** (onset of menstruation) is commonly very welcome in dance. However, regarding **health**, it is **unfavorable** for the development of high **bone mineral density**. From a purely competitive point of view, girls with late menarche seem to have an advantage over those who reach puberty early. The effects of hormone levels and cycles can be felt differently in adolescent girls, and in some cases, they cannot be felt at all.[716] In contrast to menstrual pain and other noticeable effects of altered hormone levels, **a negative impact on bone metabolism and bone mineral density due to late menarche is not noticeable to the outside world**! The girl bears the **consequences** much later **in** her **adult life**.

Severe "side effects" of menarche can significantly influence a female young dancer's wellbeing, coping abilities, and performance, which is very often deliberately ignored in the overall goal of producing excellent dancers, increasing the intrinsic stress level of young dancers tremendously. Increased basal temperature in the second half of the cycle, triggered by the thermogenetic effect of progesterone, (pre-) menstrual lower abdominal, leg, or/and back pain, colic, bloating, increased fluid retention with weight gain, and mental or psychological instability can affect performance and wellbeing just in times where the girl is supposed to deliver higher levels of performance than ever. Although menstruation and female hormone phases are easily swept under the carpet and are often made a taboo in our society, it must nevertheless be said that the female hormone phases and the related menstruation can have significant impact on female high-performance athletes for multiple reasons. Changing resilience, pain, mood swings, and the like accompany many young dancers month after month, and can multiply the usually high degree of exhaustion of some, while they are/seem non-existent in others. Many teachers argue that they had never had any support with their own problems themselves when they were in education and that they now consider any support for their students in related matters as effeminacy. However, when young dancers are severely affected by period pain resulting from cramps due to muscle hypertonia or related issues, they need to have attention and support.

First, to make sure that severe pain is not related to any pathologies, e.g., endometriosis[717, 718], which has the potency to cost careers. Second, when that is hopefully to be ruled out, to reduce affected girls' stress levels "just" by showing and giving support. That creates relatedness on the one hand, and is a matter of injury prevention on the other, because higher stress levels make a dancer more prone to injury. Third, increased levels of training load have shown to be significantly influencing the functionality of the pelvic floor, which becomes rigid. As such, it can significantly increase period pain and also already introduce issues such as urinal incontinence or increasing susceptibility for urethra tract infections in girls. Some of the reasons why a training related dysfunctional pelvic floor is associated with decreased quality of life in athletes.[719720,721,722]

Volume 3 includes an extensive chapter on the role and importance of the pelvic floor in dancers and athletes, further related to all aspects of training, alignment, endurance, core stability, breathing, and overall wellbeing.

Forth, girls' weight gain through the impact of hormonal changes in early and middle puberty can lead to the introduction of **dieting and (forced) weight loss**, all factors further increasing stress levels and kindling feelings of shame and insufficiency in young artistic athletes, which can lead to severe consequences such as eating disorders. The girl's (perceived) need to starve can backfire by multiplying period pain and related symptoms, and might eventually lead to amenorrhea, laying the groundwork for the Female Athletic Triad. The girl's monthly burden and any weight gain associated with the period can reduce performance in addition to all

[716] Constantini NW, and MP Warren MP. *Physical activity, fitness and reproductive health in women: clinical observations.* In: Bouchard C, Shepard RJ, and T Stephens T (eds.) Physical activity, fitness and health: international proceedings and consensus statement. Champaign (IL). Human Kinetics. 1994. p. 955-966.

[717] Bulun SE, Yilmaz BD, Sison C, Miyazaki K, Bernardi L, Liu S, Kohlmeier A, Yin P, Milad M, and Wei J. *Endometriosis.* Endocr Rev. 40(4). 1048-1079. 2019.

[718] Poli-Neto OB, Oliveira AMZ, Salata MC, Cesar Rosa-E-Silva J, Machado DRL, Candido-Dos-Reis FJ, and Nogueira AA. *Strength Exercise Has Different Effects on Pressure Pain Thresholds in Women with Endometriosis-Related Symptoms and Healthy Controls: A Quasi-experimental Study.* Pain Med. 21(10). 2280-2287. 2020.

[719] Giagio S, Salvioli S, Pillastrini P, and Innocenti T. *Sport and pelvic floor dysfunction in male and female athletes: A scoping review.* Neurourol Urodyn. 40(1). 55-64. 2021.

[720] Thyssen HH, Clevin L, Olesen S, and Lose G. *Urinary incontinence in elite female athletes and dancers.* International Urogynecological Journal and Pelvic Floor Dysfunction. 13(1). 15-17. 2002.

[721] Pires T, Pires P, Moreira H, Gabriel R, Viana S, and Viana R. *Assessment of pelvic floor muscles in sportswomen: Quality of life and related factors.* Phys Ther Sport. 43. 151-156. 2020.

[722] Louis-Charles K, Biggie K, Wolfinbarger A, Wilcox B, and Kienstra CM. *Pelvic Floor Dysfunction in the Female Athlete.* Curr Sports Med Rep. 18(2). 49-52. 2019.

other pubertal effects. Weight fluctuations due to growth and seasons (in spring usually the size and thus weight increase[723]) must be taken into consideration but need the so often mentioned content knowledge in teachers. However, what one usually sees instead is that the training is intensified when a girl experiences performance plateaus or setbacks. The response to weight gain, for various reasons mentioned, comes in the form of criticism and often even sanctions and restrictions to lose weight. As a result, the adolescent dancer may further reduce her already low food intake – and all the problems mentioned above multiply. Since dancers commonly tend to make themselves responsible for "mistakes" due to traditionally misguided self-discipline and "dancer's identity", possibly related stress becomes a vicious circle.

Fifth, when the teacher can show social support, aware of its importance, feelings of relatedness are kindled between teacher and dancer, supporting empowering motivational climates, which again are essential for the dancer's injury prevention, performance enhancement and future sense of identity. Such aspects, for instance, are later essential, when many female dancers find increasing desire looming up in their souls and minds to have children. However, practice shows how such wishes are still not welcomed in the 21st century. Moreover, practice also shows, how often a female athletic triad or an overlooked pathology such as endometriosis can lead to infertility in the dancer's adult life. All such issues have to be avoided and are *partly* in the teacher's hands. By installing empowering motivational climates, the teacher provides vital aspects of social support, leading to high levels of perceived relatedness and autonomy in the young dancers. Such results support **self-concept**, self-esteem and therefore the future **identity** of a dancer. She might gain enough emotional and social competence through the groundwork a caring and knowledgeable teacher has provided, to stand up for her own[724] in all (future) matters of health and wellbeing and might thus be more protected against dance related issues such as overtraining, eating disorders, or injuries.

Boys who enter puberty early, and girls who enter puberty late seem to have a temporary advantage compared to their classmates who experience the opposite. Boys with early onset show better performance than boys who do not yet gain muscle mass. In girls, those with late onset stay thinner for longer than those who already undergo hormone-related increase in body weight / fat percentage. The chapters on nutrition discusses this misguided assumption. For both sexes, puberty should be characterized by focusing on healthy and sufficient nutrition and exercise, diversity instead of early specialization and a **monitored balance of training load and loadability**. [725, 726, 727] The **foundations** for **aerobic endurance** should be laid here through accurate and dance medicine-based planning of training, based on periodization at best.[728] The benefits of summer breaks, staying in the sun and fresh air, focusing on hobbies and family life instead of dancing should not be underestimated with respect to overall health and wellbeing of the young dancer but also to performance enhancement and injury prevention.[729] Simultaneously, young dancers in vocational training should have enough free time and recovery breaks to have and cherish social and private lives: **Activities outside of dance, living their young lives** with all its revolts and the vital part of forging identity is a further essential aspect in wellbeing, related to performance enhancement and injury prevention.

Reducing the high number of smokers in dance can also be influenced by schools and teachers.[730, 731] Targeted education on the matter, teachers as role-models, stress-free and reasonable recovery breaks, and above all, avoiding any steps towards hunger and starvation in dancers, which only increase the desire to smoke, should be the most critical topics in this matter. Teamwork among teachers, evidence-based scheduling, and the **adherence to scheduled rehearsal and training timetables** are a major aspect in the prevention of smoking as well as eating disorders among dancers. While many reach for cigarettes to kill their hunger, many dancers also realize that smokers have (more) breaks than non-smokers, which leads to high numbers of smokers among dancers. Such responsibility lies with the teachers, trainers and institutions, who, first, have to be aware of the issue and take it seriously, and second, have to make sure that breaks and rest phases are granted to

---

[723] Stace JM. *The physiological development of the adolescent dancer*. J Dance Med Sci. 3(2). 59-65. 1999.

[724] Hecht, Thom. Emotionally Intelligent Ballet Training. Facilitating Emotional Intelligence in Vocational Dance Training. Saarbrücken. VDM Verlag Dr Müller. 2007.

[725] Sousa M, Carvalho P, Moreira P, and VH Teixeira. *Nutrition and nutritional issues for dancers.* 28(3). 119-123. 2013.

[726] IADMS. *Fueling the dancer* Fact sheet. IADMS International Assoziation for Dance Medicine & Science. www.iadms.org.

[727] Kraft EM. Richtig essen im Tanz. tamed infoblatt Nr 10. 2010.

[728] Wyon M. *Preparing to perform: periodization and dance.* J Dance Med Sci. 14(2). 67-72. 2010.

[729] Koutedakis Y, Myszkewycz L, Soulas D, Papapostolou V, Sullivan I, and Sharp NC. *The effects of rest and subsequent training on selected physiological parameters in professional female classical dancers.* Int J Sports Med. 20(6). 379-383. 1999.

[730] Clippinger KS. *Smoking in Young Dancers.* J Dance Med Sci. 3(3). 115-125. 1999.

[731] Teenage Tobacco Use. American Lung Association Fact Sheet. September 1998 Update. J Dance Med Sci. 3(3). 113-114. 1999.

every dancer equally. They are never a privilege – neither to smokers nor to those who "earned" their breaks through hard work. **Breaks and rest are an integrating part of training and scheduling** of every dancer's work environment and life. The importance of preventing smoking, any other substance abuse such as addictions to pain killers or other drugs, as well as the promotion of healthy eating behaviors are not only relevant for immediate health issues. They also play an essential role in the prevention of long-term health issues such as e.g., osteoporosis or infertility.

In any case, it must be clear to the teacher that psychological and physiological changes need to be understood and not reacted to with threats or even sanctions![732] **Puberty is a natural process and must not become a trauma for young athletes.**

WATER BALANCES, SCHEDULES, COMMUNICATION & FURTHER ASPECTS VITAL IN GROWTH

Children and adolescents need to **drink a lot** because their **thermoregulation** requires a lot of water. Children sweat less than adults, and as with so many changes, puberty brings about the transition from child to adult with respect to water household and perspiration as well. The teacher must keep an eye on the children's and the adolescents' **drinking behavior** and educate them towards frequent and sufficient water intake.

Drinking less water to promote weight loss is a common and dangerous mistake. Dancing children, young people in training and adult dancers need to drink enough water to prevent dehydration caused by training, sweating, and excessive muscle heat. Besides, measures such as wrapping the pubescent girl's body in cling film or any other plastic during training to lose more water and reduce body weight due to increased sweating are highly dangerous. These measures verge on bodily harm and lead to severe injuries. Such provoked unnatural and substantial increase in body core temperature under the plastic and the increased water loss can lead to fatigue, thus injury, reduced circulation and cardiovascular collapse. Practice shows how many countries and schools still use these and other obscure measures to promote weight loss!

Water bottles must be allowed in the (work) environment of dancers. The argument that children who drink a lot need to interrupt their training too often because they need to constantly **use the bathroom** is not justifiable. By **warming-up** sufficiently, the body changes its vegetative control from the parasympathetic **nervous system** responsible, for urination and excretion, among many other, to the **sympathetic nervous system** accountable for action and movement. If the warm-up does not only consist of traditional stretching but follows the guidelines of dance medicine and sports science (for instance neuromuscular warm-up[733]), children and adolescents who are focused on training do not have to use the bathroom until they enter the rest and recovery phase physically and mentally after a good cool-down: **Sufficient (not excessive) water intake** about 15-20 minutes **before training**, using the **bathroom** before **warming-up** and **frequent water sips every 20-25 minutes during training** support performance by balancing body temperature, supporting blood flow, and increasing concentration already in the young. **Rehearsal** and **training plans** must be designed as such that the adolescents (as all dancers) have enough **time** to **drink**, **eat** and **recover**.

Already child dancers can be educated to use the water bottles in small breaks, which the teacher has to give during classes, or are raised with autonomy. In the case of the latter, teachers clearly communicate that the child or young dancer can take a sip of water during short explanations or when other groups are dancing, under the premise that the dancer stays mentally focused and does not stop paying attention to the teacher.

Practice has shown that such situations, when clearly and mindfully communicated to the children are already working in the very young. They foster responsibility and autonomy by allowing children to make their own informed decisions. Comparable situations are handling of warm-up or other aspects of training, discussed in further volumes of this series.

The physical and accompanying psychological changes which the adolescents experience demand a lot from them. Education and personal conversations between teachers and students are vital during puberty. In

[732] Brenner JS. *Overuse injuries, overtraining, and burnout in child and adolescent athletes*. Pediatrics. 119. 1242-1245. 2007.

[733] Kaufmann J-E, Nelissen RGHH, Stubbe JH, Gademan, MGJ. Neuromuscular warm up is associated with less overuse injuries in ballet dancers, compared to traditional ballet specific warm up routines.

addition to healthy nutrition[734] and acknowledgement of individuality in training, honest, mindful communication help adolescents maintain their self-esteem and emerge from puberty with high levels of self-concept and -esteem. The knowledgeable teacher is aware of the importance to communicate the background of hormonal changes and the impact of puberty to the young dancer. By doing so, pressure and stress is taken of the adolescent, things might become clearer, and issues can be prevented before they evolve into problems. A teacher experienced in mindful communication can build essential bridges over setbacks and performance plateaus, ensuring the dancer that the longed-for **body control returns quicker when the given circumstances are accepted, supporting the dancer by adjusting training and schedules in most demanding phases.** This will bring all involved further than if the student becomes ashamed of their changes and tries to fights them.[735]

---

[734] Robson B, and A Chertoff. *Bone Health and Female Dancers: Physical and Nutritional Guidelines*. IADMS Fact Sheet. 2008-2010.

[735] Brenner JS. *Overuse injuries, overtraining, and burnout in child and adolescent athletes*. Pediatrics. 119. 1242-1245. 2007.

...AND WHAT ABOUT THE TEACHERS, TRAINERS & CHOREOGRAPHERS?

Have you as teacher/trainer/choreographer ever critically observed whether you drink enough while working? Whether a water bottle accompanies you during your daily routine and makes it into the dance studio? Not only do the teachers themselves need sufficient water to ensure their mental and physical ability to perform and concentrate. They also function as role models, an effect that must not be underestimated. With respect to drinking, eating or other behavior as well as with reference to communication skills, as shortly introduced above.

Volume 4 of this series is dedicated to health and wellbeing, performance enhancement and injury prevention of the trainer, teacher, ballet master, artistic director, choreographer. All aspects mainly discussed for the perspective of the dancer in the first 3 volumes are related to the instructor's viewpoint, needs, loads and benefits.

Even though children and adolescents (all dancers) often do not seem to notice it, they unconsciously (and silently consciously) perceive the teacher's behavior. If the most revered teachers/choreographers/trainers present themselves completely naturally, (young) dancers, of course, notice this. That includes language, respect, politeness, their warm-up and cool-down, the use of a water bottle for themselves and consistent drinking, focused breaks where they make sure that the dancers and they themselves can enjoy real silence, regular food intake, etc.

Apart from their role model effect, which can create a self-evident responsibility in dance education (!) this is also important regarding the teacher's injury prevention. Repeatedly, dance medicine is asked **how dance teachers/trainers/choreographers themselves can carry out their own injury prevention**: the small list mentioned above are only basic aspects, which fall under this category.

An essential part of health and wellbeing in dance is rarely recognized as such: Nutrition is the **most crucial component to provide dancers with sufficient energy** for their demanding (daily) work.[736,737] While it is essential for performance, nutrition is a vital aspect of the **prevention of injuries and ill-health**. When the dancer is not sufficiently fueled, performance as well as health can only decline. Literature on nutrition and eating disorders in dance already exists in large numbers (also use the bibliography of this volume).[738,739,740,741] However, far too many people – including teachers and trainers – still ask the astonishing question of what the discussion about undernourishment and malnutrition in dance has to do with **injury prevention**.

Nutrition can be regarded as essential aspect for health and performance of everybody and in every profession or sportive environment. As such, nutrition is handled as an efficient tool to positively and deliberately influence both aspects. This book is not meant to be a discussion of how to eat correctly as a dancer or teacher, because so many good books on the topic are available already (also take a look at the bibliography).[742,743,744] However, consequences of malnutrition, energy deficiency, or eating disorders, such as osteoporosis or stress fractures are discussed in the following, because they belong to the overall topics of this volume.

For the basic understanding it is essential to know that it is not only eating disorders which are to be concerned about. They probably can be called the symptom(s) we can observe in a person. The underlying problem is **low energy availability (Relative Energy Deficiency – RED)**[745], which comes in combination with a broad variety of different causes, influencing factors and triggers and can affect all genders, all ages, and all levels of expertise.[746] Reasons can be that somebody is deliberately restricting calory intake, overexercises, or both. That again can be based on intrinsic factors, including weight-control or ambition, performance- and/or appearance-related, but can also be extrinsically triggered, with society, media, schools, sport specific rules and regimentation, trainers, teachers, peers, parents, etc. as the external risk factors influencing the athlete or dancer.

Regarding eating disorders, many understand that dancers suffering from eating disorders have restricted energy supply at their disposal, which will affect their performance and add to injury risk sooner or later. However, further and most essential short- and long-term effects of nutrition imbalances of any kind in (young) dancers are much more complex and far-reaching. They include **decreased overall health, fatigue, burnout, fear, anxiety, low self-concept, perfectionistic tendencies, increased injury risk, they influence bone and organ health and can therefore lead to many diseases such as osteopenia, osteoporosis, infertility**, and many more. Equally far-reaching are the consequences for all parties involved in the life and work environment of a person suffering from eating disorders.[747,748,749]

Eating disorders are always a co-product of many factors. Teachers, peers, media, society, stress, fear and many others are contributing. Many of these influences still favor or support a particularly low ideal weight as a

---

736 Zanker CL. *Bone metabolism in exercise associated amenorrhoea: the importance of nutrition.* Br J Sports Med. 33. 228-229. 1999.

737 Robson B, and A Chertoff. *Bone Health and Female Dancers - Physical and Nutritional Guidelines.* IADMS International Association for Dance Medicine & Science. 2008.

738 Piran, Niva, Levine Michael P, and Catherine Steiner-Adair. Preventing Eating Disorders – A Handbook of Interventions and Special Challenges. Philadelphia London. Brunner/Mazel A Member of the Taylor & Francis Group. 1999.

739 Mastin, Zerlina. Nutrition for the Dancer. Hampshire. Dance Books Ltd. 2009.

740 Bartl, Eva. Essstörungen im Leistungssport: Die Negation eines Tabuthemas. Hamburg. Diplomica Verlag. 2011.

741 Challis J, Stevens A, and IADMS. *Nutrition Resource Paper.* International Association for dance Medicine & Science. 2019. Free resource: https://iadms.org/resources/publications/resources-paper/#nutr1

742 Simmel, Liane, and Eva-Maria Kraft. Nutrition for Dancers: Basics, Performance Enhancement, Practical Tips. Abington-on-Thames. Taylor & Francis. 2017.

743 Katch FI, Katch VL, and WD McArdle. Exercise physiology: energy, nutrition, and human performance. Philadelphia. Lippincott Williams & Wilkins. 2010.

744 Fitt, Sally Severy, and Robin D. Chmelar. Diet For Dancers. A Complete Guide to Nutrition and Weight Control. Princeton. Dance Horizons Books, Princton Books Co. 1990.

745 Elliott-Sale KJ, Tenforde AS, Parziale AL, Holtzman B, and Ackerman KE. *Endocrine Effects of Relative Energy Deficiency in Sport.* Int J Sport Nutr Exerc Metab. 28(4). 335-349. 2018.

746 Areta JL, Taylor HL, and Koehler K. *Low energy availability: history, definition and evidence of its endocrine, metabolic and physiological effects in prospective studies in females and males.* Eur J Appl Physiol. 121(1). 1-21. 2021.

747 Stefanini MC, Troiani MR, Caselli M, Dirindelli P, Lucarelli S, Caini S, and Martinetti MG. *Living with someone with an eating disorder: factors affecting the caregivers' burden.* Eat Weight Disord. 224(6). 1209-1214. 2019.

748 Stefanini MC, Troiani MR, Caselli M, Dirindelli P, Lucarelli S, Caini S, and Martinetti MG. *Living with someone with an eating disorder: factors affecting the caregivers' burden.* Eat Weight Disord. 224(6). 1209-1214. 2019.

749 Milano W, Milano L, and Capasso A. *Eating Disorders in Athletes: From Risk Management to Therapy.* Endocr Metab Immune Disord Drug Targets. 20(1). 2-14. 2020.

superficial ideal of beauty. Additionally, many esthetic or competitive sports, such as dance, stress a low BMI and body fat mass, and the pressure to adhere is continuously increasing in today's performance-oriented society. That exacerbates the problem of eating disorders, with women and children/adolescents particularly at risk of developing eating disorders. **Anorexia nervosa** is the most common eating disorder, also among dancers.[750] Nevertheless, eating disorders also occur in young men and are most common in esthetic sports and those that have different weight classes correlating with a chance to win.[751] In addition to social and psychosomatic factors, disorders affecting the endocrine system can also be among the triggers. Apart from **anorexia nervosa**, **bulimia** and **binge-eating-disorders** (cravings and related loss of control), are the most common eating disorders.

Anorexia athletica is a further problem that occurs in sports. However, this form of anorexia is not treated as an eating disorder per se from a psychiatric point of view[752, 753] although it is commonly clinically treated similarly to eating disorders. Anorexia athletica is an **intentionally provoked/increased imbalance** between excessive athletic **loading and** purposefully **low energy intake** through restricted diet or starving, resulting in severe underweight. In contrast to eating disorders, however, the athlete is not primarily concerned with being thin with the aim to correspond to an ideal of beauty, but to get admission to certain weight classes and/or win in sports competitions.

Not least in dance, there is no exact line between sports anorexia and anorexia nervosa. Especially because Anorexia athletica in dance might be regarded as the link between Anorexia nervosa as psychiatric disorder and Anorexia athletica as tool to manipulate sportive performance: dancers are restricting their dietary intake to be thin and adhere to their professional necessities and standards (e.g., to be light enough for lifts). However, they also have to follow tradition-imposed ideals of esthetic beauty. Thus, the line between eating disorder and Anorexia athletica in dance is a fine line to tread.

The occurrence of eating disorders in dance is strongly linked to the dance style[754], which means that the focus on the maximum ideal weight is handled much more rigorously in disciplines such as classical ballet, dancesport, or rhythmic gymnastics than in most modern dance styles. Generally, **dancers have a significantly high risk of suffering from eating disorders**[755,756] with a meta-analysis on eating disorders in ballet[757] reporting that anorexia nervosa and eating disorders not otherwise specified (EDNOS) in general are reported with 12.0% but in ballet affecting 16.4% of dancers. Anorexia nervosa had a general risk of 2.0% versus 4% for ballet dancers, while bulimia showed to be generally higher (4.4%) than in dancers (2%). However, EDNOS was much higher for ballet dancers with 14.9% versus 9.5% as general prevalence. Among these EDNOS, eating disorders not otherwise specified, Anorexia athletica might have its place. The problem of eating disorders **especially affects adolescents**. Thus, the high risk of eating disorders in dance in general makes adolescent dancers even more at risk, when **body dissatisfaction** and **body dysmorphic disorders** are taken into account, often as the starting points for eating disorders.[758]

Aside from increased injury risk and decrease in performance through severe related lack of energy leading to fatigue, loss of concentration, susceptibility to infections, among many other, eating disorders negatively affect endocrine (hormone related), neuropsychological and cerebral (brain) health, **introducing far-reaching, long-term endocrinological, metabolic, neuropsychological and social changes, which mark an affected dancer for a lifetime**. Eating disorders can also lead to death, above all occurring in young girls during puberty and holding the sad record of the highest mortality rate among psychiatric diseases in children and adolescents.[759]

---

[750] Arcelus J, Witcomb GL, and Mitchell A. *Prevalence of eating disorders amongst dancers: a systemic review and meta-analysis.* Eur Eat Disord Rev. 22(2). 92-101. 2014.

[751] Modan-Moses D, Yaroslavsky A, and Novikovet I. *Stunting of growth as a major feature of anorexia nervosa in male adolescents.* Pediatrics. 111. 270-276. 2003.

[752] Sudi K, Öttl K, and Payerl D. *Anorexia athletica.* Nutrition. 20. 657-661. 2004.

[753] Tappauf M, Scheer PJ, Trabi T and Dunitz-Scheer M. *Anorexia athletica. Sportanorexie. Wenn Sport krank is(s)t.* Monatsschr Kinderheilkd. 155. 558-559. 2007.

[754] Stensland SH, and Sobal J. *Dietary practices of ballet, jazz, and modern dancers.* J Amer Dietetic Association. 92. 3. 319-324. 1992.

[755] Sundgot-Borgen J, and Klungland Torstveit M. *Prevalence of eating disorders in elite athletes is higher than in general population.* Clin J Sport Med 14. 25-32. 2004.

[756] Nascimento AL, and Fontenelle LF. *Body dysmorphic disorder and eating disorders in elite professional female ballet dancers.* Annals Clin Psychatry. 24(3). 191-194. 2012.

[757] Arcelus J, Witcomb GL, and Mitchell A. *Prevalence of eating disorders amongst dancers: a systemic review and meta-analysis.* Eur Eat Disord Rev. 22(2). 92-101. 2014.

[758] Garcia-Dantas A, Alonso DA, Sánchez-Miguel PA, and Del Río Sánchez C. *Factors Dancers Associate with their Body Dissatisfaction.* Body Image. 25. 40-47. 2018.

[759] Holtkamp K and Herpertz-Dahlmann B. *Neuropsychological performance in anorexia and bulimia nervosa. [Anorexia und Bulimia nervosa im Kindes- und Jugendalter].* Monatsschr Kinderheilkd. 150. 164-171. 2002.

The most often unknown issue is that **many of the irreversible damages to the dancers' health caused by the compulsion to be thin will only come into effect much later in their lives. This happens when society, media, audiences, teachers, and institutions which have co-caused these health conditions are usually no longer in contact with the dancer**. Even though many dancers may not suffer from clearly discernible eating disorders, education favoring starving, dieting and low BMI can lead to a serious, complex outcome, called "Female Athletic Triad".[760,761,762] Although it is attributed only to women and girls, the F.A.T. can also affect young men, albeit under other conditions, which will be discussed. The danger of **low energy availability cannot be overstressed. And the obsession with being thin among dancers is dangerous, while falsely considered a sign of discipline and good performance measurement.**[763]

FEMALE ATHLETIC TRIAD: BONE HEALTH & ENERGY AVAILABILITY IN FEMALE DANCE

The term **"Female Athletic Triad"** (F.A.T) **was first mentioned by the American College of Sports Medicine in 1992** and has reached the attention of many people working with competitive athletes to this day.[764,765,766,767,768] The F.A.T. is a widespread problem in dance and sports, which commonly goes widely unnoticed. On the one hand, the provoked damage is usually only visible much later, and on the other hand, due to its complexity, the problem can hardly be considered "a disease", as in something being acutely visible in the dancer.

As introduced above, the underlying problem of the F.A.T. and everything related to eating disorders is low Energy Availability or, more often referred to as R.E.D., Relative Energy Deficiency.[769,770] The F.A.T. goes beyond eating disorders, can often lead to them or can also be the result of eating disorders or anorexia athletica. And to put the record straight: The Triad can affect all ages and all levels of expertise (professional and amateur dancer or other sportive people), as well as all genders.

The F.A.T. **results from** three different conditions: A **very high training load** has to face or leads to

- severe **energy deficiency** or **low energy availability** (e.g., malnutrition, restricted caloric intake, or eating disorder)**,**
- leading to **hormonal imbalances** (e.g., amenorrhea, or oligomenorrhea)
- resulting in **disordered bone metabolism** (e.g., osteopenia, osteoporosis.

Osteoporosis is one of the "common diseases" in industrialized countries.[771] The disease often called "bone loss" in colloquial speech emerges from an imbalance in bone metabolism, which leads to increased deterioration of bone substance. This results in bone demineralization, i.e., it reduces bone mineral density, leading to an unstable and easily fractured bone architecture.[772]

Two medical appearances of osteoporosis have to be differentiated:

Primary osteoporosis (95%) refers to that form of osteoporosis which was not caused by any other disease. That includes both adolescent osteoporosis, the origin of which is idiopathic (unknown), and common osteoporosis among the elderly.

---

760 Gordon, Cathrine M, and Merryl M. LeBoff. The Female Athletic Triad. A Clinical Guide. Wien-New York. Springer Verlag. 2015.

761 Yeager KK, Agostini R, Nattiv A, and Drinkwater B. *The female athletic triad: disordered eating, amenorrhea, osteoporosis*. Med Sci Sports Exerc. 25(7). 775-777. 1993.

762 American College of Sports Medicine. The Female Athletic Triad. by Otis CL, Drinkwater B, Johnson M, Loucks A, and Jack Wilmore. Med Science Sports Exerc. 29(5). 1997.

763 Barker PR, Petroczi, and Quested E. *Assessment of nutritional knowledge in female athletes susceptible to the Female Athletic Triad syndrome*. J Occup Med Toxicol. 2(10). 2007.

764 Barker PR, Petroczi, and Quested E. *Assessment of nutritional knowledge in female athletes susceptible to the Female Athletic Triad syndrome*. J Occup Med Toxicol. 2(10). 2007.

765 Otis CL, Drinkwater B, and Johnson M. *American College of Sports Medicine position stand: The Female Athletic Triad.* Med Sci Sports Exerc. 29(5). i-ix. 1997.

766 Wilmore JH. *Relation of level of exercise, age, and weight-cycling history to weight and eating concerns in male and female runners*. Health Psychology. 11. 418-442. 1992.

767 Yeager KK, Agostini R, Nattiv A, and Drinkwater B. *The female athletic triad: disordered eating, amenorrhea, osteoporosis*. Med Sci Sports Exerc. 25(7). 775-777. 1993.

768 Areta JL, Taylor HL, and Koehler K. *Low energy availability: history, definition and evidence of its endocrine, metabolic and physiological effects in prospective studies in females and males*. Eur J Appl Physiol. 121(1). 1-21. 2021.

769 Elliott-Sale KJ, Tenforde AS, Parziale AL, Holtzman B, and Ackerman KE. *Endocrine Effects of Relative Energy Deficiency in Sport.* Int J Sport Nutr Exerc Metab. 28(4). 335-349. 2018.

770 Areta JL, Taylor HL, and Koehler K. *Low energy availability: history, definition and evidence of its endocrine, metabolic and physiological effects in prospective studies in females and males*. Eur J Appl Physiol. 121(1). 1-21. 2021.

771 Meunier, Pierre. Osteoporosis: Diagnosis and Management. London. Taylor & Francis. 1998.

772 Kanis JA, Melton LJ III, Christiansen C, Johnston CC, and Khaltaev N. *The diagnosis of osteoporosis*. J Bone Miner Res. 9(8).1137-1141. 1994.

Secondary osteoporosis (5%) is caused by another disease, medication, smoking, malnutrition, or for instance, underweight, among other. On an affected athlete's way to osteoporosis, **injuries can be caused by overloading already insufficiently adjusted bones due to energy deficiency**. Overuse injuries, such as stress fractures or acute injuries (accidents) resulting from a lack of concentration and fatigue due to the underlying energy deficiency can be the consequences.[773]

The triad takes place quietly and gradually in the dancer. Very low bone density is not visible from the outside, and often only **stress fractures draw attention to it** (provided that those responsible recognize the association.[774,775,776] Their location varies depending on the strain or sport, but it most frequently affects – not least in dance – the lower extremities, and women are exposed to a higher risk than men.[777,778,779,780] The reason for this can be found in their hormonal situation in competitive sports on the one hand, but also in the smaller muscle percentage, the wider pelvis, and thus more unfavorable biomechanical conditions due to different hip and knee joint angles than in men.

Volume 3 discussed such gender differences (e.g., the female quadriceps angle) in the chapters on biomechanics and anatomy.

Besides, women generally have a lower basal bone mineral density (basic bone density) than men. Of course, all of this can hardly be recognized from the outside. What can be seen, however, is the absolute underweight of many young dancers, the often enormous levels of fatigue, possible recurrent **colds**[781,782,783] resulting from a fundamentally impaired immune system in many due to overtraining, and last but not least the daily struggle with energy deficiency, which teachers can see in the eyes of the child/dancer – if they only looked at them (and knew enough to recognize)!

Healthy and sufficient nutrition intake as well as adequate physical activity would be **essential means of prevention of osteopenia and osteoporosis**. To be preventive, exercise has to happen in a **controlled manner with regard to intensity, frequency and duration**. Exercise, which is too much might be as detrimental[784] as is a lack of physical activity, which is why dance would be healthy, if it was not associated to overtraining too often already in the young. Again, knowledge, evidence-based and precise goal setting based on optimal nutrition intake as well as planning and scheduling of training are essential. It is vital that young dancers can benefit from teacher/trainer/administrator-knowledge, optimal scheduling and education, and are allowed to experience their growth spurts and puberty without the compulsion to keep weight low or lose weight. That would increase their bone mineral density through **a combination of sufficient fueling through healthy nutrition and controlled mechanical loading (i.e., training)** onto their bones, which **prevents osteoporosis**.

Essential for prevention is a balance of all factors involved, which again shows how essential the practical implementation of dance medicine and science is for the daily lives and wellbeing of dancers:

- Balanced nutrition and sufficient fueling
- Control of stress levels and sufficient recovery time (including sufficient sun-exposure for Vitamin D)
- Knowledge on nutrition in general
- Knowledge on related aspects of dance medicine in particular (from F.A.T. to science of training)
- Avoidance of chronic stress, fear, anxiety, overloading etc.
- Monitoring of training load
- Evidence-based scheduling
- Periodization to ensure the two previously mentioned aspects
- Healthy approach to weight (BMI, fat mass, lean mass)

[773] Korsten-Reck U. *Female Athletic Triad und Stressfrakturen.* Gynäkol Endokrinologie. 8.230-235. 2010.
[774] Korsten-Reck U. *Female Athletic Triad und Stressfrakturen.* Gynäkologische Endokrinologie. 8. 230-235. 2010.
[775] Barrow GW, and S Saha. *Menstrual irregularity and stress fractures in collegiate female distance runners.* Am J Sports Med. 16. 209-216. 1988.
[776] Bennell K, Matheson G, Meeuwisse W, and P Brukner. *Risk factors for stress fractures.* Sports Med 28. 91-122. 1999.
[777] Bruckner P, and K Bennell. *Stress fractures in female athletes. Diagnosis, management and rehabilitation.* Sports Med. 24(6). 419-429. 1997.
[778] Burrows M, Shepherd H, Bird S et al. *The components of the female athlete triad do not identify all physically active females at risk.* J Sports Sci. 25. 1289-1297. 2007.
[779] Bennell K, Matheson G, Meeuwisse W, and P Brukner. *Risk factors for stress fractures.* Sports Med 28. 91-122. 1999.
[780] Protzman RR, Griffis CG. *Stress fractures in men and women undergoing military training.* J Bone Joint Surg Am 59(6). 825. 1977.
[781] Cohen S. et al. *Psychological stress and susceptibility to the common cold.* New Engl J Med. 325.606-612.1991.
[782] Stone AA et al. *Secretory IgA as a measure of immunocompetence.* J Human Stress.13. 136-140.1987.
[783] Clover, RD et al. *Family functioning and stress as predictors of influenza B infections.* J Familiy Practice. 28. 1989.
[784] Burrows M, Nevill AM, Bird S, and Simpson D. *Physiological factors associated with low bone mineral density in female endurance runners.* Br J Sports Med. 37(1). 67-71. 2003.

- and weight gain/fluctuations during puberty
- Recurrent screening for dance technical errors
- Recurrent screening for all dancer related health aspects
- Recurrent screening of teachers'/trainers' work
- Avoidance of smoking and drug (e.g., painkillers) abuse
- i.e., avoiding of excessive distress, e.g., through pressure, pain, or avoidable injury

Bone mineral density increases in a person, starting above all with the onset of sex hormones in puberty until about the age of 30, where it reaches its highest density and then begins to decrease steadily. That is physiological and, therefore, normal. What is essential, though, is that the highest possible value of bone mineral density up to the moment of its peak should be reached, the so-called **"peak bone mass"**, i.e., the moment of an individual's highest bone mass. For this purpose, sufficient nutrition and nutritional intake, weight-bearing and a fair (not overreaching) amount of aerobic endurance sports, healthy diets, and a lifestyle without (too many) drugs (e.g., painkillers) and non-smoking is recommended. The higher the bone mineral density is at the time of the peak, the more "bone capital" a person has at their disposal as a hopefully high baseline to start off from, when the density begins to decrease.

Concerning bone mineral density, dance itself comes along with a paradox: Since dancers move a lot due to their profession, the bone metabolism in the involved bone structures is also stimulated more than, for instance, in sedentary professions and people. The bone structures, such as the femoral neck or spinal column, which are highly endangered when suffering from osteoporosis, are used intensively in dance training.

For the bones, adequate mechanical loading happens through **weight bearing** activities: bouncing, swinging, full body motion, stretching, jumping or running, basically everything where muscles and their tendons pull at bones and where ground reaction forces impact. Through the provoked biological adaptation as natural response of tissues to loading, e.g., training, the body strengthens the tissues and improves their internal structures. Therefore, sportive activities promote bone metabolism and prevent osteoporosis. [785], [786], [787], [788] Suitable, comprehensive amateur dance classes can be among the best and most far-reaching preventive measures for young people concerning osteoporosis (besides many other positive effects!).[789,790,791]

Professional dancers should also have an excellent bone density considering their daily movements. However, measurements showed that bone mineral density was not better than in not-dancing population, with density in the head of male and arms of female dancers being even less. [792] Recent studies showed that vocational ballet dancers had lower density at impact and non-impact sites than age-matched controls, which was associated with maturation.[793] However, professional female dancers still showed lower density at non-impact sites in the same study. When lower or unadjusted bone mineral density can be identified in vocational ballet dancers, it can be concluded that in any way, healthy eating and a focus on promotion of the importance of nutrition for health and performance is essential during phases of growth and adolescence.[794]

Hence, the obligation to restrict calories in dance could change what would basically be considered an advantage. 80% of professional dancers keep their daily amount of calories below 85% of their recommended intake. Their average working hours range from four to more than nine hours per working day.[795,796] Here, too low an energy level

---

[785] Young N, Formica C, and Szmukler G. *Bone density at weight-bearing and nonweight-bearing sites in ballet dancers: the effects of exercise, hypogonadism, and body weight.* J Clin Endocrinol Metab. 78.449-454. 1994.

[786] Chestnut III CH. *Bone mass and exercise.* Am J Med 95:5A/34S-36S. 1993.

[787] Taaffe DR, Tracey IR, Snow CM, and Marcus R. *High-impact exercise promotes bone gain in well-trained female athletes.* J Bone Miner Res. 12.255-260. 1997.

[788] Body JJ, Bergman P, and Boonen S. Non-pharmacological management of osteoporosis: a consensus of the Belgian Bone Club. Osteoporosis Int. 22(11). 2769-2788. 2011.

[789] Matthews B, Bennell K, and McKay H. *Dancing for bone health: a 3-year longitudinal study of bone mineral accrual across puberty in female non-elite dancers and controls.* Osteoporos Int. 17. 1043-1054. 2006.

[790] Daly, R.M. and M.A. Petit. (Eds.) Optimizing bone mass and strength: The role of physical activity and nutrition during growth. Basel. Karger. 2007.

[791] McKay HA, MacLean L, Petit M, MacKelvie-O'Brien K, Janssen P, Beck T, and Khan KM. *"Bounce at the Bell": a novel program of short bouts of exercise improves proximal femur bone mass in early pubertal children.* Br J Sports Med. 39(8). 521-526. 2005.

[792] Kahn KM, Warren MP, Stiehl A, McKay HA, and Wark JD. *Bone mineral density in active and retired ballet dancers.* J Dance Med Sci. 3(1). 15-23. 1999.

[793] Amorim T, Koutedakis Y, Nevill A, Wyon M, Maia J, Machado JC, Marques F, Metsios GS, Flouris AD, Adubeiro N, Nogueira L, and Dimitriou L. *Bone mineral density in vocational and professional ballet dancers.* Osteoporos Int. 28(10). 2903-2912. 2017.

[794] Wewege MA, and Ward RE. *Bone mineral density in pre-professional female ballet dancers: A systematic review and meta-analysis.* J Sci Med Sport. 21(8). 783-788. 2018.

[795] Frusztajer NT, Dhuper S, Warren MP, Brooks-Gunn J, and Fox RP. *Nutrition and the incidence of stress fractures in ballet dancers.* J Clin Nutr. 51. 779-783. 1990.

[796] Twitchett E, Angioi M, Koutedakis Y, and Wyon M. *The demands of a working day among female professional ballet dancers.* J Dance Med Sci. 14(4). 127-132. 2010.

meets too high a workload. As a result, a very low body mass index (BMI) starting in puberty can indicate low available energy which could have complex consequences as mentioned above. High training load and far-reaching nutritional deficiency could then prepare young dancers early for osteoporosis.[797, 798] Combined with amenorrhea risks of injury increase drastically.[799] Also, disturbing the neuroendocrine balance (hormonal balance) can negatively affect fertility.[800, 801, 802, 803, 804]

Bones are **highly dynamic tissues**, which, like all tissues, undergo daily and, under stress intensified, highly physiological reconstruction processes. Bone loss occurs relatively quickly while forming new bones takes several weeks, comparable to growing a tree, which can take a hundred years, while cutting it might take (a high maximum) of 100 hours. An imbalance in the activity of **osteoblasts** (bone formation) and **osteoclasts** (bone remodeling and destruction) among dancers as described above, can result in weakened bone tissue, which is unable to sufficiently adjust to loading – at least temporarily. As a consequence, excessive training can lead to recurring, small tissue damages. This imbalance of micro-traumata (small tissue injuries), and often only insufficient repairing processes due to maladaption lead, in the worst case, to stress fractures.[805] The risk of stress fractures increases with increasing workload, making the dancer prone to overuse injuries. Incorrect alignment and technical errors in dance (e.g., excessive pronation of the foot[806] in forced turnout) leading to suboptimal joint mechanics, contribute to this risk, especially when the bone is not able to adjust to the strain anymore.[807,808,809,810]

The still common **education favoring underweight or malnutrition** in dance has to be considered abnormal.[811] However, it is still a traditional matter of course – which on closer inspection should be declared a bodily injury because it is based on exploiting the discipline, devotion, and obedience of children, adolescents, and adult dancers, and is associated with severe consequences in females as well as males.[812] As practice shows, incredible measures still occur in various dance environments, such as confiscation of young dancers' lunch bags, public weighing, provoking weight-related social competition and other **dubious measures** to lose weight such as the compulsion to vomit, wrapping the body in cling film to reduce the body weight by losing water, or sanctions, such as the threat to lose the cast or training position, if the young dancers do not reduce their weight. Such issues must not be called educational measures but should be labelled **exertions of pressure on minors** (as well as older dancers) instead. Weight loss and eating disorders, as well as troubles with sensibly assessing one's own body, can already be considered severe and dangerous conditions in adolescent growth. However, the mechanism underlying the female (and male) triad, a negative energy balance, results in a multiplication of far-reaching changes that affect not only the young dancers' growth but also their life.

The **absence of menstruation**, which can be observed in many young female dancers, is **the external sign of a hormonal disturbance based on decreased energy availability paired with increased levels of stress.** What is disturbed is the "hypothalamic-pituitary-ovarian-axis", the cooperation between the hypothalamus monitoring the pituitary gland (in the brain) and the ovaries. If this cooperation (named "axis") is disturbed, far-reaching,

---

797 Burckhardt P, Wynn E, Krieg MA, Bagutti C, and Faouzi M. *The effects of nutrition, puberty and dancing on bone density in adolescent ballet dancers.* J Dance Med Sci. 15(2). 51-60. 2011.

798 Muños MT, C de la Piedra, Barrios V, Garrido G, and Argente J. *Changes in Bone Density and Bone Markers in Rhythmic Gymnasts and Ballet Dancers:Implications for Puberty and Leptin Levels.* Europ J Endocrinology. 151(4).491-496. 2004.

799 Lloyd T, Triantafyllou SJ, and Baker ER. *Women athletes with menstrual irregularity have increased musculoskeletal injuries.* Med Sci Sports Exerc. 18. 374-379. 1986.

800 Loucks AB, Mortola JF, Girton L, and Yen SSC. *Alterations in the hypothalamic-pituitary-ovarian and the hypothalamic-pituitary-adrenal axes in athletic women.* J Clin Endocrinol Metab. 68.402-441. 1989.

801 De Souza MJ, Maguire MS, Maresh CM, Kraemer WJ, Rubin KR, and Loucks AB. *Adrenal activation and the prolactin response to exercise in eumenorrheicand amenorrheic runners.* J Appl Physiol. 70.2378-2387. 1991.

802 Loucks AB, Laughlin GA, Mortola JF, Girton L, Nelson JC, and Yen SSC. *Hypothalamic-pituitary-thyroidal function in eumenorrheic and amenorrheic athletes.* J Clin Endocrinol Metab. 75.514-518. 1992.

803 Keay N, Fogelman I, and Blake G. *Bone mineral density in professional female dancers.* Br J Sports Med. 31.143-147. 1997.

804 Khan KM, Bennell KL, and Hopper JL. *Self-reported ballet classes undertaken at age 10–12 years and hip bone mineral density in later life.* Osteoporos Int 8. 165-173. 1998.

805 Bohndorf K. *Ermüdungsfrakturen.* In: Bohndorf Klaus, Imhof Herwig und Klaus Wörtler (eds.). Radiologische Diagnostik der Knochen und Gelenke. Stuttgart. Thieme. 2002. p. 18.

806 Taunton JE, Ryan MB, Clement DB. *A retrospective case-control analysis of 2002 running injuries.* Br J Sports Med 36:95-101. 2002.

807 Taunton JE, McKenzie DC, and Clement DB. *The role of biomechanics in the epidemiology of injuries.* Sports Med 6. 107-120.1988.

808 Kadel NJ, Teitz CC, Kronmal RA. Stress fractures in ballet dancers. Am J Sports Med. 20(4). 445-449. 1992.

809 Frusztajer NT, Dhuper S, Warren MP, Brooks-Gunn J, and Fox RP. *Nutrition and the incidence of stress fractures in ballet dancers.* Am J Clin Nutr. 51(5). 779-783. 1990.

810 Warren MP, Brooks-Gunn J, Hamilton LH, Warren LF, Hamilton WG. *Scoliosis and fractures in young ballet dancers. Relation to delayed menarche and secondary amenorrhea.* N Engl J Med. 314(21). 1348-1353. 1986.

811 Berz K, and McCambridge T. *Amenorrhea in the Female Athlete: What to Do and When to Worry.* Pediatr Ann. 45(3). 97-102. 2016.

812 Melin AK, Heikura IA, Tenforde A, and Mountjoy M. *Energy Availability in Athletics: Health, Performance, and Physique.* Int J Sport Nutr Exerc Metab. 9(2). 152-164. 2019.

long-term effects can be found in the female body.[813,814] The retroactive effect of intense physical activity on hormonal regulation changes the hormonal balance to the athlete's disadvantage. The body perceives high loading as well as energy deficiency as stress, thus, suffers from respectively multiplying stress levels, which impair the **hormonal regulation**: hypothalamus and pituitary gland cooperating with the ovaries in females reduce the release of LH (luteinizing hormone, also called "lutropin") and FSH (follicle-stimulating hormone). Both hormones are responsible for the production and maturation of the reproductive cells (the female egg, and the male sperm). That leads to insufficient or ceased estradiol production in the young female dancer. Such endocrinological (hormonal) disorders can lead to changes in the menstrual cycle[815], visible through a delayed menarche or a primary or secondary amenorrhea. [816] **Primary amenorrhea** describes an absence of menstruation up to the age of 16, whereby **secondary amenorrhea** means menstruation with breaks of three to six months, i.e., the menstruation has already been here in a girl but becomes interrupted. **Oligomenorrhoea** means a cycle duration of more than 36 days or irregular menstruation cycles. In sports, associated with a high weekly training load and a focus on low weight, the menarche's onset (menstruation) is generally delayed by a few years.[817] It is medically discussed whether menarche's occurrence before the age of 18 is sufficient to prevent damage or reduced fertility.[818]

But how is the functionality of the hormone system, visible through menstruation as well as injury risk, related to stress through overtraining and energy deficiency?

First, when a high training load meets low energy availability, the discrepancy of **energy-needed and energy-used up** results in a minus, leading to **severe levels of stress for the body**. With the overall goal to survive, the affected nervous system monitored by its "wise" hypothalamus default to the only possible solution: all systems which are not necessarily needed for **survival** in the first place are shut down. One of them is fertility in the young dancer, visible through the onset of menstruation after the peak of the second growth spurt, so menstruation stops or does not start. (Cave: in males, there is no menstruation as visible sign for the problem, meaning that in male dancers, this dysbalance only becomes visible when injuries already occur!) In dance, a sudden end of menstruation or failing onset very often is appreciated by all those, who do not know about the underlying survival mode of the young body and its consequences. However, the menstruation is only the visible sign of the availability of estrogen in the body. Estrogen, as will be explained, is directly related to bone health. So is testosterone in the male dancer.

Second, the other connection to stress disturbing the hormonal balance is cortisol, which is released while experiencing stress, introducing a vicious circle: Cortisol [819] regulates glucose levels and is increasingly released in the blood when the glucose level is low, since **hunger** as well as **overtraining** mean **stress for** the **body**.[820,821] As a **consequence** of increased cortisol levels over a longer period, the mental **ability to concentrate decreases**, and the **risk** of suffering from **burnout** and **injuries** increases dramatically. The problem multiplies itself because cortisol, being a catabolic (destructing) hormone, decreases lean body mass and thus again adds to the low energy availability in dancers, worsening stress levels from the top.

As much as dancers (and teachers) and their understanding of an "ideal body" may despise the word "fat", it is a vital part of human health: Besides being in charge of thermoregulation, **adipose tissue** (body **fat**) produces several important hormones that are mainly responsible for growth and are in permanent exchange with the ovaries, through which reproduction is regulated (monitored by the hypothalamus). The hormone **leptin**, which is formed in fat cells, shows higher levels in the blood when there is enough adipose tissue. It signals the brain that reproduction and growth are possible. If the leptin sinks, the brain knows that the body has too little fat and, therefore, too little energy reserved to perform

813 Meczekalski B, Katulski K, Czyzyk A, Podfigurna-Stopa A, and Maciejewska-Jeske M. *Functional hypothalamic amenorrhea and its influence on women's health.* J Endocrinol Invest. 37(11). 1049-1056. 2014.

814 Hurvitz M, and Weiss R. *The young female athlete.* Pediatr Endocrinol Rev. 7(2). 43-49. 2009.

815 Enatsu A. *Musculoskeletal rehabilitation and bone. Abnormal bone metabolism in female elite athletes.* Clin Calcium 20:543–550. 2010.

816 Shufelt CL, Torbati T, and Dutra E. Hypothalamic Amenorrhea and the Long-Term Health Consequences. Semin Reprod Med. 35(3). 256-262. 2017.

817 Torstveit MK, Rosenvinge JH, Sundgot-Borgen J. *Prevalence of eating disorders and the predictive power of risk models in female elite athletes: a controlled study.* Scand J Med Sci Sports 18:108-118. 2008.

818 Rowland TW. *The physiological impact of intensive training on the prepubertal athlete.* In: Cahill Bernard R, Pearl Arthur J, and American Othrthopaedic Society for Sports Medicine (eds.) Intense participation in children's sport. Champaign (IL). Human Kinetics Publication. 167-193.1993.

819 Chang, AY, and Auchus RJ. *Endocrine Disturbances Affecting Reproduction.* IN: Jerome F. Strauss, Robert L. Barbieri (Eds). Yen & Jaffe's Reproductive Endocrinology (6th Edition). W.B. Saunders. 2009. 561-575.

820 Constantini NW, Dubnov G, Lebrun CM. *The menstrual cycle and sport performance.* Clin Sports Med 24:51–82. 2005.

821 Loucks AB. *Exercise training in the normal female.* In: Warren Michelle P., and Naama W. Constantini (eds.) Sports endocrinology. Tatowa (NJ). Humana Press Inc. 2000. p. 165-180.

energy-consuming actions such as reproduction, adaptation, or significant repairs (e.g., wounds, tissue adaption to loading etc., which is why reduced levels of energy can lead to decreased immune system, i.e., the body has no energy to defend itself). If the fat percentage decreases drastically, the brain must shut down many physical processes to ensure survival. Primarily, all growth and reproduction processes belong to this category. If reproduction is hindered, stopped, or never even started at all, the hormone level of young female dancers decreases or remains so low that the girls' **estrogen production** is stopped or does not get started.[822,823,824,825]

Especially in vocational education, the female sex hormone estrogen very often is a red flag in the dancers' and teachers' eyes, because the young girl seems to be better off in dance education without the burden of menstruation, weight fluctuations, etc. What is always neglected here is that apart from its function as a sex hormone, **estrogen** is necessary to stimulate **bone metabolism**: estrogen hinders osteoclasts, bone cells that break down bone tissue. Estrogen creates a balance in favor of the slower bone building cells (osteoblasts) and slows down the faster destructing cells. Thus, bone mineral density can increase through estrogen, which is essential for bone and overall health. If girls have low body fat mass or/and are forced to lose weight, it can lead to the Female Athletic Triad, as already described:

An unnaturally **low energy availability** leads to **low percentage of fat,** introducing a **shortage** of **estrogen** as well as **lower levels of leptin** in the blood, resulting in **hormonal dysbalances** and **impaired bone health**, making the dancer prone for osteopenia and osteoporosis.

Apart from a healthy bone metabolism and the possibility of reproduction (which could and may become very important for a female dancer after or even during her career!), **estrogen** also guarantees numerous other essential physiological processes. It regulates the first half of the female cycle, forms the woman's secondary sex characteristics (which are not well appreciated in professional dance and education), it clears free radicals, and helps stabilize the brain's thermoregulation. It is involved in lowering cholesterol and blood lipid levels, promoting circulation, healthy sleep, and a good mood. In addition to boosting bone metabolism, which is particularly important for the young dancer, estrogen's encouraging effect on concentration should also be mentioned. And last but (especially for the dancer) not least: estrogen has weight-regulating characteristics: Estrogen controls the appetite, promotes movement behavior, and could thus contribute to regulating the lowering of the body weight.[826,827,828,829]

Studies on F.A.T. and osteopenia in dancers show that a lack of bone density caused by amenorrhea cannot simply be corrected by hormone therapy, including "the pill".[830] Practice shows how many (teachers, dancers, parents) think that taking the pill would just save the problem. However, the estrogen used in the pill is not a natural estrogen, as produced only by the body. Although the dancer seems to have a normal period, ovulation and estrogen production in the ovaries are inhibited. While energy deficiency can more or less quickly be reversed (within weeks to months if the dancer is allowed to eat sufficiently and healthily), the already committed effects on bone health are not correctable as easily as that – if anyway. Hence, it does not matter how intense the aversion to fat in dancers may be: A certain individual **optimal percentage of adipose tissue is vital for a functional bone metabolism.**

Dance, as all sports, can only be performed healthily = successfully, if the dancer is sufficiently fueled through optimal and sufficient nutrition, and only then!

Suppose a low body mass index negatively affects young female dancers' hormonal regulation in the second growth spurt's critical phases. In that case, the bone density remains low even with hormone therapy. Whereas it was shown that **gaining one to two kilos (!!!)**

[822] Muños MT, C de la Piedra, Barrios V, Garrido G, and Argente J. *Changes in Bone Density and Bone Markers in Rhythmic Gymnasts and Ballet Dancers: Implications for Puberty and Leptin Levels.* Europ J Endocrinology. 151(4).491-496. 2004.

[823] Cervero A, Domínguez F, Horcajadas JA, Quiñonero A, Pellicer A, and Simón C. *The role of the leptin in reproduction.* Curr Opin Obstet Gynecol. 18(3). 297-303. 2006.

[824] Moschos S, Chan JL, and Mantzoros CS. *Leptin and reproduction: a review.* Fertil Steril. 77(3). 433-444. 2002.

[825] Thong FS, and Graham TE. *Leptin and reproduction: Is it a critical link between adipose tissue, nutrition, and reproduction?* Can J Appl Physiol. 24(4). 317-336. 1999.

[826] Gao Q, Mezei G, Nie Y, Rao Y, Choi CS, ... and Horvath TL. *Anorectic estrogen mimics leptin's effect on the rewiring of melanocortin cells and Stat3 signaling in obese animals.* Nat Med. 13(1). 89-94. 2007.

[827] Wallen WJ, Belanger MP, and Wittnich C. *Sex hormones and the selective estrogen receptor modulator tamoxifen modulate weekly body weights and food intakes in adolescent and adult rats.* J Nutr. 131(9). 2351-2357. 2001.

[828] Riant E, Waget A, Cogo H, Arnal JF, Burcelin R, and Gourdy P. *Estrogens protect against high-fat diet-induced insulin resistance and glucose intolerance in mice.* Endocrinology. 150(5). 2109-2117. 2009.

[829] Xu P, Cao X, He Y, Zhu L, Yang Y, ... and Xu Y. *Estrogen receptor–α in medial amygdala neurons regulates body weight* J Clin Investigation. 125(7). 2861-2876. 2015.

[830] Warren MP, Brooks-Gunn J, Fox RP, Holderness CC, Hyle EP, Hamilton WG, and L Hamilton. *Persistent osteopenia in ballet dancers with amenorrhea and delayed menarche despite hormone therapy: a longitudinal study.* Fertility and Sterility. 80(2). 398-404. 2003.

in body weight could already bring about the (re-)onset of menstruation and **solve the problem from scratch**! Only the healthy hormonal balance in puberty, adipose tissue, and sufficient nutrition guarantee the health of the person affected.[831]

Especially in competitive sports and professional dance, examining the hormonal situation and education on all topics of nutrition both in the classroom and during the regular **screening**[832] must be just as present as the reliable cooperation of dance teachers, therapists, and physicians. Moreover, a professionally close, empowering relationship between teachers and dancers is essential to enable confidential conversations, preventing such problems before they occur. Teaching and living self-responsibility can only work with well-trained teachers in proactive cooperation with trained medical professionals.

MALE ATHLETIC TRIAD: BONE HEALTH & ENERGY AVAILABILITY IN MALE DANCE

Within the last three years, research has indicated that the same underlying issues responsible for the Female Athletic Triad also leads to severe consequences for male health and functioning.[833,834,835] Directly comparable to the Female Athletic triad (F.A.T.) the Male Athletic Triad has been investigating causal relationships between

- **Low Energy Availability** (e.g., nutritional deficiency, eating disorders)
- **Disturbances in the male hormonal production** and function (e.g., low testosterone levels, infertility)
- **Impacting bone health and metabolism** (e.g., high risk for stress fractures) and **strength**

Low levels of energy availability due to overtraining/overexercising or low caloric intake, or both, is associated with reduced bone mineral density in men and thus with high incidences of stress-related injuries to the bone, e.g., stress fractures. Comparable to the same mechanism leading to reduced or inhibited estrogen release in women, dysbalances in the hypothalamic-pituitary-gonadal-axis through low energy availability or energy deficiency results in low testosterone concentration, impacts spermatogenesis (the ability to produce functional, healthy sperm), libido, fertility and strength.

Under healthy circumstances, the hypothalamus is the gland monitoring the pituitary gland and gonads, the testicles in men, the ovaries in women. This so-called glandular axis is the cooperation of the glands, responsible for androgenic (i.e., male) hormonal development. Dysbalances can severely disturb male hormones such as testosterone and androsterone, affecting strength, bone health and fertility, comparable to the women's triad. Men seem to be more resilient when it comes to the consequences of energy deficiency and overtraining than women, and it takes longer to identify altered hormonal and metabolic mechanisms and their manifestations, while such perturbations are more quickly reversible. However, their high risk for related injuries must not be underestimated.

VITAMIN D AND HEALTH IN MALE & FEMALE DANCERS

A further essential aspect in dancers has been highlighted in dance medicine: Dance training normally takes place in closed rooms, most commonly without any windows, and a lot of time is spent in darkened theaters with electrical light. Only in the rarest exceptions training and/or performances are held outdoors, under big skylights, or in dance halls equipped with huge windows. Moreover, many (professional) dancers train too many months a year, with too little time spent on vacation (outdoors). That can lead to fundamental **vitamin D deficiency in dancers.**[836]

---

[831] Misra M, and Klibanski A. *Anorexia nervosa and bone.* J Endocrinol. 221(3). 163-176. 2014.

[832] Bonbright JM. *Developing screening and education programs for detecting and preventing eating disorders at the subclinical level in dancers.* Impulse. 3(4). 303-311. 1995.

[833] Melin AK, Heikura IA, Tenforde A, and Mountjoy M. *Energy Availability in Athletics: Health, Performance, and Physique.* Int J Sport Nutr Exerc Metab. 9(2). 152-164. 2019.

[834] De Souza MJ, Koltun KJ, and Williams NI. *The Role of Energy Availability in Reproductive Function in the Female Athlete Triad and Extension of its Effects to Men: An Initial Working Model of a Similar Syndrome in Male Athletes.* Sports Med. 49(Suppl 2). 125-137. 2019.

[835] De Souza MJ, Koltun KJ, and Williams NI. What is the evidence for a Triad-like syndrome in exercising men? Curr Opinion in Physiology. 10. 27-34. 2019.

[836] Ducher G, Kukuljan S, Hill B, Garnham AP, Nowson CA, Kimlin MG, and Cook J. *Vitamin D status and musculoskeletal health in adolescent male ballet dancers. A pilot study.* J Dance Med Sci. 15(3). 99-107. 2011.

It must be said that vitamin D deficiencies are common in latitudes where the solar radiation over the winter months or year in general is low. However, vitamin D deficiencies can also affect people who use strong sun blockers (sun lotion) in the summer, which also impairs vitamin D productions. A study conducted in 2012 estimated that 80% of all Europeans have a vitamin D deficiency.[837]

In 2014, another report stated that 87% of all German children suffer from hypovitaminosis D, 57% of men, 58% of women, and 75% of over-65-year-olds. The population's deficiency in vitamin D has personal health consequences for those affected and economic significance for the state and health system.[838,839] In the USA, an annual burden of vitamin D deficiency and its direct consequences on the health of bones, all soft tissues, organs, nervous system, and immune system of 56 billion dollars was recorded.[840]

The production of vitamin D, also known as "the sun vitamin", takes place in the skin when exposed to sunlight.[841, 842, 843] Since humans can produce it themselves through UV-B-radiation, the term "vitamin" is medically discussed. It is a fat-soluble secosteroid (steroid group), and its subgroups vitamin D2 and D3[844] are more likely to be considered hormones that have numerous vital tasks in the body. The ability to resorb calcium through the small intestine and our bones' health depend on vitamin D just as much as all muscles and organs since vitamin D has numerous effects on the metabolism and even our genes.[845,846,847,848]

For a long time, vitamin D was treated as highly toxic and allowed only in small doses, which had no significant effect on the body.[849] The much too low daily dose, which public authorities had recommended for years, was declared a calculation error in 2014.[850] Today the importance of the hormone/vitamin for almost all metabolic and growth processes in the body is discussed, including its effect on osteoporosis.[851] Additionally to the production of vitamin D in the human skin caused by sunlight, some foods such as fish (especially trout and herring) and healthy fats (e.g., sesame oil), eggs, milk, cheese, broccoli, algae, and sesame seeds provide vitamin D.

While (young) dancers spend most of their time in the dance studio, they are also encouraged to spend summers with additional training and to avoid getting tanned due to traditional so-called beauty standards, which favor pale skin. The consequence can be **vitamin D deficiency**. That, however, does not only affect **injury risk**, **strength** and overall wellbeing, but is in addition to the problem of malnutrition negatively associated with bone metabolism: Vitamin D enables the **absorption, transport, and storage of calcium** in the bones and has numerous other positive effects on metabolism and health.

Volume 3 discussed the pelvic floor, its health and function, in the professional and private lives of dancers. Vitamin D is vital for the functionality of the pelvic floor (as for all muscles).

It has been shown that dancers with vitamin D deficiency suffer more injuries. In contrast, an increased vitamin D level significantly increases dance performance, such as jump heights or isometric muscle strength, and lowers

[837] Gonzalez-Gross M, Valtuena J, et al. *Vitamin D status among adolescents in Europe: the healthy lifestyle by nutrition in adolescence study*. Br J Nutr. 107(5). 755-764. 2012.
[838] Kunz C and Zittermann A. *Vitamin D im Kindes- und Jugendalter in Deutschland. Dringlichkeit und Probleme der Umsetzung von Zufuhrempfehlungen.* Monatsschr Kinderheilkd. 163. 776-782. 2015.
[839] Hinzpeter B et al. *Higher prevalence of Vitamin D deficiency is associated with immigrant background among children and adolescents in Germany*. J Nutr 138. 1482-1490. 2008.
[840] Grant WB, and MF Holick. *Benefits and requirements of vitamin D for optimal health: A Review.* Alternat Med Rev. 10. 94-111. 2005.
[841] Barvencik F und M Amling. *Vitamin-D-Stoffwechsel des Knochens.* Orthopäde. 44(9). 686-694. 2015.
[842] Carpenter KJ, and L Zhao. *Forgotten mysteries in the early history of Vitamin D.* Nutrition. 129(5). 923-927. 1999.
[843] Rajakumar K, Greenspan SL et al. *Solar ultraviolet radiation and Vitamin D. A Historical Perspective*. Am J Public Health. 97(12). 1746-1754. 2007.
[844] Trang HM, Cole DE, Rubin LA, Pierratos A, Siu S, Vieth R. *Evidence that vitamin D3 increases serum 25-hydroxyvitamin D more efficiently than does vitamin D2.* Am J Clin Nutr. 68(4). 854-858. 1998.
[845] Goltzmann D. *Vitamin D action: lessons learned from genetic mouse models*. Ann NY Acad Sci. 1192. 145-152. 2010.
[846] Amling M, Priemel M, Holzmann T, Chapin K, Rueger JM, Baron R, and MB Demay. *Rescue of the skeletal phenotype of vitamin D receptor-ablated mice in the setting of normal mineral ion homeostasis: formal histomorphometric and biomechanical analyses.* Endocrinology.140(11). 4982-4987. 1999.
[847] Li YC, Pirro AE, Amling M, Delling G, Baron R, Bronson R, Demay MB. *Targeted ablation of the vitamin D receptor: an animal model of vitamin D-dependent rickets type II with alopecia.* PNAS. 94(18). 9831-.9835. 1997.
[848] Haussler MR, Whitfield GK, Kaneko I, Haussler CA, Hsieh D, Hsieh JC, and PW Jurutka. *Molecular mechanisms of vitamin D action.* Calcif Tissue Int. 92(2). 77-98. 2013.
[849] Kunz C und Zittermann A. *Vitamin D im Kindes- und Jugendalter in Deutschland. Dringlichkeit und Probleme der Umsetzung von Zufuhrempfehlungen.* Monatsschr Kinderheilkd. 163. 776-782. 2015.
[850] Veugelers P, and J Ekwaru. *A Statistical Error in the Estimation of the Recommended Dietary Allowance for Vitamin D.* Nutrients. 6(10). 4472-4475. 2014.
[851] Mastaglia SR, Mautalen CA, Parisi MS, and Oliveri B. *Vitamin D2 dose required to rapidly increase 25OHD levels in osteoporotic women.* Eur J Clin Nutr. 60(5). 681-687. 2006.

injury rates.[852, 853] Besides, the positive effect of the "vitamin" on all soft tissues and the nervous system leads to better coordination, which reduces the risk of bone fractures in dancers and makes them generally fitter. If the dancers usually already suffer a nutritional deficiency due to starving, missing vitamin D because of a lack of sunlight multiplies the bone metabolism problem. However, as with all interventions for dancers benefits, the compliance of the dancers themselves is an essential aspect for the success of any dance medical intervention.[854]

And last but not least, as with all **nutritional supplements**, vitamin D (or anything else) must not be supplemented only for good measure. Supplemental intake of any kind has to be checked with medical professional assistance, e.g., blood samples are essential to take a look first, whether vitamin or mineral (etc.) supplies in the body are low and need supplementation!

EDUCATION, EATING HABITS & DISORDERS

The collaboration with nutritionists, dietitians, and serious nutrition consultants, to whom dancers must have access but whose consultation must not have negative consequences for the dancers, has proved incredibly successful. **Education is crucial for preventing eating disorders, and related problems in dance.** Education and awareness in dancers as well as teachers are the most important first steps. However, such initiating steps are only successful, when institutions such as schools or companies provide the necessary environment for their practical implementation. The most effective situation would be that institutions enforce related regulations and insist on targeted educational programs in dancers and, first and foremost, teaching personnel. That is the only way to prevent eating disorders or the Female/Male Athletic Triad from scratch.[855,856,857]

A further important aspect is misunderstood and one-sided dietetics based on fractions of knowledge in dancers and teachers, which are too small to really be beneficial.[858,859] It is essential for injury prevention and performance enhancement, to have sufficient, professional in-depth knowledge on a topic, in order to prevent, for instance, deficient diet plans, which were composed by dancers or teacher based on a smidge of knowledge. That can backfire, and is a loss of resources and time. Again, the (will for) cooperation with dance medical professionals, such as dance specialized nutritionists, is essential. Any lack of nutrients, minerals, vitamins, etc. puts the body under stress, because it needs all necessary components in balanced form for efficient metabolism. Only a healthy metabolism enables the dancer to achieve their optimal performance, because it allows for biological adaptation to adjust to dance training, while it supports injury prevention. **For optimal overall health and performance, a balance of all factors involved is essential.**

Equally crucial is to specifically relate to dancers why, how, and what happens in the body if they do not eat sufficiently and purposefully. Such behavior can ruin their career, and comes along with pain, fear, and lifelong consequences that must be openly stated and discussed. **Dancers are very intelligent human beings with a strong body sense, good intuition, open minds and souls. They can understand and learn how they themselves can make a change and actively contribute to their own health and performance enhancement, as long as they can see that their personal responsibility is supported based on an empowering environment supporting their autonomy.**

The teacher/trainer, again, can be regarded as the most important significant other, as in so many aspects of a dancer's life. If teachers have experience and training in

[852] Wolman R, Wyon MA, Koutedakis Y, Nevill AM, Eastell R, and Allen N. *Vitamin D status in professional ballet dancers: winter vs. summer.* J Sci Med Sport. 16(5). 388-391. 2013.

[853] Wyon MA, Koutedakis Y, Wolman R, Nevill AM, and Allen N. *The influence of winter vitamin D supplementation on muscle function and injury occurrence in elite ballet dancers: a controlled study.* J Sci Med Sport. 17(1). 8-12. 2014.

[854] Rowan FE, Benjamin-Laing H, Kennedy A, De Medici A, Beasley I, and Haddad FS. *Self-Directed Oral Vitamin D Supplementation in Professional Ballet Dancers: A Randomized Controlled Trial Pilot Study.* J Dance Med Sci. 23(3). 91-96. 2019.

[855] Yannakoulia M, Sitara M, and Matalas AL. *Reported eating behavior and attitudes improvement after a nutrition intervention program in a group of young female dancers.* Int J Sport Nutrition and Exercise Metabolism. 12. 24-32. 2002.

[856] Raymond-Barker P, Petroczi A, and Quested E. *Assessment of nutritional knowledge in female athletes susceptible to the Female Athlete Triad syndrome.* J Occup Med Toxicol. 2(10). 2007.

[857] Liu CY, Tseng MC, Chang CH, Fang D, and Lee MB. *Comorbid psychiatric diagnosis and psychological correlates of eating disorders in dance students.* J Formos Med Assoc. 2015. [Epub ahead of print]

[858] Frusztajer NT, Dhuper S, Warren MP, Brooks-Gunn J, and Fox RP. *Nutrition and the incidence of stress fractures in ballet dancers.* Am J Clin Nutr. 51. 779-783. 1990.

[859] Burckhardt P, Wynn E, Krieg MA, Bagutti C, and Faouzi M. *The effects of nutrition, puberty and dancing on bone density in adolescent ballet dancers.* J Dance Med Sci. 15(2). 51-60. 2011.

this field, they can positively contribute to the conversation about nutrition and proactively support its practical implementation. Their role model-effect must also never be underestimated.

However, even if the teachers are specifically educated on the subject and are willing to help and understand the student, it helps to provide specialists who are not the dancers' teachers or trainers. It may help dancers if they are allowed to talk about nutritional or similar "intimate" questions with professionals, who are not their leading teacher or trainer. Together with cooperative teachers, psychologists, therapists, and/or nutritionists can contribute more to the dancers' health, as a team. Awareness and the **conscious, targeted fight against eating disorders and other injury mechanisms is essential for the success of injury preventive strategies.** [860] Lectures and workshops with invited experts, who can specifically instruct dancers how, when and what to eat, can eliminate a lot of stress, frustration, hunger and add new joy to the fact that as a dancer one may eat without fear and restriction if one only knows how.[861,862,863,864,865,866,867,868,869,870,871,872]

[860] Lai EYJ, Krasnow D, and M Thomas. *Communication Between Medical Practitioners and Dancers.* J Dance Med Sci. 12(2). 47-53. 2008.
[861] Mastin, Zerlina. Nutrition for the Dancer. Hampshire. Dance Books Ltd. 2009.
[862] Andreu, Helene. Dance, Movement, and Nutrition: Fitness Minutes for a Healthier Life. London. Author House. 2006.
[863] Fitt, Sally Severy, and Robin D. Chmelar. Diet For Dancers. A Complete Guide to Nutrition and Weight Control. Princeton. Dance Horizons Books, Princton Books Co. 1990.
[864] Fueling the dancer. Fact sheet. IADMS International Assoziation for Dance Medicine & Science. Resource paper. (Nutrition for the dancer).
[865] Challis J. *Nutrition for Dancers*. dance UK Information Sheet 12. 2003.
[866] Kraft EM. *Richtig essen im Tanz*. tamed infoblatt Nr 10. 2010.
[867] Wanke EM. *Essstörungen im Tanz*. tamed infoblatt Nr 6. 2007.
[868] Piran, Niva, Levine Michael P, and Catherine Steiner-Adair. Preventing Eating Disorders – A Handbook of Interventions and Special Challenges. Philadelphia London. Brunner/Mazel A Member of the Taylor & Francis Group. 1999.
[869] Koutedakis, Yannis, and NC. Craig Sharp. The fit and healthy dancer. Chichester. John Wiley & Sons Ltd. 1999.
[870] Ryan, Allen J, and Robert L. Stephens. The Dancer's Complete Guide to Healthcare and a Long Career. Chicago. Bonus Books. 1998.
[871] Katch FI, Katch VL, and WD McArdle. Exercise physiology: energy, nutrition, and human performance. Philadelphia. Lippincott Williams & Wilkins. 2010.
[872] Gordon, Cathrine M, and Merryl M. LeBoff. The Female Athletic Triad A Clinical Guide. Wien-New York. Springer Verlag. 2015.

It is nothing new that smoking is bad for health.[873] It is also known that smoking regularly negatively affects overall physical and mental performance.[874,875,876] In dancers, the number of smokers is very high, which frighteningly starts in early adolescence.[877,878,879,880,881]

Smoking adolescents have a higher heart rate, which **affects** their **basic endurance** ability to **recover** after mental and physical activity as well as **bone metabolism.**[882] The heart rate's ability to adapt to stress (heart rate variability, HRV), for instance to training, is reduced, and the average maximum heart rate corresponding to one's age can no longer be reached. In (adolescent) dancers, smoking increases the risk and consequences of the Female Athletic Triad and/or eating disorders with relation to overall health and bone metabolism: **Smoking** (nicotine) **promotes osteopenia and osteoporosis**, while it inhibits estrogen production and its effects on the body.[883]

Dancers smoke because of different reasons.[884,885] On the one hand, using cigarettes is an attempt to control hunger and keep their weight low. On the other hand, it is commonly but falsely assumed that smoking helps to cope with high stress levels and decreasing energy levels. If dancers psychologically, mentally, and with their metabolism enter this vicious circle, it is difficult to escape without getting into a complex vortex of body weight and stress management loops based on the related withdrawal. An alarming aspect, however, is the indirectly but recurrently reported cry for recovery breaks: dancers perceive that smokers are more likely to take a break than non-smokers. Instead of basing dancers' education and training on evidence -based planning (e.g., periodization) to ensure the fair availability of breaks, it is commonly accepted that dancers smoke. An easier way out. Other reasons are related to social aspects such as a sense of belonging, group pressure, lack of emotional intelligence, and the search for something to hold on to are, like many other reasons of and for smokers, also true for dancers.

As with all aspects, early education and the teacher's influence and knowledge are crucial, especially since smoking is directly related to **healthy eating behavior** and **targeted weight control in dance**. Not only the harmfulness of smoking and its importance in reducing performance must be explained clearly. Too many (young) people are still unaware of smoking's harmfulness or refuse to become aware of it.[886, 887] Already the youngest dancers need help to learn alternative solutions for weight and stress control.

Teaching, explaining and implementing coping strategies for stress situations such as training or performance peaks in combination with an evidence-based control of training load to avoid high levels of stress and pressure are essential. This includes **emphasizing hobbies and circles of friends outside of dancing** to eliminate the dancers' social isolation and offer new and **healthy alternatives in life, social contacts, and opportunities for creating identity**. Again, the teacher and trainer serves as a role model. Dancers look up to teachers and choreographers, as well as to older dancers. Their behavior and awareness of their role-model-effect is vital.

Not only in adolescents, smoking leads to increased risk and occurrence of respiratory diseases, but it can also

---

873 Suttorp N und S Nitschmann. *Rauchen.Kardiovaskuläre Auswirkungen und Abstinenzstrategien.* Internist. 56. 1325-1328. 2015.

874 Papathanasiou G, Georgakopoulos D, Georgoudis G, Spyropoulos P, Perrea D, and A Evangelou. *Effects of chronic smoking on exercise tolerance and on heart rate-systolic blood pressure product in young healthy adults.* Eur J Cardiovasc Prev Rehabil. 14(5). 646-652. 2007.

875 Bernaards CM, Twisk JW, Van Mechelen W, Snel J, and HC Kemper. *A longitudinal study on smoking in relationship to fitness and heart rate response.* Med Sci Sports Exerc. 35(5). 793-800. 2003.

876 Sidney S, Sternfeld B, Gidding SS, Jacobs DR Jr, Bild DE, Oberman A, Haskell WL, Crow RS, and JM Gardin. *Cigarette smoking and submaximal exercise test duration in a biracial population of young adults: the CARDIA study.* Med Sci Sports Exerc. 25(8). 911-916. 1993.

877 Clippinger KS. *Smoking in Young Dancers. J* Dance Med Sci. 3(3). 115-125. 1999.

878 American Lung Association Fact Sheet. *Teenage Tobacco Use September 1998 Update.* J Dance Med Sci. 3(3). 113-114. 1999.

879 Robson B, Snell E, Danek I. *A questionnaire for adolescent dance students.* Paper presented at Medical Problems of Musicians & Dancers Symposium, Aspen, CO, June 1999.

880 American Lung Association: Trend Report on Cigarette Smoking. New York. ALA. 1999.

881 Koutedakis Y, Pacy PJ, Carson RJ, and F Dick. *Health and fitness in professional dancers.* Med Probl Perform Art. 12. 23-27. 1997.

882 Papathanasiou G, Georgakopoulos D, Papageorgiou E, Zerva E, Michalis L, Kalfakakou V, and A Evangelou. *Effects of smoking on heart rate at rest and during exercise, and on heart rate recovery, in young adults.* Hellenic J Cardiol. 54(3). 168-177. 2013.

883 Bartl R und C Bartl. *Aktuelle Osteoporoseprophylaxe und -therapie. Frakturorientiert, effektiv, nebenwirkungsarm, kostengünstig.* Internist. 56.1445-1457. 2015.

884 Clippinger KS. *Smoking in Young Dancers. J* Dance Med Sci. 3(3). 115-125. 1999.

885 Robson B, Snell E, Danek I. *A questionnaire for adolescent dance students.* Paper presented at Medical Problems of Musicians & Dancers Symposium, Aspen, CO, June 1999.

886 Kropp RY, and BL Halpern-Felsher. *Adolescents' beliefs about the risks involved in smoking "light" cigarettes.* Pediatrics. 114(4). 445-451. 2004.

887 Kozlowski LT, Goldberg ME, Yost BA, White EL, Sweeney CT, LJ Pillitteri. *Smokers' misperceptions of light and ultra-light cigarettes may keep them smoking.* Am J Prev Med. 15(1). 9-16. 1998.

affect the development of the lungs and thus lay a negative foundation for the entire adult life. Although smoking seems to have an energizing effect on the smoker, it significantly lowers the cardiorespiratory fitness, metabolism (also fat metabolism!), and bone metabolism.

Thus, smoking limits performance. The pollutants released by the fire when lighting a cigarette are numerous and have different effects on the body. Especially tar, nicotine, and carbon monoxide (CO) should be considered here. [888] **Tar** is carcinogenic. It forms a sticky layer on the inside of the lungs and thus impairs their function.[889,890] It inhibits the exchange of substances through inflammation of the alveoli and irritates the mucous membranes. Their inflammatory reaction is the increased formation of mucus, which smokers must cough up, but only can to a certain extent. **Carbon monoxide** prevents the uptake and transport of oxygen in the body by occupying the oxygen-carrying hemoglobin (red blood cells), which leads to an undersupply of all tissues and cells.[891]

Dancers who are already prone to a deficit of aerobic endurance further limit their energy metabolism by smoking. Oxygen is the basis of life and the energy supply of the body. The heart muscle, all skeletal muscles, connective tissues, and the metabolism of all body cells, their repairing processes, and their ability to adapt are thus blocked and therefore put under a lot of stress. After injuries, the healing processes are slower, the healing takes longer, and the risk of injury is increased due to damaged tissues. Blood pressure increases, the heart rate variability and the maximum oxygen intake decrease, the immune system is weakened. **The oxygen capturing carbon monoxide leads to fatigue. It thereby increases the risk of injury.**

Smoking affects the respiratory tract and blood circulation, which is reflected in the blood vessels' permeability and cardiac output. The usually very thin dancers often tend to freeze, tense, and have difficulties warming up and recovering their body. Smoking exacerbates all of this. The body cannot fully metabolize the already minimal food intake to which many dancers restrict themselves if all the harmful effects of smoking block the metabolism.

However, stress through smoking is not only caused by a lack of oxygen and energy: **Nicotine** reaches the brain through the bloodstream, where it triggers the release of adrenaline. Adrenaline is one of the neurotransmitters of the sympathetic nervous system, thus responsible for action. However, ongoing adrenaline levels are as detrimental as cortisol, as discussed in the chapters before, because they increase heartbeat, blood pressure, and breathing rate – their task for moments of action which but should be curbed again after the action has ceased.

On the one hand, this explains why cigarettes make smokers feel invigorated and empowered. They believe smoking fights fatigue and lack of energy. However, this feeling is deceptive. The adrenaline released by cigarettes is addictive, which ultimately becomes a habitual action, the stimulating effect of which, in turn, subsides with the course of the habit. Despite the habituation, the release of adrenaline, cortisol, and all hormones involved keeps leading to increased stress for the body. In case of stress cell growth, regeneration, and adaptation of tissues are hindered. **Smoking multiplies the dancers' already high load of stress considerably.**

Supporting that, a study [892] looked at nicotine dependence and sleep quality in 116 conservatory dancers. The study showed that compared to non-smokers the smoking dancers had a higher risk of poor quality of sleep [OR = 4.39]. 59.5% of the dance students reported poor sleep quality (Pittsburgh Sleep Quality Index scores > 5) of which 20.7% smoked. Compared to non-smokers, smoking dancers scored higher on the Pittsburgh Sleep Quality Index ($p = 0.001$), slept fewer hours ($p = 0.05$), took longer to fall asleep ($p = 0.001$), reported worse efficiency of their sleep ($p < 0.001$) as well as more diurnal dysfunctions resulting from sleep deprivation ($p = 0.023$). Since dancers need a lot of sleep due to their heigh training loads it can be concluded that smoking is detrimental to their health and wellbeing.

For non-smoking dancers, the contact with smokers is detrimental in terms of passive smoking. Dance means a

[888] Uchiyama S, Hayashida H, Izu R, Inaba Y, Nakagome H, and Kunugita N. *Determination of nicotine, tar, volatile organic compounds and carbonyls in mainstream cigarette smoke using a glass filter and a sorbent cartridge followed by the two-phase/one-pot elution method with carbon disulfide and methanol.* J Chromatogr A. 1426. 48-55. 2015.

[889] Lindner D, Smith S, Leroy CM, and Tricker AR. *Comparison of exposure to selected cigarette smoke constituents in adult smokers and nonsmokers in a European, multicenter, observational study.* Cancer Epidemiol Biomarkers Prev. 20(7).1524-1536. 2011.

[890] Kaufman DW, Palmer JR, Rosenberg L, Stolley P, Warshauer E, and Shapiro S. *Tar content of cigarettes in relation to lung cancer.* Am J Epidemiol. 129(4).703-711. 1989.

[891] McDonough P, and Moffatt RJ. *Smoking-induced elevations in blood carboxyhaemoglobin levels. Effect on maximal oxygen uptake.* Sports Med. 27(5). 275-283. 1999.

[892] Arbinaga F. *Dependence on Nicotine and Subjective Quality of Sleep in Conservatory Dance Students.* J Dance Med Sci. 23(3). 97-103. 2019.

lot of physical contact and close cooperation among all professionals in dance. Dancers usually are persons for whom cleanliness and "esthetic hygiene" are paramount. The stench of smoke in clothes, hair, skin, and breath is a disgrace for all non-smokers – fascinatingly for many smokers themselves. Justin Howse, dance medical expert and physician, presented an impressive list of facts[893], which want to be listed as a conclusion:

- Twenty minutes after the last cigarette blood pressure, and heart rate can decrease again.
- Eight hours after the last cigarette the oxygen concentration in the blood regenerates, and the carbon monoxide level drops.
- Two days after the last cigarette the smell dwindles, and the sense of taste returns.
- Three days after the last cigarette the lung capacity begins to increase, and breathing becomes easier, the airways begin to relax.
- Two weeks after the last cigarette the body stops asking for nicotine.
- Three months after the last cigarette blood circulation and lung functions normalize.
- Nine months after the last cigarette the lungs begin to clean themselves, and the risk of infection starts to decrease.

[893] Howse, Justin, and Moira McCormack. Anatomy, Dance Technique and Injury Prevention. New York London. Methuen Drama. 2009. p 109.

CONCLUSION: WHY "THE SYMBIOSIS OF THE FUTURE" BECAME THE TITLE

The chapters of this book have addressed topics which too often remain unaddressed. But as stated in the introductory chapters, such diplomatic handling of outdated traditions has not shown to pay off for dancers or teachers. Neither have they earned them the respect, the health and wellbeing nor the success they deserve, because their health but also their reputation so often is impaired. For that reason, some things have to be said out loud to protect those who deserve and need it. And to politely but courageously ask the others to make a change, or leave. Because after decades of dance medicine, dance science, as well as dance medical dance pedagogy in the making, times are ready to address issues directly, based on evidence, courage and love for dance as probably the most wonderful athletic artform ever, and dancers, as the most impressive athletic, high-performing artists, who undoubtedly deserve all care and support they can be given.

The **basis for a maximum of individual performance in dance is a maximum of individual health**, the motto to which this series is dedicated. This motto refers to dancers' as well as teachers'/trainers' health and performance. Preparing dancers to achieve this state begins in early dance education. Several chapters have highlighted the essential role of the teacher and trainer in this very complex scenario. While teachers, trainers, ballet masters, artistic directors etc. are the first on the list of measures needed for efficient injury prevention in dancers, they also depend on the institutions, thus administrations and organizational bodies they work for, including governments. Also on the list are **dancers themselves**. However, they have to be provided with an adequate education and environment in order to be able to become self-responsible and autonomous.

The aspects discussed in this volume and all others in this series can only be primarily met if professional associations for dance teachers and above all politics and society realize and accept that dance, teaching dance and training dancers have to be based on dance medicine and science. That includes compulsory education, training and examination for dance teachers, trainers and all professions in the second career of a dancer, with the overall goal to protect and support dancers of all ages and levels of expertise. Compulsory teachers' education will raise the teacher's reputation, their own motivation, health and job satisfaction.

Such regulations also protect the dance teachers/trainers themselves and demand from states and governments to legally anchor this protection, i.e., their job as a high-level profession. For that it has to be based on sufficient scientific education and background, otherwise it cannot be taken seriously as a high-level profession – coming full circle. This will sort out all teachers and trainers who cannot or do not want to be aware of their responsibility to professionally guide a dancer through their dance practice.[894,895] In the long run, dance teaching can be transferred into dance pedagogy, an evidence-based profession with scientific and social accreditation. In the short run, dancers' health and wellbeing can already be enhanced.

Only such described team work of all representatives of all sciences involved can make a change to outdated traditions of dance practice, which so often come along with detrimental effects for the dancer's overall health and wellbeing but also for their performance. Moreover, making a change towards new pathways of dance inevitably connected to dance medicine and science, will also lead to a change in how society, politics, media etc. perceive dance, dancers, dance teachers and related professions. Only then can dance be anchored and accepted in its exceptionally virtuous uniqueness, and dancers as the artistic high performing athletes who they are. Such changes again will be reflected in increasing medical and financial support for dancers, companies, schools and so forth. To be taken seriously one has to act accordingly!

Beginning in the education of the youngest, the teacher as role model for dance pedagogy and dance medicine is essential in the young dancer's life. Children see and thus imitate how the teacher handles important aspects like self-reflectiveness, education, courtesy, communication, outspokenness and emotional/social intelligence, management of conflicts, training and regeneration, eating and drinking behavior, pain and injury, and so many aspects of a dancer's life and environment. Teachers of the young as well as trainers of adult dancers create a motivational climate through which they have the power to lay the foundation for high levels of self-

[894] Lee SA. *The Artist as Teacher: A Psychological Perspective.* Med Probl Perform Art. 12(2). 38-41. 1997.

[895] Lakes R. *The Messages behind the Methods: The Authoritarian Pedagogical Legacy in Western Concert Dance Technique Training and Rehearsals.* Arts Education Policy Review. 106(5). 3-18. 2005.

concept, identity, self-esteem and self-efficacy, self-assessment, injury prevention – dancers' health, wellbeing and performance.

If teachers/trainers/masters etc. possess sufficient knowledge, are supported by their employing institutions, but also government, politics, media, society and audiences, they will be able to make a change away from outdated traditions. Such a change will come along with

- teamwork of all professions involved in the proactive care for dancers
- healthy, successful and empowered dancers
- acknowledgement of dance as artistic high-performance sport
- involving medical, social, political and economic support
- the elevation of dance teaching into dance pedagogy as an evidence-based science
- away from unsuccessful passing-on of unfounded so-called "knowledge"
- increasing reputation of dancers and dance pedagogues
- new generations of dancers who are more autonomous with respect to their own performance and their injury prevention through their own knowledge, education, and thus self-concept
- new generations of dancers who will then, one day, become a new generation of teachers, trainers, artistic directors, dance specialized physicians, therapists, and so forth...
- new generations, who, as a matter of course, will naturally think of dancing, dance medical dance pedagogy, dance medicine and dance science as the inseparable symbiosis, which they are meant to be in order to be able to live up to their full potential:

The Symbiosis of the Future in Dance

PART 4

GETTING STARTED:
THE BASICS OF HOW TO FIND AND USE SCIENCE

The Inspiration Part I

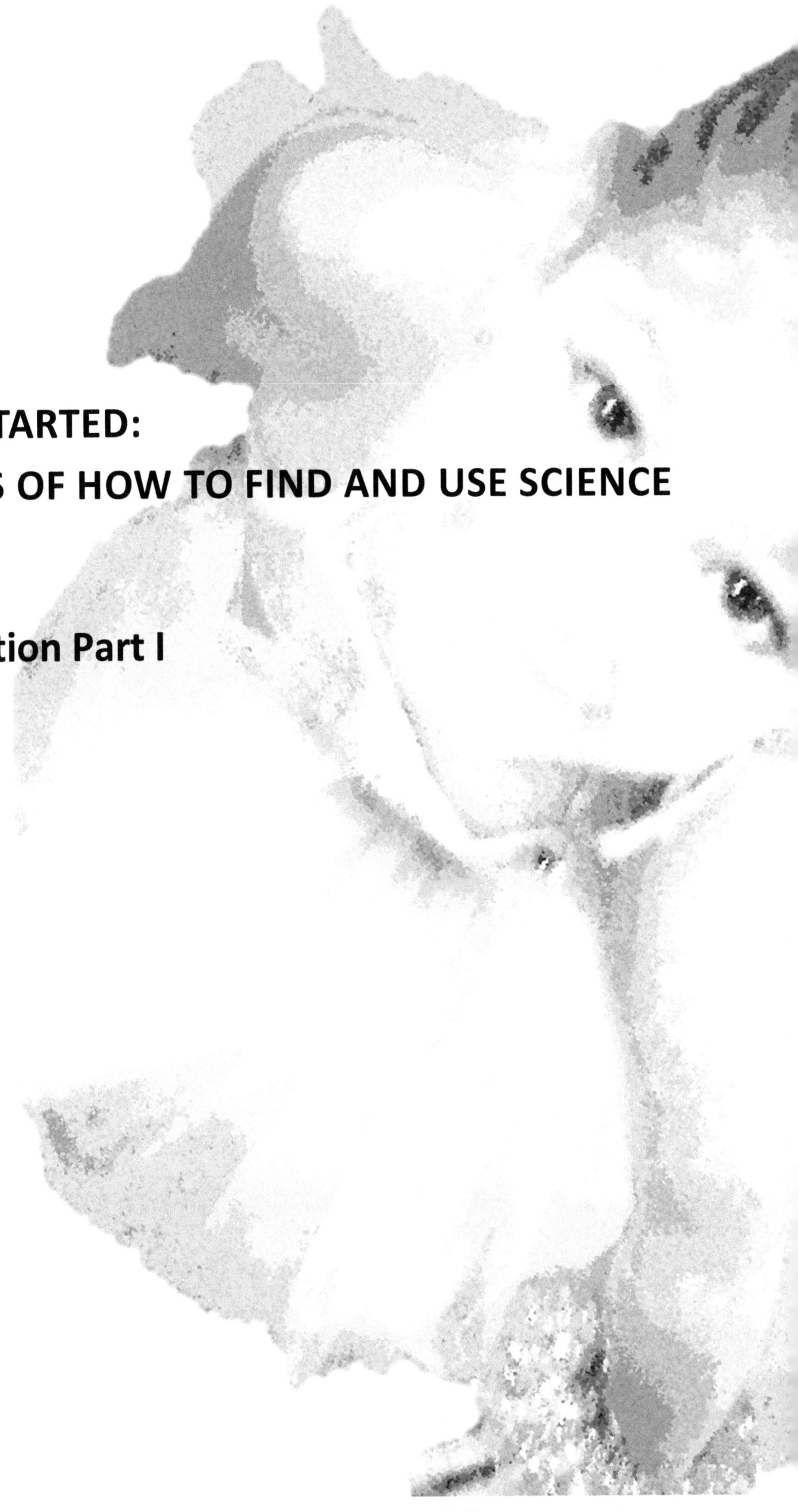

PART 4 GETTING STARTED: HOW TO FIND & USE SCIENCE – THE INSPIRATION PART I

This chapter was introduced to this series at the request of so many dancers, teachers, parents, or other caring for dancers, who would like to engage in science but do not know how or where to start. After having been inspired by (my) lectures, books etc. to engage in dance medicine and science, so many get in touch and state that they would like to read scientific publications, but don't know how to search and find them, or if found, how to actually read them, which is frustrating.

For that matter, I would like to offer a very basic and brief overview on how you can get started, for example using Google Scholar as a kickstart and Pubmed & Co for further research. The chapters explain which basic study designs exist, e.g., meta-analysis, systematic review, cohort studies, and which purpose they serve.

Taking it from there, the chapters relate what the reader can expect to find when retrieving and reading a scientific article. The common internal structure (e.g., abstract, introduction, methods, results, discussion, conclusion) of scholarly literature is explained. This shows which information can normally be found in which part of a scientific article, allowing the reader to make informed decisions on how and why to read which part of a study, depending on the information they want to retrieve.

Moreover, the following chapters aim at inspiring new (and experienced) researchers to look into the great body of research (again), which dance medicine and science as well as dance medical dance pedagogy have compiled for ***you*** throughout decades.

I wish you joy with your first steps (and hopefully many more steps to follow!). Sometimes, after your first searches, just think back to how you started, look at your own collection, perhaps how neatly you sorted and labelled your treasures (see below), and bathe in the sensations of inspiration, enjoyment, and pride you might find in yourself through the knowledge you gained.

Knowledge is something nobody can ever take away from you. It is one of the greatest treasures you can have, and it leads to inspiration, motivation, and curiosity; sensations related to the satisfaction of autonomy and perceived competence, which is why knowledge is power and power of motivation, at that.

I always enjoy seeing the pride and new levels of self-esteem arise, when one of my students or dancers embarked on this very journey and ended up with many new thoughts, possibilities, and horizons, which had opened up: The more you know the more you will be able to protect yourself and others by making informed decisions, – or knowing where you can find somebody to ask for help in making such decisions!

By the way: The latter is an important part of intelligence coming along with increasing sophistication: knowing where to look things up or where or whom to ask for help! Do not hesitate to do exactly that.

In order to get your head around a topic, it has become common practice to simply ask Google. However, when you type in "dance injuries", you will end up with a myriad of search results, for instance 66.500.321 today. Since Google provides so much information from such a variety of sources, it takes ages to get down to evidence-based publications, and you have to dig yourself through blogs, news, trivia, videos etc. Hence, it makes sense to leave Google out of that and start off with Google Scholar: https://scholar.google.com.

Google Scholar presents scholarly resources from various databases, regardless of their indexing or the topics of the scientific journals, in which they appear. In other words, Google Scholar gathers a broad overview of existing literature but, other than Google, only searches for scientific publications such as theses, research articles ("studies"), conference presentations, or books. Within the broad array of scholarly literature, one of the many advantages of Google Scholar as a computer-generated database is that the platform collects and offers many open access sources, i.e., publications which you can download in full version as a pdf document. The database also helps you by offering first search key-combinations or "key strings", which are combinations of search terms you might be interested in: When you type in "dance", Google Scholar sets out to offer you a broad array of possible further specifications in order to narrow down your search *(Figure 2).*

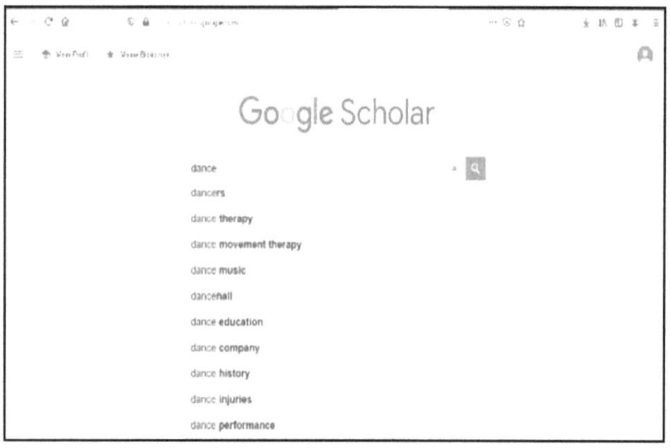

Figure 2: Key words offered by google scholar

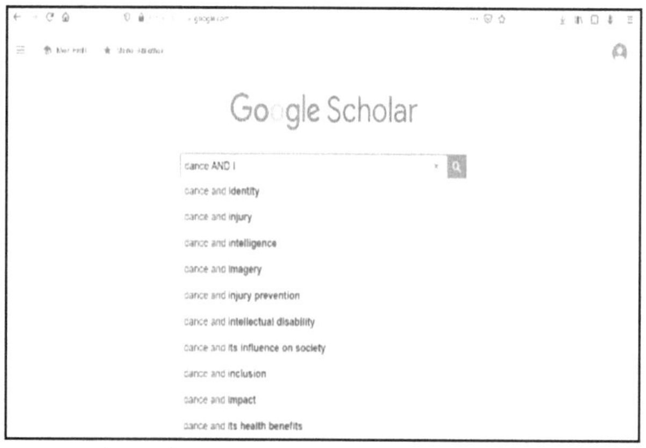

Figure 3: Choice of key words

So, one of your first steps would be to **make up your mind what you actually want to find**, i.e., which are the main **key words** you want to use and gather information on. For instance, you are interested in publications, which discuss dance injuries. Then a basic combination such as "dance AND injuries" might be helpful to start off with *(Figure 3).*

As you can see, Google Scholar already starts to offer possible combinations of keywords, for which the search engine holds search strings (i.e., the underlying connection of key words the computer is using to narrow down your search) at the ready for you. Try out your combination of "dance AND injury" and hit enter:

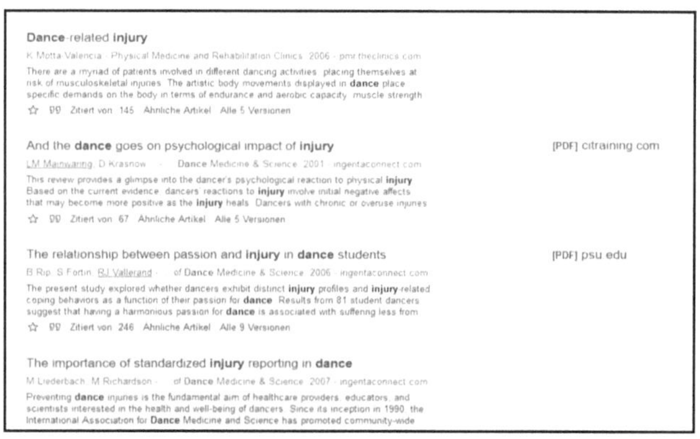

Figure 4: First search results

Google Scholar will offer you scholarly literature on the topic *(Figure 4).* And as you can see on the right margin of the page, many of the publications will be already linked to their **original source**. When it gives you "**[PDF]**" in this link, you mostly have **free access to the publication**. As such, you can compile your own, private database and can stay posted on thousands of evidence-based publications, which dedicated researchers in dance medicine and science have provided for you.

Already the first results in Google Scholar will give you vital information already on the first glimpse. In blue and hyperlinked you can find the **title** of the publication. Below, in green, you will see the **authors**, or at least the first author's name, followed by the **scientific journal**, in which the article was published, the **year of publication** and the **source of the link**. Below these first details, you can read into the abstract, in which your own key words will be bold. The **abstract is the summary of a scholarly publication**, with the aim to report the most essential results in brief. Although Google Scholar cuts it short you can already find out whether this publication could be of interest for you. Otherwise click on the title and you will be able to read the whole abstract, most likely in another database, where the article is indexed.

You will see that Google Scholar often redirects you to the webpage of a scientific journal or links to further databases, which offer the **free PDF**. You can then either browse in the journals or in the various scientific databases or you return to your original Google Scholar search. In case you go on in another database or a journal, be aware that such searches often need **specific search techniques**, which again might differ from database to database (see below). Also, you might get off track very fast, because databases and journals offer you a lot of additional but maybe different and not always related articles you may get lost in when starting to browse.

Databases you could use for further (and already high levels of) scholarly search are for instance pubmed.ncbi.nlm.nih.gov or researchgate.net. For many databases, e.g., Web of Science, you will need institutional access or pay for your access. Databases such as **Pubmed** or **Web of Science** are based on specific search techniques, as mentioned above. You would benefit from taking a user tutorial, which are offered by databases, such as Pubmed, for free (go to https://learn.nlm.nih.gov/ or google "pubmed tutorial") https://learn.nlm.nih.gov/documentation/training-packets/T0042010P/

How ever you decide to go on with further search, to start off into any research in dance medicine and science as a novice or to generally get yourself an overview, what actually exists on a topic, enjoy Google Scholar. You will end up with a wonderful compilation of high-level scientific publications, which will bring you far into the world of dance science already. Then enjoy taking it up a notch, use the tutorials of, e.g., Pubmed and go into depth. You might not be able to retrieve all studies you find as pdf, because many are dependent on institutional access, such as university accounts. However, more and more research articles are published "**open access**", which means that the researchers themselves or their institutions pay the publisher to be able to provide *you* with the free and full document (!). In the case of open access, you can also get the full article on Pubmed. It pays off to give it a try.

HOW TO CREATE YOUR VERY OWN RESEARCH COLLECTION

The following tips will help you to start your very own scholarly collection with the many articles, you can already harvest on Google Scholar (or through further research in Pubmed, Researchgate, & Co). Start off by entering your key word(s) into Google Scholar and then decide, which articles you would like to keep and read in full. When you are lucky, you will find the [PDF] and can access the full publication. Otherwise, perhaps you might want to save the abstract in a word doc or related programs. In any case you want to keep a retrieved publication, abstract etc., here are some tips you might find helpful:

- **File names**: When you create your own research-collection, make sure to name the files properly from the beginning. When you are full with inspiration you might get into a flow and end up with a great number of interesting publications you cannot wait to dive into. However, scholarly literature very often is not stored under the author's name or the publication's title, but for instance under the article reference number of the respective scientific journal, which published it. Since there are thousands of scientific journals serving the great number of available topics, you might end up with a motley assortment of quite interesting (but not helpful) file names.
- **Find one uniform way to name your files**: The sense behind your own database (collection of literature) is to collect publications which support your topic(s) of interest and especially, to easily find information again, which you have once read. Click into the pdf file name and start your own database by naming all your articles in the same way. As such, you will be able to find them again easily. One of the most common ways to name files is by the first author's family name, the publication year and if you want, the title. Be aware that titles can be long, which would make re-naming of files impossible. In such a moment shorten the title, if you want to include the title (which makes sense for easier search in your own collection).
- **Find quoted articles in your collection**: To name your file after the first author and year will be an advantage in the future: After you have read some publications you might want to look up a publication, which you find cited in a study you are

just reading and check whether you possess the full-text article already. Most commonly, publications are cited in texts by (at least) the first author's family name and the year (the whole reference you can find in the reference list at the end of the article). However, when you have archived your publications under the first author's name and year, you can immediately find it in your collection by just typing this name into your search field on your computer.

- **Group your findings**: According to your level of inspiration and resulting flow, you might end up with many publications on various topics. Try to group them in files, which you can name after the most important key word or topic, for instance: "injuries", etc.
  When you want to take it further already, you can make sub-files such as: "ballet", "modern", ... etc., and then subdomains such as "prospective studies", "retrospective studies", "reviews" etc., or you file in any other way to keep your very personal overview.
- **Create keyword documents for quick find**: While you read an article, you might find a lot of information which you would like to remember later. Especially, you might want to remember in which article you had read a special information, which will become harder and harder the more papers you are going to read. Thus, you might want to be really smart already from the beginning: Open a file such as Excel, Word, Pages, or Numbers, and make your own "key words" document. Noting down keywords while you read a publication and save them under the reference (FirstAuthor'sName_Year_Title) can help you access it again later: Programs such as the named allow you to open a "search" field. There you type in a key word you are looking for and the program will guide you to all the publication notes you filed upon reading, which contain this very word. As such, you even create your very own search system in your very own database. It is enough to note down key words, you don't need to copy sentences. Creating such personal (keyword-) summaries, by the way, is called "excerpting or extracting" literature, i.e., noting vital information on a publication for further and quick access. (The following chapters will give you some more ideas and details.)
- **Use the following chapters** to take a look, which possible publications you may find and how they can serve your very specific purpose.

Another tip: **IADMS**, The International Association for Dance Medicine & Science, offers a broad variety of **IADMS resource papers** for free (https://iadms.org/resources/publications/resources-paper/). The association, among many others, is dedicated to support dancers and all involved in and interested in dance. Aside from their resource papers, **IADMS offers the Bulletin for Dancers and Teachers**, a nice compilation of publications especially dedicated to dancers, teachers, trainers, instructors, ballet masters etc. (https://iadms.org/resources/publications/iadms-bulletin/). Feel free to visit them and enjoy their generous offer, which is compiled especially for you by various researchers dedicated to dance medicine and science! Becoming a member of IADMS holds even more benefits at the ready!

TYPES & GOALS OF SCHOLARLY LITERATURE

As stated above, scholarly literature differs (a lot) from what you can commonly find with a normal Google search. Scientific literature does not include non-scholarly magazine articles, news, or blogs, etc. As such, you can be sure that what you read is based on certain evidence-based standards of scientific research and reporting. Other than trivial information, scholarly literature aims at researching and presenting a topic as objectively and unbiased as possible, i.e., to provide scientific evidence on a topic, and not the authors' personal opinion. In the publication of scientific articles, ethic committees as well as peer review procedures are involved to make sure that the publication follows certain rules and reaches specific levels of sophistication.

One of many of these rules is that high level scientific literature always **cites further publications**, where they have used and gathered information from. On the one hand, not citing (directly or indirectly) quoted literature is plagiarism, and simply a no-go in real science. On the other hand, it is a matter of courtesy to cite properly so that previous researchers are credited for their hard work appropriately. (When you read a 5–10-page article you might want to keep in mind that such a publication might have cost the researcher 1-10 years or even more to design, research, evaluate, compose, and publish!). Moreover, through the thorough referencing of the author(s), the reader is presented with a high number of further study references on a topic just by reading one article. Hence, also enjoy and use the reference lists of articles you read.

In science, a variety of different designs exist, how research can be executed and presented to the public.

They all have their legitimacy, because they mostly follow a specific purpose. It might be of interest to know about the most important research designs in order to decide, which publication will best serve your special interest and purpose. Various designs represent different levels of evidence in research.

- **Meta-Analysis** and **Systematic Literature Review** are publications which present filtered information and are therefore excellent for you to start with and get an impression of what evidence is already existing on a certain topic. The Meta-Analysis presents a statistical analysis of combined results from a number of similar studies. The Systematic Literature Review uses clearly pre-defined methods to gather studies, which have investigated (and can give answers to) a certain topic. Both present you with filtered information (they have **created an overview** for you already), which is why they rank highest in the pyramid of scholarly research: They offer overviews on research topics for other researchers to see what has already been done, and for every reader to be able to quickly access previous literature on one topic without having to gather and read and analyse the related papers themselves.
- **Review** or **Narrative (Review)** are simple forms of reviews. However, they are reviews most commonly based on the author's opinion and methods (if they have any), but not on methodological research approach. In comparison, Meta- and Systematic Literature Reviews follow specific methods and are not meant to present the author's view of a topic but summarize existing evidence in the most objective way possible. A Narrative (or any non-systematic review) can serve as interesting source of information but always include the author's opinion, which Meta-Analysis or Systematic Literature Reviews specifically aim to avoid. You have to keep that in mind when reading and analysing a paper.
- **Randomized Controlled Trials** (RCT) are prospective, experimental designs, which randomly allocate participants to two or more groups in order to investigate the effect of a certain treatment or intervention (e.g., one group, the experimental group, performs a certain training, while the control group does not). RCTs investigate, how such treatment or intervention influences an outcome, e.g., whether they are effective against injuries or illness, which would be examples for outcomes. The process of randomization allows to reduce bias, because the researchers cannot influence (and mostly don't know) in which group which participants will be. Hence, RCTs are the highest level of studies investigating exposure (i.e., what participants were exposed to, such as treatment or intervention; also named determinant) with respect to a certain outcome (i.e., the point of interest an exposure leads to, e.g., injuries).
- **Cohort studies** are studies which investigate a certain group of people, whose participants are linked in some way (form a cohort), for example "dancers", and compare this group with a control group (e.g., non-dancers) with respect to a certain variable they were exposed to, like a treatment, intervention, or medication (i.e., the exposure or determinant).
- **Case control studies** are studies in which researchers identify and select certain participants ("cases") who are exposed to something with the purpose of studying these very cases and compare them to a control group ("control"), who did not have this exposure.

Both designs, cohort and case control studies, are **observational** designs, in which researchers observe the effect of an exposure. Randomized Controlled Trials, in comparison, are **experimental** studies, in which the researchers introduce and investigate the exposure, e.g., a certain intervention like a specific training, which is meant to reduce injury risk etc. All three designs deliver **unfiltered information**, compared to Meta-Analysis or Systematic Reviews, which aim to filter information and present you with the summary.

Lower in the hierarchy of scientific evidence are case reports, in which researchers describe specific single cases of an illness, injury, etc. At the bottom line of level of scientific evidence are animal and in vitro studies followed by narratives (mentioned above to compare with systematic reviews) as well as letters to editors or authors, editorials, and opinion papers, etc.

The study designs briefly described all have their purpose and value. Specific topics need specific designs, because they cannot be investigated in another way. The reader knows (or will find out) which design serves which specific purpose.

For you this might be helpful when you aim to find specific studies. For instance, you want to know whether there is any systematic review published on injuries in hip hop, because you would like to gain an overview on existing literature before you search for the details. Then combine the keyword(s) "review" or "systematic literature review" to your search (with your key words) or use the filter "systematic review" in databases such as Pubmed by ticking the box, and you will come up with reviews first in your search, which help you get an already filtered, comprehensive overview on a topic.

The following introduction, again, is only in brief, to give you a certain basic guideline and "kickstart".

When you retrieve and read scientific literature, you will mostly find it presented in a certain structure. Such a structure is essential, because the researcher provides the reader with a very clear "storyline" or "red thread" throughout the document. All the various parts of an article serve a different purpose. When you know which purpose, you know exactly where to find which information in a publication:

- **Abstract**: The abstract of a research publication is a **brief summary** with the aim to give the most essential information, such as possible background, the objectives (research question, aims), methods, results, and conclusion of the study. Since many publishers restrict abstracts to approximately 250 words and abstracts will never contain all vital information to really get the whole picture of a study, it will be important that you read through the following sections of the publication, too.
- **Introduction**: In an introduction the author(s) aim(s) to present the background of a paper, i.e., is there any existing literature already (in brief) and how does is support the background of this very paper. At the end of the introduction, you should be able to find the **research question** (objectives, purpose, aim), which is the "conclusion" of the introduction, i.e., the authors' reason, why and with which purpose the study was conducted.
- **Methods**: The methods section will tell you specifically, which approach was undertaken, so you will find out which design the study had (e.g., meta-analysis, RCT, etc). Furthermore, the methods give you details on how participants or studies were selected, grouped, interpreted, etc., which is called "**inclusion**" and "**exclusion criteria**". If statistical procedures are underlying the study, the researchers will give their details on how they approached their choice of statistical analysis. The clearer the methods section the better the study can be understood (because the researchers themselves were very clear about what they were about to do and therefore can present the following sections clearly).
- **Results**: in the results section you find, mostly very short and based on statistical analysis, the results of the study, uninterpreted at best. The aim is to objectively present the results of what was done, without any interpretation or further comment.
- **Discussion**: Such interpretation and further comments are reserved for the discussion, which is mostly the longest part of a study. As a starter, the authors might sum up in only some sentences, what was done with which goal and what was found. Taking it from there, background and previously conducted research is being discussed with reference to the findings of the very study you read. As such, a discussion literally **discusses the background** information and literature briefly presented in the introduction **in direct reference to the new results**, which their very own study can contribute to the topic and to science.
- **Strengths and limitations**: This is the last part of the discussion, where authors critically analyse their own design and approach. No study is perfect, and there is just as much of an effort a researcher can put into the methodological approach or the conduction of a study in pursuit of excellence. There are always biases, limitations or confounders to address, which should be addressed. Such a section makes a publication even more valuable, because the more you are able to (try to) objectively look at a topic, the better you can understand the contribution of the results. However, as much as every paper has its limitations, the specific strengths of a research should also be mentioned here, because every paper will also have special strengths.
- **Conclusion**: In a few sentences the authors conclude **which new insights** their study was able to provide and how it can contribute to science.
- **References**: At the end of a scientific paper, you should always find a list of references quoted in the paper and ready for you to dive into additional information and further read. The bibliographic section of an academic publication might be quoted in different styles (such as "APA", "MLA", or "Chicago"), but every style is meant to contain all relevant information, such as author(s) name(s), title, year of publication, journal of publication including volume and issue, page numbers, and probably the "doi" (i.e., Digital Object Identifier, a permanent identification of a document, which will help to easily identify and locate a publication on the web).

If you have catalogued your pdfs by author_year_title (or a similar choice) you will immediately be able to have a look, whether you already possess a specific interesting publication you find cited in another article by just searching for the first author's name. If you do not find the pdf in your very own database yet, copy the doi or title into google or google scholar and have a look whether the browser offers you a free pdf, or at least you will find the abstract somewhere.

And again, you might have retrieved many more interesting articles just by reading one paper and browsing its reference list. As such, you will, first, see how many wonderful academic publications dance medicine and science can offer, and, second, how awesome it is to dive into the world of knowledge and broaden your horizon.

In case you do not want to or do not have the time to study a whole paper, I would recommend you read the abstract, introduction and discussion, to get the basic gist. However, you might soon find out that you are left with certain questions you would like to have answered. If that's the case, give at least the methods section a try. A good methods section is like the "FAQ" (frequently asked questions) of a paper.

SCIENTIFIC LANGUAGE: EXCERPTING & EXTRACTING VITAL INFORMATION

As stated above, it comes in handy when you document what you read and note down your own key words. To extract vital information while/after reading a publication is called "**excerpting**" or "**extracting**": After you read it you try to summarize the most important information in order to document it for yourself or summarize it for somebody else. For this procedure there are some guidelines you could follow, which result in very targeted extraction of vital information for further use, storage, and retrieval. If you want to learn more about how to search for publications, read, interpret, excerpt, or present them, feel free to contact us and book one of our Academy's online courses on the topic: www.tanzpaedagogik.eu

One more important final comment: When you start to engage in the reading of scholarly publications, you might find it very difficult at first to understand the language or even the whole paper. This can be the case even when you read a paper in your mother tongue. **Do not throw in the towel**. Such difficulties are normal at the beginning and all they say is that you only have to get your head around academic writing and language, which you will, when you just keep on trying. Take small steps, but keep going. After you have read some papers you will soon be able to read them easily. – And find out again what you have learned just because you did not give up, and where you can be really proud of yourself!

You are welcome to join the Academy for Dance Pedagogy and Dance Medicine's round table discussions, presentations of excerpted literature (journal club) or Special Lecture Series open to the public. Don't hesitate to get in touch or contact the author of this series.

Enjoy & take care!

PART 5

BIBLIOGRAPHY
& RECOMMENDED READING

ON DANCE, DANCE MEDICINE, SCIENCE, HISTORY, PEDAGOGY…

The Inspiration Part II

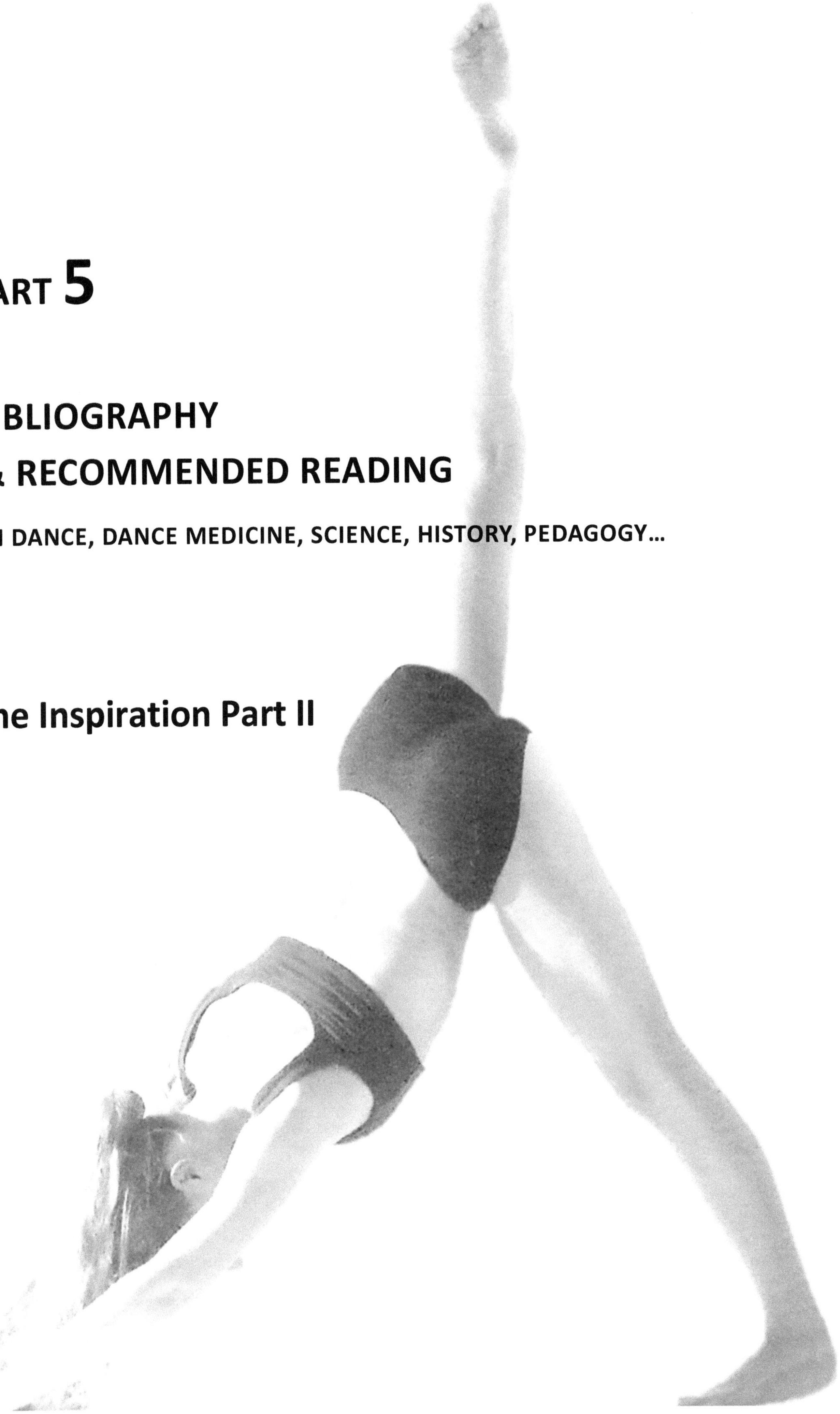

A

- Abernethy Bruce, Hanrahan, Stephanie J., Kippers, Vaughan, MacKinnon, Laurel T., Pandy, Marcus G., and McManus, Ali. Biophysical foundations of human movement (3rd edition.). Champaign, IL. Human Kinetics. 2013.
- Acosta, Carlos. No Way Home: A Dancer's Journey from the Streets of Havana to the Stages of the World. New York. Simon and Schuster. 2008.
- Adair Christy, and Burt, Ramsay. British Dance: Black Routes. Abington-on-Thames. Routledge. 2016.
- Adshead-Lansdale, Janet, and June Layson (eds.). Dance History – An Introduction (2nd edition). London. Abington-on-Thames. Routledge. 1994.
- Afifi, Adel K., and Ronald A. Bergman. Functional Neuroanatomy: Text and Atlas (2nd edition). New York. McGraw-Hill Education. 2005.
- Albers, S. Eating Mindfully (2nd edition). Oakland. New Harbinger Publications. 2012.
- Alexander, FM. The use of self: Its conscious direction in relation to diagnosis functioning and the control of reaction. London. Orion. 1985.
- Aloff, Mindy. Dance in America: A Reader's Anthology: A Library of America Special Publication. New York. Library of America. 2018.
- Alter, Michael J. The Science of Flexibility. Champain, IL. Human Kinetics Publishers, Inc. 2004.
- Anderson, Jack. Ballet and Modern Dance: A Concise History (2nd Ed). Princeton. Princeton Book Company. 1993.
- Andreu, Helene. Dance, Movement, and Nutrition: Fitness Minutes for a Healthier Life. London. Author House. 2006.
- Angyal, Chloe. Turning Pointe: How a New Generation of Dancers Is Saving Ballet from Itself. New York. PublicAffairs. 2021.
- Arnheim, Daniel D. Dance injuries: Their prevention and care. St.Louis. Mosby. 1991.
- Au, Susan. Ballet & Modern Dance. London. Thames and Hudson. 1988.

B

- Bailey, Diane. History of Dance. Minneapolis. ABDO. 2015.
- Bales, Melanie, and Karen Eliot. Dance on Its Own Terms: Histories and Methodologies. Oxford. OUP USA. 2013.
- Bales, Melanie, and Rebecca Nettl-Fiol. The Body Eclectic: Evolving Practices in Dance Training. Champaign. University of Illinois Press. 2008.
- Banes, Sally, Baryshnikov, Mikhail, and Andrea Harris. Reinventing Dance in the 1960s: Everything was Possible. Madison. Univ of Wisconsin Press. 2003.
- Banes, Sally. Dancing Women: Female Bodies On Stage. Abington-on-Thames. Routledge. 1998.
- Banes, Sally. Democracy's Body: Judson Dance Theater, 1962-1964. Durham. Duke University Press. 1993.
- Banes, Sally. Terpsichore in Sneakers: Post-Modern Dance. Middletown. Wesleyan University Press. 2011.
- Barringer Janice, and Sarah Schlesinger. The Pointe Book: Shoes, Training and Technique. Pennington. Princeton Books Co. 2012.
- Bartenieff, L, and D Lewis. Body movement: Coping with the environment. New York. Gordon and Breach Science. 1980.
- Bartlett, Roger. Introduction to sports biomechanics (1st edition). New York, NY. Routledge. 1997.
- Bean, A. Food for Fitness: How to Eat for Maximum Performance (4th edition). London. Bloomsbury Sport. 2014.
- Bean, A. The Complete Guide to Sports Nutrition (7th edition). London. Bloomsbury Sport. 2013.
- Beaumont, Cyril W., and Stanislas Idzikowski. The Cecchetti Method of Classical Ballet: Theory and Technique. North Chelmsford. Courier Corporation. 2003.

- Bell-Kanner, Karen. Frontiers: The Life and Times of Bonnie Bird: American Modern Dancer and Dance Educator. New York. Psychology Press. 1998.
- Benbow-Pfalzgraf, Taryn. International Dictionary of Modern Dance. Farmington Hills. St. James Press. 1998.
- Berardi, Gigi. Finding Balance: Fitness, Training, and Health for a Lifetime In Dance. Abington-on-Thames. Routledge. 2013.
- Bernard, Andre, Steinmuller, Wolfgang, and Stricker, Ursula. Ideokinesis: A Creative Approach to Human Movement and Body Alignment (*1st edition*). Berkeley. North Atlantic Books. 2006
- Bittar, Adriano, Wyon, Matthew, Figueiredo, Valéria, Brown, Derrick, and Aline Haas. Dance Medicine & Science Guide: From the Brazil-United Kingdom DMS Network. St Marechal Rondon. Editora Kelps. 2021.
- Blakey, Paul. The Muscle Book. Honesdale. Himalayan Institute Press. 1992.
- Bläsing, Bettina, Puttke, Martin, and Thomas Schack. The Neurocognition of Dance. Mind, Movement and Motor Skills. New York. Psychology Press. 2010.
- Blom, Lynne Anne, and L. Tarin Chaplin. The Intimate Act Of Choreography. Pittsburgh. University of Pittsburgh Press. 1982.
- Blom, Lynne Anne, and L. Tarin Chaplin. The Moment Of Movement: Dance Improvisation. Pittsburgh. University of Pittsburgh Press. 1988.
- Boulpaep, Emile L., and Walter F. Boron. Medical physiology: a cellular and molecular approach. St. Louis. Elsevier Saunders. 2005.
- Bracilovic, Ana. Essential Dance Medicine. New York. Humana Press – Springer. 2009.
- Bradley, Karen K. Rudolf Laban. Abington-on-Thames. Routledge. 2018.
- Brodie, Julie A., and Elin E. Lobel. Dance and Somatics: Mind-Body Principles of Teaching and Performance. Jefferson. McFarland. 2014.
- Brown, Carolyn. Chance and Circumstance: Twenty Years with Cage and Cunningham. Evanston. Northwestern University Press. 2009.
- Brown, Jean M. The Vision of Modern Dance: In the Words of Its Creators. Princeton. Princeton Book Company. 1998.
- Burke, L. The Complete Guide to Food for Sports Performance (3rd edition). Crows Nest. Allen & Unwin. 2010.
- Burke, L., and V. Deakin. Clinical Sports Nutrition (5th edition). Singapure. McGraw-Hill Education. 2015.
- Burt, Ramsay. Alien Bodies: Representations of Modernity, 'Race' and Nation in Early Modern Dance. Abington-on-Thames. Routledge. 1998.
- Burt, Ramsay. Judson Dance Theater: Performative Traces. Abington-on-Thames. Routledge. 2007.
- Burt, Ramsay. The Male Dancer: Bodies, Spectacle, Sexualities. Abington-on-Thames. Routledge. 2007.
- Burt, Ramsay. Ungoverning Dance: Contemporary European Theatre Dance and the Commons. Oxford. Oxford University Press. 2016.
- Bussell, Darcey. Pilates for Life: A Practical Introduction to the Core Programme. London. Penguin Michael Joseph. 2005.

C

- Calais-Germain, Blandine. Anatomy of Breathing. Seattle. Eastland Press. 2006.
- Calais-Germain, Blandine. Anatomy of Movement (2nd revised edition). Vista. Eastland Press. 2008.
- Camerino, Oleguer, Castaner, Marta, and Teresa M. Anguera. Mixed Methods Research in the Movement Sciences: Case Studies in Sport, Physical Education and Dance. London-New York. Routledge. 2014.
- Cardwell, G. Gold Medal Nutrition (5th edition). Champaign (IL). Human Kinetics. 2012.
- Carriere, Beate. Fitness for the Pelvic Floor. Stuttgart. Thieme Publishing Group. 2002.
- Carter, Alexandra, and Janet O'Shea. The Routledge Dance Studies Reader (2nd edition). Abington-on-Thames. Taylor & Francis. 2010.
- Carter, Alexandra, Morris, Geraldine, and Larraine Nicholas. Rethinking Dance History: A Reader. New York. Psychology Press. 2004.
- Carter, Alexandra. Dance and Dancers in the Victorian and Edwardian Music Hall Ballet. Farnham. Ashgate. 2005.

- Celichowska, Renata, and Erick Hawkins. The Erick Hawkins Modern Dance Technique. Princeton. Princeton Book Company. 2000.
- Chaiklin, Sharon, and Hilda Wengrower. The Art and Science of Dance/Movement Therapy: Life Is Dance. Abington-on-Thames. Taylor & Francis. 2009.
- Chandler-Vaccaro, Kimberley, and Lorraine Person-Kriegel. Jazz Dance Today Essentials: The $6 Dance Series. Scotts Valley. CreateSpace Independent Publishing Platform. 2014.
- Chasteen, John Charles. National Rhythms, African Roots: The Deep History of Latin American Popular Dance. Albuquerque. UNM Press. 2004.
- Chodorow, Joan. Dance Therapy and Depth Psychology: The Moving Imagination. London-New York. Routledge. 2013.
- Clark, N. Nancy Clark's Sports Nutrition Guidebook (5th edition). Champaign (IL). Human Kinetics. 2013.
- Clarkson, Pricilla M, and Margret Skrinar. The Science of Dance Training. Champaign. Human Kinetics. 1992.
- Clayton, Paula. Sacroiliac Joint Dysfunction and Piriformis Syndrome: The Complete Guide for Physical Therapists. Chichester. Lotus Publishing. 2016.
- Climenhaga, Royd. Pina Bausch (2nd edition). Abington-on-Thames. Routledge. 2018.
- Climenhaga, Royd. The Pina Bausch Sourcebook: The Making of Tanztheater. Abington-on-Thames. Routledge. 2012.
- Clippinger, Karen Sue. Dance Anatomy and Kinesiology. Champaign. Human Kinetics. 2007.
- Cohan, Robert. The Dance Workshop. London. Dance Books Ltd Cecil Court. 1986.
- Coker, Cheryl A. Motor Learning and Control for Practitioners. London-New York. Routledge. 2017.
- Cone Purcell, Theresa, and Stephen L. Cone. Teaching Children Dance. Champaign, IL. Human Kinetics. 2004.
- Cook, Rena, and Jane Boston. Breath in Action: The Art of Breath in Vocal and Holistic Practice. London. Jessica Kingsley Publishers. 2009.
- Cooper Albright, Ann. Choreographing Difference: The Body and Identity in Contemporary Dance. Middletown. Wesleyan. 1997.
- Copeland, Misty. Life in Motion: An Unlikely Ballerina. London. Sphere. 2017.
- Copeland, Roger. Merce Cunningham: The Modernizing of Modern Dance. Abington-on-Thames. Routledge. 2003.
- Costa, R. Cooking for Sport and Exercise. Coventry. Coventry University Enterprises. 2012.

D

- Daly, R.M. and M.A. Petit (Eds.). Optimizing bone mass and strength: The role of physical activity and nutrition during growth. Basel. Karger. 2007.
- Dance UK (ed.) Dance Teaching Essentials. London. ATP Europe Dance UK. 2002.
- Das, Joanna Dee. Katherine Dunham: Dance and the African Diaspora. Oxford. Oxford University Press. 2017.
- Davies, Eden. Beyond Dance: Laban's Legacy of Movement Analysis. London-New York. Routledge. 2007.
- DeFrantz, Thomas F. Dancing Revelations: Alvin Ailey's Embodiment of African American Culture. Oxford. Oxford University Press. 2004.
- Denniston, Christine.The Meaning Of Tango: The Story of the Argentinian Dance. London. Pavilion Books. 2007.
- Desmond, Jane C. Meaning in Motion: New Cultural Studies of Dance. Durham. Duke University Press Books. 1997.
- DeVito, Joseph A. Human Communication: The Basic Course, Global Edition. New York. Pearson Higher Education. 2015.
- Dickinson, Edward Ross. Dancing in the Blood: Modern Dance and European Culture on the Eve of the First World War. Cambridge. Cambridge University Press. 2017.
- Dils, Ann, and Cooper Albright, Ann. Moving History/Dancing Cultures: A Dance History Reader. Middletown. Wesleyan. 2001.
- DK. Dance: From Ballet to Breakin'—Step into the Dazzling World of Dance. London. DK Publishing. 2012.
- Dodds, Sherril. The Oxford Handbook of Dance and Competition. Oxford. Oxford University Press. 2018.
- Dolin, Anton. Pas de Deux: The Art of Partnering. New York. Dover Publications. 2005.
- Dow, Allen, and Mike Michaelson. The Official Guide to Jazz Dancing. Secaucus, NJ. Chartwell Books. 1980.
- Drake, Richard L., Vogel, A. Wayne, und Adam W.M. Mitchell. Gray's Atlas of Anatomy. Philadelphia. Elsevier/Churchill Livingstone. 2008.
- Driver, Ian. A Century of Dance. New York. Cooper Square Press. 2001.

- Dunbar, June. Jose Limon: An Artist Re-viewed. Abington-on-Thames. Routledge. 2013.
- Dunning, Jennifer. Alvin Ailey: A Life In Dance. New York. First Da Capo Press. 1998.

E

- Elswit, Kate. Theatre and Dance. London-New York. Macmillan International Higher Education. 2018.
- Elswit, Kate. Watching Weimar Dance. Oxford. Oxford University Press. 2014.
- Everett, William A., and Paul R. Laird. Historical Dictionary of the Broadway Musical. Lanham. Rowman & Littlefield. 2015.
- Exner-Grave, Elisabeth (Hrsg). TanzMedizin. Die medizinische Versorgung professioneller Tänzer. Stuttgart-New York. Schattauer Verlag. 2008.

F

- Farhi, Donna. The Breathing Book: Good Health and Vitality Through Essential Breath Work. New York. Owl Books/Henry Holt and Company. 1996.
- Fay, Maya. Maria Fay's Floor Barre. London. Dance Books UK. 2000.
- Feldenkrais, Moshe, and Yochanan Rywerant. The Feldenkrais Method. Richmond. Readhowyouwant. 2011.
- Feldenkrais, Moshe. Awareness Through Movement. London. Thorsons. 2011.
- Feldenkrais, Moshe. Body And Mature Behavior: A Study of Anxiety, Sex, Gravitation, and Learning. Berkeley. North Atlantic Books. 2011.
- Fernandes, Ciane. Pina Bausch and the Wuppertal Dance Theater: The Aesthetics of Repetition and Transformation. Wien. Peter Lang International Academic Publishers. 2001.
- Fernandes, Ciane. The Moving Researcher: Laban/Bartenieff Movement Analysis in Performing Arts Education and Creative Arts Therapies. London. Jessica Kingsley Publishers. 2014.
- Fitt Sally S. Dance kinesiology. New York. Schirmer Books. 1996.
- Fitt, Sally Severy, and Robin D. Chmelar. Diet For Dancers. A Complete Guide to Nutrition and Weight Control. Princeton. Dance Horizons Books, Princton Books Co. 1990.
- Fitt, Sally Severy. Dance Kinesiology. New York. MacMillan Books. 1988.
- Flatt, Kate. Choreography: Creating and Developing Dance for Performance. Ramsbury. Crowood Press. 2020.
- Flynn, Arthur. Irish Dance. Gretna. Pelican Publishing Company. 1998.
- Foley, Cathrine E. Step Dancing in Ireland: Culture and History. Abington-on-Thames. Routledge. 2016.
- Forti, Simone. Handbook in Motion. New York. New York University Press. 1974.
- Foster, Rory. Ballet Pedagogy: The Art of Teaching. Tampa, Gainsville. University Press of South Florida. 2010.
- Foulkes, Julia L. Modern Bodies: Dance and American Modernism from Martha Graham to Alvin Ailey. Chapel Hill. Univ of North Carolina Press. 2003.
- Fox, K. (ed.) Physical activity and psychological well-being, London: Routledge. 2000.
- Franklin, Eric. Conditioning for Dance. Training for peak performance in all dance forms. United Kingdom. Human Kinetics. 2004.
- Franklin, Eric. Dance Imagery for Technique and Performance (2nd edition). Champaign, IL. Human Kinetics. 2013.
- Franklin, Eric. Dynamic Alignment through Imagery. Champaign, IL. Human Kinetics. 2012.
- Friedler, Sharon E., and Susan Glazer. Dancing Female: Lives and Issues of Women in Contemporary Dance. Abington-on-Thames. Taylor & Francis. 1997.
- Friedman, Sharon. Post-Apartheid Dance: Many Bodies Many Voices Many Stories. Newcastle upon Tyne. Cambridge Scholars. 2014.
- Fuhrer, Margaret. American Dance: The Complete Illustrated History. Minneapolis. Quarto Publishing Group USA. 2014.

G

- Gamble, Nikki. Tap and Jazz. Portsmouth. Heinemann Library. 2008.
- Gibbons, John. Functional Anatomy Of The Pelvis And The Sacroiliac Joint: A Practical Guide. Berkeley. North Atlantic Books. 2017.
- Gibbons, John. Muscle Energy Techniques: A Practical Guide for Physical Therapists. Berkeley. North Atlantic Books. 2013.
- Gibney, MJ., Lanham-New, SA., Cassidy, A., and HH. Vorster (eds.). Introduction to human nutrition. Oxford. John Wiley & Sons. 2013.
- Gibson, Laurieann. Dance Your Dance: 8 Steps to Unleash Your Passion and Live Your Dream. Nashville. W Publishing. 2021.
- Gift, Virginia. Tango: A History of an Obsession. Charleston. BookSurge. 2008.
- Gilroy, Anne M. Anatomy An essential textbook. Stuttgart, New York. Thieme Medical Publishers. 2017.
- Gilroy, Anne M., MacPherson, Brian R, and Ross, Lawrence M. Thieme Atlas of Anatomy. Stuttgart, New York. Thieme Medical Publishers. 2017.
- Glass, Barbara S. African American Dance: An Illustrated History. Jefferson. McFarland, Incorporated, Publishers. 2012.
- Goldberg, K. Meira, Bennahum, Ninotchka Devorah, and Michelle Heffner Hayes. Flamenco on the Global Stage: Historical, Critical and Theoretical Perspectives. Jefferson. McFarland. 2015.
- Goodill, Sharon W. An Introduction to Medical Dance/Movement Therapy: Health Care in Motion. London. Jessica Kingsley Publishers. 2005.
- Gordon, Catherine M. The Female Athletic Triad: A Clinical Guide. New York. Springer. 2014.
- Gordon, Cathrine M, and Merryl M. LeBoff. The Female Athletic Triad A Clinical Guide. Wien-New York. Springer Verlag. 2015.
- Gordon, Susanne. Off Balance. The real world of ballet. New York. McGnaw-Hill. 1984.
- Graham, Martha. Blood Memory: An Autobiography. London. Sceptre. 1993.
- Grant, Gail. Technical Manual and Dictionary of Classical Ballet (3rd edition). North Chelmsford. Courier Corporation. 1982.
- Grant, Mark. The Rise and Fall of the Broadway Musical. Lebanon. Northeastern University Press. 2005.
- Grau, Andrée, and Stephanie Jordan. Europe Dancing: Perspectives on Theatre Dance and Cultural Identity. Abington-on-Thames. Routledge. 2000.
- Grau, Andrée. Dance. London. Dorling Kindersley Limited. 2003.
- Gray, Judith A. Dance Instruction: Science Applied to the Arts of Movement. Champaign. Human Kinetics. 1989.
- Green, Diana F. Choreographing From Within: Developing the Habit of Inquiry as an Artist. Champaign. Human Kinetics. 2010.
- Greig, Valerie. Inside Ballet Technique. London. Dance Books. 1994.
- Guarino, Lindsey, and Wendy Oliver. Jazz Dance: A History of the Roots and Branches. Gainsville. University Press of Florida. 2015.

H

- Haas, Jacqui Greene. Dance Anatomy (2nd edition). Champaign, IL. Human Kinetics. 2017.
- Hackney, Peggy. Making Connections: Total Body Integration Through Bartenieff Fundamentals. Abington-on-Thames. Taylor & Francis. 2004.

- Hahn, Tomie. Sensational Knowledge: Embodying Culture through Japanese Dance. Middletown, CT. Wesleyan University Press. 2007.
- Haibach, Pamela, Reid, Greg, and Douglas Collier. Motor Learning and Development (2nd edition). Champaign, IL. Human Kinetics. 2017.
- Hall, Karen. So You Want to Sing Music Theater: A Guide for Professionals. Lanham. Rowmann & Littlefield. 2014.
- Halprin, Daria. The Expressive Body in Life, Art, and Therapy: Working with Movement, Metaphor and Meaning. London. Jessica Kingsley Publishers. 2003.
- Hamil, Joseph, and Kathleen M. Knutzen. Biomechanical Basis of Human Movement. Philadelphia. Lippincott Williams & Wilkins. 2014.
- Hamilton, Linda H. The Person Behind the Mask: A Guide to Performing Arts Psychology. New York. Ablex Publishing Corporation. 1997.
- Hamilton, Linda H., and New York City Ballet. The Dancer's Way: The New York City Ballet Guide to Mind, Body, and Nutrition. St. Martin's Publishing Group. 2015.
- Hamilton, Linda. Advice for Dancers. Emotional Counsel and Practical Strategies. Sussex-New York. Jossey-Bass. 2002.
- Hamilton, Trenton. The History of Western Dance. Chicago. Encyclopaedia Britannica. 2015.
- Hatchett, Frank, and Nancy Myers Gitlin. Frank Hatchett's Jazz Dance. Champaign, IL. Human Kinetics. 2000.
- Hays, Joan F. Modern Dance: A Biomechanical Approach to Teaching. Maryland Heights. C.V. Mosby Company. 1981.
- Haywood, Kathleen M, and Nancy Getchell. Life span motor development (6th edition). Champaign. Human Kinetics. 2014.
- Haywood, Kathleen M., and Mary A. Robertson. Advanced analysis of motor development. Champaign, IL. Himan Kinetics. 2012.
- H'Doubler, Margaret N. Dance: A Creative Art Experience. Madison. University of Wisconsin Press. 1959.
- Hecht, Thom. Emotionally Intelligent Ballet Training. Facilitating Emotional Intelligence in Vocational Dance Training. Saarbrücken. VDM Verlag Dr Müller. 2007.
- Heffner Hayes, Michelle. Flamenco: Conflicting Histories of the Dance. Jefferson. McFarland. 2014.
- Heyward V. Advanced Fitness Assessment and Exercise Prescription. Champaign. Human Kinetics. 2010.
- Hodge, Susie. Latin and Ballroom. Portsmouth. Heinemann Library. 2009.
- Hodgson, John. Mastering Movement: The Life and Work of Rudolf Laban. New York. Psychology Press. 2001.
- Homans, Jennifer. Apollo's Angels: A History of Ballet. Random House Publishing Group. 2010.
- Hooch, DJ. Street Dance: The Best Moves. London. Hachette UK. 2015.
- Hopgood, Jeromy. Dance Production: Design and Technology. New York-Abington. Focal Press. 2016.
- Horosko, Marian, and Nikolai Serebriakov. Pas de Deux: A Textbook on Partnering. Tampa. University Press of Florida. 2000.
- Horosko, Marian. Martha Graham. The Evolution of her Dance Theory and Training. Gainsville. University Press of South Florida. 2002.
- Horosko, Marian. May O'Donnell: Modern Dance Pioneer. Gainsville. University of Florida. 2005.
- Howse, Justin, and Moira McCormack. Anatomy, Dance Technique and Injury Prevention. New York-London. Methuen Drama. 2009.
- Howse, Justin, and Shirley Hancock. Dance Technique and Injury Prevention. Abington-on-Thames. Routledge. 2014.
- Humphrey, Doris. The Art of Making Dances. Princeton. Princeton Book Company (1991). 1958.
- Hutchinson Guest, Ann. Labanotation: The System of Analyzing and Recording Movement. Abington-on-Thames. Routledge. 2005.
- Hutchinson Guest, Ann. Your Move: A New Approach to the Study of Movement and Dance, Volume 1. New York. Psychology Press. 1983.
- Hutchinson Guest, Ann. Your Move: A New Approach to the Study of Movement and Dance, Volume 2. New York. Gordon and Breach. 1983.
- Huxley, M. The Dancer's World, 1920 - 1945: Modern Dancers and their Practices Reconsidered. New York. Springer. 2015.

I

- Janesick, Valerie J. "Stretching" Exercises for Qualitative Researchers (4th edition). Thousand Oaks. SAGE Publications. 2015.
- Janevski, Ana, and Thomas J. Lax. Judson Dance Theater: The Work is Never Done. New York. Museum of Modern Art. 2018.
- Johnson, Anne E. Jazz Tap: From African Drums to American Feet. New York City. The Rosen Publishing Group. 1999.
- Jowitt, Deborah. Time and the Dancing Image. Berkeley. University of California Press. 1989.
- Joyce, Mary. Dance Technique for Children. California City. Mayfield Publishing Company. 1984.
- Jukendrop, A., and M. Gleesen. Sports Nutrition (2nd edition). Champaign (IL). Human Kinetics. 2010.

K

- Kaltenbrunner, Thomas. Contact Improvisation: Moving, Dancing, Interaction. Aachen. Meyer & Meyer Verlag. 2003.
- Karina, Lilian, and Marion Kant. Hitler's Dancers: German Modern Dance and the Third Reich. Oxford-New York. Berghahn Books. 2004.
- Kassing, Gayle. History of Dance (2nd edition). Champaign. Human Kinetics, Inc. 2017.
- Katch FI, Katch VL, and WD McArdle. Exercise physiology: energy, nutrition, and human performance. Philadelphia. Lippincott Williams & Wilkins. 2010.
- Kavanagh, Julie. Nureyev: The Life. New York. Knopf Doubleday Publishing Group. 2011.
- Kellmann, Michael. Enhancing Recovery. Under-recovery and overtraining: Different concepts - similar impact? Champaign. Human Kinetics. 2002.
- Kelly, Deirdre. Ballerina: Sex, Scandal, and Suffering Behind the Symbol of Perfection. Vancouver. Greystone Books. 2012.
- Kendall F, McCreary E, Provance P. Muscles: Testing and function. Philadelphia-Lippincott. Williams & Wilkins. 1993.
- Kimmerle, Marliese and Paulette Cote-Laurence. Teaching dance skills: A motor learning and development approach. Andover (New Jersey). J. Michael Ryan Publishing, Inc. 2003.
- Kimmerle, Marliese and Paulette Côté-Laurence. Teaching Dance Skills. A Motor Learning and Development Approach. Andover (NJ). J. Michael Ryan Publishing Inc. 2003.
- Kirkland Gelsey, and Lawrence, Greg. Dancing On My Grave. South Yarmouth. J. Curley. 1986.
- Kislan, Richard. Hoofing on Broadway: A History of Show Dancing. Upper Saddle River. Prentice Hall Press. 1987.
- Kislan, Richard. The Musical: A Look at the American Musical Theater. Montclair. Applause Books. 1995.
- Knapp, Mark L., Hall, Judith A., and Horgan, Terrence G. Nonverbal Communication in Human Interaction (8th edition). Boston. Wadsworth Publishing. 2013.
- Knowles, Mark. Tap Roots: The Early History of Tap Dancing. Jefferson. McFarland. 2002.
- Knudson, Duane. Fundamentals of Biomechanics. Wien-New York-Heidelberg-Berlin. Springer Science & Business Media. 2007.
- Koch, Liz. Core Awareness, Revised Edition: Enhancing Yoga, Pilates, Exercise, and Dance. Berkeley. North Atlantic Books. 2012.
- Koegler, Horst. The Concise Dictionary of Ballet. Oxford-New York. Oxford University Press. 1987.
- Kolb, Brian and Ian Q. Whinshaw. Fundamentals of Human Neuropsychology (7th edition). New York. Worth Publishers. 2015.
- Kosstren, Hannah. Honest Bodies: Revolutionary Modernism in the Dances of Anna Sokolow. Oxford. Oxford University Press. 2017.
- Kostelanetz, Richard. Merce Cunningham: Dancing in Space and Time. Boston. Da Capo Press. 1998.
- Kostrovitskaya, Vera S. 100 Lessons in Classical Ballet the Eight-Year Program of Leningrad's Vaganova Choreographic School: Eight-year Programme of Leningrad's Vaganova Choreographic School. New York. Proscenium Publ/Limelight. 1987.

- Koutedakis, Yannis, and N.C. Craig Sharp. The Fit and Healthy Dancer. Chichester. John Wiley & Sons Ltd. 1999.
- Kraft, Eva Maria, and Liane Simmel. Nutrition for Dancers. Basics. Performance Enhancement. Practical Tips. Milton Park, Oxfordshire. Taylor and Francis. 2017.
- Krasnow, Donna H., and Mary Virginia Wilmerding. Motor Learning and Control for Dance: Principles and Practices for Performers and Teachers. Champaign, IL. Human Kinetics. 2015.
- Kraus, Richard G., Chapman Hilsendager, Sarah, and Brenda Dixon. History of the Dance in Art and Education. Upper Saddle River. Prentice Hall. 1991.
- Kuhlke, Olaf, and Adam M. Pine. Global Movements: Dance, Place, and Hybridity. Minneapolis. Lexington Books. 2014.
- Kwan, SanSan. Kinesthetic City: Dance and Movement in Chinese Urban Spaces. Oxford. OUP USA. 2013.

L

- Laane, Rose-Marie. Danse Classique et Mechanismes Corporels. Paris. Editions Amphora. 1991.
- Lalagia. Spanish Dancing A Practical Handbook. London. Dance Books Cecil Court. 1985.
- Lambert-Beatty, Carrie. Being Watched: Yvonne Rainer and the 1960s. Cambridge. The MIT Press. 2011.
- Lanham-New, S., Stear, S., Shirreffs, S., and A. Collins. Sport and Exercise Nutrition. Oxford. Wiley-Blackwell. 2011.
- Laws Helen, Apps Joanna, Bramley Ian, and Diane Parker (Eds). Fit to Dance 2: Report of the Second National Inquiry Into Dancers' Health and Injury in the UK. London. Dance UK Books. 2005.
- Laws, Kenneth, and Cynthia Harvey. Physics, Dance, and the Pas de Deux. New York. Schirmer Books. 1994.
- Laws, Kenneth. Physics and the Art of Dance: Understanding Movement. Oxford. Oxford University Press. 2008.
- Lax, Thomas J., and David Velasco. Ralph Lemon. New York. Museum of Modern Art. 2016.
- Leblon, Bernard. Flamenco. Heidelberg. Palmyra Verlag. 2001.
- Lee, Carol. Ballet in Western Culture: A History of Its Origins and Evolution. New York. Psychology Press. 2002.
- Leger, Dawn L. Fundamentals of Biomechanics: Equilibrium, Motion, and Deformation. Wien-New York-Heidelberg-Berlin. Springer Science & Business Media. 2013.
- Legg, Joshua. Introduction to Modern Dance Techniques. Princeton. Princeton Book Company. 2011.
- Leigh Foster, Susan. Choreographing Empathy: Kinesthesia in Performance. Abington-on-Thames. Routledge. 2010.
- Lepecky, Andre. Exhausting Dance: Performance and the Politics of Movement. Abington-on-Thames. Routledge. 2006.
- Lepecky, Andre. Planes of Composition: Dance, Theory and The Global. Kolkata. Seagull Books. 2010.
- Lesondak, David. Fascia : What it is and Why it Matters. Pencaitland. Handspring Publishing Limited. 2017.
- Levy, Fran J. Dance/Movement Therapy. A Healing Art. Waldorf. AAHPERD Publications. 1988.
- Lexová, Irena. Ancient Egyptian Dances. North Chelmsford. Courier Corporation. 2000.
- Limón, José. José Limón: An Unfinished Memoir. Middletown. Wesleyan University Press. 2001.
- Louis, Murray, and Alwin Nikolais. The Nikolais/Louis Dance Technique: A Philosophy and Method of Modern Dance. Abington-on-Thames. Routledge. 2016.
- Love, Paul. Modern Dance Terminology. Princeton. Dance Horizons Books, Princeton Books Co. 1997.
- Luigi, Kriegel, Luigi, Person Kriegel, Lorraine, and Francis Roach. Luigi's Jazz Warm Up: And Introduction to Jazz Style & Technique. Princeton. Princeton Book Company. 1997.
- Lynn, Graeme. Awakening Somatic Intelligence: Understanding, Learning & Practicing the Alexander Technique, Feldenkrais Method & Hatha Yoga. London. Singing Dragon. 2016.

M

- Magee David J. Orthopedic Physical Assessment. Philadelphia. Saunders. 2008.
- Magill, Richard A. Motor Learning. Concepts and Applications (5th edition). Boston. McGraw-Hill. 1996.
- Magill, Richard, and David Anderson. Motor Learning and Control. Concepts and Applications (10th edition). Singapore. McGraw-Hill Education. 2014.

- Malone, Jacqui. Steppin' on the Blues: The Visible Rhythms of African American Dance. Champaign. University of Illinois Press. 1996.
- Manning, Susan, and Lucia Ruprecht. New German Dance Studies. Champaign. University of Illinois Press. 2012.
- Manning, Susan, Ross, Janice, and Rebecca Schneider. Futures of Dance Studies. Madison. University of Wisconsin Press. 2020.
- Manning, Susan. Ecstasy and the Demon: Feminism and Nationalism in the Dances of Mary Wigman. Berkeley. University of California Press. 1993.
- Manning, Susan. Ecstasy and the Demon: The Dances of Mary Wigman. Minneapolis. University of Minnesota Press. 2006.
- Manning, Susan. Modern Dance, Negro Dance: Race in Motion. Minneapolis. University of Minnesota Press. 2004.
- Marieb, Elaine, and Suzanne Keller. Essentials of Human Anatomy & Physiology, Global Edition (12th edition). Harlow. Pearson Education Limited. 2017.
- Martins, Peter. New York City Ballet Workout. New York. Harper Collins Publishers. 1997.
- Mastin, Zerlina. Nutrition for the Dancer. Hampshire. Dance Books Ltd. 2009.
- Matlin, MW. Cognition (Textbook). (8 ed.). Hoboken. Wiley. 2013.
- Mazo, Joseph H. Prime Movers, The Makers of Modern Dance in America. New York City. William Morrow and Company. 1977.
- McCarthy-Brown, Nyama. Dance Pedagogy for a Diverse World: Culturally Relevant Teaching in Theory, Research and Practice. Jefferson. McFarland. 2017.
- McDonagh, Don. Complete Guide to Modern Dance. New Yorkk. Popular Library.1976.
- McDonagh, Don. Martha Graham. New York. Praeger. 1973.
- McDonagh, Don. The Rise and Fall and Rise of Modern Dance (Rev edition). Atlanta. A Cappella Books. 1970.
- McGinnis, Peter M. Biomechanics of Sport and Exercise. Champaign, IL. Human Kinetics. 2013.
- McGrath, Aoife. Dance Theatre in Ireland: Revolutionary Moves. London. Palgrave Macmillan. 2012.
- Mears, Patricia. Ballerina: Fashion's Modern Muse. New York City. Vendome Press. 2019.
- Meyer, Marion. Pina Bausch - The Biography: The Biography. London. Oberon Books. 2017.
- Midgelow, Vida. Reworking the Ballet: Counter-narratives and Alternative Bodies. Abington-on-Thames. Routledge. 2007.
- Mille, Agnes de. Dance to the Piper. Boston. An Atlantic Monthly Press Book. 1953.
- Mille, Agnes de. Martha: The Life and Work of Martha Graham. New York. Vintage Books. 1992.
- Miller, Abby Lee. Everything I learned about Life, I learned in Dance Class. New York. Harper Collins. 2014.
- Mindlin, Naomi. Doris Humphrey: A Centennial Issue. New York. Psychology Press. 1998.
- Moore, Carol-Lynne, and Kaoru Yamamoto. Beyond Words: Movement Observation and Analysis. Abington-on-Thames. Routledge. 2012.
- Morgenroth, Joyce. Dance Improvisations. Pittsburgh. University of Pittsburgh Press. 1987.
- Morgenroth, Joyce. Speaking of Dance: Twelve Contemporary Choreographers on Their Craft. Abington-on-Thames. Routledge. 2004.
- Morris, Gay. A Game for Dancers: Performing Modernism in the Postwar Years, 1945-1960. Middletown. Wesleyan. 2006.
- Morris, Mark, and Stace, Wesley. Out Loud: A Memoir. London. Penguin Press. 2019.
- Murphy, Jacqueline Shea. The People Have Never Stopped Dancing: Native American Modern Dance Histories. Minneapolis. University of Minnesota Press. 2007.
- Musmon, Margaret. Latin and Caribbean Dance. New York. Infobase Publishing. 2010.
- Myers, Thomas, and James Earls. Fascial Release For Structural Balance (Revised Edition). Berkeley. North Atlantic Books. 2017.
- Myers, Tom W. Anatomy Trains. Edinburgh-London. Elsevier. 2009.

N

- Nagrin, Daniel. Dance and the specific image: improvisation. Pittsburgh. University of Pittsburgh Press. 1994.

- Nagrin, Daniel. How to Dance Forever. Surviving against the Odds. New York. William Morrow. 1988.
- Neal, Nelson D. Hemsley Winfield: Pioneer of Modern Dance: A Biography. San Diego. Nelson D. Neal. 2020.
- Nelson, Arnold G. Stretching Anatomie. München. Human Kinetics. 2007.
- Nelson, Tom. Tango and Related Dances. London-Bloomington. AuthorHouse. 2009.
- Nettl-Fiol, Rebecca, and Luc Vanier. Dance and the Alexander Technique: Exploring the Missing Link. Champaign. University of Illinois Press. 2011.
- Newlove, Jean, and John Dalby. Laban for All. London. Nick Hern Books. 2004.
- Newman, Barbara. Never Far from Dancing: Ballet artists in new roles. Abington-on-Thames. Routledge. 2016.
- Noisette, Phillipe. Talk About Contemporary Dance. Paris. Flammarion. 2011.
- Noland, Carrie. Merce Cunningham: After the Arbitrary. Chicago. University of Chicago Press. 2019.
- Northouse, Peter G. Leadership: Theory and practice. (7th edition). Thousand Oaks, CA. Sage. 2015.
- Novack, Cynthia J. Sharing the Dance: Contact Improvisation and American Culture. Madison. University of Wisconsin Press. 1990.
- Noverre, Jean-Georges. Lettres sur la danse, et sur les ballets. Lyon. Aimé Delaroche. 1760.

O

- Ohno, Kazuo, and Yoshito Ohno. Kazuo Ohno's World: From Without & Within. Middletown. Wesleyan University Press. 2004.

P

- Pagett, Matt. The best dance moves in the world ever!. London-NY-Toronto. Simon & Schuster. 2007.
- Pallant, Cheryl. Contact Improvisation: An Introduction to a Vitalizing Dance Form. Jefferson. McFarland & Company. 1996.
- Partsch-Bergsohn, Isa, and Harold Bergsohn. The Makers of Modern Dance in Germany: Rudolph Laban, Mary Wigman, Kurt Jooss. Princeton. Princeton Book Company. 2003.
- Paskevska, Anna. Ballet Beyond Tradition. New York. Psychology Press. 2005.
- Paskevska, Anna. Both Sides of the Mirror. The Science and Art of Ballet. Pennington. Princeton Books Co. 1992.
- Payne, Helen. Essentials of Dance Movement Psychotherapy: International Perspectives on Theory, Research, and Practice. London-New York. Routledge. 2017.
- Payne, Helen. Supervision of Dance Movement Psychotherapy: A Practitioner's Guide. London-New York. Routledge. 2008.
- Pearson, Judy. Human Communication (2nd edition). New York. McGraw-Hill Education. 2005.
- Perces, Majorie B., Forsythe, Ana-Marie, and Cheryl Bell. The Dance Technique of Lester Horton. Princeton. Dance Horizons Books, Princeton Books Co. 1992.
- Person-Kriegel, Lorraine, and Kimberly Chandler-Vaccaro. Jazz Dance Today Essentials: The $6 Dance. Series. North Charleston. CreateSpace Independent Publishing Platform. 2014.
- Petterson Royce, Anya. The Anthropology of Dance. Hampshire. Dance Books Ltd. 2002.
- Phelan, Sharon A. Dance in Ireland: Steps, Stages and Stories. Newcastle upon Tyne. Cambridge Scholars Publishing. 2014.
- Pine, Adam M., and Olaf Kuhlke. Geographies of Dance: Body, Movement, and Corporeal Negotiations. Minneapolis. Lexington Books. 2013.
- Piper, Heather (ed). Touch in Sports Coaching and Physical Education. Fear, Risk and Moral Panic. London. Abington-on-Thames. Routledge. 2014.
- Piran, Niva, Levine Michael P, and Catherine Steiner-Adair. Preventing Eating Disorders – A Handbook of Interventions and Special Challenges. Philadelphia-London. Brunner/Mazel A Member of the Taylor & Francis Group. 1999.

- Price Boday, Mary. A Dancer's Journey: It All Began with a Lie the Biography of Mary Anthony. Indianapolis. Dog Ear Publishing. 2013.
- Puh, Megan. America Dancing: From the Cakewalk to the Moonwalk. London. Yale University Press. 2015.
- Purves, Dale, Augustine, George J. Fitzpatrick, David, Hall, William C., and LaMantia, Anthony-Samuel (eds.). Neuroscience (6th edition). Oxford. Oxford University Press. 2018.

Q

- Quin, Edel, Rafferty, Sonia, and Charlotte Tomlinson. Safe Dance Practice. Champaign, IL. Human Kinetics. 2015.

R

- Rees, Heather. Tap Dancing Rhythm in their feet. Wiltshire. The Corowood Press Ltd. 2003.
- Reynolds, Nancy, and Malcolm McCormick. No Fixed Points: Dance in the Twentieth Century. London. Yale University Press. 2003.
- Rinkel, Lindsay A. Lack of Nutritional Knowledge Puts Female College Athletes at Nutritional Risk for the Female Athlete Triad. Ann Arbor. Proquest Uni Dissertation Publishing. 2011.
- Rogers, Carl, and Richard A. Farson. Active Listening. Mansfield Centre. Martino Publishing. 2015.
- Rolf, Ida P. Rolfing : Reestablishing the Natural Alignment and Structural Integration of the Human Body for Vitality and Well-Being. Rochester. Inner Traditions Bear and Company. 1999.
- Rolland, John. Inside Motion. Toronto. Contact Editions. 1984.
- Romita, Nancy, and Allegra Romita. Functional Awareness: Anatomy in Action for Dancers. Oxford. Oxford University Press. 2016.
- Rosenbaum, David A. Human motor control. San Diego, CA. Academic Press. 1991.
- Rosenberg, Susan. Trisha Brown: Choreography as Visual Art. Middletown. Wesleyan University Press. 2016.
- Ross, Janice. Moving Lessons: Margaret H'Doubler and the Beginning of Dance in American Education. Madison. University of Wisconsin Press. 2000.
- Rossen, Rebecca. Dancing Jewish: Jewish Identity in American Modern and Postmodern Dance. Oxford. Oxford University Press. 2014.
- Royal Academy of Ballet. Step by Step Ballet Class. London. Ebury Press. 1993.
- Ruben, Brent D., & Stewart Lea P. Communication and human behavior (6th edition). Dubuque. Kendall Hunt. 2016.
- Ruyter, Nancy Lee Chalfa. Reformers and Visionaries: The Americanization of the Art of Dance. Princeton. Dance Horizons. 1979.
- Ruyter, Nancy Lee Chalfa. The Cultivation of Body and Mind in Nineteenth-century American Delsartism. Santa Barbara. Greenwood Press. 1999.
- Ryan, Allen J, and Robert L. Stephens. The Dancer's Complete Guide to Healthcare and a Long Career. Chicago. Bonus Books. 1998.
- Ryan, Allen J, and Robert L. Stephens. The Healthy Dancer. London. Dance Books. 1987.

S

- Saladin, Kenneth S. Anatomy & Physiology: The Unity of Form and Function. New York. McGraw-Hill. 2011.
- Santos Newhall, Mary Anne. Mary Wigman. Abington-on-Thames. Routledge. 2017.
- Schleip, Robert. Fascia Research. München. Elsevier Urban Fischer. 2007.
- Schmidt, Richard A., and Timothy D. Lee. Motor control and learning: a behavioral emphasis. Champaign, IL. Human Kinetics. 2011.

- Schmidt, Richard A., and Timothy D. Lee. Motor Learning and Performance – From Principle to Application (5th edition). Champaign, IL. Human Kinetics. 2013.
- Schrader, Constance A. A Sense of Dance: Exploring Your Movement Potential. Champaign, IL. Human Kinetics. 2005.
- Schreiner, Claus. Flamenco. Cleckheaton. Amadeus Press. 1996.
- Schuenke, Michael, Schulte, Erik, Schumacher, Udo, MacPherson, Brian R., Stefan, Cristian, and Hugo Zeberg. Head, Neck, and Neuroanatomy (THIEME Atlas of Anatomy), Latin nomenclature (English). New York. Thieme. 2016
- Schulze, Janine und Susanne Traub. Moving Thoughts. Tanzen ist Denken. Berlin. Verlag Vorwerk 8. 2004.
- Schurman, Nona. Modern Dance Fundamentals (2nd edition). Morrisville. Lulu Press. 2011.
- Scolieri, Paul A. Ted Shawn: His Life, Writings, and Dances. Oxford. Oxford University Press. 2019.
- Seed, Patricia. José Limón and La Malinche: The Dancer and the Dance. Austin. University of Texas Press. 2008.
- Seibert, Brian. What the Eye Hears: A History of Tap Dancing. New York. Farrar, Straus and Giroux. 2016.
- Sellers-Young, Barbara. Belly Dance, Pilgrimage and Identity. New York. Springer. 2016.
- Sellers-Young, Barbara. Breathing, Movement, Exploration. Montclair. Applause Theatre & Cinema Books. 2001.
- Serebrennikov, Nikolai Nikolaevich. Pas de Deux: A Textbook on Partnering. Gainsville. University of Florida. 2000.
- Sharif, Keti. Bellydance: A Guide to Middle Eastern Dance, Its Music, Its Culture and Costume. Crows Nest. Allen & Unwin. 2004.
- Shawn, Ted, and H. R. Haweis. Ruth St. Denis - Pioneer & Prophet, Being a History of Her Cycle of Oriental Dances. Volume I - The Text. Shbeen-Menoufia. Read Books. 2009.
- Shawn, Ted. Every Little Movement: A Book about François Delsarte, the Man and His Philosophy, His Science and Applied Aesthetics, the Application of this Science to the Art of the Dance, the Influence of Delsarte on American Dance. Princeton. Dance Horizons. 1968.
- Shawn, Ted. Shawn's Fundamentals of Dance, Volume 1. Abington-on-Thames. Taylor & Francis. 1988.
- Shell CG. The dancer as athlete: 1984 Olympic Scientific Congress Proceedings. Champaign, IL. Human Kinetics. 1986.
- Shelton, Suzanne. Ruth St. Denis: A Biography of the Divine Dancer. Austin. University of Texas Press. 1990.
- Shelver, Bradley. Performance Through The Dance Technique Of Lester Horton (2nd edition). Bradley Shelver. 2020.
- Sherrill, Claudine. Adapted Physical Activity, Recreation and Sport: Crossdisciplinary and Lifespan (5th edition). Dubuque. WCB/McGraw-Hill. 1998.
- Shook, Karen. Elements of Classical Ballet Technique. New York. Dance Horizons. 1977.
- Shumway-Cook Anne (ed.), and Marjorie H. Woollacott. Development of posture and gait: Across the life span. Columbia. University of South Carolina Press. 1989.
- Shumway-Cook Anne, and Marjorie H. Woollacott. Motor control: Theory and practical applications. Baltimore. Williams & Wilkins. 2001.
- Siegel, Marcia B. Howling Near Heaven: Twyla Tharp and the Reinvention of Modern Dance. New York. Macmillan. 2007.
- Siegel, Marcia B. Mirrors and Scrims: The Life and Afterlife of Ballet. Middletown. Wesleyan University Press. 2011.
- Siegel, Marcia B. The Tail of the Dragon: New Dance, 1976-1982. Durham. Duke University Press. 1991.
- Simmel, Liane, and Eva-Maria Kraft. Nutrition for Dancers: Basics, Performance Enhancement, Practical Tips. Abington-on-Thames. Taylor & Francis. 2017.
- Simmel, Liane. Dance Medicine in Practice: Anatomy, Injury Prevention, Training. Abington-on-Thames. Routledge. 2013.
- Smith, Karen Lynn. Popular Dance: From Ballroom to Hip-hop. New York. Infobase Publishing. 2010.
- Smith, Laura K, Weiss Elisabeth, and Don Lehmkuhl. Brunnstrom's Clinical Kinesiology. Philadelphia. F.A.Davis Company. 1996.
- Smith-Autard. Jacqueline M. Dance Composition: A Practical Guide to Creative Success in Dance Making. London. Bloomsbury Publishing. 2015.
- Solomon, Ruth, and John Solomon. Dance Medicine & Science Bibliography, 7th Edition. Aurora. International Association for Dance Medicine & Science. 2017.
- Solomon, Ruth, Minton, Sandra C., and John Solomon. (Eds). Preventing Dance Injuries. Champaign. Human Kinetics Pub Inc. 2005.
- Solomon, Ruth, Solomon, John, and Lyle J. Micheli. Prevention of Injuries in the Young Dancer. New York. Springer. 2017.

- Spain, Kent de. Landscape of the Now: A Topography of Movement Improvisation. Oxford. Oxford University Press. 2014.
- Sparger, Celia. Anatomy and Ballet. London. Adam and Charles Black. 1970.
- Speer, Dean. On Technique. Gainsville. University Press of Florida. 2010.
- Spitzer, Manfred. The Mind Within the Net: Models of Learning, Thinking, and Acting. Cambridge. Bradford Book. MIT Press. 2000.
- Squire, Larry R., Berg, Darwin, Bloom, Floyd E., du Lac, Sascha, Ghosh, Anirvan, and Nicholas C. Spitzer (eds). Fundamental Neuroscience (4th edition). San Diego, CA. Academic Press. 2014.
- Stearns, Marshall, and Jean Stearns. Jazz Dance: The Story Of American Vernacular Dance. Boston. Da Capo Press. 1994.
- Stephens, Robert E., and Allan J. Ryan. Dance medicine: a comprehensive guide. Chicago. Pluribus Press. 1987.
- Sternberg, Robert J, Sternberg, Karin, and Jeff Mio. Cognitive Psychology (Textbook). Wadsworth. Cengage Learning. 2012.
- Svendler Nielsen, Charlotte, and Stephanie Burridge. Dance Education around the World: Perspectives on dance, young people and change. Abington-on-Thames. Routledge. 2015.
- Sweigard, Lulu E. Human Movement Potential: Its Ideokinetic Facilitation. United States. Allegro Editions. 2013.

T

- Taylor, Jim, Taylor, John D., and Ceci Taylor. Psychology of Dance. Champaign. Human Kinetics Publishers. 1995.
- Tharp, Twyla. Keep It Moving: Lessons For The Rest Of Your Life. London-New York-Toronto. Simon & Schuster. 2019.
- Tharp, Twyla. The Creative Habit: Learn It and Use It for Life. London-New York-Toronto. Simon & Schuster. 2005.
- Thomas, Helen. Dance, Modernity, and Culture: Explorations in the Sociology of Dance. New York. Psychology Press. 1995.
- Thomasen, Eivind and Rachel-Ann Rist. Anatomy and Kinesiology for Ballet Teachers. London. Dance Books Ltd. 1996.
- Todd, Mabel Elsworth. The Thinking Body. Princeton. Princeton Book Company. 1937.
- Traguth, Fred. Modern Jazz Dance. Upper Saddle River. Prentice-Hall. 1983.

V

- Vaganova, Agrippina. Basic Principles of Classical Ballet. North Chelmsford. Courier Corporation. 2012.
- Valis Hill, Constance. Tap Dancing America: A Cultural History. Oxford. Oxford University Press. 2014.
- Vincent, LM. The Dancer's Book of Health. Kansas City. Andrews & McNeel. 1978.

W

- Walker, Brad. The Anatomy of Stretching, Second Edition : Your Illustrated Guide to Flexibility and Injury Rehabilitation (2nd edition). Berkeley. North Atlantic Books. 2013.
- Walther, Suzanne. The Dance Theatre of Kurt Jooss. Reading. Harwood Academic. 1993.
- Wang, Yunyu, and Stephanie Burridge. Identity and Diversity: Celebrating Dance in Taiwan. Abington-on-Thames. Taylor & Francis. 2020.
- Wanke, Eileen M. TanzSportMedizin. Handbuch für Tänzer, Trainer, Therapeuten und Ärzte. Köln. Sportverlag Strauß. 2011.
- Ward Warren, Gretchen. Classical Ballet Technique. Tampa, Florida. University Press of South Florida. 1989.
- Warren, Larry. Anna Sokolow: The Rebellious Spirit. New York. Psychology Press. 1998.
- Watkins, Andrea, and Priscilla Clarkson. Dancing longer, Dancing stronger. Pennington. New Jersey. Princeton Books Co. 1990.

- Wayland Barber, Elizabeth. The Dancing Goddesses: Folklore, Archaeology, and the Origins of European Dance. New York City. W.W. Norton & Company. 2013.
- Weeks, Molly. The BalletCore® Workout. New York. Ballantine Books. 2005.
- Weigelt, Linda. Berührungen und Schule - Deutungsmuster von Lehrkräften: Eine Studie zum Sportunterricht.
- White, John. Teaching Classical Ballet. Gainsville. University Press of South Florida. 1996.
- Wigman, Mary. The Language of Dance. London. MacDonald & Evans. 1966.
- Williams, Drid. Teaching Dancing with Ideokinetic Principles. Champaign. University of Illinois Press. 2011.
- Wilmerding, Mary Virginia, Krasnow, Donna, and IADMS. Dancer Wellness. Champaign, IL. Human Kinetics. 2016.
- Wood, Catherine, and Yvonne Rainer: The Mind is a Muscle. London. Afterall. 2007.
- Wooliams, Ann. Ballet Studio. New York. Mereweather Press. 1978.
- Wulff, Helena. Ballet Across Borders: Career and Culture in the World of Dancers. Oxford. Berg Publishers. 1998.
- Wyon M. The cardiorespiratory demands of contemporary dance. Saarbrücken. VDM Verlag Dr. Müller. 2009.

Z

- Zakkai, Jennifer Donohue. Dance as a Way of Knowing. York. Stenhouse Publishers. 1997.
- ZeeRay. Hip Hop. Move to the Music. Aachen. Meyer & Meyer Verlag. 1999.
- Zeller, Jessica. Shapes of American Ballet: Teachers and Training before Balanchine. Oxford. Oxford University Press. 2016.

INDEX